Structured Reading

Sixth Edition

Lynn Quitman Troyka

Queensborough Community College,
The City University of New York

Joseph Wayne Thweatt

Southwest Tennessee Community College

Prentice
Hall

Upper Saddle River, New Jersey 07458

Library of Congress Cataloging-in-Publication Data

Troyka, Lynn Quitman, date
  Structured reading / Lynn Quitman Troyka, Joseph Wayne Thweatt—6th ed.
    p. cm.
  Includes index.
  ISBN 0-13-045076-6
    1. College readers.   I. Thweatt, Joseph Wayne.   II Title.

PE1122.T76 2002
428.6—dc21

20022766249

VP, Editor-in-Chief: Leah Jewell	Art Director: Jayne Conte
Sr. Acquisition Editor: Craig Campanella	Cover Designer: Bruce Kenselaar
Editorial Assistant: Joan Polk	Cover Art: Getty Images, Inc./Artville LCC
AVP, Director of Manufacturing and Production: Barbara Kittle	Permission Specialist: Frederick T. Courtright
Executive Managing Editor: Ann Marie McCarthy	Director, Image Resource Center: Melinda Lee Reo
Production Liaison: Fran Russello	Manager, Rights & Permissions: Kay Dellosa
Project Manager: Karen Berry/Pine Tree Composition, Inc.	Interior Image Specialist: Beth Boyd
	Photo Researcher: Jerry Marshall/Picture Research & Editing
Manufacturing Manager: Nick Sklitsis	
Prepress and Manufacturing Buyer: Ben Smith	Marketing Manager: Rachel Falk

This book was set in 10/12 Palatino by Pine Tree Composition, Inc. and printed and bound by R. R. Donnelly & Sons Company. The cover printer was Phoenix Color Corp.

© 2003 by Prentice Hall
Upper Saddle River, New Jersey 07458

Printed in the United States of America
10 9 8 7 6 5 4 3 2 1

ISBN 0-13-045076-6
ISBN 0-13-047512-2 Instructor's Edition

Pearson Education, Ltd., *London*
Pearson Education Australia Pty, Limited, *Sydney*
Pearson Education Singapore, Pte. Ltd.
Pearson Education North Asia Ltd., *Hong Kong*
Pearson Education Canada, Ltd., *Toronto*
Pearson Educación de Mexico, S.A. de C.V.
Pearson Education—Japan, *Tokyo*
Pearson Education Malaysia, Pte. Ltd.
Pearson Education, *Upper Saddle River, New Jersey*

For our students:
If we sometimes forget names after all these years,
we never forget you as the people
whose dedication to learning inspires us daily
as we write and teach.

Contents

v

Part 2   Thinking: Getting Started   81

Part 3   Thinking: Getting Started   137

*New for this edition

Part 4   Thinking: Getting Started   195

*New for this edition

Part 6 Thinking: Getting Started   323

*New for this edition

Appendix

Preface

In writing *Structured Reading,* Sixth Edition, we remained convinced that students learn best from guided, hands-on experience with complete, not partial, reading selections. We believe, too, that the best approach starts with detailed instruction in the separate skills areas that assure movement to college-level reading abilities, followed by extensive, repeated practice with many complete reading selections that comprise five-sixths of this book.

In flight training, student pilots spend some instructional time in a training simulator. But within a short time, the instructors move students from the simulator to the cockpit of the airplane to give the students hands-on practice in flying the plane. Few passengers would fly with a pilot who had only simulator experience. Most want a pilot who has logged many hours of real flight time in the cockpit. Likewise, we want students to move quickly from the skills (the simulator) to actual reading (the cockpit) for extended practice. This method has worked well since the first edition of *Structured Reading* and is evidenced by its continued use by hundred of teachers and thousands of students in the United States and Canada.

We've consistently had our students in mind as we've talked through our revision decisions for this Sixth Edition of *Structured Reading.* We've learned from our reviewers and teaching colleagues that many students look for a detailed introduction to the separate college-level reading skills they need ("Central Theme and Main Ideas"; "Major Details"; "Inferences"; "Critical Thinking"; and "Reader Response"). To that end, we offer in this Sixth Edition a comprehensive, new Part One, "Skills for Reading." This fourteen-chapter part explains and demonstrates each reading skill. It also offers extensive skills-based exercises to prepare students for their hands-on experience with the thirty complete reading selections in Parts Two through Six.

Another demonstration of our focus on students in *Structured Reading* is the topics of the thirty complete reading selections. Some students say that they avoid reading because nothing they're assigned to read interests them. While we know that such feelings derive as much from a lack of confidence in reading abilities as from specific topics, we've always strived to provide engaging topics that appeal to a diverse audience. To this end, we've replaced five reading selections with new ones on more current, absorbing issues.

Here are the major features of *Structured Reading*, Sixth Edition:

- NEW! Part One, "Skills for Reading" explains the reading process. Using an FAQ approach, it gives students down-to-earth advice—with lots of chances for practice—about how to improve reading speed, expand vocabulary, make useful predictions during reading, read "on, between, and beyond" the lines, find central themes and main ideas, identify major and minor details, make inferences, read critically, and respond to ideas.

- Thirty reading selections, with five new for this edition, represent our desire to offer an instructive, stimulating balance of readings from books, magazines, newspapers, and textbooks in disciplines across the curriculum. The final mix represents male and female writers, as well as writers from a variety of ethnic groups.

- Exercises are deliberately structured to promote analytic and critical reasoning. Indeed, our structured sequences of exercises following every reading selection are the key feature that teachers and students have been praising from the first edition of *Structured Reading*: "Vocabulary," "Central Theme and Main Ideas," "Major Details," "Inferences," "Critical Thinking" ("Fact vs. Opinion" and "The Writer's Craft"), and "Reader Response." This structured sequence demands concentrated work in **reading for literal meaning, for inferential meaning, and for critical thinking.** This approach, used repeatedly, leads students to internalize successfully complex reading and thinking skills.

- The answer options for our structured exercises may look to some like multiple-choice items, but the similarity stops there. *Structured Reading* exercises are unique, which can be seen as soon as anyone looks beneath the surface. We've written the incorrect answers (called "distracters") to propel students into close reading and active analysis. They're forced to marshal their higher-order reasoning powers to think through mental challenges. Students' powers of persistence and focus can become habit when teachers require them not only to identify a correct answer (called "the key") but also to analyze and articulate why other choices are incorrect.

- Complete, authentic dictionary entries accompany each reading selection to help students tackle the more difficult words in the piece.

This unique, popular feature of *Structured Reading* provides students hands-on experience with dictionary use. We have again been fortunate to offer entries from *Webster's New World College Dictionary*, Fourth Edition. Our Appendix, "Guide to Dictionary Use," helps students—in plain English—retrieve information from dictionary entries.

- The book has six parts. Part One teaches the reading process and its college-level skills. Parts Two through Six contain reading selections with increasingly difficult readability levels (see the *Instructor's Edition* of *Structured Reading*), and with short-to-longer selections within each part.

- "Thinking: Getting Started" sections, another unique feature of *Structured Reading,* open Parts Two through Six to help students engage in predictive reading. We use posters, photographs, advertisements, cartoons, and other visuals to prepare students for the topics to come.

Here are highly useful supplements for our Sixth Edition:

- NEW! The *Instructor's Edition* (ISBN 0-13-047512-2) of our Sixth Edition of *Structured Reading* marks another milestone on behalf of teachers. For the first time, we provide instructors with a special edition that includes answers to all exercises right on the student text pages, along with a 45-page "Instructor's Guide" bound at the back of the text. The "Instructor's Guide" contains additional teaching strategies, readability levels for the thirty Reading Selections, and tips on using *Structured Reading* in either a classroom setting or a self-paced lab. We hope this special edition will help new teachers along with their more experienced colleagues. Free to instructors.

- An *Instructor's Resource Manual* (ISBN 0-13-047515-7) provides additional material for instructors as they prepare for class. This manual contains transparency masters, comprehension boosters, extra vocabulary exercises, and supplementary dictionary exercises. We have designed these materials to support instructors and lab tutors as they work with students. Free to instructors.

- NEW! Companion Website for *Structured Reading* at www. prenhall.com/troyka. This website includes additional textbook readings at varying reading levels. For these readings, we offer the same structured exercise sequence as in the print book: Vocabulary, Central Theme and Main Ideas, Major Details, Inferences, Critical Reading, and Reader Response. Exercises (excluding Reader Response) are self-grading for students, and they can e-mail the results directly to their instructor.

- NEW! The Prentice Hall Reading Skills Test Bank, which contains 100 exercises on each of eleven different reading skills. Available online, designed for use with any text, this test bank has over 1,000 exercises, covering word analysis, context clues, stated main idea, implied main idea, tone and bias, details, major vs. minor details, style, study reading,

reading rate, and visual aids. Questions are multiple choice, matching, or true/false. The test bank is available in printed format or electronically. ISBN (printed): 0-13-041249-X. Instructors can contact their Prentice Hall representative to request the electronic version. Free to instructors upon adoption.

• NEW! Free dictionary offer: Students can receive a **free** *New American Webster Handy College Dictionary* packaged with their text when instructors adopt *Structured Reading,* Sixth Edition. This dictionary has over 1.5 million Signet copies in print with over 115,000 definitions, including current phrases, slang, and scientific terms. It offers more than 1,500 new words, with over 200 not found in any competing dictionary, and it features boxed inserts on etymologies and language. It also includes foreign words and phrases and an international gazetteer with correct place-name pronunciations. Instructors can ask their Prentice Hall sales representative for the ISBN of the package.

ACKNOWLEDGMENTS

We thank the many colleagues and students who have contributed suggestions and comments about the prior editions of *Structured Reading.* With their active participation, our Sixth Edition has evolved with the dynamic changes in theory and practice.

At Southwest Tennessee Community College, we thank Ruth Sowell and Joshua Baney for specific feedback on our new reading selections and related structured exercises, and we are grateful to Donna Overstreet and Jean McDonald for their ever-ready willingness to listen and respond throughout our writing process. At Lambuth University, Jackson, Tennessee, we appreciate the students who reacted to some of the new material in our Sixth Edition.

For their invaluable reviews of our Fifth Edition as we prepared our revision plan for this Sixth Edition, we thank Susan Ford, Thomas University; Patricia Illing, Longview Community College; Robert W. Rigdon, Highline Community College; and Lisa Tittle, Harford Community College. Our prior editions benefited from the reviews of William Bean, Daytona Beach Community College; Elaine Chakonas, Rosary College; Nadine A. Gandia, Miami-Dade Community College; Lynna Geis, Rose State College; Bertilda Garnica Henderson, Broward Community College; Jossie A. Moore, Southwest Tennessee Community College; Peggy S. Myers, Indian River Community College; Karen Patty-Graham, South Illinois University at Edwardsville; Karen Houck Rothman, Bellevue Community College; Ted Walkup, Clayton State College; Joyce Weinsheimer, University of Minnesota; Donna Wood, Southwest Tennessee Community College; and Beverley J. Young, Oxnard College. We, however, retain responsibility for any flaws that remain.

At Prentice Hall, Craig Campanella, Senior Editor for Developmental English, cheered us on with his special brand of outstanding wisdom, efficiency, and humor. Joan Polk, Administrative Assistant, supported us invaluably with continuity and practical help. At Pine Tree Composition, Karen Berry, Production Manager, steered our course from manuscript through bound book with patient grace, steady craft, and admirable professionalism. Maggi Miller, Austin Community College, gave us exceptionally fine first drafts of the activities in Part One.

On a personal level, we thank Ida Morea, Administrative Assistant to Lynn Quitman Troyka, for her efficiency, energy, warmth, and acumen. Lynn Quitman Troyka also thanks her husband David for his robust moral support and selfless love. Joseph Wayne Thweatt thanks his wife, Marilyn Thweatt, for her consistently wise counsel; his son, Rob Thweatt, and his mother, June Thweatt, for their patience when the book took precedence over family.

Lynn Quitman Troyka, *New York City*
Joseph Wayne Thweatt, *Memphis, Tennessee*

▪ Part 1 ▪

Skills for Reading

A s a college student, why do you need a textbook called *Structured Reading*? After all, you already know how to read. Yet, a placement test score or an academic advisor says you need a course to show you how to read successfully at a college level. Our purpose in writing this textbook is to provide you with a concrete, structured method—with lots of opportunity for practice—that can assure that you reach your goal.

Reading is a challenge for many people. As a college student, however, you're more advanced than the 90 million Americans who are unable to read well enough to function productively in today's world. Over 40 million adults cannot fill out a simple form. Another 50 million are unable to read newspapers or magazines. College students aren't in these groups. Rather, they need to master reading strategies needed for college success.

In *Structured Reading*, we draw on excellent, convincing research about how adults improve their reading skills most efficiently. The best approach involves a structured system of skill building that is applied repeatedly to complete, whole reading selections. Part One, the section you're now reading, explains the overall approach of *Structured Reading*, introducing you to the structured reading strategies that successful adult readers use. Part One also gives you much initial practice with each skill presented separately.

Parts Two through Six of *Structured Reading* provide you with multiple opportunities to combine all the skills introduced in Part One. After each of the thirty complete reading selections, you'll find structured questions that reinforce the strategies you've learned. The whole selections are representative of material that adults encounter in books, newspapers, magazines, and textbooks. Within Parts Two through Six, the reading selections get longer. Also, each successive Part increases in difficulty. (In Part One, we include some short excerpts so that you can practice initially with isolated skills.)

SETTING *YOUR* GOALS

Now that we, the authors of *Structured Reading*, have set our goals, we invite you to set yours. Please list below what you consider your strengths as a reader before starting your college-level reading class. Then, please list the areas in which you'd like to improve as a reader. These are your personal lists, so make them informal and honest.

What are My Strengths as a Reader?

In What Areas Would I Like to Improve as a Reader?

Chapter 1

What Is the Reading Process?

Reading is not just looking at words. Reading is a complex, diverse process. It involves your eyes (looking at the page) working together with your memory (accessing the store of information you already know). To learn new material by reading, you "hook" it to what's in your memory. Knowledge builds on knowledge. To build the knowledge base required in college, you need to marshal your self-discipline so that you actively engage with all interactions between your eyes and your memory.

Because learning involves your "hooking" new knowledge to old, you read best when you already know something about the topic at hand. Even a little helps. Your first concern when beginning a reading selection is to determine your level of prior knowledge about the topic.

PREVIEWING AND PREDICTING IN THE READING PROCESS

To check your prior knowledge about a topic, use the technique called *previewing*. For example, would you go to a movie without knowing something about it? Most likely, no—unless you specifically want to be totally surprised. Perhaps you or a friend has heard people say good things about the movie, has read a review of it, or knows one of the actors. Having an idea about the movie, you can predict in a broad sense what to expect.

The same holds tenfold for reading. Before you read, you need some knowledge of what you're about to read. By engaging in the act of previewing and predicting, you establish all-important connections between what you already know and what's new to you. Students often avoid previewing and predicting because they aren't willing to take the time to do it. Yes, previewing and predicting take time, but the payoff is tremendous. Without previewing and predicting as you start each reading selection, you float in an open sea without oars and a compass.

To preview, do these three things (to yourself or aloud):

1. Based on your looking over the material, consciously predict what the topic and its development are likely to be about.

2. Ask yourself consciously what you already know about the topic.

3. Predict what your reading the material will add to what you already know.

No one previewing method works for all material. Writers present material in huge varieties of ways. Here are guidelines for one approach to try out—and to adapt to your needs and preferences.

- For an essay or article, read the opening and closing paragraphs, which is often where main ideas are found. Then, stop to decide what you predict the essay or article is about. Next, read the first lines of the paragraphs (as you become more skilled, you can skip some paragraphs if a few seem to cluster around one idea). Then, stop to revisit your first prediction and modify it, if necessary.

- For a textbook chapter, read the title, the first paragraph or introduction, the subheadings (often appearing in **boldface print** or *italics*), and the conclusion or summary. Then, stop to decide what you predict the textbook material will cover.

The discipline for, and skill of, predicting as you read is so important that Chapter 6 in Part One discusses it in depth. (In the meantime, consider this section a preview about previewing!)

CONCENTRATING DURING THE READING PROCESS

The ability to use the reading process skillfully takes concentration and self-discipline. Before you start a reading session, seek out places where, and times of day when, you'll not be interrupted or distracted by people or noise. Never mislead yourself into thinking you can concentrate adequately when you're in a room where people are talking, or the TV is on, or music is playing loudly, or when you're expecting phone calls. If you are uncomfortable with silence, as some people tend to be, experiment *honestly* with what gives you comfort: soft non-distracting music, a clock that ticks reassuringly, etc. If there's little private time where you live, schedule yourself to read in a quiet corner of the library or a spot in a park or public building with minimum human traffic. Check out which college classrooms are empty during off-peak class hours.

Aside from external influences on your concentration, internal factors can also get in your way. These include daydreams, personal problems, anxiety, and failure to stick with what you set out to accomplish. Concentration takes your total mental immersion in what you're doing. Developing an outstanding ability to concentrate is a major challenge facing college students. At all times, try to work with fierce determination to concentrate and focus with razor-sharp intensity. This is a learned ability. It doesn't come to most people automatically. The good news is that everyone can learn to concentrate and focus. You'll find that the more you practice, the stronger and more stubborn becomes your refusal to tolerate distractions, external or internal.

One way to monitor your powers of concentration is to place a short stroke (vertical mark) on a sheet of paper each time your mind wanders. Doing this reminds you that you're not concentrating. At the end of the page or article, count the number of strokes you have accumulated. The next time you read, compete with yourself. Reduce the number of strokes you make per page or article. Soon, with practice, you can decrease the number of strokes.

Use the paragraph below to test your powers of concentration. Place a short stroke (vertical line) within the lines each time your mind wanders. Then, count the strokes as your baseline to measure your progress toward reducing the number of strokes as you read. The paragraph below is from a student essay about the homeless in *Steps in Composition, Seventh Edition*, by Lynn Quitman Troyka and Jerrold Nudelman.

> The largest group of homeless people consists of families with children. To save on the cost of labor, many companies have downsized their operations or moved them out of the United States. The companies' stockholders may have benefited, but the companies' workers have not. For example, May and Joe Kalson, who lost their jobs when General Motors closed its factory in New York, had to live on welfare after their unemployment insurance ran out. But the payments did not cover all of their expenses. When the Kalsons no longer could pay their rent, they piled into their old Chevy and headed for Detroit in search of work in an automobile factory. But there were no job openings. Their first night in Detroit the family stayed in a homeless shelter, where some of their clothing was stolen while they slept. The Kalsons now sleep in their car. According to the U.S. Conference of Mayors, over half of all the homeless people in this country are families like the Kalsons.

Chapter 2

What Is Your Personal Reading History?

Everyone has a history of learning to read and of being a reader. By re-calling the details of that history, people can come to understand their strengths and weaknesses as readers. Here's a questionnaire that prompts you to remember and analyze your reading history.

ACTIVITY A   MY READING HISTORY
Think about and answer these questions.

1. Before you started to read as a child, did family members or other adults read to you? _____? If yes, did you enjoy it? _____ Why or why not? _____

2. What's your first memory of starting to read (if you recall your ap-proximate age at the time, give it)? _____
_____

3. What's the title (or story outline) of one of the first books you read as a young child? _____

4. When you were in school (1st through 12th grades), did you en-counter any difficulties with reading? _____ If yes, what were they? _____

5. What's the title (or story) of your favorite book when you were in ele-mentary school? _____
What did you like about it?_____

6. What's the title (or theme) of one of the best books you've ever read?

   _____

7. In general, as you were growing up, if you could choose between watching television or reading for pleasure, which did you choose? _____ Why? _____

8. What's your estimate of the number of complete books you were assigned to read in school? _____ Did you enjoy most of them? _____ Why or why not? _____

   _____

9. How often did you read for your own pleasure (fill in the table below)?

SCHOOL YEARS	almost daily	once a week	once a month	once or twice a year	never
Elementary					
Middle					
High					

10. How often do you currently read for your own pleasure? _____

    Do you read newspapers? _____ magazines? _____

    books? _____

11. Other memories or comments: _____

    As you reflect on your answers, what do they suggest about your current reading ability? Your answers might hold a clue about why you're enrolled in a college-level reading class. For example, people who've had many reading experiences in childhood tend to be better adult readers. These people had many chances to practice regularly. If you didn't have such chances, the reading class you're enrolled in offers you the chance to start catching up. Anything you do well requires continued, disciplined practice—whether it is participating in a sport, playing a musical instrument, or cooking a favorite dish.

Chapter 3

What Is the Role
of Speed During Reading?

Research indicates a close relation between speed and understanding. But that connection is not what you might assume it to be. Speed-reading, even though various commercial sources claim to teach it, isn't the major skill you need to read college-level material. Rather, you need the mental flexibility to adjust your reading pace according to your purpose for reading—just as you adjust your speed in a car to the terrain, such as hills or curves or flat roadway. A fast look at words in complex material isn't suited to understanding and remembering new information. Conversely, too slow a pace for fairly simple, straightforward information tends to distract your concentration. You can usually pick up your speed with information that confirms what you already know. Expect, however, to slow down as you encounter new information.

RELATING SPEED TO PURPOSES FOR READING

Always expect to adjust your reading speed to your purpose for reading. The following box lists the major reading purposes and the relative speeds they usually demand.

If you're like many college students, you're probably holding down a full- or part-time job. With classes, work, and family commitments, you might have little time left over for studying—not to mention a social life. To meet the demands on your life, and to fit in well-used study time, you want to call upon the most effective reading strategies available. This effort starts with becoming aware of the relativity of reading speed according to your purposes for reading.

The average college student reads between 250 and 300 words per minute (wpm) with at least 70 percent comprehension on fiction and

Purposes for Reading

Casual Reading *Reading for relaxation, amusement.* Casual reading means catching the basics without worrying about minor details, though sometimes you might find the reading is so pleasurable that you prefer not to miss anything. You adjust your speed according to how much you want to retain the material.

Scanning *Reading for specific information, such as a telephone number, street address, or the time of an event.* Scanning requires you to move quickly through the material with a specific word or phrase in mind.

Skimming *Reading for the overall idea or gist of the material.* Skimming is accomplished by omitting unnecessary words, phrases, and sentences. This method is useful for getting an overview of a topic or for reviewing major ideas and concepts after you have studied the material. You adjust your speed according to your goals, sometimes speeding ahead and sometimes slowing down.

Study *Reading for a thorough understanding of central themes, main ideas, supporting details, and inferences.* Reading to learn and remember takes time. The pace is slow, not because you read word-by-word, but because you need to think about the material and consciously associate it with knowledge that you already have. Often, you need to read the material a few times. This is what college-level readers do.

nontechnical materials. Textbook material, especially that involving complex ideas in the social sciences and in mathematics and science, demands a slower pace. That rate might go down to 100 or 150 wpm for difficult material. Your reading speed is influenced by many factors, including your desire to improve, your willingness to try new techniques, and your motivation to practice.

USING RAPID WORD DISCRIMINATION

If you find yourself daydreaming as you read, you actually may need to increase your rate of movement through words. The "Rapid Discrimination Drills" coming up show you how to push yourself to read more quickly when necessary. They demand that you look at words and pick out, at very rapid rates, those that are alike or different. Using a watch or clock with a second hand, note the time you begin on a sheet of paper. Then note the time you finish. Subtract the time you began from the time you finished to determine the total time you read. Then go back and carefully check to see if your responses are correct. Give yourself five points for each correct answer.

ACTIVITY B   RAPID DISCRIMINATION DRILL 1.

In each line, circle the word that is different.

Key Word	1	2	3	4
1. fight	fight	fight	light	fight
2. side	side	side	side	site
3. than	then	than	than	than
4. sail	nail	nail	nail	nail
5. foot	food	foot	foot	foot
6. ride	ride	hide	ride	ride
7. flood	flood	flood	floor	flood
8. hump	bump	hump	hump	hump
9. tool	fool	fool	fool	fool
10. hold	hold	hold	hold	sold
11. sack	rack	sack	sack	sack
12. took	book	book	book	book
13. real	seal	seal	seal	seal
14. cook	cook	cool	cook	cook
15. maps	maps	maps	maps	mops
16. bore	bore	bore	tore	bore
17. lamp	lamp	lump	lamp	lamp
18. trick	trick	trick	track	trick
19. mail	mail	mail	mail	nail
20. cave	cave	cove	cave	cave

ACTIVITY C   RAPID DISCRIMINATION DRILL 2.

Circle the word that matches *the key word on each line.*

Key Word	1	2	3	4	5
1. pore	tore	bore	pore	gore	more
2. jack	sack	jack	tack	pack	rack
3. cake	take	make	bake	fake	cake
4. hats	hats	cats	mats	pats	rats
5. call	fall	mall	tall	call	pall
6. hide	hide	ride	side	tide	wide
7. rap	cap	sap	map	tap	rap
8. hook	cook	took	hook	book	look
9. mart	cart	mart	tart	part	dart
10. park	bark	dark	hark	park	lark
11. tear	bear	tear	fear	sear	hear
12. chide	pride	hide	tide	side	chide
13. tan	can	man	tan	fan	pan
14. rash	cash	rash	mash	bash	sash
15. mold	sold	fold	told	mold	bold
16. kill	fill	kill	pill	till	bill
17. tone	tone	bone	cone	done	lone

Key Word	1	2	3	4	5
18. take	make	take	cake	bake	fake
19. leach	beach	reach	teach	peach	leach
20. sunny	puny	runny	sunny	funny	bunny

ACTIVITY D   RAPID DRILL DISCRIMINATION 3.
Circle the word that is different in each line.

Key Word	1	2	3	4
1. stove	cove	stove	stove	stove
2. their	their	their	their	there
3. hall	hall	hall	fall	hall
4. belief	belief	relief	belief	belief
5. redo	redo	undo	redo	redo
6. unless	unless	unless	unless	unlock
7. confine	confide	confine	confine	confine
8. trestle	trestle	trestle	bustle	trestle
9. ladder	madder	ladder	ladder	ladder
10. truck	truck	truce	truck	truck
11. flip	flip	flip	skip	flip
12. cable	cable	cable	cable	table
13. tricycle	tricycle	tricycle	tricycle	bicycle
14. clammer	clammer	clammer	hammer	clammer
15. bee	see	bee	bee	bee
16. toil	toil	foil	toil	toil
17. flow	flow	flow	blow	flow
18. tip	hip	tip	tip	tip
19. liking	liking	liking	liking	hiking
20. carry	carry	marry	carry	carry

Scanning at appropriate speeds is another essential discrimination technique for reading. Without scanning, imagine how long using the dictionary, telephone directory, or encyclopedia would take. People do not want to start at the beginning of such reference works and look at every entry until they find what they're seeking. Here's an activity to involve you in a scanning situation that many people need for everyday life.

ACTIVITY E   SCANNING A COMMUTER TRAIN SCHEDULE.
For this activity, accuracy is more important than speed. Look at the commuter train schedule on page 12 that shows the times for trips from Little Neck to Penn Station on weekdays and on weekends and holidays. Answer the questions placed after the schedule. Before you begin, scan read the timetables, getting used to the variety of column headings. Each of the smaller column headings names a train station between Little Neck and Penn Station. Next, figure out how to determine the days of operation and the times of departures and arrivals. To determine those times, move your eyes across each row.

TO WOODSIDE AND NEW YORK
MONDAY TO FRIDAY EXCEPT HOLIDAYS

Morning Service

Note	Little Neck	Douglaston	Bayside	Flushing	Woodside	Penn Station
			Leave		Arrive	
	12:51	12:53	12:56	1:05	1:14	1:24
	1:38	1:40	1:43	1:52	2:00	2:10
	3:35	3:37	3:40	3:49	3:57	4:06
	5:21	5:23	5:26	5:36	5:42	5:52
Peak	5:48	5:50	5:53	6:02	6:10	6:20
Peak	6:30	6:32	6:35	6:44	6:52	7:03
Peak	6:40	6:42	6:45	6:55	7:03	7:14
Peak			7:02	·····	·····	7:24
Peak	7:23	7:26	7:30	·····	·····	7:55
Peak	7:55	7:57	8:00	·····	·····	8:26
Peak	8:07	8:10	8:14	·····	8:26	8:38
Peak			8:32	8:41	·····	8:59
Peak	8:32	8:35		·····	·····	9:02
	8:41	8:43	8:46	8:55	9:03	9:14
	9:01	9:03	9:06	9:15	9:23	9:34
	9:29	9:31	9:34	9:43	9:50	10:01
	9:52	9:54	9:57	10:03	10:12	10:22
	10:21	10:23	10:26	10:33	10:42	10:52
	10:52	10:54	10:57	11:03	11:12	11:22
	11:21	11:23	11:26	11:33	11:42	11:52
	11:52	11:54	11:57	12:03	12:12	12:22

Afternoon and Evening Service

Note	Little Neck	Douglaston	Bayside	Flushing	Woodside	Penn Station
	12:21	12:23	12:26	12:33	12:42	12:52
	12:52	12:54	12:57	1:03	1:12	1:22
	1:21	1:23	1:26	1:33	1:42	1:52
	1:52	1:54	1:57	2:03	2:12	2:22
	2:21	2:23	2:26	2:33	2:42	2:52
	2:52	2:54	2:57	3:03	3:12	3:22
	3:21	3:23	3:26	3:33	3:42	3:52
	3:52	3:54	3:57	4:03	4:12	4:23
	4:19	4:21	4:24	4:32	4:39	4:51
	4:49	4:51	4:54	5:02	5:10	5:23
	5:12	5:14	5:17	5:26	5:35	5:45
	5:46	5:48	5:51	5:57	6:04	6:17
	6:23	6:25	6:27	6:36	6:44	6:55
	6:47	6:49	6:52	6:58	7:05	7:15
	7:21	7:23	7:26	7:35	7:42	7:53
	7:51	7:53	7:56	8:05	8:12	8:23
	8:21	8:23	8:26	8:35	8:42	8:53
	8:51	8:53	8:56	9:05	9:12	9:22
	9:21	9:23	9:26	9:35	9:42	9:52
	9:51	9:53	9:56	10:05	10:12	10:22
	10:21	10:23	10:26	10:35	10:42	10:53
	10:51	10:53	10:56	11:05	11:12	11:22

TO WOODSIDE AND NEW YORK
SATURDAY, SUNDAY, AND HOLIDAYS

Morning Service

Note	Little Neck	Douglaston	Bayside	Flushing	Woodside	Penn Station
			Leave		Arrive	
	12:51	12:53	12:56	1:05	1:14	1:24
	1:51	1:53	1:56	2:05	2:14	2:24
	3:51	3:53	3:56	4:05	4:14	4:24
	5:51	5:53	5:56	6:05	6:14	6:24
	6:51	6:53	6:56	7:05	7:14	7:24
	7:51	7:53	7:56	8:05	8:14	8:24
	8:51	8:53	8:56	9:05	9:14	9:24
	9:51	9:53	9:56	10:05	10:14	10:24
	10:51	10:53	10:56	11:05	11:14	11:24
	11:51	11:53	11:56	12:05	12:14	12:24

Afternoon and Evening Service

Note	Little Neck	Douglaston	Bayside	Flushing	Woodside	Penn Station
	12:51	12:53	12:56	1:05	1:14	1:24
	1:51	1:53	1:56	2:05	2:14	2:24
	2:51	2:53	2:56	3:05	3:14	3:24
	3:51	3:53	3:56	4:05	4:14	4:24
	4:51	4:53	4:56	5:05	5:14	5:24
	5:51	5:53	5:56	6:05	6:14	6:24
	6:51	6:53	6:56	7:05	7:14	7:24
	7:51	7:53	7:56	8:05	8:14	8:24
	8:51	8:53	8:56	9:05	9:14	9:24
	9:51	9:53	9:56	10:05	10:14	10:24
	10:51	10:53	10:56	11:05	11:14	11:24
	11:51	11:53	11:56	12:05	12:14	12:24

1. To take a train on a weekday at Douglaston Station to go to Penn Station, what's the earliest time you can leave after 6 a.m.? _____

2. How many stops are scheduled between Douglaston Station and Penn Station leaving at the earliest time after 6 a.m.? _____

3. To leave from the Little Neck Station to meet a friend at Penn Station at noon on Saturday, what time do you need to leave the Little Neck Station? _____

4. How long does it take on a holiday to travel from Douglaston Station on the 8:53 p.m. train to Woodside Station? _____

5. How many trains run nonstop from Bayside Station to Penn Station? _____

6. How many minutes does it take to make the nonstop trip from Bayside Station to Penn Station leaving at 7:30 a.m.? _____

7. What's the last time before midnight on a holiday that you can take a train from Little Neck Station to Penn Station? _____

8. How much time do you save on a weekday by taking the 8:41 a.m. train rather than the 8:55 a.m. train from Flushing Station to Penn Station? _____

9. How many trains run on a weekday between 7:50 a.m. and 9 a.m. from Bayside Station to Penn Station? _____

10. To leave from Little Neck Station to go to Penn Station on a weekday, what train would reach your destination by 7:10 a.m.? _____

Chapter 4

How Do Eye Movements Affect Reading?

Skilled readers benefit from the mind's tendency to think in concepts, pulling ideas into a meaningful whole of information. Weak readers, on the other hand, read word by word. Their eyes stop at each word as they try to piece together ideas from the reading. It often leads to the destructive habits of reading *regression* (needless or unconscious rereading of material) and *sub-vocalization* (always repeating the words in your head) while reading. Breaking old habits and replacing them with new ones require practice. Three techniques can help you progress rapidly in establishing new habits. The key to your success with these three techniques is always to exaggerate for the eye what you want the mind to train itself to do.

AVOIDING "WHITE SPACE"

Approximately one-third of a page of print—the part in the margins—is blank. This is called "white space," no matter what color the paper. Efficient readers automatically indent with their eyes at each new line so that their field of vision eliminates the surrounding white space.

ACTIVITY F   EYE MOVEMENTS
Here are the first two paragraphs from "In Praise of the F Word" by Mary Sherry. Notice that the shaded areas are placed about five letter spaces in from each margin. Focus your eyes on these shaded areas, and let your peripheral (outer) vision take in the rest. Don't let your eyes drift over to the material to the left and right of the shaded areas.

14

(A) Tens of thousands of 18-year-olds will graduate this year and be handed meaningless diplomas. These diplomas will not look any different from those awarded their luckier classmates. Their validity will be questioned only when their employers discover that these graduates are semiliterate.

(B) Eventually a fortunate few will find their way into education-repair shops—adult-literacy programs, such as the one where I teach basic grammar and writing. There, high school graduates and high school dropouts pursuing graduate-equivalency certificates will learn the skills they should have learned in school. They will also discover they have been cheated by our educational system.

Indenting your eyes to avoid white space saves time and can, therefore, increase your speed. To make practical use of this technique, take a minute before you read any selection, including the ones in this textbook, and lightly draw vertical lines about a half-inch inside the left and right margins. When you read the material, use these lines as boundaries. Soon, you'll automatically adjust the way you approach print. You'll no longer waste your time or eye movements to look at white space.

EXPANDING EYE FIXATIONS

To read, your eyes must stop. These stops, called fixations, last a fraction of a second. On average, 5 to 10 percent of reading time is spent on fixations. Therefore, if you reduce the amount of time you spend on fixations, you can increase your reading rate. This calls for you to enlarge your span of recognition, increasing the number of words you take in per fixation or stop. For example, read the following phrase:

down the street

How many fixations did you make—one, two, or three? One is ideal. Next, read this word:

comprehensive

Did you read this word whole, or did you stop at each syllable for a total of four fixations?

Both examples above contain thirteen letters. Your goal is to read each with one fixation. Your eye fixations while you are reading affect your ability to understand and remember what you're reading. To read skillfully, you need to read for ideas. Ideas are rarely contained in a single word. They reside in groups of words.

To train yourself to read two or three words per eye fixation, practice using your peripheral vision on either side of the fixation point. As you decrease the number of your eye fixations, you'll see that taking in phrases and thought units go together automatically. To illustrate, here's

15

a sentence of eleven words grouped into four thought units. Use it to practice your eye fixations. By expanding what you take in with each eye fixation, you can read the sentence with four fixations or fewer.

- More and more states are requiring students to pass competency exams.

Write out your own sentences to practice with. The more you modify your eye muscle habits to handle fewer fixations, the faster will be your reading rate.

PACING THROUGH THE PRINT

Many young readers are discouraged from using their fingers to point to individual words because adults worry that the children will become word-by-word readers. However, a version of this pointing can help you learn the habit of focusing on ideas, not words, as you read. Using either hand, begin by indenting as previously discussed and then move line by line under the print. Focus on thought units as you read. Speed up on familiar materials, and slow down on unfamiliar or difficult material.

During these practices, try not to look back—to regress—and reread. (Controlled rereading is an advanced study strategy discussed in Chapter 7 in Part One.) If you habitually regress because you aren't concentrating while reading, use your hand as a pacer to help you break this harmful habit. Keep pushing on until you come to the end of the section. Only then do you want to go back and reread what you missed. Practice with this technique as long as you need it to train your mind and eyes.

ACTIVITY G   EYE FIXATIONS

Here are passages for you to practice eye fixations. The first, "Rice," is printed here in columns with six words on each line. The second, "Bees," is printed in columns with ten words on each line. Using your hand as a pacer, read the passages trying to make only two fixations per line. A dashed line has been placed down the middle of the column to help you with the fixations.

Rice

Rice is one of the world's
most important food crops. More than
half of the people in the
world eat this grain as the
main part of their meals. Nearly
all the people who depend on
rice for food live in Asia.
In some Asian languages, the same

word means *eat* and *eat rice*.
Most rice is eaten as boiled,
white grain.

Bees

When the temperature of the air in a hive of
honeybees falls to about 57 degrees Fahrenheit, the bees of
that hive begin to form their winter cluster. As the
temperature continues to fall, the cluster becomes well defined, approximately
30,000 individuals forming a hemispherical mass upon the comb. The
bees in the center of the cluster and in contact
with the honey reserves feed on the high-energy food and
begin to generate heat. Those on the surface of the
cluster act as insulation.

The cluster, like a living thermostat, reacts to changes in
the temperature within the hive by expanding and contracting. When
it gets too hot and needs to cool down, the
mass expands, losing heat, and when it must raise its
temperature, it contracts, retaining heat. It is a thing of
constant mass but variable surface area.

The layer of bees on the outside of the mass,
those acting as insulation, may be one to three inches
thick. They are more tightly packed than the innermost bees
that are doing the eating and generating the heat. The
goal of the bees in that outer layer is to
maintain a temperature of 45 degrees. A drop below that
level causes them to tighten up. Above that, they loosen.
Forty-five degrees happens to be the temperature at which the
hive most efficiently uses its honey reserves, which must last
to the end of what may prove to be a
long, cold winter.

By shifting places within the cluster periodically, each bee has
an opportunity to eat some honey. Thus, it not only
keeps itself alive but also contributes to the heating of
the entire hive. In fact, this vital system cannot endure
without the support of nearly all its members. If participation
erodes, the system fails, and the hive is lost.

The three strategies for improving your reading rate and understanding of the material are (1) eliminating "white space" (2) expanding
eye fixations, and (3) pacing yourself through the print. All three provide
you with tools to break harmful habits. Use these tools consciously as
transition techniques to move you into being a skilled, efficient reader.
Practice them frequently and seriously, and soon they'll become automatic for you. Your reward will be a new-found ability to handle with
ease the college-level reading you encounter.

CHOOSING *YOUR* FAVORITE STRATEGY FOR CONTROLLING EYE MOVEMENTS

Use the paragraphs below to discover which strategy for controlling your eye movements is best for you. The paragraphs are from a student essay about stress in *Steps in Composition*, Seventh Edition, by Lynn Quitman Troyka and Jerrold Nudelman.

The first step to coping with stress is exploring your situation and changing your attitude. What is causing your stress? Like many people, you may have taken on so many activities that you feel overwhelmed. To deal with this problem, make a list of everything that is contributing to your stress. Then rank each item according to how serious the consequences would be if you did not do it. For example, you need to do well on your mid-terms, and you need a car to get to school and to work. So as much fun as the football game would be, you should spend the weekend studying and getting your car repaired. If you have trouble ranking the items, show your list to someone who has the objectivity to see a good solution. As you accomplish each item on your list, cross it off. This technique will help you to manage your time more efficiently and will give you a sense that you are in control of your life.

The second step to reducing stress is to begin a program of regular physical exercise. When people are under a great deal of stress, their bodies produce extra adrenalin, which quickens the heartbeat, increases the sugar level in the blood, and slows up or stops digestion. These bodily changes, in turn, cause people to sweat, to have upset stomachs, to feel jittery, and to lose sleep. However, if you exercise vigorously for 20 to 30 minutes a day—run or swim, for example—you will use up the extra energy produced by the high sugar level, and the physical symptoms of stress will probably disappear. Exercise on a planned schedule so that it becomes a habit, and do not exercise too near bedtime so that it does not interfere with sleep. Exercise will calm you and give you a feeling of well-being that will allow you to deal more effectively with your hectic lifestyle.

Chapter 5

How Can I Improve My Vocabulary?

English is a rich language with over 1,000,000 words. Yet, the average English-speaking adult has a vocabulary of only 40,000 to 50,000 words. And sadly, most of us use about 500 words in our everyday speech.

When you possess a large vocabulary, you can express and think about fine shades of meaning. You can think with precision. For example, unless you're a sailor, you probably refer to all the various lines on a sailboat as "ropes." "Ropes," however, is a basic, generic term suitable only for armchair discussion. When the wind is blowing a gale, and the waves are covering the deck with solid sheets of water, you want to yell out to your crew something more specific than "tighten the rope." Sailors say such exact phrases as "harden the jib sheet," "ease the boom vang and rig a starboard preventer," or "mind the dingy painter while we back down on the anchor rode." Such phrases communicate clearly at a mature level. Whether you're reading, writing, or speaking at the college level about sailing or science, about football or philosophy, about literature or sociology, a strong vocabulary is essential.

As a young child, you learned words very quickly. You imitated adults and older children. When you grew old enough to start school, your vocabulary acquisition slowed down. By middle and high school, you had to work to enlarge your vocabulary. Teachers gave you vocabulary lists, perhaps ten words a week, and then tested you. Often what happened after the test was that unless you used the words, you forgot them. Now that you've reached college, your vocabulary has fossilized in a sense. The good news is that every adult, no matter what age, is capable of learning and using new vocabulary words. The simple truth is that you'll remember new words only when you make up your mind to use them as often as possible. Memorization without usage is ineffective.

Success in college, and in certain jobs, depends heavily on vocabulary. One of the best ways to learn new words is to discover them in your reading. Push yourself to try to guess the meaning of a word from the way it is used in a sentence. This method calls for using *context clues*. With context clues, you try to determine the meaning of an unfamiliar word by looking for evidence in the sentence that contains the word, in the sentences that precede the word, and even in the sentences that follow the word. Context clues can be divided into four categories:

- Restatement Context Clues
- Definition Context Clues
- Example Context Clues
- Contrast Context Clues

USING RESTATEMENT CONTEXT CLUES

For a **restatement context clue,** look for a thought that's repeated in different words in the same or a nearby sentence. Sometimes, the restatement enlarges or limits the original thought. When writers repeat a thought, often taking the form of a synonym, you need simply to think about the shared meaning of the original and the restatement. For example, what does "fray" mean in the following sentence:

- He jumped into the **fray** and enjoyed every minute of the fight.

Perhaps a reader would guess that "fray" means either "fight" or "audience." After thinking of those two possibilities, the reader would note the words "jumped into" earlier in the sentence. Those words suggest an energetic entering, rather than a passive joining. "Fight" would be the correct choice.

Sometimes a restatement is set off by punctuation, which makes the reader's job easy. For example,

- Fatty deposits on artery walls combine with calcium compounds to cause **arteriosclerosis** (hardening of the arteries). [Here the restatement appears in parentheses *after* the difficult word.]
- The upper left part of the heart—the left **atrium**—receives blood returning from circulation. [Here the restatement appears in dashes *before* the word.]

ACTIVITY H   RESTATEMENT CONTEXT CLUES
Using restatement context clues, circle the best meaning for the italicized *words in the sentences below.*

1. In searching for food, homeless people often have to *scavenge* in dumpsters.

   Scavenge means   a. sleep.   b. hunt.   c. hide.

2. Sir Edmund Hillary and his climbing partner Sherpa Temzing Norgay were famous *alpinists*. In fact, they were the first to reach the top of Mt. Everest in 1953.

   Alpinists means   a. balloonists.   b. mountain climbers.   c. parachutists.

3. An *adroit* boxer—one who can dodge, jab, and avoid being knocked out—is generally not the type of fighter a crowd wants to see.

   Adroit means   a. entertaining.   b. nervous.   c. skillful.

4. Era had the *audacity* to break line in front of me in the school cafeteria. Then she had the nerve to ask me to loan her a dollar to pay for her lunch.

   Audacity means   a. impoliteness.   b. opportunity.   c. boldness.

5. At first, I was *dubious* whether I could complete the course. After the first major test, however, I was not as doubtful.

   Dubious means   a. unsure.   b. discouraged.   c. devastated.

6. The basketball players made a *simultaneous* jump for the ball. This concurrent movement resulted in a collision.

   Simultaneous means   a. at different times.   b. at the same time.   c. at conflicting times.

7. We have informed the guests about the *postponement*. The ceremony will not take place until a later date.

   Postponement means   a. cancellation.   b. advancement.   c. delay.

8. I am glad you were able to *alleviate* Kathie's fear of airplanes. Your suggestions made it easier for her to fly.

   Alleviate means   a. lessen.   b. increase.   c. free.

9. George Washington Carver was a famous *botanist*. He developed literally hundreds of uses for the peanut.

   Botanist means one who studies   a. animals.   b. plants.   c. fish.

10. On a movie set, *surrogates* often stand in for the real stars while technicians adjust the lights and camera angles.

    Surrogates means   a. professionals.   b. amateurs.   c. substitutes.

USING DEFINITION CONTEXT CLUES

A **definition context clue** means that the word is formally defined in the same sentence. Formal definitions are direct and easy to spot.

- To say that my misunderstanding your instructions caused me **chagrin** would be like saying my daily appetite is satisfied by a grain of sugar. The Tenth Edition (2000) of *Merriam Webster's Collegiate Dictionary* defines **chagrin** as "distress of mind caused by humiliation, disappointment, or failure." Replace "distress" with agony and misery in that definition, and perhaps you can better imagine my feelings.

Some definition clues are less direct. For example, a difficult word might be defined by a detailed description rather than a formal definition. Descriptive definitions are less obvious than formal ones, but once you become aware of the descriptive approach, you can use them to your advantage.

- The most **overly aggressive** people I know are also the most successful in business. They possess great stores of energy, never hesitate to take the lead and make quick decisions, interrupt conversations, and tell others what to do.

ACTIVITY I   DEFINITION CONTEXT CLUES
Below are ten sentences, each of which defines the italicized word. Use the clues in the definition sentences to fill in the answers to items 1–10 that follow.

- *Polyester* is generally characterized as a wrinkle-resistant fabric.

- A *skeptical* thinker is one who does not question beliefs or concepts.

- *Phi, theta,* and *kappa* are Greek letters meaning *wisdom, aspiration,* and *purity.*

- A street that curves and bends best describes a *sinuated* road.

- To feel *chagrin* is to be embarrassed or annoyed.

- A paragraph has *coherence* when the sentences are arranged in a clear, logical order.

- *Geriatrics* is the diagnosis and treatment of diseases associated with the elderly.

- A breed of powerful sled dogs developed in Alaska is the *malamute.*

- An *ambiguous* answer to a simple question is unclear because it can mean at least two different things.

- A person who talks without changing the pitch of the voice speaks in a *monotone.*

1. Your explanation of your actions is _____ because it can be taken in two ways.

2. I fell asleep listening to his _____ voice.

3. We need an expert in _____ to explain my grandparents' health.

4. A city apartment is no place for a dog as large as a _____.

5. My philosophy professor was _____ about whatever she read in newspapers.

6. I felt deep _____ when I realized that I had forgotten my best friend's birthday.

7. We couldn't understand the scientist's explanation of nanoseconds because it lacked _____.

8. The spot where the old country road goes up a hill and starts to _____ has been the site of many serious car accidents.

9. The Greek letter for wisdom is _____, for aspiration is _____, and for purity is _____.

10. Fabric made of _____ saves ironing time.

USING CONTRAST CONTEXT CLUES

A **contrast context clue** means you can figure out an unknown word when its opposite—or some other type of contrast—is mentioned close by.

- We feared that the new prime minister would be a *menace* to society, but she turned out to be a great peacemaker.

This sentence suggests that "menace" means "threat" because the contrast is that "she turned out to be a great peacemaker."

As you read, watch for words that signal contrasts. Such words include *but, however, nevertheless, on the other hand, unlike, in contrast,* and others.

ACTIVITY J   CONTRAST CONTEXT CLUES
Use contrast context clues to select the best meaning for the italicized words in the sentences below:

1. Even though Raleigh insisted that she hadn't passed a red light, the police officer's videotape of her doing so was *irrefutable* proof.

   Irrefutable means   a. can't be disputed.   b. unrealistic.
   c. questionable.

2. After a ten-mile hike to reach Pike's Peak, I thought I would be *ravenous*. Yet, I was so relieved that the hike was over I couldn't eat a thing.

   Ravenous means   a. highly excited.   b. extremely lazy.
   c. very hungry.

3. The Williams enjoyed their country house on Creve Coeur, and so they found it difficult to adjust to *urban* life in St. Louis.

   Urban means   a. expensive.   b. city.   c. secluded.

4. Unlike my wife who does not approve of our children eating between meals, I *sanctioned* their eating fruit if it keeps them from crying.

   Sanctioned means   a. ignored.   b. approved of.   c. discouraged.

5. This week my bosses assigned me to the *tedious* task of proofreading every one of the ninety-four letters they wrote last week.

   Tedious means   a. envious.   b. complex.   c. boring.

6. Greg was *gregarious*, but his twin brother Rory was shy.

   Gregarious means   a. distrustful.   b. sociable.   c. outspoken.

7. An abridged dictionary, not an *unabridged* dictionary, has been shortened.

   Unabridged means   a. complete.   b. incomplete.   c. blended.

8. Although Earmonika *somnambulates*, Veronica, her sister, never walks in her sleep.

   Somnambulates means   a. snores in her sleep.   b. talks in her sleep.
   c. strolls around while asleep.

9. Dee's whistle was *inaudible* to me; however, my puppy could hear it.

   Inaudible means   a. not seen.   b. not heard.   c. not recognizable.

10. Although a tuition increase of 15 percent has been approved, the college does not expect an *attrition* in enrollment.

    Attrition means   a. decrease.   b. growth.   c. renewed interest.

USING EXAMPLE CONTEXT CLUES

You are looking at an **example context clue** when an unfamiliar word is followed by an example that reveals what the unknown word means.

> They were *conscientious* workers, never stopping until they had taken care of every detail so that everything was done correctly and precisely.

The words "never stopping until," "taken care of every detail," and "done correctly and precisely" clue you to the meaning of *conscientious*. It means responsible, thorough, and reliable.

Often, an example context clue is introduced with signal words like *such as*, *for example*, *for instance*, and *including*.

ACTIVITY K   EXAMPLE CONTEXT CLUES
Select the best meaning of the word shown in italics *in the sentences below.*

1. *Adversities*, such as poverty, poor grades, and a weak family background, can be overcome with effort.

   Adversities means   a. obstacles.   b. pleasures.   c. responsibilities.

2. Andrew had a reputation for doing *perilous* activities. For example, he loved to ride a racing bike without a helmet, climb mountains without a safety rope, and ride in a speedboat without a life preserver.

   Perilous means   a. thrilling.   b. dangerous.   c. remarkable.

3. *Pungent* odors, including those of perfume, room deodorizers, and household cleansers, can cause allergic reactions in some people.

   Pungent means   a. mild.   b. sharp.   c. weak.

4. An *obituary* generally includes the person's age, occupation, survivors, and funeral arrangements.

   Obituary means   a. death notice.   b. sermon.   c. will.

5. Brothers and sisters sometimes like to play a harmless *prank* on one another. For example, a sister might make up the idea that their mother wants the brother to do a messy household chore.

   Prank means   a. joke.   b. assignment.   c. request.

6. I could see by Carlos's *visage* he was upset. He had an angry frown on his face, and his eyes were wide with fury.

   Visage means   a. actions.   b. personality.   c. appearance.

7. *Pachyderms*, such as the rhinoceros, the hippopotamus, and the elephant, are mammals that live in Africa.

   Pachyderms means   a. sensitive.   b. hostile.   c. thick-skinned.

8. That mole on your arm is a dark color; you need to see a doctor who specializes in *dermatology*.

   Dermatology means   a. heart.   b. skin.   c. feet.

9. Servers in restaurants depend on customers to leave a *gratuity* for their services. Without tips, waiters couldn't make a living.

   Gratuity means   a. money.   b. compliment.   c. recommendation.

10. To avoid encountering fans, Mankind and The Rock of the World Federation Wrestlers, agreed to a *rendezvous* at 12 midnight at Main Street and Broadway.

    Rendezvous means   a. exhibition.   b. match.   c. meeting.

LEARNING AND REMEMBERING NEW WORDS

So that you do not have to rediscover a new word repeatedly, you want to work at reviewing and remembering new words all the time. How can you learn to remember new words? A personal method of vocabulary study that fits your learning style will work. Here's a good method to try—or to adapt to be most effective for you.

Learning New Words: The PWRA System

P = Pick   Look and listen for new words you would like to add to your vocabulary. Choose selectively so that you concentrate on the words that will serve you best. Each word that is new to you will require thorough, repeated study. Most people can learn about ten new words at a time.

W = Write   Use a 3 × 5 index card for each word you want to learn. On the front side of the card, write the word. On the backside of the card, write the definition. Below the definition, write an original sentence using the word. Here's a sample card for the word *avocado*:

avocado

Front Side

---

a pear-shaped tropical fruit

An avocado is sometimes mashed and combined with onion, lemon juice, etc. to make a dip.

Back Side

R = Review   Stack your 3 × 5 cards so that you see each card only on the side showing the word alone. Look at the word and try to recall the definition on the back. After you have been through the entire stack, turn over the cards so that you now see the sides with the definitions. This time look at the definition and your sentence to recall the word on the other side. As you work through your cards, divide them into two stacks: "know" and "don't know." Then, review the cards in your "don't know" stack. This intensifies your concentration. Before you end your study session, go through both stacks of cards again.

A = Apply   Once you have learned a word, apply it. Actively use the word in your speaking and writing. Push yourself to find occasions that allow you to fit in the word. To reinforce your mastery of the word, hold it in the front of your mind, thinking about its definition and appropriate use. Only when you're certain that you "own" the word—that is, it's in your active vocabulary—can you move it to your list for every-two-weeks or monthly review. If you've forgotten the word, put it back on your daily study list.

In *Structured Reading,* we give you actual dictionary entries for the more challenging words in each reading selection. They are from *Webster's New World College Dictionary, Fourth Edition.* Having the entries readily accessible gives you hands-on experience with a first-class dictionary. We designed this resource so that you can become familiar with dictionary entries. Dictionary entries can look more complex than they are. Take apart the sections of a dictionary entry:

- Pronunciation guide for the word.

- Material at the beginning of many entries, which tells how to pronounce the word and the origin of the word if it's derived from languages other than modern English.

- Sequence of definitions for words with more than one meaning (most-to-less frequently used? oldest use to newest? other?).

- Various forms the word can take, such as a noun that can be adapted for use as an adjective.

Along with the complete dictionary entries, *Structured Reading* offers you various types of vocabulary practice exercises. They include context clues, fill-ins, multiple choices, and crossword puzzles. Working with vocabulary exercises in this textbook gives you hands-on opportunities to master your knowledge of words. Your goal is to "own" the new words.

Many people have a mental (and sometimes written) list of words they've heard or read whose meanings they don't know—but they'd like to. Other people don't have a list but still experience a vague discomfort because they'd like to know the meaning of more words. Even if you're not sure about how to spell them, list ten of them here. Then, apply the PWRA system to each, using the guidelines on pages 26 and 27.

_____   _____

_____   _____

_____   _____

_____   _____

_____   _____

Chapter 7

What Is the Role of "SQ3R" When Reading to Study?

SQ3R stands for *Survey*, *Question*, *Read*, *Recite*, and *Review*. It's a study technique to help you maximize your comprehension while minimizing your reading time. Learning how to use these principles will help you master textbook material—that is retaining information over the long term, learning information to the point of recall, and understanding the facts and how they fit together. Try applying this five-step process to the textbook excerpts in this textbook (Selections 28 and 29). The investment of your time is worth the benefits. You'll notice improvement in your concentration, comprehension, and reading rate. The box below describes the SQ3R technique.

SQ3R for Studying

S = Survey   Before you read closely, look over the title, headings, and subheadings. Look also at the captions under pictures, charts, graphs, or maps. Consciously predict what you think the topics will be.

Q = Question   Turn each heading and subheading into a question using the "*five W's and one H*": *who, what, when, where, why, how*. By asking questions, you prepare your mind to read for the answer.

R = Read   Read closely, keeping in mind the questions you've already asked about the material. Strive to hook any new material onto what you already know. Come to understand the material.

R = Recite   After you've read two or more pages, go back to whatever headings, subheadings, or boldface words you used to form questions during the Q part of SQ3R. Cover up the specific paragraphs, and in your own words, say aloud or to yourself what the material is about.

$\longrightarrow$

SQ3R for Studying, continued

R = Review Look over the material again. Move somewhat slowly and take special notice of key spots: the title, main headings, subheading, and important paragraphs. As you review, you might highlight key areas with a see-through marking pen—but be careful to highlight only major ideas. If you fill a page with highlighter pen, you need to work harder on separating minor material from key points. Next, think through whether your predictions made during your Survey were correct. The review is intended to pull together all the pieces as if you're working on a jigsaw puzzle.

Below are a few paragraphs about the Giant Panda, from a publication of The Healthy Planet. Practice applying the SQ3R technique as you read it.

Evidence of the Giant Panda in Ancient Times

For more than three million years, the Giant Panda lived in remote, forested areas of China. Numerous fossil remains provide evidence that the mammal known to the Chinese as daxiong mao (dah-sh-WING, MAH-oo) which mean, "large cat-bear," lived in more than 48 different localities throughout China as well as one site in Burma.

The Giant Panda has appeared in Chinese books about literature, medicine and geography for more than 2,000 years. At one time, the mammal was hunted for it's beautiful and unusual coat because superstitions thought it to possess the power of prediction and protection: It was believed that having a good night's sleep on a panda pelt indicated good fortune, while the pelt itself was thought to keep ghosts at bay. Today, the Giant Panda is the much respected national symbol of China.

An Appealing Pace of Life

A slow metabolism makes the panda an energy-conserving animal, which means it uses a minimal amount of energy to find its next food source. If it didn't have to, the panda would probably not move at all. In the wild, the Giant Panda will plunk itself down in the midst of a bamboo forest and simply pull at the shoots it can reach.

Using its unique wrist bone that acts as an opposable thumb, the panda can grasp bamboo. The animal peels the bamboo like a banana by holding it between its five fingers and its wrist knob. An especially tough esophagus helps the panda swallow the fibrous bamboo.

Chapter 8

How Can Maps and Outlines Help With Reading?

Drawing maps and making outlines are two very effective ways for you to comprehend and remember what you're reading.

MAPPING OF CONTENT

Mapping creates a visual diagram of a topic's major points and sub-points. Mapping, also called *clustering* or *webbing*, is a structured method to draw ideas on paper. This visual technique has been shown to help readers clarify what they're reading, comprehend the larger chunks of material, and more easily remember what's been read. Maps demonstrate relationships between ideas by seeing how they play themselves out spatially. The technique of mapping doesn't appeal to everyone, but try it a few times to get used to it. Then, you can decide whether to put mapping into your store of reading strategies.

To map, you begin at the center of a blank sheet of paper, which you can consider the center or nucleus. Draw a circle at the center into which you write the central topic of the article or essay. Next, drawing out from the center circle, make lines that spread out in various directions. End each line with a blank circle. In each of these new circles, write a main idea that's connected to the central topic of the material—this forms "branches" off the central topic. After this, work outward from each main idea by drawing shorter lines ending with circles into which you write supporting details for each main idea. As you work out from the center of the sheet of paper in all directions, you generate a growing, organized structure of what you're reading, which is composed of key words and phrases. Adapt this technique to what you're reading or rereading. Maps can be drawn in all sorts of patterns and shapes, so you can decide how you prefer to display it on a map.

ACTIVITY L MAPPING

Read this paragraph twice. First, read it for its meaning. Second, reread it with an eye toward drawing a map of it.

Elephants are the largest animals that live on land. There are two chief kinds of elephants: African and Asiatic. African elephants live only in Africa south of the Sahara. Asiatic elephants live in parts of India and Southeast Asia. An African elephant is about the same height at the shoulder and rump. Its back dips slightly in the middle. However, an Asiatic elephant has an arched back that is slightly higher than the shoulder and the rump. The ears of an African elephant measure as wide as four feet and cover their shoulders while the ears of an Asiatic elephant are about half as large as those of the African elephant and do not cover the shoulders. The forehead of an Asiatic elephant forms a smooth curve, but the Asiatic elephant has two humps on its forehead just above the ears. The trunk of an African elephant has two finger-like knobs of flesh on the tip; whereas, the trunk of an Asiatic elephant has only one finger-like knob on the tip. The trunk provides a keen sense of smell, and elephants depend on this sense more than on any other.

Fill in this map of the paragraph about elephants. Some answers are provided to get you started.

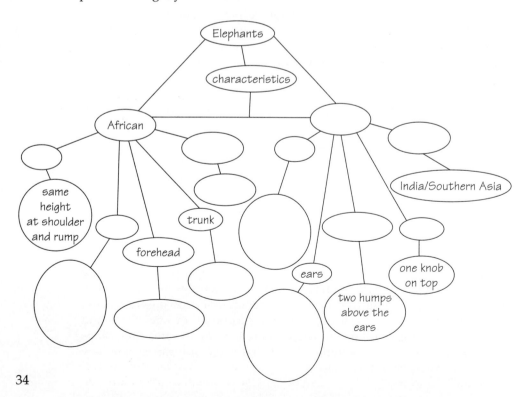

Many people like to work at understanding ideas by using mapping techniques. These people report that mapping feels like drawing a picture. They let their hand glide across the page, capturing ideas within circles. Many "mappers," who often prefer not to write outlines, say that they relax and think better when they map. Many other people, however, feel that a map seems cluttered, unorganized, and difficult to use to identify the main and sub points. They prefer to outline.

OUTLINING

Outlining is a structuring process that helps you organize, understand, and remember information. You might find that outlining isn't appropriate for everything you read (for example, fiction), but it can assist you particularly well when you need to master a sizable amount of material. Two common methods of outlining are informal and formal outlines.

CREATING AN INFORMAL OUTLINE

An informal outline breaks down material into sections that correspond roughly to different parts of the material. Its purpose is to increase your awareness of the separate parts of what you've read. No strict format exists for informal outlines. Writers often use informal outlines to create their working plans, a way to lay out the major parts of an essay. Here's an informal outline for an essay about weight lifting for women.

Informal Outline

<u>weights/how to use</u>

safety is vital

free weights

don't bend at waist

do align neck and back

do look straight ahead

weight machines—safety is easier

CREATING A FORMAL OUTLINE

A formal outline takes the concept of an informal outline a few steps further. It adheres to strict format requirements, using Roman numerals, letters, and numbers to show how ideas relate to another. Roman numerals identify main ideas. Letters identify major details. Numbers identify minor details if they're necessary to include. Here's a formal outline for an essay about weight lifting for women. Following it is a Box that summarizes guidelines for creating formal outlines.

Formal Outline

Title: Weight Lifting for Women

I. Avoiding massive muscle development
   A. Role of women's biology
   B. Role of combining exercise types
      1. Anaerobic (weight lifting)
      2. Aerobic (swimming)
II. Using Weights Safely
   A. Free weights
   B. Weight Machines (built-in safeguards)

Guidelines for a Formal Outline

FORMAT

I. First main idea
   A. First major detail
   B. Second major detail
      1. First minor detail
      2. Second minor detail
         a. First smaller detail
         b. Second smaller detail
II. Second main idea
   A. First major detail
   B. Second major detail

RULES

- *Groupings:* Numbers, letters, and indentations identify groupings and levels of importance. Roman numerals (I, II, III) signal major subdivisions of the topic. Indented capital letters (A, B) signal the next level of generality. Even more indented Arabic numbers (1, 2, 3) show the third level of generality. And, finally, if absolutely necessary, indented lowercase letters (a, b) show the fourth level. Remember, all subdivisions must be at the same level of generality. For example, a main idea can't be paired with a supporting detail.

- *Levels:* Each level *must* have more than one entry. Don't enter a *I* unless there's a *II*; don't enter an *A* unless there's a *B*; don't enter a *1* unless there's a *2*; don't enter an *a* unless there's a *b*. If only one entry is possible, that entry is part of the heading in the next higher level. ⟶

Guidelines for a Formal Outline, continued

NO   A. Free weights
       1. Safe lifting technique
     B. Weight machines
YES A. Free weights
     B. Weight machines
YES A. Free weights
       1. Unsafe lifting techniques
       2. Safe lifting techniques
     B. Weight machines

- *Headings:* Headings don't overlap. For example, whatever is covered in subdivision 1, must be distinct from whatever is covered in subdivision 2.

NO   A. Free weights
       1. Unsafe lifting techniques
       2. Not aligning head and neck
YES A. Free weights
       1. Unsafe lifting techniques
       2. Safe lifting techniques

- *Parallelism:* Entries are grammatically parallel (all items start with a verb, or with a noun, or with any other word form). For example, all start with the *-ing* forms of verbs (*Helping, Assisting, Guiding*).

NO   A. Free weights
     B. Using weight machines
YES A. Using free weights
     B. Using weight machines

- *Capitalization and Punctuation:* The first word of each entry is capitalized, and proper nouns are always capitalized. The items in a sentence outline end with a period (or a question mark, if needed). The items in a topic outline don't end with punctuation.
- *Introductory and Concluding Paragraphs:* These aren't part of a formal outline.

Here's a useful way to outline. Divide each sheet of paper in two, as follows: from the top to the bottom draw a straight line down the sheet, with about one-third of the paper's space to the left of the vertical line and about two-thirds of the space to the right. To the right of the vertical line, write your outline. To the left of the line, write key words or phrases that hint what's outlined on the right side.

Key Words	Outline
Long-term Memory Organization	Organization 1. Semantic memory 2. 3. 4.

Processes	Processes
	1. Depth of processing
	   a. Semantic codes
	   b. Pair-associates recall
	2.
	3.
	   a.
	   b.

When you go back later to re-study the material, first move your eye down the left side of the paper, looking at the key words and phrases to check your recall. Then, to refresh your memory, slowly read the outline on the right side, thinking about the material as you read. Then, once again move your eye down the left side of the page to see how much you can recall without looking at the right side. Doing this repeatedly will help you train your memory.

Your outline form itself depends on the material you're reading, your purpose in reading it, and how much you want to recall. If you're reading for a class or a test, your outline should include all the important main points and their supporting details. If you're reading for general recall only, your outline requires less detail.

Although you will not always outline everything you read, you might want to practice the technique so it becomes an easy way for you to make notes when thorough recall is important. Apply this technique to Selection 28, "Long-Term Memory," with the idea in mind that you can use your notes in a discussion on how memory affects test performance in a study skills class. The outline has been started for you above.

When you complete the outline, you might want to compare what you have with what others in your class have done. You may find that wordings vary among different students, but be sure to check that the main ideas are the same. Be certain, also, that you have included all the supporting details used by the author. Whenever you're not completely sure that you've captured the author's points, go back and reread the material.

Chapter 9

What Is Reading On, Between, and Beyond the Lines?

Reading **on, between,** and **beyond** the lines means reading closely. You can practice intensive and extensive practice in reading closely in all the exercises that follow each reading selection in *Structured Reading*.

Reading **on the lines** means understanding the stated meaning of the material. Here you look for the exact, literal meaning of what's written. In *Structured Reading,* three kinds of exercises have been designed especially to help you develop your ability to read on the lines: "Vocabulary" (explained in Chapter 5 in Part One); "Central Theme and Main Ideas" (Chapter 10); and "Major Details" (Chapter 11).

Reading **between the lines** means understanding what's implied but not stated outright. When ideas are implied, you need to read between the lines to figure out what's not said directly, but is meant for the reader to realize nevertheless. To do this, look for these underlying assumptions or attitudes:

- Attitude toward you, the reader (respectful, condescending, playful, etc.), as reflected in the writing.

- Assumptions concerning what you, the reader, are expected to know before you begin reading the material.

- Attitude toward the topic (objective, biased, passionate, etc.).

To figure out authors' assumptions and attitudes, depend on how the authors express what they say. What words and phrases hint at something that's not stated? What alternatives of word choice were at the authors' disposal, and why did the authors choose the words used? Also, how do authors use evidence? Do they distort facts and information only to make their point? What line of reasoning do the authors use? Do the points being raised progress in a logical pattern, or do the authors try to mislead the reader by using faulty logic? Your answers to such questions provide a portrait of the author's tone. Just as you can tell how people feel about a topic from their tone of voice, so can tone also emerge from the writing. In *Structured Reading,* two kinds of exercises have been designed especially to give you practice with reading between the lines: "Inferences" (Chapter 12) and "Critical Reading" (Chapter 13).

Reading **beyond the lines** means you develop informed opinions about the subject being discussed in the material you're reading. To do this, come to your own conclusions based on what's been stated (on the lines) and what has been implied (between the lines). In *Structured Reading,* "Reader Response" exercises (Chapter 14) offer you opportunities to think and talk about your personal point of view about the subject of what you're reading. The subjects vary so that you can practice in diverse realms of thought.

In Parts Two through Six, every reading selection in *Structured Reading* provides you structured practice with reading on, between, and beyond the lines. The entire purpose of *Structured Reading*'s exercises is *not* merely to test whether you've read a selection. That would be a simplistic waste of time. Rather the purpose of all the exercises is to guide you along a structured path that leads to your being comfortable and skilled with reading at a college level.

The driving force behind the structure and content of the exercises is this: "If a person can't make a mistake, that person can't make anything." The learning moment is at hand if you choose a wrong answer to a question. Seize that moment! Figure out *why* your answer is wrong. If your answer is incorrect, examine your personal line of reasoning to figure out what you misunderstood. The exercises in *Structured Reading* are designed so that students learn as much, if not more, from an incorrect answer than from a correct one. Did the misunderstanding come from forgetting to read closely, with your full focus? Did the misunderstanding result from having missed what's implied but not stated?

Learning the reading habits and thinking strategies for college-level performance takes time. Don't get discouraged, and don't give up. *Structured Reading* challenges you to grow as a reader by deliberately asking you to stretch beyond what you're used to as your personal reading method. The ultimate goal is for you to make giant strides toward upgrading your reading ability.

Chapter 10

What Are "Central Theme" and "Main Ideas"?

In *Structured Reading*, the term **central theme** refers to what an entire reading selection is about. The term **main idea** refers to what a paragraph or group of paragraphs is about. To identify a reading selection's central theme and main ideas you usually need to "read on the lines"—see Chapter 9 in Part One. Sometimes, however, a central theme or the main ideas aren't stated outright. They're implied, which calls for you to "read between the lines," explained in Chapter 9. To figure out the central theme and main ideas of a passage, you need to read closely and give yourself the time to reflect on what you've read.

FINDING A CENTRAL THEME

The **central theme** of a reading selection is your answer to the question "What's the key point here?" A central theme is the key, the core, the significant message of a reading selection. To get to the central theme, try imagining this scene: A close friend stops by to visit you for a few minutes on the way to work. You invite him in and ask him to sit down. He glances briefly at the headlines on the front page of the newspaper lying on the floor. Not having time to hear all the details, he asks, "What's this about?"

The summary you give—neither too long nor too short—is a statement of the central theme, in this case of the newspaper article. For example, a good statement of a central theme would be "A high school coach is accused of receiving $200,000 for convincing one of his players to sign with a nearby college."

FINDING MAIN IDEAS

The **main idea** is the key message in a paragraph or several paragraphs. The main idea is the thesis, the topic, the subject of a subsection of paragraphs within a whole piece of reading. For example, what's the topic in the following paragraph?

Many students believe teachers can prevent cheating. In other words, cheating would not be a problem if teachers took certain steps to prevent it. For example, students believe that cheating could be prevented if teachers announced tests early and the material to be covered on the test. They believe that in small classes teachers who work with students in a personal manner discourage cheating. Seating arrangements can also aid in combating cheating. They also believe that cheating could be prevented if penalties were made clear and firmly enforced. In short, cheating is perceived to be a teacher's responsibility, not a student's responsibility.

To find the main idea do this: First, locate one or two words that represent what the paragraph is about. In the above paragraph, the word is *cheating*. Using *cheating* as your key word, ask yourself *what* the paragraph says about cheating. The answer is the main idea: "Many students believe teachers can prevent cheating." (By the way, usually you need to state the main idea in your own words, even though here a quotation is appropriate.)

A good way to think of a main idea in a paragraph is to think about the design of an umbrella. Main ideas are "umbrella ideas." The main idea can be compared to the fabric covering an umbrella. All the major details are the supporting ideas—reasons, examples, names, statistics, and other material that supports the main idea—make up the metal spines of the umbrella. The diagram on the next page shows the relationship between a main idea and its supporting details.

Main ideas usually appear at the beginning of paragraphs, especially in textbooks, articles, and essays. Yet, many times, authors place the main idea at the end of a paragraph so that they can lead up to a small climax. Sometimes, writers put the main idea in the middle of the paragraph so that related material can surround it.

A main idea stated at the beginning of a paragraph is illustrated by the passage about cheating, shown earlier in this chapter. Here's a paragraph with the main idea stated in the final sentence. It's from "Dr. Ice Cream," in the *Washington Post*.

Since Wendell Arbuckle retired, he has worked as a consultant—often traveling to ice cream factories to taste what they produce and evaluate it, much as tea tasters taste tea and wine tasters, wine. The tasting usually is done with two spoons, Arbuckle said, one for scooping the ice cream out of the package, the other for putting it into his mouth. Arbuckle said he usually stands over a sink, and spits out each sample without swallowing. "Sometimes I sample 90 batches a day," he said. "If I swallowed just a little bit of each one that would be too much." He evaluates the ice cream not only for flavor but also for texture as well, and gives advice on how to improve it.

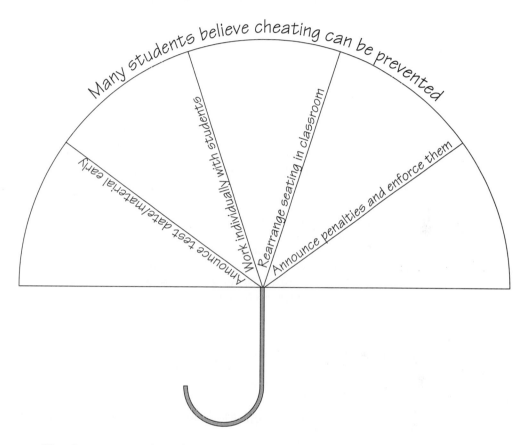

Here's a paragraph with the main idea implied, not stated directly. It's from "Things Are Seldom What They Seem," in *Pageant* magazine.

Just because a body's in a hearse or on a body cart covered with a sheet in a funeral home doesn't mean it's dead, although the casual onlooker has every right to think so. However, policemen in Fresno, California, being of more suspicious mind, detected breathing coming from the bodies and arrested the two suspects they had been pursuing. Both were very much alive.

You need to "read between the lines" to determine when main ideas are implied, not stated. You want to identify the main point from the reasons, examples, and other details mentioned in the passage. In the

43

paragraph from *Pageant* magazine above, the author comments about appearance versus reality. What appeared to be two dead bodies are actually two fugitives who had tried to elude the police.

OBSERVING CENTRAL THEMES AND MAIN IDEAS IN ACTION

Structured Reading provides two types of practice in finding central themes and main ideas. One type asks you to select the correct statement of a central theme or main idea from among four options (multiple choice). Read the choices closely and think about them so that you're ready to justify why you chose what you did and why you rejected what you did. Reasons for not choosing an option are as important as reasons for choosing. Here's an example from *Black Belt* magazine:

> Lookout Mountain School for boys in Colorado is a school for boys who will not stay, voluntarily, at other places. They've been in trouble, in some cases deep trouble, with society. But the school, like other confining institutions, can't always offer total rehabilitation programs. The boys develop a certain amount of social retardation, being retained and confined. As one counselor puts it, "They can't function in society so they come here. Then we try to teach them to function in society." It's a tough job because, as he says, "The question remains: How can we teach them to function in society when they can't go out there?"

_____ 1. What's the main idea of this paragraph?
   a. Because Lookout Mountain School is a confining institution, it can't offer a total rehabilitation program.
   b. There's no attempt to rehabilitate the boys at Lookout Mountain School.
   c. Most boys at Lookout Mountain School are too "hardened" to be rehabilitated.
   d. Teaching delinquent boys to function in society is a tough job.

Answer: *a*

The second type of practice for finding central themes and main ideas is *open ended*. This type asks you to state a central theme or main idea in your own words. Here's an example from "People Are the Attraction," by Bill and Sonia Freedman. (Another passage from this essay appears in Chapter 11 in Part One.)

Among the Pennsylvania Dutch, married couples travel in covered horse-drawn buggies. Unmarried ones drive in open carts without a roof. You guessed it: so the entire community can see that no hanky-panky is going on. On top of which, Mama sees to it that instead of hooks-and-eyes, daughter's dress is fastened with straight pins—sharp ones placed in strategic locations. It may be a coincidence, but it is rumored any bachelor worth his salt always wears three or more Band-Aids on his pinkies.

In your own words, give the main idea of the paragraph above.

_____

_____

Answer: In your own words, convey this idea: Among the Pennsylvania Dutch, the romantic morals of an unmarried couple are watched over all the time.

PRACTICING WITH CENTRAL THEMES AND MAIN IDEAS

ACTIVITY M   CENTRAL THEME AND MAIN IDEAS 1
Read the paragraphs below and answer the questions that follow them. (Answers on page 78.)

From "Dealing with Unhappy and Difficult Customers," by Eric Tyson

(1) Some people say, "The customer is always right." In other words, even if a customer is being a jerk and trying to take advantage of you or is just being all-around difficult, you should bend over backward to please a customer.

(2) I don't buy this way of thinking. You should give the benefit of doubt to customers because they can do lots of good for your business if you keep them happy and lots of harm if you don't. But some customers are a major pain in the posterior and impossible to please. Trying to keep them happy can be a time-consuming, costly process.

(3) Difficult people often don't have many friends so you probably won't get referrals anyway, and those customers they do refer to you may be as difficult as they are.

(4) If your business didn't do right by a customer, apologize, and bend over backward to make the customer happy. Offer a discount on the problem purchase or, if possible, a refund on product purchases. Also, be sure that you have a clear return and refund policy. Be willing to bend that policy if doing so helps you satisfy an unhappy customer or rids you of a difficult customer.

_____ 1. What's the central theme of "Dealing with Unhappy and Diffi-cult Customers"?
  a. A business's customers are always right, so it's wise business practice to please them no matter how difficult they are.
  b. Some customers can never be pleased, no matter what you do, because they enjoy being unhappy and making others miserable.
  c. Business benefits when customers are happy, but getting rid of some difficult customers can help a business sometimes.
  d. Because of their never-can-be-satisfied personalities, difficult customers probably have few friends—or potential customers to refer to you.

_____ 2. What's the main idea of paragraph 2?
  a. The author thinks that pleasing customers, even when they're difficult, is a bad idea.
  b. A business must give customers the benefit of the doubt, no matter how difficult they become.
  c. Unhappy customers can cause trouble for a business by spreading their opinions to other people.
  d. Keeping difficult customers happy can be a time-consuming, costly, frustrating process.

_____ 3. What's the main idea of paragraph 4?
  a. If your business has clear policies—with room to make ex-ceptions—for handling complaints, most customers are usu-ally satisfied.
  b. Clear policies for handling complaints help a business get rid of impossibly difficult customers without making the matter seem personal.
  c. Most businesses are better off without impossibly difficult customers, even if official policy says all customers must be satisfied.
  d. When a business can offer discounts and refunds, unhappy and difficult customers alike can be satisfied.

ACTIVITY N   CENTRAL THEME AND MAIN IDEAS 2

Read the paragraphs below and answer the questions that follow them. (Answers on page 79.)

From *Direct from Dell*, by Michael Dell with Catherine Fredman.

(1) Dell is the kind of company where everyone rolls up his sleeves and gets personally involved. We may be an $18 billion company, but our entire management team, myself included, is involved in the details of our business every day. This is, in fact, how we got to be successful: As

managers, it's not enough to sit around theorizing and reviewing what those who report to us do. We frequently meet with customers and attend working-level meetings about products, procurement, and technology, to tap into the real source of our company's experience and brainpower.

(2) Why bother? It's a way to get close to our people, for certain. But that's not all. Our day-to-day involvement in the business helps us establish and allows us to maintain one of Dell's critical competitive advantages: speed. In this case, "staying involved in the details" allows for rapid decision making because we know what's going on.

(3) For example, when a problem crops up, there's no need for us to do more research or assign someone the job of figuring out what the issues are. Because we often have all the information at our fingertips, we can gather the right people in one room, make a decision, and move forward—fast. The pace of business moves too quickly these days to waste time noodling over a decision. And while we strive to always make the right choice, I believe it's better to be first at the risk of being wrong than it is to be 100 percent perfect two years late.

_____ 1. What's the central theme of this excerpt from *Direct from Dell*?
   a. Dell's managers stay involved in day-to-day issues so that they can make informed decisions.
   b. Almost everyone at Dell likes being part of an $18 billion company.
   c. The pace of most businesses today is slower than the pace at Dell, a fact that makes many people uncomfortable.
   d. Dell is successful because its managers do the theorizing and reviewing without having to consult its customers.

2. What's the main idea of paragraph 1?

_____

_____

_____ 3. What's the main idea of paragraph 3?
   a. Problems are solved more easily when research has been completed.
   b. It's important for people to have information at their fingertips.
   c. Making decisions quickly is more valuable than making correct decisions.
   d. Today's rapid pace of business makes quick decision-making important.

ACTIVITY O   CENTRAL THEME AND MAIN IDEAS 3
Read the paragraphs below and answer the questions that follow them. (Answers on page 79.)

From *Catfish and Mandala*, by Andrew X. Pham

(1) The engine was running, but the sea had us in its palm. Our poor fishing vessel bobbed directionless, putting no distance between us and the mysterious ship in pursuit. The crew looked defeated. Mom muttered that it was terrible luck. First, the net fouling the propeller, now this. She said to Dad, "How could this be?" The calendar showed today to be auspicious. All the celestial signs were good—clear sky, good wind. She shook her head, looking at her Japanese flag, a patch of red on a white sheet, flapping noisily. Our hopes were pinned on that fraudulent banner.

(2) We waited. Time sagged. I counted the waves beneath our keel. There was nothing to do. The men's lips were moving, mumbling prayers. Eyes closed. Mom had her jade Buddha in her palms. Miracle. Miracle. Our boat seemed to plead with the ocean. Please send a miracle.

(3) It happened. The men stirred, but no one uttered a word. They looked hopeful, fearing that saying something might jinx whatever was happening. Another minute I could tell that the ship was veering away from us. They cheered. Tai instructed us to stay hidden, knowing that the ship had us in its binoculars. Mom was shaking with relief. Eventually, the ship went over the horizon and the men celebrated with a meal.

_____ 1. What is the central theme of this excerpt from *Catfish and Mandala*?
   a. A family hiding on a fishing vessel prays they will not be discovered.
   b. A family hidden by a boat's crew experiences several instances of terrible luck.
   c. People hiding on a fishing vessel are relieved when a crew from another ship chooses not to investigate them more closely.
   d. A ship's crew mistakes an illegal fishing vessel as Japanese.

_____ 2. What's the main idea of paragraph 1?
   a. The fishing vessel is not Japanese, even though it's flying the Japanese flag.
   b. The people hiding on the disguised ship are unhappy about their terrible luck.
   c. The people on the fishing vessel are strong believers in good luck and bad luck.
   d. The two examples of bad luck are the net fouling the propeller and a pursuing ship.

_____ 3. What's the main idea of paragraph 3?
   a. The men celebrate when a pursuing ship turns away.
   b. Tai, as the captain of the fishing vessel, gave the orders and everyone obeyed.

    c. The men stayed silent as the "miracle" happened before their eyes.

    d. The author's mother shook with relief when the ship went over the horizon.

ACTIVITY P   CENTRAL THEME AND MAIN IDEAS 4

Read the paragraph below and answer the questions following it. (Answers on page 79.)

From *Fish for All Seasons,* by Kitty Crider

(1) There is a lot of hoopla in the summer about wild salmon, especially the Copper River fish, which has had a highly successful marketing program in recent years. And it's a fine fish, to be sure.

(2) But the thing about salmon today is that it's like a strawberry. You can buy it fresh any time of the year, from somewhere. Salmon is no longer a seasonal item, found only in the wild. It's also farm-raised—in about 40 countries—and shows up on plates in the middle of the desert as well as near the coasts.

(3) Salmon illustrates how much the fresh-fish platter has changed in the past 10 years, primarily because of improved airline distribution and farm raising of more species. Fish that were once available only near their waters have become frequent fliers. And species that were only eaten in certain areas or months are being farmed in a variety of locations for year-round distributions.

    1. What's the central theme for "Fish"?

    _____

    _____

_____   2. What's the main idea for paragraph 2?
    a. Salmon is like a strawberry because both decay quickly.
    b. People almost anywhere can buy fresh salmon any time of the year.
    c. Salmon is farm-raised in about 40 countries.
    d. People can eat fresh fish, even in the desert.

_____   3. What's the main idea of paragraph 3?
    a. All kinds of fresh fish can be flown to almost anywhere in the world.
    b. Fish farming in a variety of locations means year-round salmon distribution.
    c. Fresh fish can be found in the wild and on fish farms in 40 countries.
    d. Fast airline distribution and fish farming have led to increased availability of salmon.

Chapter 11

What Are "Major Details"?

Major details support and develop a main idea. They emerge as you read "on the lines," a concept discussed in Chapter 9. Being able to tell the difference between a major detail and a minor detail is an important reading skill. Major details are the metal spines in the umbrella diagram shown on page 43. If you view all details as equally important, you'll become overloaded by details. To remember efficiently, you want to sort out the major details from the rest. Minor details can be interesting, but they're not basic to the understanding of the material you're reading.

FINDING MAJOR DETAILS

Differentiating between major and minor details takes practice. You can make such judgments only in the context of a complete reading selection. Depending on the framework in which the major detail is used, the same detail can be major or minor. For example, a person's age can be a major detail if the material is about the person's tragic, early death. On the other hand, a person's age can be a minor detail if the material is about the person's thoughts on global warming. Outlining (explained in Chapter 8) can help you figure out what's major, because it must be written on the outline, and what's minor, because it can be skipped without losing the main drift of the material.

Another way to identify major details is to look for words of transition such as *first, one, next, moreover, another, furthermore, in addition, also,* and *finally.* You are more likely—but not positively—looking at a minor detail when it follows words such as *for example, to illustrate, in particular, and for instance.* (For a complete list of words of transition, see the end of Chapter 14 in Part One.)

Categories for Major Details: REFS-NNDQ

- **R** = **R**easons
- **E** = **E**xamples
- **F** = **F**acts
- **S** = **S**enses (sight, hearing, touch, smell, taste)
- **N** = **N**ames
- **N** = **N**umbers (statistics)
- **D** = **D**efinitions
- **Q** = **Q**uotations

Yet another method for deciding what are major details is this formula: **REFS NNDQ** (hint: pronounce REFS, and name the letters NNDQ). Be aware, however, that this formula doesn't include the more obscure categories for major details.

Many writers depend solely on major details to imply the main idea of their material. For example, in the paragraphs below, details accumulate and build to give the whole picture. They explain why the doctor has recommended that his patient's leg be amputated. As you read this passage from *Mortal Lessons: Notes on the Art of Surgery,* by Richard Selzer, M.D., underline each detail.

> I invited a young diabetic woman to the operating room to amputate her leg. She could not see the great shaggy black ulcer upon her foot and ankle that threatened to encroach upon the rest of her body, for she was blind as well. There upon her foot was a Mississippi Delta brimming with corruption, sending its raw tributaries down between her toes. Gone were all the little web spaces that when fresh and whole are such delights to loving men. She could not see her wound, but she could feel it. There's no pain like that of the bloodless limb turned rotten and festering. There's neither unguent nor anodyne to kill such a pain yet leave intact the body.
>
> For over a year, I trimmed away the putrid flesh, cleansed, anointed, and dressed the foot, staving off, delaying. Three times each week, in her darkness, she sat upon my table, rocking back and forth, holding her extended leg by the thigh, gripping it as though it were a rocket that must be steadied lest it explode and scatter her toes about the room. And I would cut away a bit here, a bit there, of the swollen blue leather that was her tissue.
>
> At last we gave up, she and I. We could no longer run ahead of the gangrene. We had not the legs for it. There must be an amputation in order that she might live—and I as well.

It was to heal us both that I must take up knife and saw, cut it off. And when I could feel it drop from her body to the table, see the blessed space appear between her and that leg, I too would be well.

OBSERVING MAJOR DETAILS IN ACTION

Structured Reading provides you with three types of practice for finding major details. The first type asks you to decide if a listed detail is major or minor *in the context of the entire reading selection*. As you read the example below from *Read Magazine*, identify each detail and then decide whether it's major or minor. Be ready to defend your choice each time.

Where he lives, the air is so clean that sunsets are never red, not even purple. There's simply not enough dust in the atmosphere to break up the light. Instead, the purple evening sky is tinged with green from the forests below. Where he lives, the mountain slopes tumble downward from the sky, picking up trees as they go along and ending in the rush of a clear and unpolluted river. Eagles soar high above on the swirling air currents. Bighorn sheep bounce with sure hooves along the mountain peaks. Bears, deer, elk, and mountain lions roam the lower slopes. Where he lives is America, as it existed long before the coming of white settlers. He lives where Five Mile Creek flows into The River of No Return in a country named Light on the Mountains. He is one-sixteenth Apache but most of his forbearers came to America 300 years ago and kept moving westward in a search for freedom and elbowroom. Even his name is appropriate—Sylvan Hart. Sylvan comes from a Latin root meaning "forest," and a hart is one of nature's most elusive creatures, the male red deer.

_____ 1. Where Sylvan Hart lives, eagles soar high above on the swirling air currents.

_____ 2. Sylvan Hart lives in the rugged north central section of Idaho.

_____ 3. Sylvan Hart is one-sixteenth Apache.

_____ 4. Sylvan comes from a Latin root meaning "forest."

Answers: 1. minor; 2. major; 3 minor; 4. minor

TRUE, FALSE, or NOT DISCUSSED is a second type of exercise for Major Details. This type asks you to decide whether a listed detail is true, false, or isn't discussed in the material. To decide whether a major detail is *true* or *false*, read and reread carefully so that your concept of what the author wrote is clear. Only with close reading can you avoid jumping to the wrong conclusions. To decide whether an item is *not discussed* in the material, avoid allowing your mind to add in what's missing, no matter how much sense it makes. As you answer each question, be prepared to point to the source of each of your decisions.

Here's an example of a TRUE/FALSE/NOT DISCUSSED exercise for Major Details. It's from "People Are the Attraction" by Sonia and Bill Freedman. (Another passage from this essay appears in Chapter 10 in Part One.)

> In most places that tourists go to, things are the attraction—cathedrals and museums and pyramids and the like. In Pennsylvania Dutch country, it is the people. The Mennonites and Amish and Dunkers doggedly and picturesquely manage to live 17th-century lives in the 20th century. You've seen pictures of them: bearded men in black clothes, always hatted, and regardless of what *Esquire* says, holding their trousers up with suspenders. The women are no less severely clad, usually in black, but never without a white, frilled cap on their heads. They are stern looking, perhaps even dour, but in five minutes flat, you'll find out that they are the friendliest, most sincere people you have ever met.

Decide whether each detail is true (T), false (F), or not discussed (ND).

_____ 1. Pennsylvania Dutch country is located in Lancaster County, Pennsylvania.

_____ 2. The Pennsylvania Dutch consists of Mennonites, Amish, and Dunkers.

_____ 3. The Pennsylvania Dutch women do not wear severe clothes.

_____ 4. The Pennsylvania Dutch people look stern, but they are friendly.

Answers: (1) ND; (2) T; (3) F; (4) T

FILL-INS are the third type of practice with major details. By filling in the missing words in a statement, your mind works to retrieve accurate information. As you work with fill-ins, be prepared to point to the material that led you to complete the statements the way that you did. (Consider a close synonym of the answer given to be correct.)

Here's an example of a fill-in exercise for Major Details. It's from a newspaper article published by United Press International.

> Kim Jung-Sup's tragic man-against-mountain saga has made him a bitter man. He says he will find no peace until he conquers the Himalayan peak that killed two of his brothers.

"I am a sick man, badly sick, sick with Mt. Manaslu," said the 42-year-old veteran climber. "I cannot fall asleep, haunted by the snow-covered mountain that keeps beckoning me. Unless it is conquered, I can never feel free." Kim has just returned home from his third unsuccessful attempt to scale the 26,915-foot-high Manaslu and was soaking his frostbitten feet in a bowl of medicated water. But his five-year battle against the mountain is not over, he said. He will try again next year. One of his two dead brothers still lies in a crevasse, his body in plain sight. The body of the other has never been found. Korean expeditions have lost 16 persons in Manaslu, including a Japanese cameraman and 10 Nepalese Sherpa guides.

Fill in the word that correctly completes each statement.

1. Kim Jung-Sup wants to conquer Mt. _____ in the _____ mountain range.

2. The mountain is _____ feet high.

3. Kim's battle against the mountain was unsuccessful _____ times.

4. Of Kim's dead brothers, the body of one has never been found, and the body of the other lies at the bottom of a _____ on the mountain.

Answers: 1. Manaslu/Himalayan; 2. 26,915; 3. three; 4. crevasse

PRACTICING WITH MAJOR DETAILS

ACTIVITY Q MAJOR DETAILS 1
Read the paragraph below and answer the questions that follow it.

From *Learn Horseback Riding in a Weekend*, by Mark Gordon Watson

Learning how to behave with your horse is the first step towards building a good working relationship with him. A well-treated horse is trusting but a frightened horse can be very strong and dangerously unsafe. Always speak calmly. Horses are sensitive to tone of voice, so never shout. Avoid noises like road drills or motorbikes. Don't move suddenly or carelessly when around horses. Use persuasion to encourage your horse. Horses never forget a bad experience, but you can use their memory to your advantage, as they will also remember praise and rewards. Horses work best when they are in a happy environment and they like routine.

Fill in the word that correctly completes each statement.

1. Use a _____ tone when speaking to a horse.

2. Horses can become frightened by shouting and other loud _____

3. Horses work best when in a routine, _____ environment.

ACTIVITY R   MAJOR DETAILS 2
Read the paragraphs below and answer the questions that follow them.

"Diamonds" in *Mammoth Book of Fascinating Information*, by Richard B. Manchester

(1) "Diamonds in the rough" are usually round and greasy looking. But diamond miners are in no need of dark glasses to shield them from the dazzling brilliance of the mines for quite another reason: even in a diamond pipe, there is only one part diamond per 14 million parts of worthless rock. Approximately 46,000 pounds of earth must be mined and sifted to produce the half-carat gem you might be wearing. No wonder diamonds are expensive!

(2) After diamond-bearing ore is brought up from the mine, it is crushed into smaller rocks no larger than one-and-a-quarter inches in diameter, and then washed to remove loose dirt. At the recovery plant, the ore is spread on tables covered with grease and sprayed with water. The water moves the rocks off the table, but the diamonds adhere to the grease. Then the grease is boiled off, leaving "rocks" of quite another sort.

Decide whether each detail is true (T), false (F), or not discussed (ND).

_____ 1. Out of 14 million parts of certain rocks, only a small part is diamond.

_____ 2. A diamond's worth is determined by how many carats it has.

_____ 3. No one has ever found a diamond larger than 1¼ inches in diameter.

_____ 4. Radioactive substances are used to separate the diamonds from the ore.

ACTIVITY S MAJOR DETAILS 3

Read the paragraph below and answer the questions that follow it.

The Cake Mix Doctor, by Anne Byrn

In addition to their shortening preparation time, cake mixes are a reliable friend. Cakes "from scratch" require some practice to pull off, and you fuss over the ingredients—the right flour, room-temperature butter. Yet, the doctored-up mixes are easily assembled using the dump method in which all ingredients are mixed in one bowl. And they bake up looking pretty, time after time. Plus, cake mixes adapt to new ingredients, be it a can of cherry pie filling or a handful of fresh strawberries. Tweak them with the right number of eggs and a suitable amount of fat and liquid, and they bake up not only into cakes, but also into bars, cookies, cheesecakes, crisps, pies, even a gingerbread house.

Decide whether each detail is MAJOR or MINOR based on the context of the reading selection.

_____ 1. Doctored-up cake mixes are easily assembled.

_____ 2. Baked cake mixes look pretty, time after time.

_____ 3. Pie fillings can be a can of cherries.

_____ 4. Cake mixes can be used to make bars, cookies, cheesecakes, crisps, and pies.

ACTIVITY T MAJOR DETAILS 4

Read the paragraphs below and answer the questions that follow them.

Careers and Occupations, by Catherine Dubiec Holm

(1) A variety of information is available on the Internet, including job listings and job search resources and techniques. Internet resources are available 7 days a week, 24 hours a day. No single network or resource will contain all information on employment or career opportunities, so be prepared to search for what you need. Job listings may be posted by field or discipline, so begin your search using keywords.

(2) A good place to start your job search is America's Job Bank <http://www.ajb.dni.us/>. America's Job bank, run by the U.S. Department of Labor's Employment and Training Administration, provides information on preparing resumes and using the Internet for job searches, as well as trends in the U.S. jobs market and approximately 1.4 million openings. The

Internet is completely unregulated, so if you come across a job offer that seems too good to be true, it probably is.

Fill in the word that correctly completes each statement.

1. Job listings are available at any time on the _____.

2. _____ from a field or discipline can help you search for information about jobs.

3. America's Job Bank is an Internet resource provided by the U.S. Department of _____.

Chapter 12

What Are "Inferences"?

To make an **inference** in reading is to "read between the lines," a concept discussed in Chapter 9 in Part One. To make an inference, you arrive at a decision or opinion by drawing on what's said "on the lines," such as facts or evidence, to infer what isn't said but is nevertheless intended to be understood.

MAKING INFERENCES

In everyday life, everyone makes inferences. When we deal with people, ride in a car, or watch television, we make inferences. We use the five senses—sight, sound, touch, taste, and smell—to figure out what's going on. For example, when people smile sincerely, the look on their faces implies that they're happy or pleased. When you walk into a kitchen or restaurant filled with delicious smells, the scent implies that the person cooking is an excellent chef.

Here are more examples of your making inferences all the time:

- On your way to a classroom, you wave to a friend, but she does not wave back. You may infer that she is angry, that she is displeased with you, that her mind is on something else, or that she did not see you.

- As you're driving home, you come to a traffic light. On the side of the road sits an unshaven man wearing wrinkled, dirty clothes. He holds a sign that says, "Will work for food." You might infer that he is homeless, has no job, and is hungry. Or you might infer that this is a rip-off. Rather than passers-by offering him a job, the man expects people to give him a couple of dollars to buy food.

- You turn on the television to watch a program. The announcer mentions rolling blackouts, nuclear power, and conservation. You know that all the guests are environmentalists, so you infer that the program will be about an energy plan.

Making inferences is as natural for everyone as being human is. To use inference making in reading, however, isn't as automatic. In reading, you think about what the author says "on the lines" to lead you to make an inference about what the author doesn't say outright.

The ability to make inferences while you read is a learned skill. To make inferences, your take hints from what's stated and then fill in the gaps. You need to practice consciously so that you can easily understand more than what is said. Here are questions to keep in mind as you look for inferences:

- What does the author take for granted that I already know on the subject?

- What does the author take for granted about my attitudes toward the subject? Is the author's assumption accurate? Does the author give me room to have an open mind?

- What is the tone of the material? That is, how does the author say what's said? Are the words chosen to make the material clear or complicated? Honest or manipulative? Respectful or superior sounding? When humor is used, is the goal to help me understand the material or to distract me from thinking seriously about the subject?

- Does the author demonstrate a bias toward the material and try to make me accept the same bias?

- What unstated assumptions or conclusions does the author expect me to come to from reading the material?

To make correct inferences, a clear understanding of exactly what the author states is essential. You don't want to draw incorrect conclusions because you understood only part of the information given. Also, to make correct inferences, you are expected to draw upon your prior knowledge. For example, if an author names a famous person without giving any details about him or her, the author is assuming that you know who the person is. Without that knowledge, you'll likely miss the message of the material. Therefore, you'll want to do research about the person so that the author's point is clear.

College-level readers dislike being manipulated by an author. For example, suppose an author seeks to convince readers that elderly parents should be put in nursing homes rather than cared for at home. You want to ask yourself whether the author is an expert on family life, on the elderly, or related areas. The answer should affect your reaction to the material. Perhaps the author is the owner of a nursing home, which means the author wants people to give him business by placing their elderly parents in his facility. This means that the author is biased and is trying to manipulate readers. Or, suppose that the author is a health-care professional, such as a doctor of internal medicine, a psychiatrist, or a rehabilitation specialist. You would want to see whether that professional provides only a medical view of the elderly without consideration of life in a nursing home from a resident's standpoint. Of course, sometimes information about the author is not revealed by what the writer says or implies. In such cases, especially if you're being influenced to change your mind on an issue, you want to do research about the author so that you'll be well informed.

OBSERVING INFERENCES IN ACTION

Often, the basic understanding of the main point of a piece depends on your ability to make good inferences. In "How to Stay Alive," Reading Selection 25 in this textbook, the author begins this way:

> Once upon a time, there was a man named Snadley Klabberhorn who was the healthiest man in the whole wide world. Snadley wasn't always the healthiest man in the whole wide world. When he was young, Snadley smoked what he wanted, drank what he wanted, ate what he wanted, and exercised only with young ladies in bed.

Much in the above paragraph implies that the author is using exaggeration and humor to drive home a point about some people's excessive concern with their health. The hints include the opening storybook phrase, "Once upon a time . . ."; the unusual, deliberately humorous name "Snadley Klabberhorn"; and the exaggerated statement that Snadley was the "healthiest man in the whole wide world." It takes reading inferentially to catch the message of the material. Also, if you happen to have prior knowledge about the author, Art Hoppe, you know that he usually writes humorous satire, poking fun at the problems and whims of human life. That's a further clue about the spirit of the essay.

Here are two examples of drawing inferences for you to observe. Both contain paragraphs from "Coretta Scott King: A Woman of Courage," by Paul Taylor. The message concerns Mrs. King's inner strength and courage in her devotion to her husband and the civil rights movement.

> Shortly before Dexter was born, Coretta again feared for her husband's life. He was arrested for leading a sit-in at a lunch counter in Atlanta. For this minor offense, the judge handed down a harsh sentence of 6 months hard labor at the State Penitentiary. Coretta was terribly upset. The penitentiary was 300 miles from the Kings' home in Atlanta. Pregnant and with two small children, she could rarely make the 8-hour trip to visit her husband. She knew how black prisoners were treated in southern jails. Martin might be beaten—or worse.

Which of these statements can you infer from the paragraph above?

Coretta Scott King knew that black prisoners were poorly treated in southern jails because

a. black prisoners complained more than white prisoners about poor food and health care in prison.

b. the guards resented the civil rights movement and took out their anger on black prisoners.

c. Coretta Scott King had been in jail and therefore knew that black prisoners were mistreated.

d. The U.S. South had a long history of mistreatment of blacks both in and out of prison.

Answer: d

Here's another paragraph from the same source as the paragraph above.

Before lawyers had time to appeal the judge's decision, Martin was roughly dragged from his Atlanta jail cell. He was chained and handcuffed. In the middle of the night, he was taken to the penitentiary. When Coretta heard what had happened, she was distraught. Just as she was about to give up hope, the telephone rang. "Just a moment, Mrs. King," the long-distance operator said, "Senator John F. Kennedy wants to speak to you." "How are you, Mrs. King?" a warm voice inquired. After chatting a few minutes about her family and the new baby they were expecting, Senator Kennedy told Coretta he was concerned about Martin's arrest. "Let me know if there's anything I can do to help," he told her. The next day, Martin was released.

Which of these four statements can you infer from the paragraph above?

Coretta Scott King was about to give up hope because she felt that

a. the lawyers were not very capable and therefore were unable to help her husband.

b. the lawyers were secretly plotting with the judge to make sure that her husband was in jail.

c. after the rough treatment given her husband in the Atlanta jail, there was almost no hope he could survive the even tougher world of the penitentiary.

61

    d. she would not be allowed to visit her husband while he was in the penitentiary.

Answer: c

PRACTICING WITH INFERENCES

Structured Reading offers much practice in the art of drawing inferences from reading. Below are four practices for you to try your skill at inference making. Then, every reading selection in the rest of this textbook includes a structured exercise to guide you into the patterns of thought that make someone a college-level reader.

ACTIVITY U   INFERENCES 1
Read the paragraph below and answer the questions that follow it.

Travels With Lizbeth, by Lars Eighner

I find it hard to believe that anyone would have thought I had anything of much value. My clothes, besides being worn, would not fit many other people, and this should have been obvious to look at me. The little radio was of no appreciable value. Besides my papers, most of the bulk of what was taken was the remainder of Lizbeth's food and the bedding, which was warm enough, but could not have been sold. Other than a few dollars in postage, nothing could have been readily converted to cash. I was left with what I was wearing, a football practice jersey and my most ragged pair of jeans.

_____ 1. Read the paragraph again. What happened to the author's belongings?
    a. They were destroyed in a fire.
    b. They were borrowed but never returned.
    c. They were stolen.
    d. They were thrown out.

_____ 2. Read the paragraph again. Why does the author remark, "My clothes [. . .] would not fit many other people, and this should have been obvious to look at me"?
    a. The author wants people to look at him so he can show off his unusual appearance.
    b. By saying his size is unusual, the authors implies he's hugely obese.
    c. Only a fool would be interested in the author's clothes.
    d. The author is happy to be rid of his ill-fitting, ragged clothes.

ACTIVITY V   INFERENCES 2

Read the paragraph below and answer the questions that follow it.

Let's Get Well, by Adelle Davis

A study of the eating habits of individuals who could not reduce showed that they ate little throughout the day, obtained most of their food at dinner and during the evening, and had no appetite for breakfast. Anyone who has tried to reduce knows this pattern only too well. In the morning while the blood sugar is still high from food eaten the night before, will power is strong and resolutions firm. One vows he is going to stop feeling like the anchor on the *Queen Mary* and thinking of himself as a baby blimp; hence he forgoes or merely samples breakfast and lunch. As the bright star of success begins to glitter brilliantly before him, his blood sugar drops and he becomes exhausted, irritable, and starved. His undoing was not that he ate too much, but that he ate too little.

Decide whether each statement below can be inferred (YES) or cannot be inferred (NO) from the reading selection.

_____ 1. People need to eat three meals a day.

_____ 2. Fasting helps build moral character in people.

_____ 3. Lunch is the most important meal of the day.

_____ 4. Bad moods can be caused by low blood sugar.

ACTIVITY W   INFERENCES 3

Read the paragraph below and answer the questions that follow it.

From "Saint Valentine's Day" in the *New Yorker*

There are at least two saints after whom Saint Valentine's Day may have been named. One, known as "the lover's saint," was a third-century Italian bishop. In defiance of an edict of Claudius II, abolishing marriage, on the ground that it made restless soldiery, the good bishop secretly officiated at a number of wedding ceremonies, was pitched into jail, and died there. Or (there are a couple of other versions of his end) he was burned at the stake, at the behest of a Roman senator who objected to his marrying the senator's son to the daughter of an impoverished miller; or he choked to death on a fishbone. The other Saint Valentine was beheaded in 270 A.D., for refusing to renounce Christianity. While awaiting execution, he is supposed to have dashed off a farewell message to his jailer's blind daughter, signed "From Your Valentine." How he expected a blind girl to read the note the story doesn't say.

63

Decide whether each statement below can be inferred (YES) or cannot be inferred (NO) from the reading selection.

_____ 1. The saint who inspired Saint Valentine's Day might never be identified.

_____ 2. A Roman senator was held in greater respect than was a miller.

_____ 3. One requirement for sainthood is to have died by execution.

_____ 4. One Saint Valentine was in love with a jailer's daughter.

ACTIVITY X INFERENCES 4

Read the paragraph below and answer the questions that follow it.

From *Computers*, by Larry Long and Nancy Long

At the Skalny Basket Company, in Springfield, Ohio, Cheryl Hart insisted on daily backups of the small family-owned company's accounts receivables files [records of who owed money to the company]. The backups were inconvenient and took 30 minutes each day. Cheryl took the backup home each day in her briefcase, just in case. On December 23, she packed her briefcase and left for Christmas holidays. Five days later, Skalny Basket Company burned to the ground, wiping out all inventory and its computer system. The company was up in smoke, all except for a tape cassette that contained records of $600,000 accounts receivables. Cheryl said, "We thought we were out of business. Without the tape, we couldn't have rebuilt."

_____ 1. Read the paragraph again. What do the authors mean when they say, "Cheryl took the backup home each day in her briefcase, just in case"?
   a. Cheryl worried that someone would steal the information from the office.
   b. Cheryl wanted an extra copy of the files in case of disaster.
   c. Cheryl was considering stealing the company's files and escaping to Canada.
   d. Cheryl intended to work on the company's files while she was at home.

_____ 2. Read the paragraph again. Why did having the files of accounts receivables mean the company could rebuild?
   a. The accounts receivable had the original floor plans for the company's building.
   b. Cheryl Hart held all details of the company's inventory and operations in her head.

c. The company had fire insurance, so there would be money to reconstruct its building.

d. By knowing whom to bill for purchased baskets, the company's income wouldn't stop.

Chapter 13

What Is "Critical Reading"?

Critical reading calls for "reading between the lines," a concept explained in Chapter 9 in Part One. Here the concept has a different focus: the one needed for making inferences (explained in Chapter 12 in Part One). Reading critically means analyzing how each author presents the ideas in each piece of writing. Critical reading is much like critical thinking. Both require you to *question, compare,* and *evaluate.* The two most important areas for critical reading are (1) being able to tell the difference between a fact and an opinion, so that the material doesn't manipulate you, and (2) being able to recognize how the craft of the writer influences your thinking about the material.

CRITICAL READING: DECIDING BETWEEN FACT AND OPINION

As a reader, you're often called upon to make judgments about whether the material is objective rather than subjective, or whether it's honest or distorted. Here are two statements, one a fact and the other an opinion, each followed by a critical analysis.

- Rebecca is the friendliest contestant in the pageant. ["Friendliest" is an opinion. Being friendly means something different to each of us. Even if you happen to agree that Rebecca is the friendliest contestant, your assessment is still an opinion.]
- Rebecca's peers elected her as the friendliest contestant in the pageant. ["Friendliest" is not the issue here. Rather it's the fact that Rebecca has been *voted* the friendliest contestant in the pageant. The vote is a fact.]

Test for Facts: E R O

E = Experiment For example, "The Glaser study showed that elder residents of retirement homes in Ohio who learned progressive relaxation and guided imagery enhanced their immune function and reported better health than did the other residents."

R = Research For example, "According to the Americans' Use of Time Project, when we don't have to do anything else, most Americans mainly watch television."

O = Observation For example: "After a perfectly miserable, aggravating day, a teacher comes home and yells at her children for making too much noise. Another individual, after an equally stressful day, jokes about what went wrong during the all-time most miserable moment of the month. [. . .] The first is displacing anger onto someone else. The second uses humor to vent frustration."

Facts are statements that can be verified. You can "test" whether a statement is a fact or opinion by applying to it the three tests listed in the box above. If the statement passes any one of the three tests, it's a fact. The examples in the box are from "A Personal Stress Survival Guide," which is Reading Selection 29 in this textbook.

Opinions are statements of personal beliefs. They contain ideas that can't be verified or confirmed. As such, opinions are open to debate. Opinions often contain abstract ideas, information that can't be proven, and/or emotionally charged words.

Sometimes an opinion is written so that it appears to be a fact. This is especially true when a quotation is involved. A quotation isn't automatically a fact. True, someone made the statement, but whether the content of the quotation expresses a fact or an opinion is what counts. For example, an author might quote a horse owner as follows: "Having a healthy horse to ride, work, show, or even keep as a pet is a rare privilege." The content of the quotation expresses an opinion, one certainly not shared by all. In contrast, the following quotation expresses a fact: A horse owner reports, "It costs me $600 a year to feed my horse."

OBSERVING "FACT AND OPINION" IN ACTION

Sometimes, even without doing any reading, you can decide whether a statement is a fact or an opinion. Write F or O in the blank.

_____ 1. Health investigators have not found the cause of illness that affected two dozen workers at a hazardous waste processing plant.

_____ 2. Last year Jarred and Jossie missed school nine days.

_____ 3. Sometimes the best way to judge a truck is to look under one.

_____ 4. Nothing is better on a cold, winter day than a warm bowl of soup or stew—except maybe a loaf of homemade bread.

_____ 5. Bull sharks are common along beaches in the South.

_____ 6. "You have to love mushrooms to work here," says the owner of Oakhaven Mushroom Farm.

_____ 7. When I was a youngster, my grandfather used to bring me rusty bicycles, old rope, and broken toys he found in the junkyard.

_____ 8. In *Bon Appetit* magazine's fourth annual reader survey, cheesecake topped the list of dessert favorites.

_____ 9. Clark LaGrange, drama director at ECS, will be remembered for his enthusiasm, sense of humor, and patience under production pressure.

_____ 10. No healthy child is going to suffer because Shelby County Schools are turning the thermostat down to 68 degrees.

Answers: 1. F; 2 F; 3 O; 4 O; 5 F; 6 O; 7 F; 8 F; 9 O; 10 O.

Now try reading a passage and then deciding whether the statements following are facts or opinions. These paragraphs, published in *The Washington Post*, speak about Wendell Arbuckle who was an expert on ice cream, who wrote a major book on the topic, and who served as an ice cream consultant throughout the world.

(1) During the past four years, he has been doing this sort of tasting throughout the United States, but also in Germany, France, Switzerland, Britain, and Japan. He also has done consulting work by mail with firms in about 20 countries [. . .] all of which, he said, signals an "explosion of interest" around the world in American-style ice cream.

(2) He refused to say, though, which brand of ice cream he likes best. "It depends on what people want," he said. "They all can be good for you." His own favorite flavor, he said, is plain vanilla. "It's the basis of the industry and it goes with almost everything."

Decide if the content of each statement, whether or not it's a quotation, is a fact or an opinion. Write F or O in the blank.

_____ 1. *From paragraph 1:* During the past four years he has been doing this sort of tasting throughout the United States, but also in Germany, France, Switzerland, Britain, and Japan.

_____ 2. *From paragraph 2:* "He refused to say, though, which brand of ice cream he likes best."

_____ 3. *From paragraph 2:* All brands of ice cream "can be good for you," according to Arbuckle.

Answers: 1. F; 2. F; 3. O.

PRACTICING WITH "FACT OR OPINION"

ACTIVITY Y   CRITICAL READING: FACT OR OPINION 1
Read the paragraph below and answer the question that follows it. (Answers on page 79.)

From *Warriors Don't Cry*, by Melba Pattillo Beals

> I don't remember life without Grandmother India. Mother and Daddy had lived with her in North Little Rock even before I was born. When they purchased our Little Rock house, Grandma came with them. Unlike Mother, who was delicate and fair, Grandma was tall and copper-skinned. She had pronounced cheekbones and huge deep-set almond-shaped eyes that peered at me from behind wire-rimmed spectacles. She had a regal posture and a fearless attitude. My happiest evenings were spent listening to her read aloud from the Bible, from Archie comic books, or from Shakespeare. I sometimes gave up my favorite radio programs like the *Edgar Bergen and Charlie McCarthy Show, Our Miss Brooks*, and *The Aldrich Family* to hear her read to me.

Decide whether the content of each statement, even if it's a quotation, is a FACT or an OPINION.

_____ 1. "Mother and Daddy had lived with her in North Little Rock even before I was born."

_____ 2. "She had a regal posture and a fearless attitude."

_____ 3. Grandma wore wire-rimmed spectacles.

_____ 4. "My happiest evenings were spent listening to her read aloud."

ACTIVITY Z   CRITICAL THINKING: FACT OR OPINION 2
Read the paragraphs below and answer the questions that follow them. (Answers on page 79.)

From *Words Still Count with Me*, by Herbert Mitgang

> Octavio Paz, poet-diplomat, won the Nobel Prize in literature in 1990—the first Mexican writer to achieve the high

honor. Since many authors and civilians consider the Nobel political and geographical, I thought it would not be impolite to ask him if the prize was for him or for his country. He didn't seem surprised, and his answer was philosophical: "To me, a poet represents not only a region but the universe. Writers are the servants of language. Language is the common property of society, and writers are the guardians of language. A writer has two loyalties. First, he belongs to the special tribe of writers. Then he also belongs to a culture, to his own country. Mine is Mexico."

Decide whether the content of each statement, even if it quotes someone, is a FACT or an OPINION.

_____ 1. Octavio Paz was the first Mexican writer to win the Nobel Prize in literature.

_____ 2. "a poet represents not only a region but the universe."

_____ 3. "Writers are the servants of language."

_____ 4. Writers should be loyal to the tribe of writers and to their cultures.

ACTIVITY AA   CRITICAL READING: FACT OR OPINION 4
Read the paragraphs below and answer the questions that follow them. (Answers on page 79.)

From *Hispanics*, "Top Ten Cities for Hispanics," by Diana A. Terry-Azios

Tampa, located on Florida's West Coast, just 84 miles from Orlando, is an ideal location for outdoor activities. *Runner's World* magazine named it one of the top ten cities for runners, and more than 200 species of fish, including sport fish, inhabit the bay. The climate is semi-tropical; temperatures average 62 degrees during the winter and 81 degrees in the summer. The Meyers Group, of Irvine, California, ranked Tampa thirteenth of the nation's top twenty hottest real estate markets. Although Tampa is one of the nation's oldest cities, its residents make it one of the youngest cities, with the median age around 35. The crime rate is higher than average in Tampa, but the cost-of-living is relatively low. And with jobs, transportation, recreation and climate receiving top-tenth percentile ratings, Tampa offers the best in quality-of-life.

Decide whether the content of each statement, whether or not it's a quotation, contains a FACT or an OPINION.

_____ 1. *Runner's World* magazine named Tampa one of the top ten cities for runners.

_____ 2. The median age of Tampa's residents is around 35.

_____ 3. "Tampa offers the best in quality-of-life."

_____ 4. For someone interested in outdoor activities, Tampa is ideal.

ACTIVITY BB CRITICAL READING: FACT OR OPINION 3
Read the paragraph below and answer the questions that follow it.

Total Television, 4th edition, by Alex McNeil

Because of its impact on American audiences and on the style of television comedy, *All in the Family* is perhaps the single most influential program in the history of broadcasting. In terms of production techniques, the series added nothing new; in some ways, it represented a return to the old days of television: one basic set, a small cast, and little reliance on guest stars. *I Love Lucy*, TV's first smash hit sitcom, was the first to be filmed before a live audience; *All in the Family* was the first sitcom to be videotaped, and unlike the vast majority of sitcoms of the 1960s, it was performed before a live audience.

Decide whether the content of each statement, whether or not it quotes someone, contains a FACT or an OPINION.

_____ 1. *All in the Family* is perhaps the single most influential program in the history of broadcasting.

_____ 2. *I Love Lucy* was the first sitcom to be filmed before a live audience.

_____ 3. *All in the Family* was the first sitcom to be videotaped and performed before a live audience.

CRITICAL READING: RECOGNIZING THE WRITER'S CRAFT

The writer's craft refers to the skill and artistry of an author. Such talent can often overly influence your critical response to the content of the message. At the same time, appreciating the art of the writer adds considerably to a reader's enjoyment. To read on a college level, you want to balance these two considerations. Stay aware of how the author gets and holds your attention. What techniques of good writing style does the author employ?

Such techniques can include the method of presentation (for example, using description, persuasion, or comparison and contrast). Another technique relates to the use of words for emphasis (perhaps deliberate repetition of a chosen word) and for variety (perhaps deliberate use of many synonyms for one word). Yet another technique concerns the images an author uses to make a point.

71

Techniques of good writing are varied and powerful. At the same time that you want to appreciate the artistry of the author, you also don't want to be so impressed with that artistry that you're lured to accept the author's point of view.

OBSERVING THE WRITER'S CRAFT

Questions about a writer's craft are best answered after you've finished your first pass at reading the material. You can reflect on the author's technique most clearly when you have mastered the contents and are ready to analyze the material.

To guide you in observing a writer's craft, *Structured Reading* provides two types of multiple-choice questions. One type asks you to select the correct answer from among four. Here's an example from "Home" found in *Steps in Composition*, by Lynn Quitman Troyka and Jerrold Nudelman.

These days Americans of all ages lead such hectic lives that home is often little more than a place to sleep and change clothes. Family members see each other in passing; they seldom share activities, let alone a daily meal. In the morning, Mom and Dad rush off to work at 7:30 and the children leave for school a half hour later. At 3:30, Betty goes directly from school to her part-time job at Burger King. After returning to an empty house, Jason goes out to play for a while and then eats dinner alone. When his parents arrive home at 6:30, he is in his bedroom doing his homework. When Betty comes in the door a few hours later, she yells a quick hello to her parents, grabs some leftovers from the refrigerator, and heads for her room to eat and relax. Because the family members have different schedules, they have little chance to spend time with each other.

_____ 1. In the second sentence, the author uses a semicolon to indicate
    a. a close relationship.
    b. a contrast.
    c. what comes before and after the semicolon are items in a series.
    d. a cause-and-effect relationship.

Answer: a

A second type of writer's craft question asks you to select which among the four choices of answers is *not* correct. Here's an example from "American Schools Should Take a Lesson from Japan" found in *Steps in Composition*, by Lynn Quitman Troyka and Jerrold Nudelman.

It is a widely accepted fact that many of America's schools are doing a poor job of educating the nation's young people. Research studies indicate that about 30 percent of American high school students drop out before graduating. In some high school systems, fewer than half of the students who enter ever graduate. We should not be surprised, then, that one in four Americans is illiterate—unable to read and write at the most basic level. What can be done? American schools should take a lesson from Japan, where strict rules of behavior, very demanding school schedules, and high academic standards have produced nearly 100 percent literacy.

_____ 1. By using a short question among longer sentences, the author employs all these techniques *except:*
  a. arouses interest
  b. varies the sentence rhythm
  c. uses an illustration
  d. places a short sentence among long ones

Answer: c

PRACTICING WITH THE WRITER'S CRAFT

ACTIVITY CC   CRITICAL THINKING: WRITER'S CRAFT 1
Read the paragraph below and answer the questions that follow it. (Answers on page 79.)

From *Yellow Woman and A Beauty of Spirit,* by Leslie Marmon Silko

My great-grandmother's house had a tall bookcase full of my great-grandfather's books. My grandparents' house also had rooms with shelves of books. We had books. My parents kept books at their bedsides. My father used to read at the table at lunchtime, and we did, too. It was years before I realized it is considered impolite to read at the table.

_____ 1. What is the effect of the repetition of the word *books*?
  a. emphasis
  b. clarity
  c. lack of conciseness
  d. lack of synonyms

_____ 2. What is the effect of the author's using this pattern of sentence length: long, short, short, longest?
  a. repetition
  b. difficulty
  c. unity
  d. variety

73

ACTIVITY DD   CRITICAL READING: WRITER'S CRAFT 2
Read the paragraph below and answer the questions that follow it.

From *A Lady's Life in the Rocky Mountains*, by Isabella L. Bird

> I had gone to sleep with six blankets on, and a heavy sheet over my face. Between two and three I was awakened by the cabin being shifted from underneath by the wind, and the sheet was frozen to my lips. I put out my hands, and the bed was thickly covered with fine snow. Getting up to investigate matters, I found the floor some inches deep in parts in fine snow, and a gust of fine, needlelike snow stung my face. The bucket of water was solid ice. I lay in bed freezing till sunrise, when some of the men came to see if I "was alive," and to dig me out. They brought a can of hot water, which turned to ice before I could use it. I dressed standing in snow, and my brushes, boots, and etceteras were covered with snow.

_____ 1. The tone of this selection delivers the information by
    a. complaining.
    b. being nostalgic.
    c. being bitter.
    d. being matter-of-fact.

_____ 2. What technique of development does the author use?
    a. narration
    b. description
    c. persuasion
    d. definition

ACTIVITY EE   CRITICAL READING: WRITER'S CRAFT 3
Read the paragraph below and answer the questions that follow it. (Answers on page 79.)

Excerpt from Letter by Jack London (to his daughter Joan)

> Please remember that your Daddy is a very busy man. When you write to society people, or to young people, who have plenty of time, write on your fine stationery and write on both sides of the paper. But, please, when you write to Daddy, take any kind of paper, the cheapest paper for that matter, and write on one side only. This makes it ever so much easier for Daddy to read. A two-sheet letter, such as yours that I am now looking at, written on both sides, is like a Chinese puzzle to a busy man. I take more time trying to find my way from one of the four portions into which your two-sided sheet is divided than I do in reading the letter itself.

_____ 1. Jack London, a famous author, wrote this letter to his daughter, Joan. What word would describe his attitude toward her?
   a. proud
   b. anxious
   c. irritated
   d. amused

_____ 2. In this letter, Jack London speaks of himself in the
   a. first person singular (I).
   b. second person (you).
   c. third person (Daddy).
   d. first person plural (we).

ACTIVITY FF   CRITICAL READING: THE WRITER'S CRAFT 4

Read the paragraphs below and answer the questions that follow them. (Answers on page 79.)

From *Baseball Anecdotes*, by Daniel Okrent and Steve Wulff

A baseball reporter once asked a coach of long and varied experience what were his fondest memories of a lifetime in the game. The coach was removing his uniform after a spring training workout, an aging man whose shrunken chest and loose-fitting skin made him seem—to anyone but an experienced denizen of baseball clubhouses—incredibly out-of-place in that world of speed and muscle and skill. Yet, at the same time, the entire history of baseball seemed to reside in the gray stubble on his face, the wrinkles in his neck, the dry flesh on his arms and legs.

"Which stories do you want?" he asked the reporter. "The true ones or the other ones?"

_____ 1. The purpose of this passage is to
   a. inform and entertain.
   b. explain and surprise.
   c. describe and reveal.
   d. impress and persuade.

_____ 2. What technique of development does the author use?
   a. description
   b. explanation of a process
   c. comparison and contrast
   d. narration

Chapter 14

What Is
"Reader Response"?

A **reader's response** means that you are expected to express your own opinions by answering three open-ended questions. Based on what you've read, your previous experience, and your best reasoning, here's the opportunity for *your* response, *your* opinion, *your* thinking. This is the realm of questions with no right or wrong answers. They express *your* point of view. Of course, if your peers or instructor challenges your viewpoint, you want to be ready to explain your line of reasoning and defend your conclusion.

Whether you express your responses through discussion or writing, always start by restating the question. Doing this reminds your listeners or readers what has prompted your response. Follow immediately with a clear one- or two-sentence statement of your point of view (in writing, called a "topic sentence"). Next, support your opinion with specific details in the form of facts, examples, names, incidents, and other concrete material.

If you supply more than one supporting detail, tie your presentation together with transitional words so that your audience knows what's coming next. Just as a driver watches for traffic signals and road signs to anticipate what's ahead, listeners and readers need directional signals (in the form of transitional words) to know what's coming next. Here's a list of frequently used transitional words and phrases.

Transitional Expressions

Relationship	Expressions
ADDITION	also, in addition, too, moreover, and, besides, furthermore, equally important, then, finally,
EXAMPLE	for example, for instance, thus, as an illustration, namely, specifically,
CONTRAST	but, yet, however, nevertheless, nonetheless, conversely, in contrast, still, at the same time, on the one hand, on the other hand,
COMPARISON	similarly, likewise, in the same way,
CONCESSION	of course, to be sure, certainly, granted,
RESULT	therefore, thus, as a result, so, accordingly,
SUMMARY	hence, in short, in brief, in summary, in conclusion, finally,
TIME ORDER	first, second, third, next, then, finally, afterwards, before, soon, later, meanwhile, subsequently, immediately, eventually, currently,
PLACE	in the front, in the foreground, in the back, in the background, at the side, adjacent, nearby, in the distance, here, there,

SUMMARY OF PART ONE

The goal of *Structured Reading* is to give you structured strategies for upgrading your reading skills to a college level. Part One has two purposes. First, Chapters 1 through 8 explain how the reading process works. They offer you information about reading speed, eye movements while reading, developing a college-level vocabulary, making predictions during reading, the *SQ3R* method for reading and remembering textbook material, and making maps and/or outlines after reading.

Second, Chapters 9 through 14 get you working on the six specific approaches to reading that research shows can greatly upgrade your reading ability. They are understanding "reading on, between, and beyond the lines"; finding central themes and main ideas in reading; making inferences while reading; telling the difference between facts and opinions in reading; seeing the impact of the writer's craft on reading; and bringing your personal, informed response to what you've read.

Throughout Part One, *Structured Reading* provides many opportunities for you to apply what you're learning by practicing each separate skill. Then, in Parts Two through Six, each of thirty whole—never abridged or excerpted—reading selections are followed by exercises that allow you to combine the separate skills. By using all your structured reading skills together, repeatedly, you'll have upgraded your ability to read successfully at a college level.

Answers to Activities
in Part One

Activity A: No right or wrong answers here.

Activity B: These are the mismatched words: 1. light; 2. site; 3. then; 4. sail; 5. food; 6. hide; 7. floor; 8. bump; 9. tool; 10. sold; 11. rack; 12. took; 13. real; 14. cool; 15. mops; 16. tore; 17. lump; 18, track; 19. nail; 20. cove.

Activity C: 1. three; 2. two; 3. five; 4. one; 5. four; 6. one; 7. five; 8. three; 9. two; 10. four; 11. two; 12. five; 13. three; 14. two; 15. four; 16. two; 17. one; 18. two; 19. five; 20. three.

Activity D: 1. cove; 2. there; 3. fall; 4. relief; 5. undo; 6. unlock; 7. confide; 8. bustle; 9. madder; 10. truce; 11. skip; 12. table; 13. bicycle; 14. hammer; 15. see; 16. foil; 17. blow; 18. hip; 19. hiking; 20. marry.

Activity E: 1. 6:32; 2. 3; 3. 10:51 a.m.; 4. 21 minutes; 5. 3; 6. 25 minutes; 7. 11:51 p.m.; 8. 1 minute; 9. 4; 10. 6:30 a.m.

Activity F: scanning: no answers

Activity G: scanning: no answers

Activity H: 1. b; 2. b; 3. c; 4. c; 5. a; 6. b; 7. c; 8. a; 9. b; 10. c.

Activity I: 1. ambiguous; 2. monotone; 3. geriatrics; 4. malamute; 5. skeptical; 6. chagrin; 7. coherence; 8. sinuate; 9. phi, theta, kappa; 10. polyester.

Activity J: 1. a; 2. c; 3. b; 4. b; 5. c; 6. b; 7. a; 8. c; 9. b; 10. a.

Activity K: 1. a; 2. b; 3. b; 4. a; 5. a; 6. c; 7. c; 8. b; 9. a; 10. c.

Activity L: See p. 80.

Activity M: 1. c; 2. b; 3. a.

Activity N: 1. a; 2. Answers will vary; here's one possibility: Dell's secret of success is that all managers get personally involved in the details of the business; 3. d.

Activity O: 1. c; 2. b; 3. a.

Activity P: 1. Answers will vary; here's one possibility: Salmon is now available for year-round distribution; 2. b; 3. d.

Activity Q: 1. calm; 2. noises; 3. happy.

Activity R: 1. T; 2. ND; 3. ND; 4. F.

Activity S: 1. major; 2. major; 3. minor; 4. major.

Activity T: 1. Internet; 2. keywords; 3. labor.

Activity U: 1. c; 2. c.

Activity V: 1. yes; 2. no; 3. no; 4. yes.

Activity W: 1. yes; 2. yes; 3. no; 4. no.

Activity X: 1. b; 2. d.

Activity Y: 1. fact; 2. opinion; 3. fact; 4. fact.

Activity Z: 1. fact; 2. fact; 3. opinion; 4. opinion.

Activity AA: 1. fact; 2. fact; 3. opinion; 4. opinion.

Activity BB: 1. opinion; 2. fact; 3. fact.

Activity CC: 1. a; 2. d.

Activity DD: 1. d; 2. a.

Activity EE: 1. c; 2. c.

Activity FF: 1. b; 2. d.

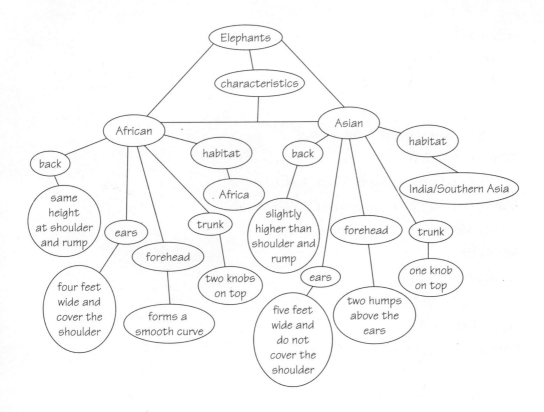

▪ Part 2 ▪

Thinking: Getting Started

Reading is an active process. During reading, your eyes and brain interact with the words on a page. This process of reading works most efficiently if you are conscious of how it operates. In addition to using your eyes, you need also to use your mind's "prior knowledge." This prior knowledge is what you know *before* you start reading; it provides a foundation for adding new knowledge to your fund of information. Learning happens when you associate new knowledge with prior knowledge.

Reading needs the active participation of your mind. The more your mind is "ready" to read actively when you start to look at a printed page, the more you will get out of your reading. Just as computers must "power up" before they begin to process information, your brain needs to "power up" before it starts to read. The next three pages of visual material are offered to help you start thinking about your prior knowledge on the subjects in the reading selections in Part 2 of this book.

Abigail Heyman, photographer/Life Classic Photographs, John Loengard, Bullfinch Press, 1996.

How would you feel about having to put a parent in a home for the elderly? (See "My World Now.")
What memories will you treasure when you are old? (See "My Mother's Blue Bowl.")

© 1993 by E.C. Publications, Inc. Artist: David Berg.

In what situations might someone's gentle, quiet voice be heard as a shout?
(See "Tyranny of Weakness.")

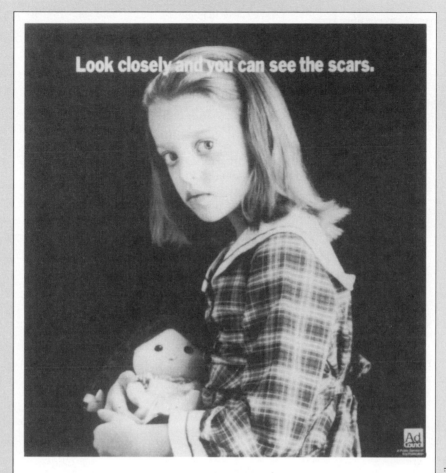

Look closely and you can see the scars.

There are no bruises.
And no broken bones.
She seems the picture of the perfect child.
But if you look closely you can see how rejection, fear and constant humiliation have left scars that have tragically affected her childhood.

So now only a shattered spirit remains.
And the light of laughter has gone out.
Remember that words hit as hard as a fist. So watch what you say.
You don't have to lift a hand to hurt your child.
Take time out. Don't take it out on your kid.

 Write: National Committee for Prevention of Child Abuse, Box 2866E, Chicago, Illinois 60690

Why should warnings about child abuse be widely publicized?
(See "A Real Loss.")

More on next page . . .

Never before has this nation
had a greater need for educated minds . . .
to help solve problems of energy,
the economy, equal rights,
employment, and the environment.
Higher education must be a higher priority
because educated people solve problems.
Support our colleges and universities!

Reprinted with permission of the Council for Advancement and Support of Education.

Why do so many people assume that if a person has a physical handicap, that person is also mentally limited? (See "Darkness At Noon.")

Grey Villet, LIFE Magazine © Time Warner.

What are the disadvantages if the land of small family farms is sold to today's super-sized farms or to housing developers? (See "The Death of a Farm.")

A Real Loss

Fern Kupfer

(1) I was sitting in back of a little girl flying as an unaccompanied minor, put on the plane by a mother who placed a Care Bear in her arms and told her to remind Daddy to call when she got to California. The girl adjusted her seat belt and sniffed back a tear, bravely setting her jaw.

(2) As we prepared for takeoff, the man next to the girl asked her the name of her bear and nodded in approval, saying Furry was a good name for a bear. When the little girl told him she was 6 years old, the man replied that he had a daughter who was 6 years old. His daughter was missing the same teeth, in fact. He asked how much money the tooth fairy was giving out in New York these days.

(3) By the time we were in the air, the man and the little girl were playing tic-tac-toe, and she revealed to him the names of her favorite friends. Somewhere over Ohio, I fell asleep, awakened by my mother instinct when I heard a child announce that she had to go to the bathroom.

(4) "It's in the back, right?" I heard the girl say to the man. She looked tentative. The flight attendants were busy collecting lunch trays.

(5) "Do you want me to take you there?" the man asked, standing.

(6) At once my antennae were up and, leaning into the aisle, I craned my neck, practically knocking heads with the woman in the seat across from me. For one moment our eyes locked. She had been listening, too, and both of us had the same idea. Would this man go into the bathroom with the child? I held my breath as he held open the bathroom door. Suddenly, he became transformed in my eyes—the dark business suit looked sinister, the friendly smile really a lure to something evil.

(7) Then the man showed the little girl how the lock worked and waited outside the door. The woman and I sighed in relief. She said, "Well, you can't be too careful these days."

(8) I've thought about that man on the plane since then, and the image of him and the little girl always leaves an empty sorrow. I know that a new heightened consciousness about child molestation is in itself a good thing. I know that sexual abuse of children is awful, and that we must guard against it. But it saddened me that I looked at someone who understood a child's fear and saw a child molester.

(9) These are trying times for men. We women say how we want men to be sensitive and nurturing, to be caring and affectionate. But my sense is that now these qualities cannot be readily displayed without arousing suspicion. Perhaps there is some sort of ironic retribution for all those

years of accepting the male stereotypes. But there is a real loss here for us all when we must always be wary of the kindness of strangers.

(498 words)

Vocabulary List

Here are some of the more difficult words in "A Real Loss."

antennae
(paragraph 6)

an·tenna (an ten′ə) *n.* ⟦L, earlier *antemna*, sail yard⟧ **1** *pl.* **··nae** (-ē) or **··nas** either of a pair of movable, jointed sense organs on the head of most arthropods, as insects, crabs, or lobsters; feeler: see INSECT, illus. **2** *pl.* **··nas** *Radio, TV* an arrangement of wires, metal rods, etc. used in sending and receiving electromagnetic waves; aerial

craned
(paragraph 6)

crane (krān) *n.* ⟦ME < OE *cran*: akin to Du *kraan,* Ger *kranich* < IE **gr-on* < base **ger-*: see CROW¹⟧ **1** *pl.* **cranes** or **crane** *a)* any of a family (Gruidae) of usually large gruiform wading birds with very long legs and neck, and a long, straight bill *b)* popularly, any of various unrelated birds, as herons and storks **2** any of various machines for lifting or moving heavy weights by means of a movable projecting arm or a horizontal beam traveling on an overhead support **3** any device with a swinging arm fixed on a vertical axis /a fireplace *crane* is used for holding a kettle/ —*vt., vi.* **craned, cran′·ing 1** to raise or move with a crane **2** to stretch (the neck) as a crane does, as in straining to see over something

heightened
(paragraph 8)

heighten (hīt″n) *vt., vi.* ⟦< prec. + -EN⟧ **1** to bring or come to a high or higher position; raise or rise **2** to make or become larger, greater, stronger, brighter, etc.; increase; intensify —*SYN.* INTENSIFY —**height′·ener** *n.*

ironic
(paragraph 9)

ironic (ī rän′ik) *adj.* **1** meaning the contrary of what is expressed **2** using, or given to the use of, irony **3** having the quality of irony; directly opposite to what is or might be expected **4** marked by coincidence or by a curious or striking juxtaposition of events: regarded by many as a loose usage Also **iron′i·cal** —**iron′i·cally** *adv.*

irony¹ (ī′rə nē, ī′ər nē) *n., pl.* **··nies** ⟦Fr *ironie* < L *ironia* < Gr *eirōneia* < *eirōn,* dissembler in speech < *eirein,* to speak < IE base **wer-,* to speak > WORD⟧ **1** *a)* a method of humorous or subtly sarcastic expression in which the intended meaning of the words is the direct opposite of their usual sense /the *irony* of calling a stupid plan "clever"/ *b)* an instance of this **2** the contrast, as in a play, between what a character thinks the truth is, as revealed in a speech or action, and what an audience or reader knows the truth to be: often **dramatic irony 3** a combination of circumstances or a result that is the opposite of what is or might be expected or considered appropriate /an *irony* that the firehouse burned/ **4** *a)* a cool, detached attitude of mind, characterized by recognition of the incongruities and complexities of experience *b)* the expression of such an attitude in a literary work **5** the feigning of ignorance in argument: often called **Socratic irony** (after Socrates' use of this tactic in Plato's *Dialogues*) —*SYN.* WIT¹

Vocabulary List

molestation
(paragraph 8)

mo·lest (mə lest′, mō-) *vt.* ⟦ME *molesten* < OFr *molester* < L *molestare* < *molestus,* troublesome < *moles,* a burden: see MOLE³⟧ **1** to annoy, interfere with, or meddle with so as to trouble or harm, or with intent to trouble or harm ☆**2** to make improper advances to, esp. of a sexual nature **3** to assault or attack (esp. a child) sexually —**mo·les·ta·tion** (mō′les tā′shən, mäl′əs-) *n.* —**mo·lest′er** *n.*

nurturing
(paragraph 9)

nur·ture (nur′chər) *n.* ⟦ME < OFr *norreture* < LL *nutritura,* pp. of L *nutrire,* to nourish: see NURSE⟧ **1** anything that nourishes; food; nutriment **2** the act or process of raising or promoting the development of; training, educating, fostering, etc.: also **nur′·tur·ance 3** all the environmental factors, collectively, to which one is subjected from conception onward, as distinguished from one's nature or heredity —*vt.* **··tured, ··tur·ing 1** to feed or nourish **2** *a)* to promote the development of *b)* to raise by educating, training, etc. —**nur′·tur·ant** *adj.* or **nur′·tural** —**nur′·turer** *n.*

retribution
(paragraph 9)

ret·ri·bu·tion (re′trə byo͞o′shən) *n.* ⟦ME *retribucioun* < OFr *retribution* < LL(Ec) *retributio* < L *retributus,* pp. of *retribuere,* to repay < *re-,* back + *tribuere,* to pay: see TRIBUTE⟧ punishment for evil done or reward for good done; requital —**re·tribu·tive** (ri trib′yo͞o tiv) *adj.* or **re·trib′u·to·ry** (-tôr′ē) —**re·trib′u·tively** *adv.*

sinister
(paragraph 6)

sin·is·ter (sin′is tər) *adj.* ⟦ME *sinistre* < L *sinister,* left-hand, or unlucky (side), orig. lucky (side) < IE base *sene-,* to prepare, achieve > Sans *sániyān,* more favorable: early Roman augurs faced south, with the east (lucky side) to the left, but the Greeks (followed by later Romans) faced north⟧ **1** *a)* [Archaic] on, to, or toward the left-hand side; left *b)* *Heraldry* on the left side of a shield (the right as seen by the viewer) (opposed to DEXTER) **2** threatening harm, evil, or misfortune; ominous; portentous [*sinister* storm clouds] **3** wicked, evil, or dishonest, esp. in some dark, mysterious way [a *sinister* plot] **4** most unfavorable or unfortunate; disastrous [met a *sinister* fate] —**sin′·is·terly** *adv.* —**sin′·is·ter·ness** *n.*

SYN.—sinister, in this connection, applies to that which can be interpreted as presaging imminent danger or evil [a *sinister* smile]; **baleful** refers to that which is inevitably deadly, destructive, pernicious, etc. [a *baleful* influence]; **malign** is applied to that which is regarded as having an inherent tendency toward evil or destruction [a *malign* doctrine]

tentative
(paragraph 4)

ten·ta·tive (ten′tə tiv) *adj.* ⟦LL *tentativus* < pp. of L *tentare,* to touch, try: see TENT²⟧ **1** made, done, proposed, etc. experimentally or provisionally; not definite or final [*tentative* plans, a *tentative* explanation] **2** indicating timidity, hesitancy, or uncertainty [a *tentative* caress] —**ten′·ta·tively** *adv.* —**ten′·ta·tive·ness** *n.*

transformed
(paragraph 6)

trans·form (trans fôrm′; *for n.* trans′fôrm′) *vt.* ⟦ME *transformen* < L *transformare* < *trans-,* TRANS- + *formare,* to form < *forma,* FORM⟧ **1** to change the form or outward appearance of **2** to change the condition, nature, or function of; convert **3** to change the personality or character of **4** *Elec.* to change (a voltage or current value) by use of a transformer **5** *Linguis.* to change by means of a syntactic transformational rule **6** *Math.* to change (an algebraic expression or equation) to a different form having the same value **7** *Physics* to change (one form of energy) into another —*vi.* [Rare] to be or become transformed —*n. Math.* the process or result of a mathematical transformation —**trans·form′·able** *adj.* —**trans·form′a·tive** *adj.*

SYN.—transform, the broadest in scope of these terms, implies a change either in external form or in inner nature, in function, etc. [she was *transformed* into a happy girl]; **transmute,** from its earlier use in alchemy, suggests a change in basic nature that seems almost miraculous [*transmuted* from a shy youth into a sophisticated man about town]; **convert** implies a change in details so as to be suitable for a new use [to *convert* an attic into an apartment]; **metamorphose** suggests a startling change produced as if by magic [a tadpole is *metamorphosed* into a frog]; **transfigure** implies a change in outward appearance which seems to exalt or glorify [his whole being was *transfigured* by love] See also CHANGE

wary
(paragraph 9)

wary (wer′ē) *adj.* **war′i·er, war′i·est** ⟦< WARE² + -Y²⟧ **1** cautious; on one's guard **2** characterized by caution [a *wary* look] —**SYN.** CAREFUL —**wary of** careful of

1A VOCABULARY

From the context of "A Real Loss," explain the meaning of each of the vocabulary words shown in boldface below.

1. *From paragraph 4:* She looked **tentative.**

   hesitant

2. *From paragraph 6:* At once my **antennae** were up and, leaning into the aisle, I **craned** my neck.

   sense organs at the top of my head/stretched

3. *From paragraph 6:* Suddenly, he became **transformed** in my eyes—the dark business suit looked **sinister.**

   changed in appearance/evil

4. *From paragraph 8:* I know that a new **heightened** consciousness about child **molestation** is in itself a good thing.

   increased/improper advances toward

5. *From paragraph 9:* We women say how we want men to be sensitive and **nurturing.**

   to promote the development of others

Name   Date

6. *From paragraph 9:* Perhaps there is some sort of **ironic retribution** for all those years of accepting the male stereotypes.

   that which has happened is the opposite of what was actually

   intended/deserved punishment

   _____

   _____

7. *From paragraph 9:* But there is a real loss here for us all when we must always be **wary** of the kindness of strangers.

   on our guard against

   _____

1B CENTRAL THEME AND MAIN IDEAS
Choose the best answer.

__d__ 1. What is the central theme of "A Real Loss"?
   a. These are trying times for men because all the media attention on child molestation has made even their simple kindnesses toward children appear to be evil.
   b. The author felt sorry for the little girl who had to fly from New York to California by herself, but at the same time the author admired the child's bravery.
   c. Child molesters can find victims everywhere, even on airplanes, so all travelers should be suspicious of anyone who is kind to children flying alone.
   d. Because of her increased awareness that some people are child molesters, the author now realizes that she has become suspicious of people who are kind to children they do not know.

__c__ 2. What is the main idea of paragraph 6?
   a. Airplane passengers often listen to other people's conversations and exchange glances about what is said.
   b. Becoming suspicious, the author leaned far into the aisle and nearly bumped heads with another watchful woman.
   c. As she waited to see what the man would do, he suddenly changed in her eyes into an evil person.
   d. The man opened the bathroom door for the little girl as the author held her breath.

1C MAJOR DETAILS

Decide whether each detail is MAJOR or MINOR based on the context of the reading selection.

MAJOR   1. The author was sitting in back of a little girl who was flying alone.

MINOR   2. The little girl's mother placed a Care Bear in the girl's arms.

MINOR   3. The little girl was going to California.

MINOR   4. The little girl knew how to adjust her seat belt.

MINOR   5. The bear's name was Furry.

MAJOR   6. Both the girl and the man's daughter were six years old.

MAJOR   7. The little girl announced that she had to go to the bathroom.

MAJOR   8. At that moment, the flight attendants were busy collecting lunch trays, so the man offered to take the girl to the bathroom.

MAJOR   9. The man showed the girl how the lock worked, and then he waited for her outside the door.

MINOR 10. The other woman sighed in relief.

MAJOR 11. The author's image of the man and the little girl on the plane left her with a feeling of loss.

MAJOR 12. A new heightened consciousness about child molestation is in itself a good thing.

1D INFERENCES

Choose the best answer.

  b 1. *Read paragraph 1 again.* Why did the little girl's mother tell her to remind Daddy to call?
    a. The mother did not want to spend the money to call California herself.
    b. The mother wanted to know that the girl had arrived safely after the long trip.
    c. The father was not considerate of the woman's feelings, so he had to be reminded to call.
    d. The mother wanted to know that the girl's father was in good health.

Name   Date

__c__ 2. *Read paragraph 2 again.* Why did the man say Furry was a good name?
  a. He had once had a bear named Furry.
  b. He wanted to make the little girl settle down so that she would not bother him and he could rest or read quietly.
  c. He wanted to make her feel comfortable and secure.
  d. The bear was very fluffy, and so Furry seemed an appropriate name.

__d__ 3. *Read paragraph 3 again.* Why did the little girl's announcement that she had to go to the bathroom wake up the author?
  a. The child was speaking very loudly and moving around in her seat, indicating that she was very uncomfortable.
  b. The author was afraid the little girl might have an accident unless someone took her to the bathroom right away.
  c. As a mother, the author thought she should be the one asked to take the little girl to the bathroom if the flight attendants were busy.
  d. As a mother, the author was used to listening—even in her sleep—for children's calls for help.

__c__ 4. *Read paragraph 7 again.* By saying "Well, you can't be too careful these days," the woman was communicating that she was
  a. annoyed at the flight attendants for being too busy to take the little girl to the bathroom.
  b. angry that the little girl had asked the man for help instead of turning to a nearby woman.
  c. slightly embarrassed that she had worried about what the man might do to the little girl.
  d. somewhat worried that the girl was too little to learn how to use the bathroom lock.

__a__ 5. *Read paragraphs 8 and 9 again.* What does the author mean when she says "there is a real loss here for us all when we must always be wary of the kindness of strangers"?
  a. Constant suspicion is a poisonous feeling, preventing people from enjoying some of the pleasanter moments in life, such as watching a man being kind to a child.
  b. Because rarely is there a way of telling who might be evil, people stop talking to strangers and miss chances to make friends.
  c. Years ago fewer child molesters existed, so children's lives were safer, and their parents had peace of mind that now has been lost.
  d. Because people today are constantly on the lookout for child molesters, nice people like the author are afraid to be kind to strangers' children for fear of being suspected of molestation.

Name   Date

___a___ 6. The word *loss* used in the title refers to the
   a. author's loss of trust of adults who are kind to children.
   b. little girl's having to leave her mother behind.
   c. negative effect on children when divorced parents live long distances apart.
   d. man's missing his own little girl who was also six years old.

1E CRITICAL READING: FACT OR OPINION

Decide whether each statement, even if it quotes someone, contains a FACT or an OPINION.

FACT 1. *From paragraph 1:* "The girl adjusted her seat belt and sniffed back a tear [. . .]."

FACT 2. *From paragraph 2:* "He asked her how much money the tooth fairy was giving out in New York these days."

FACT 3. *From paragraph 3:* "[. . .] she revealed to him the names of her favorite friends."

OPINION 4. *From paragraph 4:* "She looked tentative."

FACT 5. *From paragraph 6:* "[. . .] he became transformed in my eyes [. . .]."

OPINION 6. *From paragraph 6:* "[. . .] the dark business suit looked sinister."

FACT 7. *From paragraph 7:* "The woman and I sighed in relief."

OPINION 8. *From paragraph 7:* "[. . .] you can't be too careful these days."

OPINION 9. *From paragraph 8:* "[. . .] a new heightened consciousness about child molestation is in itself a good thing."

OPINION 10. *From paragraph 9:* "These are trying times for men."

1F CRITICAL READING: THE WRITER'S CRAFT

Choose the best answer.

___a___ 1. To get the reader's attention, the author opens with
   a. a brief anecdote.
   b. a description.
   c. a startling fact.
   d. a quotation.

Name   Date

__b__ 2. *Read paragraph 2 again.* To show how the man gains the little girl's trust, the author describes how he
    a. tells the girl jokes.
    b. asks the girl questions about herself.
    c. shows her pictures of his own daughter.
    d. talks to her stuffed bear.

__b__ 3. *Read paragraphs 4 and 5 again.* The author uses dialogue here
    a. to show she has a detailed, reliable memory of the event.
    b. to highlight that this was the most important part of the conversation.
    c. to demonstrate how to write direct dialogue.
    d. because every story should have at least one passage of direct dialogue.

__c__ 4. *Read paragraph 9 again.* The author concludes her essay with
    a. a dramatic call to action.
    b. a forecast of the future.
    c. an evaluation of the situation.
    d. a final example of the problem.

1G   READER RESPONSE: TO DISCUSS OR TO WRITE ABOUT

1. Why do some people consider it "unmanly" when men are kind, considerate, and wholesomely affectionate toward children?

2. Traditionally, American society has not encouraged men to be especially affectionate, even toward their own children. But attitudes seem to be changing. Discuss the benefits for men, for women, and for children when men are free to express wholesome affection.

3. Occasionally an adult will gain the confidence of a child and then kidnap that child. What advice would you give a child to avoid being picked up, kidnapped, and/or abused by an adult?

How Did You Do?   **1**   A Real Loss

SKILL *(number of items)*	Number Correct		Points for each		Score
Vocabulary (11)	_____	×	2	=	_____
Central Theme and Main Ideas (2)	_____	×	6	=	_____
Major Details (12)	_____	×	3	=	_____
Inferences (6)	_____	×	2	=	_____
Critical Reading: Fact or Opinion (10)	_____	×	1	=	_____
Critical Reading: The Writer's Craft (4)	_____	×	2	=	_____

(Possible Total: 100) *Total*   _____

SPEED

Reading Time: _____ Reading Rate (page 396): _____ Words Per Minute

Name   Date

The Death of a Farm

Amy Jo Keifer

(1) I am a farmer's daughter. I am also a 4-H member, breeder and showman of sheep and showman of cattle. My family's farm is dying and I have watched it, and my family, suffer.

(2) Our eastern Pennsylvania farm is a mere 60 acres. The green rolling hills and forested land are worth a minimum of $300,000 to developers, but no longer provide my family with the means to survive. It's a condition called asset rich and cash poor, and it's a hard way of life.

(3) My grandfather bought our farm when he and my grandmother were first married. He raised dairy cattle and harvested the land full time for more than 20 years. When he died, my father took over and changed the farm to beef cattle, horses and pigs, and kept the crops. But it wasn't enough to provide for a young family, so he took on a full time job, too.

(4) I can remember, when I was young, sitting on the fence with my sister and picking out a name for each calf. My sister's favorite cow was named Flower, and so we named her calves Buttercup, Daisy, Rose and Violet. Flower was the leader of a herd of more than 20. The only cattle left on our farm are my younger sister's and brother's 4-H projects.

(5) I can remember a huge tractor-trailer backed into the loading chute of our barn on days when more than 200 pigs had to be taken to market. That was before the prices went down and my father let the barn go empty rather than take on more debt.

(6) I can remember my father riding on the tractor, larger than life, bailing hay or planting corn. When prices started dropping, we began to rent some land to other farmers, so they could harvest from it. But prices have dropped so low this year there are no takers. The land will go unused; the tractor and the equipment have long since been sold off.

(7) I don't remember the horses. I've seen a few pictures in which my father, slim and dark, is holding his newborn daughter on horseback amid a small herd. And I've heard stories of his delivering hay to farms all over the state, but I can't ever remember his loading up a truck to do it.

(8) Piece by piece, our farm has deteriorated. We started breeding sheep and now have about 25 head, but they yield little revenue. My mother, who works as a registered nurse, once said something that will remain with me forever: "Your father works full time to support the farm. I work full time to support the family."

(9) I've seen movies like "The River" and "Places in the Heart." They tell the real struggle. But people can leave a movie theater, and there's a happy ending for them. There aren't many happy endings in a real

farmer's life. I was reared hearing that hard work paid off, while seeing that it didn't. My younger brother would like to take over the farm some day, but I'm not sure it will hold on much longer. Its final breath is near.

(527 words)

Vocabulary List

Here are some of the more difficult words in "The Death of a Farm."

amid
(paragraph 7)

amid (ə mid′) *prep.* ⟦ME *amidde* < *on middan* < *on*, at + *middan*, middle⟧ in the middle of; among

asset
(paragraph 2)

as·set (as′et) *n.* ⟦earlier *assets* < Anglo-Fr *assetz* (in legal phrase *aver assetz*, to have enough) < OFr *assez*, enough < VL *ad satis*, sufficient < L *ad*, to + *satis*, enough: see SAD⟧ **1** anything owned that has exchange value **2** a valuable or desirable thing to have *[charm is your chief asset]* **3** *[pl.]* *Accounting* all the entries on a balance sheet showing the entire resources of a person or business, tangible and intangible, including accounts and notes receivable, cash, inventory, equipment, real estate, goodwill, etc. **4** *[pl.]* *Law* *a)* property, as of a business, a bankrupt, etc. *b)* the property of a deceased person available to his or her estate for the payment of debts and legacies

chute
(paragraph 5)

☆**chute**[1] (sho͞ot) *n.* ⟦Fr, a fall < OFr *cheute* < *cheoite*, pp. of *cheoir*, to fall < L *cadere*: see CASE[1]⟧ **1** *a)* a waterfall *b)* rapids in a river **2** an inclined or vertical trough or passage down which something may be slid or dropped *[laundry chute]* **3** a steep slide, as for tobogganing

debt
(paragraph 5)

debt (det) *n.* ⟦altered (after L) < ME & OFr *dette* < L *debitum*, neut. pp. of *debere*, to owe < *de-*, from + *habere*, to have: see HABIT⟧ **1** something owed by one person to another or others **2** an obligation or liability to pay or return something **3** the condition of owing *[to be in debt]* **4** *Theol.* a sin

deteriorated
(paragraph 8)

de·terio·rate (dē tir′ē ə rāt′, di-) *vt.*, *vi.* **··rat′ed**, **··rat′·ing** ⟦< LL *deterioratus*, pp. of *deteriorare*, to make worse < L *deterior*, worse, inferior < *deter*, below < *de-*, from + *-ter*, compar. suffix⟧ to make or become worse; lower in quality or value; depreciate —**de·te′rio·ra′·tion** *n.*

harvested
(paragraph 3)

har·vest (här′vist) *n.* ⟦ME *hervest* < OE *hærfest*, akin to Ger *herbst* (OHG *herbist*) < IE *(s)kerp-* < base *(s)ker-*, to cut > SHEAR, SHORT, L *caro*, flesh, *cernere* & Gr *krinein*, to separate, *karpos*, fruit: basic sense "time of cutting"⟧ **1** the time of the year when matured grain, fruit, vegetables, etc. are reaped and gathered in **2** a season's yield of grain, fruit, etc. when gathered in or ready to be gathered in; crop **3** the gathering in of a crop **4** the outcome or consequence of any effort or series of events *[the tyrant's harvest of hate]* —*vt.*, *vi.* **1** to gather in (a crop, etc.) **2** to gather the crop from (a field) **3** to catch, shoot, trap, etc. (fish or game), usually in an intensive, systematic way, as for commercial purposes **4** to get (something) as the result of an action or effort **5** to remove (body parts) for transplantation —**har′·vest·able** *adj.*

reared
(paragraph 9)

rear² (rir) *vt.* ⟦ME *reren* < OE *ræran,* caus. of *risan,* to RISE⟧ **1** to put upright; elevate **2** to build; erect **3** to grow or breed (animals or plants) **4** to bring up by educating, nurturing, training, etc.; raise /to *rear* a child/ —*vi.* **1** to rise or stand on the hind legs, as a horse **2** to rise (*up*), as in anger **3** to rise high, as a mountain peak —*SYN.* LIFT

registered
(paragraph 8)

reg·is·tered (-tərd) *adj.* officially recorded or enrolled; specif., *a*) designating bonds, etc. having the owner's name listed in a register *b*) designating a dog, horse, cow or bull, etc. having its ancestry recorded and authenticated by a breeders' association established to promote the breed *c*) legally certified or authenticated

☆**registered nurse** a nurse who, after completing extensive training and passing a state examination, is qualified to perform complete nursing services

revenue
(paragraph 8)

rev·enue (rev′ə nōō′, -nyōō′) *n.* ⟦ME < MFr < fem. pp. of *revenir,* to return, come back < *re-,* back + *venir* < L *venire,* to COME⟧ **1** the return from property or investment; income **2** *a*) an item or source of income *b*) [*pl.*] items or amounts of income collectively, as of a nation **3** the income from taxes, licenses, etc., as of a city, state, or nation **4** the governmental service that collects certain taxes

2A VOCABULARY

Choose the best answer.

___c___ 1. All of the following would be **assets** except
   a. lakefront property.
   b. a charming personality.
   c. partnership in a bankrupt company.
   d. inherited government stocks and bonds.

___b___ 2. A **chute** would probably be used by a housewife to
   a. refinish all the kitchen cabinets.
   b. send laundry to the basement.
   c. plant summer vegetables in the garden.
   d. cultivate her lawn and gardens.

___a___ 3. When the farmer **harvested** his crop, he
   a. gathered in all his vegetables.
   b. made certain the crop had enough water.
   c. planted row upon row of corn.
   d. used fertilizer to grow large fruits.

___d___ 4. A **registered** dental assistant would probably
   a. work only in an approved hospital setting.
   b. have been admitted previously to dental school.
   c. be required to work before taking an examination.
   d. have had the appropriate training and passed an examination.

  d   5. If the city's **revenue** fell, the city would
      a. need to rebuild the town hall.
      b. probably share its wealth with the citizens.
      c. find good reason to lower taxes.
      d. have trouble paying all of its bills.

  a   6. If Frank sat **amid** the scholars, he
      a. was probably in the middle of the group.
      b. knew more than the rest of the members.
      c. was probably the youngest member.
      d. quit school at a very early age.

  c   7. A person in **debt** would probably
      a. be able to pay his bills monthly.
      b. have money to loan to his friends.
      c. owe money to his bank.
      d. qualify for a low-interest loan.

  b   8. A child **reared** by strict parents would
      a. be in trouble with the law.
      b. be educated or trained to be obedient.
      c. be placed with lenient foster parents.
      d. become an expert on raising children.

  b   9. As the farm **deteriorated,** the farmer
      a. was able to complete his plowing.
      b. had no equipment left to use.
      c. felt that it was time to pay off old loans.
      d. planned his crops for next season.

2B CENTRAL THEME AND MAIN IDEAS
Choose the best answer.

  b   1. The central theme of "The Death of a Farm" is the author's
      a. knowledge of raising livestock and crops.
      b. attempt to explain the painful death of her family's farm.
      c. desire to remember the good times on the farm.
      d. effort to justify her father's failure on the farm.

            Name   Date

___c___ 2. The main idea of paragraph 2 is that
  a. developers would pay more for the farm than it is worth.
  b. if the land were producing more crops, it would be worth much more.
  c. it seems to be a contradiction that the land itself is an asset and worth money even though it is not producing enough crops to make money.
  d. housing developers would make the land worth more if it were sold to them to build houses.

___c___ 3. The main idea of paragraph 9 is that
  a. movies tell the real story about farm life.
  b. the author's brother will own the farm some day.
  c. in real life hard work doesn't always pay off.
  d. the author's brother would make a success of the farm.

2C   MAJOR DETAILS

Number the following details from the story according to the order in which they occurred in the author's life. Number the events from 1 to 9, with 1 next to the event that happened first.

___5___ As a newborn, the author rode horseback with her father amid their small herd.

___8___ The author's younger brother would like to take over the farm some day.

___4___ The author's father took on a full-time job in addition to operating the farm.

___1___ The author's grandfather bought a 60-acre farm in order to raise dairy cattle and crops.

___3___ Besides farming the land, the author's father decided to raise beef cattle, horses, and pigs.

___6___ When they were children, the author and her sister named the cows.

___9___ The farm might not last long enough to pass on to a new generation.

___7___ The author's father started breeding sheep.

___2___ The author's father inherited the farm.

2D INFERENCES

Decide whether each statement below can be inferred (YES) or cannot be inferred (NO) from the reading selection.

__YES__ 1. The author is proud of her farm heritage.

__NO__ 2. The author's father was not a careful money manager.

__YES__ 3. The author's father would have had to borrow money in order to keep raising pigs.

__NO__ 4. The author's mother is resentful of having to work to support the family.

__YES__ 5. The statement by the author's mother ("Your father works full time to support the farm. I work full time to support the family.") greatly influenced the author's feelings about farm life.

__YES__ 6. Things have been bad on the farm for most of the author's life.

__NO__ 7. The author is bitter about the death of the farm because she can remember the better days.

__YES__ 8. The author is confused by the sentiment that hard work pays off when she can see that it doesn't.

2E CRITICAL READING: FACT OR OPINION

Decide whether each statement contains a FACT or an OPINION.

OPINION 1. *From paragraph 2:* "[. . .] it's a hard way of life."

FACT 2. *From paragraph 3:* "[. . .] it wasn't enough to provide for a young family, so he took on a full time job."

FACT 3. *From paragraph 4:* "My sister's favorite cow was named Flower [. . .]."

FACT 4. *From paragraph 8:* "[The sheep] yield little revenue."

OPINION 5. *From paragraph 9:* "There aren't many happy endings in a real farmer's life."

OPINION 6. *From paragraph 9:* "Its final breath is near."

2F   CRITICAL READING: THE WRITER'S CRAFT

Choose the best answer.

<u> a </u> 1. The use of expressions such as "the farm is dying" in paragraph
1 and "its final breath is near" in paragraph 9 serve to
a. give the farm human qualities that the reader can relate to.
b. gain sympathy from the reader.
c. show that the author is too involved with the farm.
d. prove that the author's father let the farm go.

2. The author begins paragraphs 4, 5, and 6 with the same three
words. What are they?

<u>I can remember</u>

<u> b </u> 3. The author repeats these words in order to
a. demonstrate the author's ability to remember exact details.
b. emphasize the solemn quality of the author's remembrances.
c. impress the reader with her knowledge of farm life.
d. stress the importance of being able to remember.

<u> b </u> 4. Although the land is worth $300,000 to housing developers, it
does not make enough money as farmland to keep animals,
crops, and family going. The author uses this as an example of
a. logic.
b. irony.
c. fantasy.
d. unity.

2G   READER RESPONSE: TO DISCUSS OR TO WRITE ABOUT

1. Do you believe that "hard work pays off"? Cite a specific example to
prove your point of view.

2. Imagine you own 60 acres of farmland worth $300,000. Because the land
does not make enough money as farmland to keep animals, crops, and
family going, you have to sell the land. What would you do with
$300,000? Give specific examples of the ways you would use the money.

3. If your family has ever suffered financially or emotionally, how did you
react? If not, what do you think your reaction would be if you watched
your family's income slowly disappear?

| Name | Date | 101 |

How Did You Do?   **2** Death of a Farm

SKILL *(number of items)*	Number Correct		Points for each		Score
Vocabulary (9)	_____	×	2	=	_____
Central Theme and Main Ideas (3)	_____	×	4	=	_____
Major Details (9)	_____	×	2	=	_____
Inferences (8)	_____	×	4	=	_____
Critical Reading: Fact or Opinion (6)	_____	×	2	=	_____
Critical Reading: The Writer's Craft (4)	_____	×	2	=	_____

(Possible Total: 100) *Total* _____

SPEED

Reading Time: _____ Reading Rate (page 396): _____ Words Per Minute

Name   Date

Tyranny of Weakness

Eda LeShan

(1) If I were to ask you who are the most aggressive people you know, chances are you would describe someone who tells other people what to do, bosses people around, has a great deal of energy—a forceful personality.

(2) Wrong! The most aggressive, the strongest people we know are the weak ones. They are people who want someone else to take care of them and have somehow managed to convince those around them that they are too sick, too weak, too helpless, too incompetent to do anything for themselves. They are not really sick or helpless at all, but they have found a way to control the world that is fool-proof.

(3) I suppose it begins in childhood when a child realizes that helplessness is a way of controlling parents and teachers and other kids. And anyone who chooses such techniques may very well believe they really are unable to function.

(4) I recall a time when I had been on a book publicity tour for 10 days and came home to face preparing Thanksgiving dinner for 14 people. I asked a friend who did not work if she could bring a salad and she said she was too tired. Or there is a man who was sure he wanted a quiet, shy helpless wife because his mother had been aggressive, competent and somewhat overpowering. So he has spent his life taking care of a wife who "gets sick" at every family crisis and takes to her own bed if a child gets sick, if the family has to move, if her husband is in a car accident.

(5) Often people who have been strong and competent become helpless after some major emotional trauma. A friend told me, "I have a full-time job and three school-age kids, and when my father died, my mother, who had always been a competent person, suddenly turned into an infant. She expected me to take her shopping, cook for her, stay at her house, drive her everywhere, listen to her endless complaints. I became so exhausted that it began to dawn on me that she wasn't weak and helpless, she was a tyrant!

(6) Weakness and helplessness can be a form of aggression. But its origins may start with feelings of incompetence, fear, lack of self-esteem.

(7) When we meet with the tyranny of weakness, we need to help the person discover strengths, ways of accepting the challenges of life.

(8) One husband, married 40 years, told me "I don't know what happened, except I finally realized my wife had made me her slave—not by yelling at me or ordering me around, but by appearing to be helpless. I was getting a few aches and pains of my own, I guess, and it wasn't fun anymore feeling I was 'The Big Man' who could do everything. Finally, one day when she told me to mop the kitchen floor because she needed to take a nap, I said, 'Do it yourself or leave it dirty!' I thought she'd faint from the shock, but it did her a world of good. It seemed to break a pattern that was bad for both of us."

(9) It's a very good idea to keep in mind that it is not only the strong who push us around, but very often it is the person who appears to be weak and helpless.

(563 words)

Here are some of the more difficult words in "Tryanny of Weakness."

Vocabulary List

aggressive
(paragraph 1)

ag·gres·sive (ə gres′iv) *adj.* **1** aggressing or inclined to aggress; starting fights or quarrels **2** ready or willing to take issue or engage in direct action; militant **3** full of enterprise and initiative; bold and active; pushing **4** *Psychiatry* of or involving aggression — **ag·gres′sive·ly** *adv.* —**ag·gres′sive·ness** *n.* —**ag·gres·siv·ity** (ag′res iv′ə tē, ə gres′-) *n.*

SYN.—aggressive implies a bold and energetic pursuit of one's ends, connoting, in derogatory usage, a ruthless desire to dominate and, in a favorable sense, enterprise or initiative; **militant** implies a vigorous, unrelenting espousal of a cause, movement, etc. and rarely suggests the furthering of one's own ends; **assertive** emphasizes self-confidence and a persistent determination to express oneself or one's opinions; **pushing** is applied derogatorily to a forwardness of personality that manifests itself in officiousness or rudeness

competent
(paragraph 4)

com·pe·tent (-tənt) *adj.* ⟦ME < OFr < L *competens*, prp. of *competere*: see COMPETE⟧ **1** well qualified; capable; fit *[a competent doctor]* **2** sufficient; adequate *[a competent understanding of law]* **3** permissible or properly belonging: with *to* **4** *Law* legally qualified, authorized, or fit —**SYN.** ABLE —**com′pe·tently** *adv.*

incompetent
(paragraph 2)

in·com·pe·tent (in käm′pə tənt) *adj.* ⟦Fr *incompétent* < LL *incompetens*: see IN-² & COMPETENT⟧ **1** without adequate ability, knowledge, fitness, etc.; failing to meet requirements; incapable; unskillful **2** not legally qualified **3** lacking strength and sufficient flexibility to transmit pressure, thus breaking or flowing under stress: said of rock structures —*n.* an incompetent person; esp., one who is mentally deficient —**in·com′pe·tence** *n.* or **in·com′pe·tency** —**in·com′pe·tently** *adv.*

personality
(paragraph 1)

per·son·al·i·ty (pʉr′sə nal′ə tē) *n.*, *pl.* **-ties** ⟦ME *personalite* < LL *personalitas* < *personalis*, personal⟧ **1** the quality or fact of being a person **2** the quality or fact of being a particular person; personal identity; individuality **3** *a)* habitual patterns and qualities of behavior of any individual as expressed by physical and mental activities and attitudes; distinctive individual qualities of a person, considered collectively *b)* the complex of qualities and characteristics seen as being distinctive to a group, nation, place, etc. **4** *a)* the sum of such qualities seen as being capable of making, or likely to make, a favorable impression on other people *b)* [Informal] personal attractiveness; engaging manner or qualities **5** a person; specif., *a)* a notable person; personage *b)* a person known for appearances on TV, radio, etc. **6** [*pl.*] remarks, usually of an offensive or disparaging nature, aimed at or referring to a person —**SYN.** DISPOSITION

self-esteem
(paragraph 6)

self-esteem (-e stēm′) *n.* **1** belief in oneself; self-respect **2** undue pride in oneself; conceit —**SYN.** PRIDE

techniques
(paragraph 3)

tech·nique (tek nēk′) *n.* ⟦Fr < Gr *technikos*: see TECHNIC⟧ **1** the method of procedure (with reference to practical or formal details), or way of using basic skills, in rendering an artistic work or carrying out a scientific or mechanical operation **2** the degree of expertness in following this *[a pianist with good technique but poor expression]* **3** any method or manner of accomplishing something

trauma
(paragraph 5)

trauma (trô′mə, trä′-) *n.*, *pl.* **-mas** or **-mata** (-mə tə) ⟦ModL < Gr *trauma* (gen. *traumatos*): for IE base see THROE⟧ **1** *Med.* a bodily injury, wound, or shock **2** *Psychiatry* a painful emotional experience, or shock, often producing a lasting psychic effect and, sometimes, a neurosis —**trau·ma′·tic** (-mat′ik) *adj.* —**trau·mat′i·cally** *adv.*

tyrant
(paragraph 5)

ty·rant (tī′rənt) *n.* ⟦ME *tirant* < OFr *tiran*, *tirant* (with *-t* after ending *-ant* of prp.) < L *tyrannus* < Gr *tyrannos*⟧ **1** an absolute ruler; specif., in ancient Greece, etc., one who seized sovereignty illegally; usurper **2** a cruel, oppressive ruler; despot **3** any person who exercises authority in an oppressive manner; cruel master **4** a tyrannical influence

3A VOCABULARY

Using the vocabulary words listed on page 104, fill in the blanks.

1. __Competent__ employees will earn not only a bonus but also praise from their employers.

2. The president of the company, while appearing to be a ____tyrant____ , was actually loved by his employees.

3. Research shows that ____aggressive____ behavior in a younger child is often learned from an older sibling.

4. A ____personality____ disorder should be diagnosed and treated by a trained professional.

5. Art students study various artists and their ____techniques____ in order to develop their own styles.

6. The teacher was judged to be highly ____incompetent____ when her students failed to learn to read.

7. Constant criticism by a spouse is likely to damage one's ____self-esteem____ .

8. The parents went into shock after the ____trauma____ of seeing their only child struck by a car.

3B CENTRAL THEME AND MAIN IDEAS
Choose the best answer.

__a__ 1. What is the central theme of "Tyranny of Weakness"?
   a. The strongest people we know are often those who appear weak and helpless.
   b. Children should always give in to the demands of parents.
   c. A wife should be able to expect household help from her husband when she is tired.
   d. Weak people often take advantage of their good-natured friends.

__c__ 2. What is the main idea of paragraph 5?
   a. Mothers should help adult daughters who have full-time jobs and children of their own.
   b. The roles of parent and child may be reversed as the parent ages.
   c. Often an emotional trauma will turn a strong individual into a helpless one.
   d. Medical studies claim that women who lose their husbands are no longer able to take care of themselves.

__b__ 3. What is the main idea of paragraph 8?
   a. After 40 years of marriage, a husband should willingly help his wife.
   b. It is never too late in a marriage to reverse an undesirable behavior pattern.
   c. After many years of marriage, a husband will become tired of being "The Big Man."
   d. Unwillingness by a husband to help his wife may signal the beginning of the end of the marriage.

3C MAJOR DETAILS

Decide whether each detail is MAJOR or MINOR based on the context of the reading selection.

MAJOR 1. Children learn early in life that helplessness can be a controlling technique.

MINOR 2. The author's friend was too tired to bring a salad for Thanksgiving dinner.

MAJOR 3. A man who marries a woman opposite in personality to his mother is trading one set of problems for another.

MAJOR 4. The intent of the incompetent individual is often to control family and friends.

MAJOR 5. Sudden helplessness in a healthy, competent individual may have been triggered by an emotional trauma.

MAJOR 6. A person may display aggressive behavior because of feelings of low self-esteem or even fear.

3D INFERENCES

Decide whether each statement below can be inferred (YES) or cannot be inferred (NO) from the story.

__NO__ 1. Aggressive behavior is bad manners.

__YES__ 2. People who appear to be incompetent and helpless may actually be very controlling.

__NO__ 3. A friend who will not help cook Thanksgiving dinner is not a true friend.

__NO__ 4. An only child will feel more responsibility toward a weak, helpless parent than toward a competent one.

__YES__ 5. Refusing to cooperate with a spouse's helpless behavior will "cure" the spouse.

__NO__ 6. A man should marry a woman whose personality is the opposite of his mother's personality.

__NO__ 7. A person who has behaved in a certain way toward a spouse for many years will not be able to change.

3E CRITICAL READING: FACT OR OPINION

Decide whether each statement, even if it quotes someone, contains a FACT or an OPINION.

OPINION 1. *From paragraph 2:* "The most aggressive, the strongest people we know are the weak ones."

OPINION 2. *From paragraph 3:* "I suppose it begins in childhood when a child realizes that helplessness is a way of controlling parents [. . .]."

FACT 3. *From paragraph 4:* "The man wanted a quiet, shy, helpless wife because his mother had been aggressive and overpowering."

FACT 4. *From paragraph 4:* "[. . .] she said she was too tired."

OPINION 5. *From paragraph 5:* "A competent mother will turn into a weak, helpless widow."

OPINION 6. *From paragraph 8:* "It seemed to break a pattern that was bad for both of us."

3F CRITICAL READING: THE WRITER'S CRAFT

Choose the best answer.

__a__ 1. The title of the selection suggests
    a. a contradiction of descriptions.
    b. a war between weak individuals.
    c. a conflict between weak and strong men.
    d. a relationship between like personalities.

__c__ 2. To make her point, the author uses all of these techniques **except**
    a. definitions of key terms.
    b. personal experience.
    c. research studies by experts.
    d. anecdotes.

__a__ 3. The author's tone in this essay is
    a. serious.
    b. sarcastic.
    c. alarmed.
    d. suspicious.

___b___ 4. The author's own attitude toward weak people who seek to manipulate others might best be described as
   a. resigned.
   b. merciless.
   c. compassionate.
   d. pessimistic.

3G   READER RESPONSE: TO DISCUSS OR TO WRITE ABOUT

1. "The most aggressive, the strongest people we know are the weak ones" (paragraph 2). Explain what you think is meant by this statement.

2. Describe someone you know personally or have observed in the television or motion picture media who tyrannizes in the way described in this essay.

3. How do you feel about yourself? Is your self-esteem high or low? Using specific examples, describe several incidents that have influenced the way you perceive yourself.

How Did You Do?   3 Tyranny of Weakness

SKILL (number of items)	Number Correct		Points for each		Score
Vocabulary (8)	_____	×	2	=	_____
Central Theme and Main Ideas (3)	_____	×	4	=	_____
Major Details (6)	_____	×	4	=	_____
Inferences (7)	_____	×	4	=	_____
Critical Reading: Fact or Opinion (6)	_____	×	2	=	_____
Critical Reading: The Writer's Craft (4)	_____	×	2	=	_____

(Possible Total: 100) *Total* _____

SPEED

Reading Time: _____ Reading Rate (page 396): _____ Words Per Minute

Name   Date

Darkness at Noon

Harold Krents

(1) Blind from birth, I have never had the opportunity to see myself and have been completely dependent on the image I create in the eye of the observer. To date it has not been narcissistic.

(2) There are those who assume that since I can't see, I obviously also cannot hear. Very often people will converse with me at the top of their lungs, enunciating each word very carefully. Conversely, people will also often whisper, assuming that since my eyes don't work, my ears don't either. For example, when I go to the airport and ask the ticket agent for assistance to the plane, he or she will invariably pick up the phone, call a ground hostess and whisper, "Hi, Jane, we've got a 76 here." I have concluded that the word "blind" is not used for one of two reasons: Either they fear that if the dread word is spoken, the ticket agent's retina will immediately detach, or they are reluctant to inform me of my condition of which I may not have been previously aware.

(3) On the other hand, others know that of course I can hear, but believe that I can't talk. Often, therefore, when my wife and I go out to dinner, a waiter or waitress will ask Kit if "*he* would like a drink" to which I respond that "indeed *he* would." This point was graphically driven home to me while we were in England. I had been given a year's leave of absence from my Washington law firm to study for a diploma-in-law degree at Oxford University. During the year I became ill and was hospitalized. Immediately after admission, I was wheeled down to the X-ray room. Just at the door sat an elderly woman—elderly I would judge from the sound of her voice. "What is his name?" the woman asked the orderly who had been wheeling me.

"What's your name?" the orderly repeated to me.

"Harold Krents," I replied.

"Harold Krents," he repeated.

"When was he born?"

"When were you born?"

"November 5, 1944," I responded.

"November 5, 1944," the orderly intoned.

(4) This procedure continued for approximately five minutes at which point even my saint-like disposition deserted me. "Look," I finally blurted out, "this is absolutely ridiculous. Okay, granted I can't see, but it's got to have become pretty clear to both of you that I don't need an interpreter."

"He says he doesn't need an interpreter," the orderly reported to the woman.

Harold Krents, inspiration for the award-winning play and movie "Butterflies Are Free," died of a brain tumor twelve years after he wrote "Darkness at Noon."

New York Times Permissions

(5) The toughest misconception of all is the view that because I can't see, I can't work. I was turned down by over forty law firms because of my blindness, even though my qualifications included a cum laude degree from Harvard College and a good ranking in my Harvard Law School class. The attempt to find employment, the continuous frustration of being told that it was impossible for a blind person to practice law, the rejection letters, not based on my lack of ability but rather on my disability, will always remain one of the most disillusioning experiences of my life.

(6) Fortunately, this view of limitation and exclusion is beginning to change. On April 16, 1976, the Department of Labor issued regulations that mandate equal-employment opportunities for the handicapped. By and large, the business community's response to offering employment to the disabled has been enthusiastic.

(7) I therefore look forward to the day, with the expectation that it is certain to come, when employers will view their handicapped workers as a little child did me years ago when my family still lived in Scarsdale. I was playing basketball with my father in our backyard according to procedures we had developed. My father would stand beneath the hoop, shout, and I would shoot over his head at the basket attached to the garage. Our next-door neighbor, aged five, wandered over into our yard with a playmate. "He's blind," our neighbor whispered to her friend in a voice that could be heard distinctly by Dad and me. Dad shot and missed; I did the same. Dad hit the rim: I missed entirely; Dad shot and missed the garage entirely. "Which one is blind?" whispered back the little friend.

(8) I would hope that in the near future when a plant manager is touring the factory with the foreman and comes upon a handicapped and non-handicapped person working together, his comment after watching them work will be, "Which one is disabled?"

(775 words)

Here are some of the more difficult words in "Darkness at Noon."

disillusioning
(paragraph 5)

dis·il·lu·sion (dis'i lōō'zhən) *vt.* **1** to free from illusion or false ideas; disenchant **2** to take away the ideals or idealism of and make disappointed, bitter, etc. —*n.* DISILLUSIONMENT

enunciating
(paragraph 2)

enun·ci·ate (ē nun'sē āt', i-; *also,* -shē-) *vt.* **-·at'ed, -·at'·ing** [< L *enuntiatus,* pp. of *enuntiare* < *e-,* out + *nuntiare,* to announce < *nuntius,* a messenger] **1** to state definitely; express in a systematic way [to *enunciate* a theory] **2** to announce; proclaim **3** to pronounce (words), esp. clearly and distinctly —*vi.* to pronounce words, esp. clearly and distinctly; articulate —*SYN.* UTTER² — **enun'·cia'·tion** (-sē ā'-) *n.* —**enun'·cia'·tive** (-āt'iv, -ə tiv) *adj.* — **enun'·cia'·tor** *n.*

exclusion
(paragraph 6)

ex·clude (eks klōōd', iks-) *vt.* **-·clud'ed, -·clud'·ing** [ME *excluden* < L *excludere* < *ex-,* out + *claudere,* CLOSE³] **1** to refuse to admit, consider, include, etc.; shut out; keep from entering, happening, or being; reject; bar **2** to put out; force out; expel —**ex·clud'·able** *adj.* —**ex·clud'er** *n.*

SYN.—**exclude** implies a keeping out or prohibiting of that which is not yet in [to *exclude* someone from membership]; **debar** connotes the existence of some barrier, as legal authority or force, which excludes someone from a privilege, right, etc. [to *debar* certain groups from voting]; **disbar** refers only to the expulsion of a lawyer from the group of those who are permitted to practice law; **eliminate** implies the removal of that which is already in, usually connoting its undesirability or irrelevance [to *eliminate* waste products]; **suspend** refers to the removal, usually temporary, of someone from some organization, institution, etc., as for the infraction of some rule [to *suspend* a student from school] — *ANT.* admit, include

ex·clu·sion (eks klōō'zhən, iks-) *n.* [ME *exclusioun* < L *exclusio* < pp. of *excludere*] **1** an excluding or being excluded **2** a thing excluded —**to the exclusion of** so as to keep out, bar, etc. —**ex·clu'·sion·ar·y** *adj.*

intoned
(paragraph 3)

in·tone (in tōn') *vt.* **-·toned', -·ton'·ing** [ME *entonen* < OFr *entoner* < ML *intonare*: IN-¹ & TONE] **1** to utter or recite in a singing tone or in prolonged monotones; chant **2** to give a particular intonation to **3** to sing or recite the opening phrase of (a chant, canticle, etc.) —*vi.* to speak or recite in a singing tone or in prolonged monotones; chant —**in·ton'er** *n.*

invariably
(paragraph 2)

in·vari·able (in ver'ē ə bəl) *adj.* [ML *invariabilis*] not variable; not changing; constant; uniform —*n.* an invariable quantity; constant —**in·var'i·abil'i·ty** *n.* or **in·var'i·able·ness** —**in·var'i·ably** *adv.*

mandate
(paragraph 6)

man·date (man'dāt') *n.* [L *mandatum,* neut. pp. of *mandare,* lit., to put into one's hand, command, entrust < *manus,* a hand + pp. of *dare,* to give: see MANUAL & DATE¹] **1** an authoritative order or command, esp. a written one **2** [Historical] *a)* a commission from the League of Nations to a country to administer some region, colony, etc. (cf. TRUSTEESHIP, sense 2) *b)* the area so administered (cf. TRUST TERRITORY) **3** the wishes of constituents expressed to a representative, legislature, etc., as through an election and regarded as an order **4** *Law a)* an order from a higher court or official to a lower one: a **mandate on remission** is a mandate from an appellate court to the lower court, communicating its decision in a case appealed *b)* in English law, a bailment of personal property with no consideration *c)* in Roman law, a commission or contract by which a person undertakes to do something for another, without recompense but with indemnity against loss *d)* any contract of agency —*vt.* **-·dat'ed, -·dat'·ing 1** to assign (a region, etc.) as a mandate **2** to require as by law; make mandatory —**man·da'·tor** *n.*

misconception
(paragraph 5)

mis·con·ceive (mis'kən sēv') *vt., vi.* **-·ceived', -·ceiv'·ing** to conceive wrongly; interpret incorrectly; misunderstand —**mis'·con·cep'·tion** (-sep'shən) *n.*

narcissistic
(paragraph 1)

nar·cis·sism (när'sə siz'əm; *chiefly Brit,* när sis'iz'əm) *n.* [Ger *Narzissismus* (< *Narziss,* NARCISSUS) + -*ismus,* -ISM] **1** self-love; interest, often excessive interest, in one's own appearance, comfort, importance, abilities, etc. **2** *Psychoanalysis* arrest at or regression to the first stage of libidinal development, in which the self is an object of erotic pleasure Also **nar'·cism'** —**nar'·cis·sist** *n., adj.* —**nar·cis·sis'·tic** *adj.*

retina
(paragraph 2)

reti·na (ret''n ə) *n., pl.* **-·nas** or **-·nae** (-ē') [ML, prob. < L *rete* (gen. *retis*), net < IE base **ere-,* loose, separate > Gr *erēmos,* solitary, Lith *rētis,* sieve & (prob.) L *rarus,* rare] the innermost coat lining the interior of the eyeball, containing various layers of photoreceptive cells that are directly connected to the brain by means of the optic nerve: see EYE, illus.

4A VOCABULARY

Using the dictionary entries on page 111, fill in the blanks.

1. The rear part of the eyeball that is sensitive to light is called the

   _____retina_____ .

2. In the United States the _____exclusion_____ of any person from employment because of his race, color, or sex is both illegal and immoral.

3. It is __disillusioning__ when we discover that a public official has used his or her office to force people to pay bribes.

4. The diplomat spoke precisely, carefully _____enunciating_____ each word clearly for his audience.

5. Some people are so self-centered and convinced of their own importance that they can easily be labeled "_____narcissistic_____ ."

6. The restaurant owners decided to _____exclude_____ all smokers from the main dining room.

7. The higher court issued a _____mandate_____ that reversed the lower court's ruling concerning discrimination.

8. A person with employable skills will _____invariably_____ have better job opportunities than will a person without such skills.

9. An adult can _____disillusion_____ a child very quickly if that adult sets a bad example by breaking the law or by being cruel to people.

10. At the funeral the minister _____intoned_____ special passages from the Bible.

11. The tenant was acting under the serious __misconception__ that he could continue to occupy his apartment without paying rent.

Name   Date

4B CENTRAL THEME AND MAIN IDEAS

Choose the best answer.

___d___ 1. What is the central theme of "Darkness at Noon"?
   a. The author leads a very fulfilling life as a lawyer and husband.
   b. Blind people often have difficulty finding jobs because employers prefer to hire sighted people.
   c. Handicapped people need to organize and campaign for better laws to protect them.
   d. People often assume that because blind people cannot see, they cannot hear, learn, or work.

___b___ 2. What is the main idea of paragraph 2?
   a. It is generally assumed that people who cannot see cannot hear.
   b. The way that many people behave in the presence of the blind can be described as downright "silly."
   c. Some people think that it is improper to use the word "blind" in the presence of blind people.
   d. Airline personnel use the number "76" to refer to blind people.

___b___ 3. What is the main idea of paragraph 5?
   a. The worst frustration for the author was when 40 or more law firms refused to hire him because he was blind.
   b. Many employers think that if a lawyer cannot see, he or she cannot work.
   c. The author got his undergraduate degree from Harvard College and his law degree from Harvard Law School.
   d. The rejection letters sent to the author were disillusioning.

4C MAJOR DETAILS

Decide whether each detail is MAJOR or MINOR based on the context of the reading selection.

MAJOR   1. The author has been blind from birth.

MAJOR   2. People often shout at blind people and pronounce every word with great care.

MINOR   3. Airline personnel use a code to refer to blind people.

MINOR   4. The author goes out to dinner with his wife, Kit.

MAJOR   5. If a blind person and a sighted person are together, other people will usually communicate with them by talking with the sighted person.

MINOR   6. The author was given a year's leave of absence from his Washington law firm to study for a diploma-in-law degree at Oxford University.

MINOR   7. The author had to be hospitalized while he was studying in England.

MAJOR   8. In 1976 the Department of Labor issued regulations that require equal employment opportunities for the handicapped.

MAJOR   9. On the whole, the business community's response to offering employment to the handicapped has been enthusiastic.

MINOR 10. The author and his father played basketball in the backyard using a special system they had worked out.

MINOR 11. The author's father shot for the basket and missed completely.

MAJOR 12. The neighbor's friend was not sure if the author or his father was blind.

4D INFERENCES

Decide whether each statement below can be inferred (YES) or cannot be inferred (NO) from the reading selection.

YES 1. The title of the essay suggests that it is sighted people, not blind people, who cannot "see."

NO 2. The author feels that he is greatly admired by people who meet him.

YES 3. The author feels that he can make his point more effectively with humor than with a stern lecture.

NO 4. The author often eats in restaurants with his wife, Kit.

NO 5. The author was highly entertained by the conversation in the hospital between the elderly lady and the orderly.

NO 6. The author got good grades at Harvard Law School because he was given special privileges reserved for blind students.

NO 7. The April 10, 1976, Department of Labor regulations were enacted because the author had complained publicly about the discrimination he experienced while looking for a job.

NO 8. The author's father was a much better basketball player than was the author.

Name   Date

4E   CRITICAL READING: FACT OR OPINION
Decide whether each statement contains a FACT or an OPINION.

FACT 1. *From paragraph 1:* "Blind from birth, I have never had the opportunity to see myself [. . .]."

OPINION 2. *From paragraph 2:* "[. . .] they fear that if the dread word is spoken, the ticket agent's retina will immediately detach [. . .]."

FACT 3. *From paragraph 3:* "I had been given a year's leave of absence from my Washington law firm to study for a diploma-in-law degree at Oxford University."

FACT 4. *From paragraph 5:* "I was turned down by over forty law firms because of my blindness [. . .]."

OPINION 5. *From paragraph 6:* "By and large, the business community's response to offering employment to the disabled has been enthusiastic."

FACT 6. *From paragraph 7:* "Dad shot [the basketball] and missed the garage entirely."

4F   CRITICAL READING: THE WRITER'S CRAFT
Choose the best answer.

b   1. The author shows the connections between each of his ideas with all of these words *except*
   a. "to date"   (paragraph 1)
   b. "obviously"   (2)
   c. "also"   (2)
   d. "conversely"   (2)
   e. "for example"   (2)
   f. "on the other hand" (3)
   g. "therefore"   (3)
   h. "finally"   (4)

c   2. In paragraph 3, rather than telling what happened in his own words, the author uses dialogue. He does this for all of these reasons *except*
   a. to help the reader experience the situation.
   b. to illustrate exactly how foolishly the people behaved.
   c. to impress the reader with his ability to recall the exact words in a conversation.
   d. to dramatize the frustration he felt

___a___ 3. The last sentence of paragraph 4 is an example of
  a. irony.
  b. calamity.
  c. odyssey.

4G READER RESPONSE: TO DISCUSS OR TO WRITE ABOUT

1. Would you avoid using a particular lawyer if he or she were blind? Explain.

2. How do you think physically handicapped people feel when they have to be with people who "can't see the person behind the handicap"? Using specific examples, explain your ideas fully.

3. In recent years our society has started to pay more attention to the needs of people who are physically handicapped. Do you think that society is doing enough? Using specific examples, explain your point of view.

How Did You Do?   4 Darkness at Noon

SKILL (number of items)	Number Correct		Points for each		Score
Vocabulary (11)	_____	×	3	=	_____
Central Theme and Main Ideas (3)	_____	×	4	=	_____
Major Details (12)	_____	×	2	=	_____
Inferences (8)	_____	×	2	=	_____
Critical Reading: Fact or Opinion (6)	_____	×	2	=	_____
Critical Reading: The Writer's Craft (3)	_____	×	1	=	_____

(Possible Total: 100) *Total* _____

SPEED

Reading Time: _____ Reading Rate (page 396): _____ Words Per Minute

Name   Date

My World Now

Anna Mae Halgrim Seaver

(1) This is my world now; it's all I have left. You see, I'm old. And, I'm not as healthy as I used to be. I'm not necessarily happy with it, but I accept it. Occasionally, a member of my family will stop in to see me. He or she will bring me some flowers or a little present, maybe a set of slippers—I've got eight pair. We'll visit for awhile and then they will return to the outside world and I'll be alone again. Oh, there are other people here in the nursing home. Residents, we're called. The majority are about my age. I'm 84. Many are in wheelchairs. The lucky ones are passing through—a broken hip, a diseased heart, something has brought them here for rehabilitation. When they're well, they'll be going home.

(2) Most of us are aware of our plight—some are not. Varying stages of Alzheimer's have robbed several of their mental capacities. We listen to endlessly repeated stories and questions. We meet them anew daily, hourly, or more often. We smile and nod gracefully each time we hear a retelling. They seldom listen to my stories, so I've stopped trying.

(3) The help here is basically pretty good, although there's a large turnover. Just when I get comfortable with someone he or she moves on to another job. I understand that. This is not the best job to have. I don't much like some of the physical things that happen to us. I don't care much for a diaper. I seem to have lost the control acquired so diligently as a child. The difference is that I'm aware and embarrassed, but I can't do anything about it. I've had three children, and I know it isn't pleasant to clean another's diaper. My husband used to wear a gas mask when he changed the kids. I wish I had one now.

(4) Why do you think the staff insists on talking baby talk when speaking to me? I understand English. I have a degree in music and am a certified teacher. Now I hear a lot of words that end in "y." Is this how my kids felt? My hearing aid works fine. There is little need for anyone to position their face directly in front of mine and raise their voice with those "y" words. Sometimes it takes longer for a meaning to sink in; sometimes my mind wanders when I am bored. But there's no need to shout. I tried once or twice to make my feelings known. I even shouted once. That gained me a reputation of being "crotchety." Imagine me, crotchety. My children never heard me raise my voice. I surprised myself. After I've asked for help more than a dozen times and received nothing more than a dozen condescending smiles and a "Yes, deary, I'm working on it," something begins to break. That time I wanted to be taken to a bathroom.

(5) I'd love to go out for a meal, to travel again. I'd love to go to my own church, sing with my own choir. I'd love to visit my friends. Most of them are gone now or else they are in different "homes" of their children's choosing. I'd love to play a good game of bridge, but no one here seems to concentrate very well. My children put me here for my own good. They said they would be able to visit me frequently. But they have their own lives to lead. That sounds normal. I don't want to be a burden. They know that. But I would like to see them more. One of them is here in town. He visits as much as he can.

(6) Something else I've learned to accept is loss of privacy. Quite often I'll close my door when my roommate—imagine having a roommate at my age—is in the TV room. I do appreciate some time to myself and believe that I have earned at least that courtesy. As I sit thinking or writing, one of the aides invariably opens the door unannounced and walks in as if I'm not there. Sometimes she even opens my drawers and begins rummaging around. Am I invisible? Have I lost my right to respect and dignity? What would happen if the roles were reversed? I am still a human being. I would like to be treated as one.

(7) The meals are not what I would choose for myself. We get variety but we don't get a choice. I am one of the fortunate ones who can still handle utensils. I remember eating off such cheap utensils in the Great Depression. I worked hard so I would not have to ever use them again. But here I am.

(8) Did you ever sit in a wheelchair over an extended period of time? It's not comfortable. The seat squeezes you into the middle and applies constant pressure on your hips. The armrests are too narrow and my arms slip off. I am luckier than some. Others are strapped into their chairs and abandoned in front of the TV. Captive prisoners of daytime television: soap operas, talk shows and commercials.

(9) One of the residents died today. He was a loner who, at one time, started a business and developed a multimillion-dollar company. His children moved him here when he could no longer control his bowels. He didn't talk to most of us. He often snapped at the aides as though they were his employees. But he just gave up; willed his own demise. The staff has made up his room, and another man has moved in.

(10) A typical day. Awakened by the woman in the next bed wheezing— a former chain smoker with asthma. Call an aide to wash me and place me in my wheelchair to wait for breakfast. Only 67 minutes until breakfast. I'll wait. Breakfast in the dining area. Most of the residents are in wheelchairs. Others use canes or walkers. Some sit and wonder what they are waiting for. First meal of the day. Only 3 hours and 26 minutes until lunch. Maybe I'll sit around and wait for it. What is today? One day blends into the next until day and date mean nothing. Let's watch a little TV. Oprah and Phil and Geraldo and who cares if some transvestite is having trouble picking a color-coordinated wardrobe from his wife's girlfriend's mother's collection. Lunch. Can't wait. Dried something with puréed peas and coconut pudding. No wonder I'm losing weight.

(11) Back to my semiprivate room for a little semiprivacy or a nap. I do need my beauty rest; company may come today. What is today, again? The afternoon drags into early evening. This used to be my favorite time of the day. Things would wind down. I would kick off my shoes. Put my feet up on the coffee table. Pop open a bottle of Chablis and enjoy the fruits of my day's labor with my husband. He's gone. So is my health. This is my world.

(1,121 words)

Here are some of the more difficult words in "My World Now."

Vocabulary List

Alzheimer's
(paragraph 2)

Alz·hei·mer's disease (älts'hī'mərz) [after A. *Alzheimer* (1864-1915), Ger physician who first described it] a progressive, irreversible disease characterized by degeneration of the brain cells and commonly leading to severe dementia

condescending
(paragraph 4)

con·de·scend (kän'di send') *vi.* [ME *condescenden* < OFr *condescendre* < LL(Ec) *condescendere,* to let oneself down, condescend < L *com-,* together + *descendere,* DESCEND] 1 to descend voluntarily to the level, regarded as lower, of the person one is dealing with; be graciously willing to do something regarded as beneath one's dignity; deign 2 to deal with others in a proud or haughty way 3 [Obs.] to make concessions; agree; assent —*SYN.* STOOP[1]

con·de·scend·ing (-sen'diŋ) *adj.* showing condescension; esp., patronizing —**con'·de·scend'·ingly** *adv.*

crotchety
(paragraph 4)

crotch·ety (-ē) *adj.* 1 full of peculiar whims or stubborn notions; cantankerous; eccentric 2 having the nature of a crotchet — **crotch'·eti·ness** *n.*

demise
(paragraph 9)

de·mise (dē mīz', di-) *n.* [Fr *démise,* fem. pp. of OFr *démettre,* to dismiss, put away < L *demittere:* see DEMIT] 1 *Law* a transfer of an estate by lease, esp. for a fixed period 2 the transfer of sovereignty by death or abdication 3 a ceasing to exist; death —*vt.* **-·mised'**, **-·mis'·ing** 1 to grant or transfer (an estate) by lease, esp. for a fixed period 2 to transfer (sovereignty) by death or abdication

diligently
(paragraph 3)

dili·gent (dil'ə jənt) *adj.* [ME < OFr < L *diligens:* see DILIGENCE[1]] 1 persevering and careful in work; industrious 2 done with careful, steady effort; painstaking —*SYN.* BUSY —**dil'i·gently** *adv.*

119

Great Depression
(paragraph 7)

de·pres·sion (dē presh′ən, di-) *n.* ⟦ME *depressioun* < OFr *depression* < L *depressio*: see DEPRESS⟧ **1** a depressing or being depressed **2** a depressed part or place; hollow or low place on a surface **3** low spirits; gloominess; dejection; sadness **4** a decrease in force, activity, amount, etc. **5** *Astron.* the angular distance of a celestial body below the horizon ☆**6** *Econ.* a period marked by slackening of business activity, widespread unemployment, falling prices and wages, etc. **7** *Med.* a decrease in functional activity **8** *Meteorol. a)* a lowering of the atmospheric pressure indicated by the fall of mercury in a barometer *b)* an area of relatively low barometric pressure; low **9** *Psychol.* an emotional condition, either neurotic or psychotic, characterized by feelings of hopelessness, inadequacy, etc. **10** *Surveying* the angular distance of an object below the horizontal plane —**the (Great) Depression** the period of economic depression which began in 1929 and lasted through most of the 1930s

plight
(paragraph 2)

plight[1] (plīt) *n.* ⟦ME *plit*, state, condition < Anglo-Fr for OFr *pleit*, a fold, way of folding, condition (see PLAIT): sense infl. by ME *plight* < OE *pliht*: see fol.⟧ a condition or state of affairs; esp., now, an awkward, sad, or dangerous situation—*SYN.* PREDICAMENT

rehabilitation
(paragraph 1)

re·ha·bili·tate (rē′hə bil′ə tāt′, rē′ə-) *vt.* -·tat′ed, -·tat′ing ⟦< ML *rehabilitatus*, pp. of *rehabilitare*, to restore: see RE- & HABILITATE⟧ **1** to restore to rank, privileges, or property which one has lost **2** to restore the good name or reputation of; reinstate in good repute **3** to put back in good condition; reestablish on a firm, sound basis **4** *a)* to bring or restore to a normal or optimal state of health, constructive activity, etc. by medical treatment and physical or psychological therapy *b)* to prepare (a disabled person, an inmate, etc.) for useful employment or successful integration into society by counseling, training, etc. —**re′·ha·bil′i·ta′·tion** *n.* —**re′·ha·bil′i·ta′·tive** *adj.*

rummaging
(paragraph 6)

rum·mage (rum′ij) *n.* ⟦aphetic < MFr *arrumage* < *arrumer,* to stow cargo in the hold < *aruner,* to arrange < *run, rum,* ship's hold < Frank **rum,* akin to OE *rum,* ROOM⟧ **1** miscellaneous articles; odds and ends **2** a rummaging, or thorough search —*vt.* -·maged, -·mag·ing **1** to search through (a place, receptacle, etc.) thoroughly, esp. by moving the contents about, turning them over, etc.; ransack **2** to get, find, or turn up by or as by searching thoroughly: with *up* or *out* —*vi.* to search diligently, now sometimes haphazardly, as through the contents of a receptacle —**rum′·mager** *n.*

transvestite
(paragraph 10)

trans·ves·tite (trans ves′tīt′, tranz-) *n.* ⟦< TRANS- + L *vestire,* to clothe (see VEST) + -ITE[1]⟧ a person who derives sexual pleasure from dressing in the clothes of the opposite sex —**trans·ves′·tism′** (-tiz′əm) *n.* or **trans·ves′·ti·tism′** (-tə tiz′əm)

utensils
(paragraph 7)

uten·sil (yōō ten′səl) *n.* ⟦ME *utensele* < MFr *utensile* < L *utensilia,* materials, utensils < neut. pl. of *utensilis,* fit for use < *uti,* to use⟧ **1** any implement or container ordinarily used as in a kitchen **2** an implement or tool, as for use in farming —*SYN.* IMPLEMENT

5A VOCABULARY

Using the vocabulary words listed on pages 119–120, fill in this crossword puzzle.

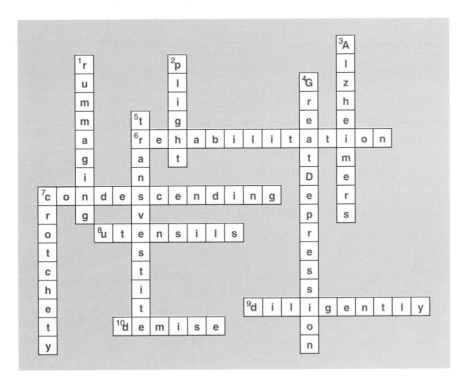

Across

6. restoration to good health
7. dealing with someone in a proud way
8. any article or device used in the kitchen
9. done carefully
10. death

Down

1. searching
2. condition
3. disease of the brain
4. period of limited business, widespread unemployment, and low salaries
5. someone who dresses in clothes of the opposite sex
7. stubborn

5B CENTRAL THEME AND MAIN IDEAS

Choose the best answer.

__d__ 1. Another title for this essay could be
   a. The Disadvantages of Growing Old
   b. If Only I Could Walk
   c. The Elderly: A Forgotten Generation
   d. The Move That Changed My Life

__c__ 2. The main idea of paragraph 3 is
   a. Overall, the help at the nursing home is good.
   b. Anna Mae Halgrim Seaver has to wear a diaper.
   c. Anna Mae Halgrim Seaver regrets that physical changes require the staff to treat her like a baby.
   d. Anna Mae Halgrim Seaver's husband wore a gas mask to change his children's diapers.

5C MAJOR DETAILS

Decide whether each detail is true (T), false (F), or not discussed (ND).

__T__ 1. Anna Mae Halgrim Seaver had received eight pairs of houseshoes from family members.

__T__ 2. Anna Mae Halgrim Seaver wishes that she had a gas mask.

__ND__ 3. Anna Mae Halgrim Seaver is confined to a wheelchair because of arthritis.

__F__ 4. Anna Mae Halgrim Seaver had only a high school education.

__T__ 5. Sometimes Anna Mae Halgrim Seaver has trouble concentrating because Seaver's mind wanders when she is bored.

__F__ 6. When Anna Mae Halgrim Seaver was younger, she often yelled at her children.

__F__ 7. All three of Anna Mae Halgrim Seaver's children live in the town where the nursing home is located.

__T__ 8. The residents at the nursing home are not given a choice of food.

__ND__ 9. Most of the residents at the nursing home are female.

__ND__ 10. Before she entered the nursing home, Anna Mae Halgrim Seaver was a piano teacher.

Name   Date

5D INFERENCES

Decide whether each statement below can be inferred (YES) or cannot be inferred (NO) from the reading selection.

__YES__ 1. The best present that Anna Mae Halgrim Seaver could receive from her family was a visit.

__NO__ 2. Anna Mae Halgrim Seaver's children put her in the nursing home when she could no longer walk.

__NO__ 3. There is a frequent turnover of staff at the nursing home because of their finding better-paying jobs.

__NO__ 4. The staff uses baby talk with Anna Mae Halgrim Seaver because they assume her mind had aged as much as her body had.

__NO__ 5. Anna Mae Halgrim Seaver's children do not visit often because they feel guilty for having put her in the nursing home.

__YES__ 6. Anna Mae Halgrim Seaver did not have a television in her room.

__NO__ 7. Nursing home workers sometimes stole items from Anna Mae Halgrim Seaver's dresser drawers.

__NO__ 8. The cheap eating utensils used in the nursing home are plastic.

__YES__ 9. The nursing home does not provide social activities, such as card games or craft classes, for the residents.

__YES__ 10. One way Anna Mae Halgrim Seaver copes with her confinement is to daydream.

__NO__ 11. The staff at the nursing home mistreated the residents.

5E CRITICAL READING: THE WRITER'S CRAFT

Choose the best answer.

__b__ 1. Anna Mae Halgrim Seaver's son compiled the essay from notes left in his mother's room after her death. Who is the intended audience?
   a. Exclusively for nursing home employees being trained for their jobs.
   b. People thinking of putting, or who have already put, a family member in a nursing home.
   c. Publishers looking at proposals for new books.
   d. Nursing home residents.

_a_ 2. The purpose of this essay is to
   a. inform.
   b. entertain.
   c. frighten.
   d. persuade.

_d_ 3. *Read paragraph 11 again.* The essay ends on a note of
   a. rejection but hope.
   b. nostalgia but regrets.
   c. anger but fear.
   d. loss but acceptance.

5F   READER RESPONSE: TO DISCUSS OR TO WRITE ABOUT

1. In some cultures, nursing homes do not exist. If an elderly parent is unable to live alone, the oldest child becomes the caregiver. What do you think of such a system? Under what circumstances should a person be placed in a nursing home? If one were available, would you place a parent in a nursing home under those circumstances? Why or why not?

2. In recent years newspaper articles and television documentaries have exposed the bad living conditions in some nursing homes. Based on Anna Mae Halgrim Seaver's notes, name three specific areas in her nursing home that need improvement. Discuss why you chose them and how you would improve them.

3. As a college student, you may have never considered the problems of growing old. But think now about your next decade. Being realistic, predict what your life will be like ten years from now. Family life? Employment? Money? Community Service?

Name   Date

How Did You Do?   5 My World Now

SKILL (number of items)	Number Correct		Points for each		Score
Vocabulary (11)	_____	×	2	=	_____
Central Theme and Main Ideas (2)	_____	×	5	=	_____
Major Details (10)	_____	×	4	=	_____
Inferences (11)	_____	×	2	=	_____
Critical Reading: The Writer's Craft (3)	_____	×	2	=	_____

(Possible Total: 100) *Total* _____

SPEED

Reading Time: _____ Reading Rate (page 396): _____ Words Per Minute

My Mother's Blue Bowl

Alice Walker

(1) Visitors to my house are often served food—soup, potatoes, rice—in a large blue stoneware bowl, noticeably chipped at the rim. It is perhaps the most precious thing I own. It was given to me by my mother in her last healthy days. The days before a massive stroke laid her low and left her almost speechless. Those days when to visit her was to be drawn into a serene cocoon of memories and present-day musings and to rest there, in temporary retreat from the rest of the world, as if still an infant, nodding and secure at her breast.

(2) For much of her life my mother longed, passionately longed, for a decent house. One with a yard that did not have to be cleared with an ax. One with a roof that kept out the rain. One with a floor that you could not fall through. She longed for a beautiful house of wood or stone. Or of red brick, like the houses her many sisters and their husbands had. When I was thirteen she found such a house. Green-shuttered, white-walled. Breezy. With a lawn and a hedge and giant pecan trees. A porch swing. There her gardens flourished in spite of the shade, as did her youngest daughter, for whom she sacrificed her life doing hard labor in someone else's house, in order to afford peace and prettiness for her child, to whose grateful embrace she returned each night.

(3) But, curiously, the minute I left home, at seventeen, to attend college, she abandoned the dream house and moved into the projects. Into a small, tight apartment of few breezes, in which I was never to feel comfortable, but that she declared suited her "to a T." I took solace in the fact that it was at least hugged by spacious lawn on one side, and by forest, out the back door, and that its isolated position at the end of the street meant she would have a measure of privacy. Her move into the projects—the best housing poor black people in the South ever had, she would occasionally declare, even as my father struggled to adjust to the cramped rooms and hard, unforgiving qualities of brick—was, I now understand, a step in the direction of divestiture, lightening her load, permitting her worldly possessions to dwindle in significance and, well before she herself would turn to spirit, roll away from her.

(4) She owned little, in fact. A bed, a dresser, some chairs. A set of living room furniture. A set of kitchen furniture. A bed and wardrobe (given to her years before, when I was a teenager, by one of her prosperous sisters). Her flowers: everywhere, inside the house and outside. Planted in anything she managed to get her green hands on, including old suitcases and abandoned shoes. She recycled everything, effortlessly. And

Alice Walker, one of eight children, was born in Eatonton, Georgia, where her parents were share-croppers. A writer since childhood, she is known today as a poet, fiction writer, essayist, biographer, and editor.

© Liaison/Getty Images

gradually she had only a small amount of stuff—mostly stuff her children gave her: nightgowns, perfume, a microwave—to recycle or to use.

(5) Each time I visited her I marveled at the modesty of her desires. She appeared to have hardly any, beyond a thirst for a Pepsi-Cola or a hunger for a piece of fried chicken or fish. On every visit I noticed that more and more of what I remembered of her possessions seemed to be missing. One day I commented on this. Taking a deep breath, sighing and following both with a beaming big smile, which lit up her face, the room, and my heart, she said: "Yes, it's all going. I don't need it anymore. If there's anything you want, take it when you leave; it might not be here when you come back."

(6) The dishes my mother and father used daily had come from my house; I had sent them years before, when I moved from Mississippi to New York. Neither the plates nor the silver matched entirely, but it was all beautiful in her eyes. There were numerous cups, used by the scores of children from the neighborhood who continued throughout her life to come and go. But there was nothing there for me to want.

(7) One day, however, looking for a jar into which to pour leftover iced tea, I found myself probing deep into the wilderness of the overstuffed, airless pantry. Into the land of the old-fashioned, the outmoded, the out-dated. The humble and the obsolete. There was a smoothing iron, a churn. A butter press. And two large bowls. One was cream and rose with a blue stripe. The other was a deep, vivid blue. "May I have this bowl, Mama?" I asked, looking at her and at the blue bowl with delight. "You can have both of them," she said, barely acknowledging them, and continuing to put left-over food away.

(8) I held the bowls on my lap for the rest of the evening, while she watched a TV program about cops and criminals that I found too horri-fying to follow. Before leaving the room I kissed her on the forehead and asked if I could get anything for her from the kitchen; then I went off to bed. The striped bowl I placed on a chair beside the door, so I could look at it from where I lay. The blue bowl I placed in the bed with me. In giv-

ing me these gifts, my mother had done a number of astonishing things, in her typically offhand way. She had taught me a lesson about letting go of possessions—easily, without emphasis or regret—and she had given me a symbol of what she herself represented in my life.

(9) For the blue bowl especially was a cauldron of memories. Of cold, harsh, wintry days, when my brothers and sister and I trudged home from school burdened down by the silence and frigidity of our long trek from the main road, down the hill to our shabby-looking house. More rundown than any of our classmates' houses. In winter my mother's riotous flowers would be absent, and the shack stood revealed for what it was. A gray, decaying, too small barrack meant to house the itinerant tenant workers on a prosperous white man's farm.

(10) Slogging through sleet and wind to the sagging front door, thankful that our house was too far from the road to be seen clearly from the school bus, I always felt a wave of embarrassment and misery. But then I would open the door. And there inside would be my mother's winter flowers: a glowing fire in the fireplace, colorful handmade quilts on all our beds, paintings and drawings of flowers and fruits and, yes, of Jesus, given to her by who knows whom—and most of all, there in the center of the rough-hewn table, which in the tiny kitchen almost touched the rusty woodburning stove, stood the big blue bowl, full of whatever was the most tasty thing on earth.

(11) There was my mother herself. Glowing. Her teeth sparkling. Her eyes twinkling. As if she lived in a castle and her favorite princes and princesses had just dropped by to visit.

(12) The blue bowl stood there, seemingly full forever, no matter how deeply or rapaciously we dipped, as if it had no bottom. And she dipped up soup. Dipped up lima beans. Dipped up stew. Forked out potatoes. Spooned out rice and peas and corn. And in the light and warmth that was her, we dined. Thank you, Mama.

(1,259 words)

Here are some of the more difficult words in "My Mother's Blue Bowl."

barrack
(paragraph 9)

bar·rack[1] (bar'ək, ber'-) *n.* [[Fr *baraque* < Sp *barraca*, cabin, mud hut < *barro*, clay, mud < VL *barrum*, clay]] **1** [Rare] an improvised hut **2** [*pl.*, *often with sing. v.*] *a*) a building or group of buildings for housing soldiers *b*) a large, plain, often temporary building for housing workmen, police, etc. —*vt.*, *vi.* to house in barracks

cauldron
(paragraph 9)

cal·dron (kôl'drən) *n.* [[ME & Anglo-Fr *caudron* < OFr *chauderon* < L *calderia*: see CALDARIUM]] **1** a large kettle or boiler **2** a violently agitated condition like the boiling contents of a caldron

divestiture
(paragraph 3)

di·vest (də vest', dī-) *vt.* [[altered < DEVEST]] **1** to strip *of* clothing, equipment, etc. **2** to deprive or dispossess *of* rank, rights, etc. **3** to disencumber or rid *of* something unwanted **4** *Law* DEVEST —*SYN.* STRIP[1]
di·vesti·ture (-ə chər) *n.* a divesting or being divested: also **di·vest'·ment** or **di·ves'·ture**

Vocabulary List

flourished
(paragraph 2)

flour·ish (flur'ish) *vi.* ⟦ME *florishen* < extended stem of OFr *florir*, to blossom < LL **florire* < L *florere* < *flos*, FLOWER⟧ **1** [Obs.] to blossom **2** to grow vigorously; succeed; thrive; prosper **3** to be at the peak of development, activity, influence, production, etc.; be in one's prime **4** to make showy, wavy motions, as of the arms **5** [Now Rare] *a*) to write in an ornamental style *b*) to perform a fanfare, as of trumpets —*vt.* **1** to ornament with something flowery or fanciful **2** ⟦first so used by John WYCLIFFE⟧ to wave (a sword, arm, hat, etc.) in the air; brandish —*n.* **1** [Rare] a thriving state; success; prosperity **2** anything done in a showy way, as a sweeping movement of the limbs or body **3** a waving in the air; brandishing **4** a decorative or curved line or lines in handwriting **5** an ornate musical passage; fanfare **6** [Obs.] a blooming or a bloom —**flour'·isher** *n.* —**flour'·ish·ing** *adj.*

frigidity
(paragraph 9)

frigid (frij'id) *adj.* ⟦ME < L *frigidus* < *frigere*, to be cold < *frigus*, coldness, frost < IE base **srīg-*, coldness > Gr *rhigos*, frost⟧ **1** extremely cold; without heat or warmth **2** without warmth of feeling or manner; stiff and formal **3** habitually failing to become sexually aroused, or abnormally repelled by sexual activity: said of a woman —**fri·gidi·ty** (fri jid'ə tē) *n.* or **frig'id·ness** —**frig'id·ly** *adv.*

itinerant
(paragraph 9)

itin·er·ant (-ənt) *adj.* ⟦LL *itinerans*, prp. of *itinerari*, to travel < L *iter* (gen. *itineris*), a walk, journey < base of *ire*, to go: see YEAR⟧ traveling from place to place or on a circuit —*n.* a person who travels from place to place —**itin'·er·antly** *adv.*

marveled
(paragraph 5)

mar·vel (mär'vəl) *n.* ⟦ME *mervaile* < OFr *merveille*, a wonder < VL *mirabilia*, wonderful things, orig. neut. pl. of L *mirabilis*, wonderful < *mirari*, to wonder at < *mirus*, wonderful: see SMILE⟧ **1** a wonderful or astonishing thing; prodigy or miracle **2** [Archaic] astonishment —*vi.* **·veled** or **·velled**, **·vel·ing** or **·vel·ling** to be filled with admiring surprise; be amazed; wonder —*vt.* to wonder at or about: followed by a clause

musings
(paragraph 1)

mus·ing (myoo'ziŋ) *adj.* that muses; meditative —*n.* meditation; reflection —**mus'·ingly** *adv.*

rapaciously
(paragraph 12)

ra·pa·cious (rə pā'shəs) *adj.* ⟦< L *rapax* (gen. *rapacis*) < *rapere*, to seize (see RAPE¹) + -OUS⟧ **1** taking by force; plundering **2** greedy or grasping; voracious **3** living on captured prey; predatory —**ra·pa'·ciously** *adv.* —**ra·pac·ity** (rə pas'ə tē) *n.* or **ra·pa'·cious·ness**

serene
(paragraph 1)

se·rene (sə rēn') *adj.* ⟦L *serenus* < IE **ksero-*, dry (> Gr *xēros*, dry, OHG *serawēn*, to dry out) < base **ksā-*, to burn⟧ **1** clear; bright; unclouded *[a serene sky]* **2** not disturbed or troubled; calm, peaceful, tranquil, etc. **3** [S-] exalted; high-ranking: used in certain royal titles *[his Serene Highness]* —*n.* [Old Poet.] a serene expanse, as of sky or water —*SYN.* CALM —**se·rene'·ly** *adv.* —**se·rene'·ness** *n.*

solace
(paragraph 3)

sol·ace (säl'is) *n.* ⟦ME < OFr *solaz* < L *solacium* < *solari*, to comfort < IE base **sel-*, favorable, in good spirits > SILLY⟧ **1** an easing of grief, loneliness, discomfort, etc. **2** something that eases or relieves; comfort; consolation; relief Also **sol'·ace·ment** (-mənt) —*vt.* **·aced**, **·ac·ing** **1** to give solace to; comfort; console **2** to lessen or allay (grief, sorrow, etc.) —*SYN.* COMFORT —**sol'·acer** *n.*

6A VOCABULARY

Match eleven of the imaginary quotations with a vocabulary word listed on pages 129–130. Write "none" for the one extra quotation.

1. "In the early 1900s, many families washed their clothes by boiling them in a kettle over an open fire."

1. ___cauldron___

2. "Farm laborers who move from place to place to harvest seasonal crops are not paid well."

2. ___itinerant___

3. "After being lost in the mountains for two days, the hungry hikers ate the beef stew greedily."

3. ___rapaciously___

4. "As Nikita lay in front of the cozy fire, her dreamy thoughts about a summer vacation brought a smile to her face."

4. ___musings___

5. "Enid Lake was calm again after the thunderstorm had passed."

5. ___serene___

6. "In his closing arguments, attorney Lance Minor made an intense plea for his client's acquittal."

6. ___None___

7. "The commander housed the soldiers in temporary buildings until their permanent quarters were completed."

7. ___barrack___

8. "Stephen's parents never visit him in Minnesota in the winter because of the extremely cold weather."

8. ___frigidity___

9. "The magician amazed us with his performance at the Orpheum Theater."

9. ___marveled___

10. "Getting rid of unwanted items can be done through a yard or garage sale."

10. ___divestiture___

11. "To ease the pain of his father's death, Paul ate junk food for comfort."

11. ___solace___

12. "Because of the moisture, the termites thrived in the wooden columns on my front porch.

12. ___flourished___

6B CENTRAL THEME AND MAIN IDEAS

Choose the best answer.

__b__ 1. What is the central theme of "My Mother's Blue Bowl"?
   a. Alice Walker's mother gave away most of her possessions except several items that her children had given her.
   b. The blue bowl filled Alice Walker with fond memories of her childhood with her mother.
   c. Alice Walker often serves food in the blue bowl her mother gave her.
   d. Alice Walker was embarrassed by the poverty she grew up in and her lack of new, pretty possessions.

__d__ 2. What is the main idea of paragraph 3?
   a. Alice Walker left home at the age of seventeen.
   b. When Alice Walker went to college, her parents moved into the projects.
   c. The projects were the best housing many poor black families in the South could afford.
   d. As she aged, Alice Walker's mother wanted to own fewer and fewer possessions.

__a__ 3. What is the main idea of paragraph 4?
   a. Alice Walker's mother owned few worldly possessions.
   b. Alice Walker's mother liked flowers inside and outside her house.
   c. Alice Walker's mother had a wealthy sister.
   d. Alice Walker's mother believed in recycling.

6C MAJOR DETAILS

Decide whether each detail is true (T), false (F), or not discussed (ND).

__T__ 1. Alice Walker's mother longed for a house of wood, stone, or brick.

__ND__ 2. The dream house of Alice Walker's mother was in Mississippi.

__F__ 3. Alice Walker was an only child.

__ND__ 4. Alice Walker was a college graduate.

__T__ 5. Alice Walker's mother had a fondness for Pepsi-Cola and fried chicken and fish.

__F__ 6. Alice Walker's mother had few items in her kitchen pantry.

__F__ 7. Alice Walker's mother did not own a television.

__T__ 8. Alice Walker's mother had a talent for growing flowers.

Name   Date

___T___   9. Alice Walker's mother worked as a cleaning lady.

___ND___   10. Alice Walker sometimes walked to school rather than ride the school bus.

6D   INFERENCES

Choose the best answer.

___c___ 1. *Read paragraph 6 again.* When Alice Walker left Mississippi for New York, she gave her old dishes to her mother because
a. Alice Walker did not have enough money to buy a new set of dishes for her mother.
b. Alice Walker knew her mother would prefer dishes that had a "history" in the family.
c. Alice Walker feared the visiting neighborhood children would break or chip new dishes.
d. Alice Walker did not want to pay for shipping her old dishes to her new home.

___b___ 2. *Read paragraph 8 again.* Why did Alice Walker hold the bowls on her lap for the rest of the evening and then take the blue bowl to bed with her? Alice Walker
a. was afraid her mother might change her mind.
b. treasured the bowls and enjoyed holding them.
c. thought her mother might break them.
d. wanted to throw them away the first thing the next morning.

___d___ 3. *Read paragraph 12 again.* What did Alice Walker imply when she wrote "And in the light and warmth that was her, we dined"?
a. Her mother hugged them as they dined in the poorly insulated house that was cold in the winter.
b. The family dined by candlelight because they had no electricity.
c. Her mother entertained the family with stories that made them laugh.
d. The children loved their mother so much that they did not notice their poor surroundings when with her.

6E   CRITICAL READING: THE WRITER'S CRAFT

Choose the best answer.

___b___ 1. The time frame used in the essay is
a. the future.
b. present to past.
c. present to future.
d. past to present.

___d___ 2. *Reread paragraph 10.* What is the strong visual impression Alice Walker had when she opened the door?
a. glowing fire
b. roughness of furniture
c. rusty old stove
d. colorful things everywhere

___c___ 3. In paragraph 10, several emotions are expressed through the use of sensory details—seeing, hearing, tasting, smelling, and touching. What two emotions are not suggested in this paragraph?
a. acceptance, love
b. shame, grief
c. jealousy, anger
d. warmth, delight

___b___ 4. *Reread paragraph 12.* By ending her essay with the words, "Thank you, Mama," Alice Walker summarizes her point by thanking her mother for
a. giving away the two bowls.
b. teaching the children many wise things.
c. being an excellent cook, even with uninteresting foods.
d. keeping the blue bowl full at all times.

6F   READER RESPONSE: TO DISCUSS OR TO WRITE ABOUT

1. Describe a woman in your family (or one whom you have read about or studied) who succeeded in spite of setbacks or obstacles. Describe her fully, but focus especially on the one outstanding quality that you think helped her succeed.

2. Think of a significant possession of your parent(s) that you would like to have. What memories do you associate with this object? Is there a significant object from your childhood that you think your child(ren) would want? Why?

3. Do you prefer to keep or give away unnecessary possessions? Give specific reasons for either keeping or giving away several items that have special significance to you.

Name   Date

How Did You Do?   6 My Mother's Blue Bowl

SKILL (number of items)	Number Correct		Points for each		Score
Vocabulary (12)	_____	×	2	=	_____
Central Theme and Main Ideas (3)	_____	×	6	=	_____
Major Details (10)	_____	×	4	=	_____
Inferences (3)	_____	×	2	=	_____
Critical Reading: The Writer's Craft (4)	_____	×	3	=	_____

(Possible Total: 100) *Total* _____

SPEED

Reading Time: _____ Reading Rate (page 396): _____ Words Per Minute

Name   Date

▪ Part 3 ▪

Thinking: Getting Started

Using your prior knowledge of a subject helps you efficiently read and remember new material on that subject. Skilled readers approach reading with a confident attitude. They believe they usually know something—even a little bit, no matter how remote—about almost any subject they encounter. That little bit of prior knowledge becomes the foundation upon which they build a larger bank of learned information.

Before you start to dive into a reading, think about the subject about which you are going to read and try to recall what you know about the subject. Use the next three pages of visuals and accompanying questions to start becoming conscious of your prior knowledge about the subjects in the reading selections in Part 3 of this book. As you finish interacting with each separate visual, turn to its related reading selection and use the technique of *survey*, explained on page 31 in Part 1.

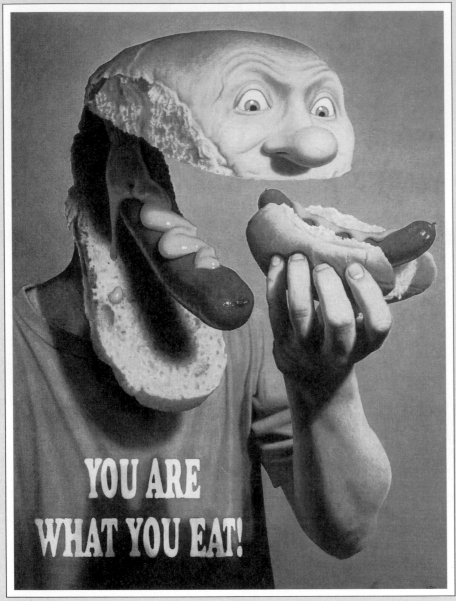

Image No. 2423 © 1998 MEIKLEJOHN GRAPHICS, London UK.

How does what you eat reflect who you are? (See "You Are How You Eat.")

TIME, 150 Years of Photo Journalism, Fall 1989, p. 61. Civil Rights–Birmingham 1963. Photo © Charles Moore/Black Star.

What sorts of events in people's lives can drastically alter the way they look at the world? (See "Summer.")

Can a child expect dreams to be fulfilled without the ability to read? (See "The Magic Words Are 'Will You Help Me?'")

You'll be flying in a jet maintained by Tommy.

When Tommy grows up, he'll be an aircraft mechanic. Perhaps he'll work on a jet that you fly in some day.

By then, the job will require an advanced knowledge of chemistry, physics, and trigonometry. Unfortunately, very few kids are being prepared to master such sophisticated subjects.

If we want children who can handle tomorrow's good jobs, more kids need to take more challenging academic courses.

To find out how you can help the effort to raise standards in America's schools, please call 1-800-96-PROMISE.

If we all pitch in and help, America will get where it needs to go.

Educational Excellence Partnership

More on next page . . .

© Jerry Marshall

How do some people show their feelings toward immigrants? (See "Mute in an English-Only World.")

"And so they were married and lived together happily for quite some time."

Drawing by Donald Reilly, © 1972. The Cartoon Bank.

Although many marriages today end in divorce, many do not, and the couple stays deeply in love. What makes some love so strong that it lasts forever? (See "The Girl with the Large Eyes.")

How can a person learn parenting skills? (See "Flour Children.")

Summer

Jonathan Schwartz

(1) I am running down an alley with a stolen avocado, having climbed over a white brick fence and into the forbidden back yard of a carefully manicured estate at the corner of El Dorado and Crescent Drive in Beverly Hills, California. I have snatched a rock-hard Fuerte avocado from one of the three avocado trees near the fence. I have been told that many ferocious   5
dogs patrol the grounds; they are killers, these dogs. I am defying them. They are nowhere to be found, except in my mind, and I'm out and gone and in the alley with their growls directing my imagination. I am running with fear and exhilaration, beginning a period of summer.

(2) Emerging from the shield of the alley I cut out into the open.   10
Summer is about running, and I am running, protected by distance from the dogs. At the corner of Crescent Drive and Lomitas I spot Bobby Tornitzer on a bike. I shout *"Tornitzer!"* He turns his head. His bike wobbles. An automobile moving rapidly catches Tornitzer's back wheel. Tornitzer is thrown high into the air and onto the concrete sidewalk of   15
Crescent Drive. The driver, a woman with gray hair, swirls from the car hysterically and hovers noisily over Tornitzer, who will not survive the accident. I hold the avocado to my chest and stand, frozen, across the street. I am shivering in the heat, and sink to my knees. It is approximately 3:30 in the afternoon. It is June 21, 1946. In seven days I will be 8 years old.   20

(215 words)

Vocabulary List

Here are some of the more difficult words in "Summer."

avocado
(paragraph 1)

☆**avo·ca·do** (av'ə kä′dō, ä′və-) *n., pl.* **-dos** [altered (infl. by earlier Sp *avocado*, now *abogado*, advocate) < MexSp *aguacate* < Nahuatl *a:wakaλ*, avocado, lit., testicle; so named from its shape] **1** a widespread, thick-skinned, pear-shaped tropical fruit, yellowish green to purplish black, with a single large seed and yellow, buttery flesh, used in salads; alligator pear **2** the tree (*Persea americana*) of the laurel family on which it grows **3** a yellowish-green color

AVOCADO

defying
(paragraph 1)

defy (dē fī′, di-; *also, for n.,* dē′fī) *vt.* **-fied′**, **-fy′·ing** [ME *defien* < OFr *defier*, to distrust, repudiate, defy < LL *disfidare* < *dis-*, from + *fidare*, to trust < *fidus*, faithful: see FAITH] **1** to resist or oppose boldly or openly **2** to resist completely in a baffling way [the puzzle *defied* solution] **3** to dare (someone) to do or prove something **4** [Archaic] to challenge (someone) to fight —*n., pl.* **-fies** a defiance or challenge

estate
(paragraph 1)

es·tate (ə stāt′, i-) *n.* [ME & OFr *estat*, STATE] **1** *a)* state or condition [to restore the theater to its former *estate*] *b)* a condition or stage of life [to come to man's *estate*] *c)* status or rank **2** [Historical] esp. in feudal times, any of the three social classes having specific political powers: the first estate was the Lords Spiritual (clergy), the second estate the Lords Temporal (nobility), and the third estate the Commons (bourgeoisie): see also FOURTH ESTATE **3** property; possessions; capital; fortune **4** the assets and liabilities of a dead or bankrupt person **5** landed property; individually owned piece of land containing a residence, esp. one that is large and maintained by great wealth **6** [Brit.] DEVELOPMENT (sense 4) **7** [Archaic] display of wealth; pomp **8** *Law a)* the degree, nature, extent, and quality of interest or ownership that one has in land or other property *b)* all the property, real or personal, owned by one

exhilaration
(paragraph 1)

ex·hila·rate (eg zil′ə rāt′, ig-) *vt.* **-rat′ed**, **-rat′·ing** [< L *exhilaratus*, pp. of *exhilarare*, to gladden < *ex-*, intens. + *hilarare*, to gladden < *hilaris*, glad: see HILARIOUS] **1** to make cheerful, merry, or lively **2** to invigorate or stimulate —*SYN.* ANIMATE —**ex·hil′a·ra′tive** *adj.*
ex·hila·ra·tion (eg zil′ə rā′shən, ig-) *n.* [LL *exhilaratio*] **1** the act of exhilarating **2** an exhilarated condition or feeling; liveliness; high spirits; stimulation

ferocious
(paragraph 1)

fe·ro·cious (fə rō′shəs) *adj.* [< L *ferox* (gen. *ferocis*), wild, untamed < *ferus*, FIERCE + base akin to *oculus*, EYE + -OUS] **1** fierce; savage; violently cruel **2** [Informal] very great [a *ferocious* appetite] —**fe·ro′·ciously** *adv.* —**fe·ro′·cious·ness** *n.*

hovers
(paragraph 2)

hover (huv′ər, häv′-) *vi.* [ME *hoveren*, freq. of *hoven*, to stay (suspended)] **1** to stay suspended or flutter in the air near one place **2** to linger or wait close by, esp. in an overprotective, insistent, or anxious way **3** to be in an uncertain condition; waver (*between*) —*n.* the act of hovering —**hov′er·er** *n.*

hysterically
(paragraph 2)

hys·teri·cal (hi ster′i kəl) *adj.* [prec. + -AL] **1** of or characteristic of hysteria **2** *a)* like or suggestive of hysteria; emotionally uncontrolled and wild *b)* extremely comical **3** having or subject to hysteria —**hys·ter′i·cally** *adv.*

manicured
(paragraph 1)

mani·cure (man′i kyoor′) *n.* [Fr < L *manus*, a hand + *cura*, care: see CURE] a trimming, cleaning, and sometimes polishing of the fingernails, esp. when done by a manicurist —*vt.* **-cured′**, **-cur′·ing** **1** *a)* to trim, polish, etc. (the fingernails) *b)* to give a manicure to **2** [Informal] to trim, clip, etc. meticulously [to *manicure* a lawn]

7A VOCABULARY

Match eight of the imaginary quotations with a vocabulary word listed on page 142. Write "none" for the two extra quotations.

1. "If you walk too near that savage animal, it will attack you."

   1. _____ferocious_____

2. "Look at those neatly trimmed bushes and that beautifully edged lawn."

   2. _____manicured_____

3. "Mr. Lloyd Dexter lives in a huge house surrounded by acres of woods."

   3. _____estate_____

4. "Sometimes my doctor prescribes pain killers for my headaches."

   4. _____none_____

5. "The young parents ran to the lifeguard in a panic when they thought their child might be drowning."

   5. _____hysterically_____

6. "While the eggs are beginning to hatch, the bird is fluttering protectively over its nest."

   6. _____hovers_____

7. "I think skydivers sometimes think they can ignore the laws of gravity."

   7. _____defying_____

8. "Wow! That ice cold shower certainly gives me a feeling of high spirits."

   8. _____exhilaration_____

9. "What do you call that pear-shaped, yellowish-green fruit on the table?"

   9. _____avocado_____

10. "No person should drive while under the influence of alcohol or drugs."

   10. _____none_____

7B MAIN IDEA AND IMAGES

Choose the best answer.

__a__ 1. Another title for this story could be
   a. June 21, 1946.
   b. Killer Dogs.
   c. My Eighth Birthday.
   d. The Alley.

Name   Date   143

   _c_ 2. The main image in paragraph 1 is of a young boy
      a. climbing a white brick fence.
      b. snatching avocados.
      c. running with fear and exhilaration.
      d. defying ferocious dogs.

   _b_ 3. The main image in paragraph 2 is of
      a. Tornitzer riding his bike.
      b. the playful, then horrified boy.
      c. the 7-year-old emerging from the alley.
      d. the hysteria of the woman driver.

7C MAJOR DETAILS

Decide whether each detail is MAJOR or MINOR based on the context of the reading selection.

MAJOR 1. The 7-year-old was running from imagined ferocious dogs.

MINOR 2. The stolen avocado was still hard.

MINOR 3. The avocado tree was on an estate.

MAJOR 4. The 7-year-old froze in horror when he saw the accident.

MAJOR 5. Bobby Tornitzer was riding his bike.

MAJOR 6. A car hit Tornitzer's bike.

MAJOR 7. Tornitzer was going to die.

MINOR 8. A woman was driving the car.

MINOR 9. The street was called Crescent Drive.

7D INFERENCES

Decide whether each statement below can be inferred (YES) or cannot be inferred (NO) from the story.

NO 1. Climbing over other people's fences is against the law.

YES 2. This experience probably left a deep emotional scar on the 7-year-old.

NO 3. The 7-year-old was being punished for stealing an avocado.

NO 4. Seven-year-old children are destructive.

YES 5. A single moment can drastically alter lives.

NO 6. The 7-year-old hated Tornitzer.

__NO__ 7. Women are poor drivers.

__NO__ 8. The driver was drunk.

__NO__ 9. Tornitzer had recently arrived in America, and so he did not understand English very well.

__NO__ 10. Tornitzer was also 7 years old.

7E CRITICAL READING: THE WRITER'S CRAFT
Choose the best answer.

__a__ 1. The story starts with the feeling of _____ and ends

with a feeling of _____ .
   a. joyful action . . . horrified inaction
   b. running . . . standing
   c. being alone . . . being with others
   d. being out in the open . . . shivering in the heat

__c__ 2. The fact that Tornitzer will die is stated in paragraph 2 at the end of a long sentence that describes the upset car driver. The author writes this way because he wants to
   a. hint that Tornitzer is the driver's son.
   b. force the reader to concentrate on the effect of the accident on the 7-year-old.
   c. convey the casual suddenness of the accident.
   d. scare the reader into realizing the importance of bicycle safety.

__c__ 3. The word "swirls" (line 16) implies
   a. a storm.
   b. curiosity.
   c. panic.
   d. calm.

__b__ 4. The phrase "hovers noisily" (line 17) conveys the image of someone who is
   a. sick.
   b. panicked.
   c. worried.
   d. happy.

__b__ 5. The phrase "shivering in the heat" (line 19) dramatically describes shock through
   a. the use of minute detail.
   b. the unexpected combination of hot and cold.
   c. its implied reference to the word "frozen."
   d. the contrast of death and play.

7F   READER RESPONSE: TO DISCUSS OR TO WRITE ABOUT

1. Was there a dramatic event, good or bad, in your childhood that you will never forget? Describe and discuss its effect on you.

2. Describe how you felt after reading "Summer."

3. What are your feelings about people who use the street rather than the sidewalk to jog, skate, or ride a bicycle? If they are hit by a car, should the driver be held responsible? Explain your point of view.

How Did You Do?   **7** Summer

SKILL (number of items)	Number Correct		Points for Each		Score
Vocabulary (10)	_____	×	3	=	_____
Main Ideas and Images (3)	_____	×	6	=	_____
Major Details (9)	_____	×	3	=	_____
Inferences (10)	_____	×	2	=	_____
Critical Reading: The Writer's Craft (5)	_____	×	1	=	_____
			(Possible Total: 100) *Total*		_____

SPEED

Reading Time: _____ Reading Rate (page 396): _____ Words Per Minute

Name   Date

The Girl with the Large Eyes

Julius Lester

(1) Many years ago in a village in Africa, there lived a girl with large eyes. She had the most beautiful eyes of any girl in the village, and whenever one of the young men looked at her as she passed through the marketplace, her gaze was almost more than he could bear.

(2) The summer she was to marry, a drought came upon the region. No rain had fallen for months, and the crops died, the earth changed to dust, and the wells and rivers turned to mudholes. The people grew hungry, and when a man's mind can see nothing except his hunger, he cannot think of marriage, not even to such a one as the girl with the large eyes.

(3) She had little time to think of the wedding that would have been had there been no drought. She had little time to daydream of the hours of happiness she would have been sharing with her new husband. Indeed, she had little time at all, for it was her job each day to find water for her family. That was not easy. She spent the morning going up and down the river bank, scooping what little water she could from the mudholes until she had a pitcher full.

(4) One morning, she walked back and forth along the river bank for a long while, but could find no water. Suddenly, a fish surfaced from the mud and said to her, "Give me your pitcher and I will fill it with water."

(5) She was surprised to hear the fish talk, and a little frightened, but she had found no water that morning, so she handed him the pitcher, and he filled it with cold, clear water.

(6) Everyone was surprised when she brought home a pitcher of such clear water, and they wanted to know where she had found it. She smiled with her large eyes, but she said nothing.

(7) The next day she returned to the same place, called the fish, and again he filled her pitcher with cold, clear water. Each day thereafter she returned, and soon she found herself becoming fond of the fish. His skin was the colors of the rainbow and as smooth as the sky on a clear day. His voice was soft and gentle like the cool, clear water he put in her pitcher. And on the seventh day, she let the fish embrace her, and she became his wife.

(8) Her family was quite happy to get the water each day, but they were still very curious to know from where she was getting it. Each day they asked her many questions, but she only smiled at them with her large eyes and said nothing.

(9) The girl's father was a witch doctor, and he feared that the girl had taken up with evil spirits. One day he changed the girl's brother into a fly and told him to sit in the pitcher and find out from where she was getting

the water. When she got to the secret place, the brother listened to the girl and the fish and watched them embrace, and he flew quickly home to tell his father what he had heard and seen. When the parents learned that their daughter had married a fish, they were greatly embarrassed and ashamed. If the young men of the village found out, none of them would ever marry her. And if the village found out, the family would be forced to leave in disgrace.

(10) The next morning, the father ordered the girl to stay at home, and the brother took him to the secret place beside the river. They called to the fish, and, when he came up, they killed him and took him home. They flung the fish at the girl's feet and said, "We have brought your husband to you."

(11) The girl looked at them and at the fish beside her feet, his skin growing dull and cloudy, his colors fading. And her eyes filled with tears.

(12) She picked up the fish and walked to the river, wondering what was to become of the child she was carrying inside her. If her parents had killed her husband, would they not kill her child when it was born?

(13) She walked for many miles, carrying her husband in her arms, until she came to a place where the waters were flowing. She knew that suffering could only be cured by medicine or patience. If neither of those relieved it, suffering would always yield to death.

(14) Calling her husband's name, she waded into the water until it flowed above her head. But as she died, she gave birth to many children, and they still float on the rivers to this day as water lilies.

(850 words)

Here are some of the more difficult words in "The Girl with the Large Eyes."

Vocabulary List

drought
(paragraph 2)

drought (drout) *n.* ⟦ME < OE *drugoth*, dryness < *drugian*, to dry up; akin to *dryge*, DRY⟧ **1** a prolonged period of dry weather; lack of rain **2** a prolonged or serious shortage or deficiency **3** [Archaic] thirst —**drought'y** *adj.* **drought'i·er, drought'i·est**

fond
(paragraph 7)

fond[1] (fänd) *adj.* ⟦ME, contr. of *fonned*, foolish, pp. of *fonnen*, to be foolish⟧ **1** [Now Rare] foolish, esp. foolishly naïve or hopeful **2** *a*) tender and affectionate; loving *b*) affectionate in a foolish or overly indulgent way **3** cherished with great or unreasoning affection; doted on *[a fond hope]* —**fond of** having a liking for

gaze
(paragraph 1)

gaze (gāz) *vi.* **gazed, gaz'·ing** ⟦ME *gazen* < Scand, as in Norw & Swed dial. *gasa*, to stare < ON *gas*, GOOSE⟧ to look intently and steadily; stare, as in wonder or expectancy —*n.* a steady look — **gaz'er** *n.*

scooping
(paragraph 3)

scoop (skōōp) *n.* ⟦ME *scope* < MDu *schope*, bailing vessel, *schoppe*, a shovel, akin to Ger *schöpfen*, to dip out, create⟧ **1** any of various utensils shaped like a small shovel or a ladle; specif., *a*) a kitchen utensil used to take up sugar, flour, etc. *b*) a small utensil with a round bowl, for dishing up ice cream, mashed potatoes, etc. *c*) a small, spoonlike surgical instrument **2** the deep shovel of a dredge or steam shovel, which takes up sand, dirt, etc. **3** the act or motion of taking up with or as with a scoop **4** the amount taken up at one time by a scoop **5** a hollowed-out place ✰**6** [Informal] *a*) the publication or broadcast of a news item before a competitor; beat *b*) such a news item *c*) current, esp. confidential, information —*adj.* designating a rounded, somewhat low neckline in a dress, etc. —*vt.* **1** to take up or out with or as with a scoop **2** to empty by bailing **3** to dig (*out*); hollow (*out*) **4** to make by digging out **5** to gather (*in* or *up*) as if with a scoop ✰**6** [Informal] to publish or broadcast a news item before (a competitor) —**scoop'er** *n.*

surfaced
(paragraph 4)

sur·face (sur'fis) *n.* ⟦Fr < *sur-* (see SUR-[1]) + *face,* FACE, based on L *superficies*⟧ **1** *a*) the outer face, or exterior, of an object *b*) any of the faces of a solid *c*) the area or extent of such a face **2** superficial features, as of a personality; outward appearance **3** AIRFOIL **4** *Geom.* an extent or magnitude having length and breadth, but no thickness —*adj.* **1** of, on, or at the surface **2** intended to function or be carried on land or sea, rather than in the air or under water *[surface forces, surface mail]* **3** merely apparent; external; superficial —*vt.* **·faced, ··fac·ing 1** to treat the surface of, esp. so as to make smooth or level **2** to give a surface to, as in paving **3** to bring to the surface; esp., to bring (a submarine) to the surface of the water —*vi.* **1** to work at or near the surface, as in mining **2** to rise to the surface of the water **3** to become known, esp. after being concealed —**sur'·facer** *n.*

8A   VOCABULARY

From the context of "The Girl with the Large Eyes," explain the meaning of each of the vocabulary words shown in boldface below.

1. *From paragraph 1:* . . . and whenever one of the young men looked at her as she passed through the marketplace, her **gaze** was almost more than he could bear.

   <u>a steady look</u>

2. *From paragraph 2:* The summer she was to marry, a **drought** came upon the region.

   <u>a prolonged period of dry weather</u>

3. *From paragraph 3:* She spent the morning going up and down the river bank, **scooping** what little water she could from the mudholes until she had a pitcher full.

   <u>taking up with a small shovel-like utensil</u>

4. *From paragraph 4:* A fish **surfaced** from the mud and said to her . . .

   <u>rose to the surface or top</u>

5. *From paragraph 7:* Each day thereafter she returned, and soon she found herself becoming **fond** of the fish.

   <u>tender and loving toward</u>

Name   Date

8B   CENTRAL THEME AND MAIN IMAGES
Choose the best answer.

__b__ 1. "The Girl with the Large Eyes" is a story about
   a. a beautiful girl who feels that the purpose of her life is to give birth to water lilies.
   b. a beautiful girl who falls in love with and marries a fish.
   c. a father and son who want to protect the beautiful girl from disgracing herself in the village.
   d. a fish that falls in love with and marries the most beautiful girl in the village.

__d__ 2. What is the moral of the underlying central theme of "The Girl with the Large Eyes"?
   a. Love is blind.
   b. Humans and fish have a right to marry each other.
   c. Families have to protect their reputations.
   d. Prejudice in all forms is destructive and cruel.

__c__ 3. The unexpected main image of paragraph 4 is
   a. the girl's walking on the river bank.
   b. a fish that surfaced from the mud.
   c. a fish that could talk.
   d. the fish's offer to fill the pitcher.

__a__ 4. The main image in paragraph 7 is of
   a. the girl and the fish falling in love.
   b. the girl who is calling to the fish.
   c. the girl who is returning every day to see the fish.
   d. the fish's smooth colorful skin and gentle voice.

__c__ 5. The main image in paragraphs 10 and 11 is of
   a. the brother and father going to the secret place at the river.
   b. the fish's skin growing dull and cloudy.
   c. the brutal murder of the fish followed by the girl's grief.
   d. the father's ordering the girl to stay at home.

__b__ 6. The unexpected main image in paragraph 12 is
   a. the girl's picking up the dead fish.
   b. the girl's being pregnant.
   c. the girl's walking to the river.
   d. the girl's knowing that her parents killed her husband.

8C MAJOR DETAILS

Fill in the word or words that correctly complete each statement.

1. The girl with the large eyes was the most ____beautiful____ girl in the village.

2. Because of the terrible drought, the girl had to spend her time ____searching____ for water.

3. One day a ____fish____ offered to bring her water.

4. On the ____seventh____ day, the girl let the fish embrace her, and she became his ____wife____ .

5. The girl's witch-doctor father turned her ____brother____ into a ____fly____ so he could discover where the girl got the water.

6. The father and brother ____killed____ the fish and ____flung____ it at the girl's feet.

7. The girl was pregnant and was afraid her parents would kill the ____child____ when they found out.

8. The girl knew that suffering could usually be cured by medicine or ____patience____ rather than death.

9. The grief stricken girl carried her dead husband to the river and waded into it until it ____flowed____ above her head.

10. As she died, she gave birth to many children which to this day float on rivers as ____water lilies____ .

8D INFERENCES

Choose the best answer.

__b__ 1. *Read paragraphs 6 and 8 again.* The girl did not tell her family about the fish because she
   a. knew the fish did not want her to say anything.
   b. knew they would not approve.
   c. was saving the news for a surprise.
   d. was embarrassed that she loved a fish.

Name   Date

___d___ 2. The creation of the water lilies at the end of the story implies that
a. water lilies are part human and part fish.
b. the deaths of the girl and the fish had a purpose.
c. people should feel sad when they see water lilies.
d. the result of true love is beauty.

8E   CRITICAL READING: THE WRITER'S CRAFT

Choose the best answer.

___d___ 1. "The Girl with the Large Eyes" is a folktale, which is a story handed down orally among the common people. The purpose of this folktale is to
a. teach the history of an African tribe.
b. warn people not to trust fish.
c. explain the effects of a drought.
d. illustrate the destructive power of prejudice.

___b___ 2. The word "embrace" in paragraph 7 means to
a. kiss.
b. hug.
c. make love with.
d. become close friends with.

___b___ 3. If the word "flung" in paragraph 10 were replaced by the word "placed," what feelings would be missing?
a. Love and concern
b. Anger and triumph
c. Embarrassment and fear
d. Tenderness and disappointment

___a___ 4. Water appears often in this folktale. Water appears in connection with all these *except*
a. the girl's eyes.
b. the girl's tears.
c. the drought.
d. the girl's death.

8F   READER RESPONSE: TO DISCUSS OR TO WRITE ABOUT

1. Was the father justified in spying on his daughter? Explain.

2. Should two people from very different backgrounds marry? Using specific examples, explain your point of view.

3. How important is family approval when a couple decides to marry? If parents don't approve of the marriage, should the couple get married anyway? What are some problems that are likely to occur if they ignore their parents' wishes?

How Did You Do? 8 The Girl with the Large Eyes

SKILL (number of items)	Number Correct		Points for Each		Score
Vocabulary (5)	_____	×	4	=	_____
Central Theme and Main Ideas (6)	_____	×	6	=	_____
Major Details* (13)	_____	×	2	=	_____
Inferences (2)	_____	×	3	=	_____
Critical Reading: The Writer's Craft (4)	_____	×	3	=	_____

(Possible Total: 100) *Total*   _____

SPEED

Reading Time: _____ Reading Rate (page 397): _____ Words Per Minute

*Questions 4, 5, and 6 in this exercise call for two separate answers each. In computing your score, count each separate answer toward your number correct.

Name   Date

You Are How You Eat

Enid Nemy

(1) There's nothing peculiar about a person walking along a Manhattan street, or any other street for that matter, eating an ice cream cone. It's the approach that's sometimes a little strange—ice-cream-cone-eating is not a cut-and-dried, standardized, routine matter. It is an accomplishment with infinite variety, ranging from methodical and workman-like procedures to methods that are visions of delicacy and grace. The infinite variety displayed in eating ice cream isn't by any means unique; it applies to all kinds of food. The fact is that although a lot of research has been done on what people eat and where they eat it, serious studies on the way food is eaten have been sadly neglected.

(2) Back to ice cream, as an example. If five people leave an ice cream store with cones, five different methods of eating will likely be on view. There are people who stick out their tongues on top of a scoop, but don't actually eat the ice cream. They push it down into the cone—push, push, push—then take an intermission to circle the perimeter, lapping up possible drips. After this, it's again back to pushing the ice cream farther into the cone. When the ice cream has virtually disappeared into the crackly cone, they begin eating. These people obviously don't live for the moment; they plan for the future, even if the future is only two minutes away. Gobble up all the ice cream on top and be left with a hollow cone? Forget it. Better to forgo immediate temptation and then enjoy the cone right to the end.

(3) On the other hand, there are the "now" types who take great gobby bites of the ice cream. Eventually, of course, they get down to an empty cone, which they might eat and, then again, they might throw away (if the latter, one wonders why they don't buy cups rather than cones, but no point in asking).

(4) The most irritating of all ice cream eaters are the elegant creatures who manage to devour a whole cone with delicate little nibbles and no dribble. The thermometer might soar, the pavement might melt, but their ice cream stays as firm and as rounded as it was in the scoop. No drips, no minor calamities—and it's absolutely not fair, but what can you do about it?

(5) Some of the strangest ice cream fans can be seen devouring sundaes and banana splits. They are known as "layer by layer" types. First they eat the nuts and coconut and whatever else is sprinkled on top. Then they eat the sauce; then the banana, and finally the ice cream, flavor by flavor. Some might feel that they are eating ingredients and not a sundae or a split, but what do they care?

(6) As for chocolate eaters, there are three main varieties, at least among those who like the small individual chocolates. A certain percentage pop the whole chocolate into their mouths, crunch once or twice and down it goes. Others pop the whole chocolate into their mouths and let it slowly melt. A smaller number hold the chocolate in hand while taking dainty little bites.

(7) Peanuts and popcorn are a completely different matter. Of course, there are always one or two souls who actually pick up single peanuts and popcorn kernels, but the usual procedure is to scoop up a handful. But even these can be subdivided into those who feed them in one at a time and those who sort of throw the handful into the open mouth, then keep on throwing in handfuls until the plate, bag or box is empty. The feeders-in-one-at-a-time are, needless to say, a rare breed with such iron discipline that they probably exercise every morning and love it.

(8) Candies like M&M's are treated by most people in much the same way as peanuts or popcorn. But there are exceptions, among them those who don't start eating until they have separated the colors. Then they eat one color at a time, or one of each color in rotation. Honestly.

(9) A sandwich cookie is a sandwich cookie, and you take bites of it, and so what? So what if you're the kind who doesn't take bites until it's pulled apart into two sections? And if you're this kind of person, and an amazing number are, the likelihood is that the plain part will be eaten first, and the one with icing saved for last. Watch Oreo eaters.

(10) A woman who seems quite normal in other respects said that although she considers her eating habits quite run-of-the-mill, she has been told that they are, in fact, peculiar. "If I have meat or chicken and a couple of vegetables on a plate, I go absolutely crazy if they don't come out even," she said. "I like to take a piece of meat and a little bit of each vegetable together. If, as I'm eating, I end up with no meat and a lot of broccoli, or no potatoes and a piece of chicken, it drives me mad."

(11) A man listening to all this rolled his eyes in disbelief. Peculiar is putting it mildly, he said. He would never eat like that. How does he eat? "One thing at a time," he said. "First I eat the meat, then one of the vegetables, then the other. How else would you eat?"

(894 words)

Here are some of the more difficult words in "You Are How You Eat."

calamities
(paragraph 4)

ca·lam·i·ty (-tē) *n., pl.* **-ties** ⟦MFr *calamité* < L *calamitas*: see CLAS-TIC⟧ **1** deep trouble or misery **2** any extreme misfortune bringing great loss and sorrow; disaster —*SYN.* DISASTER

devour
(paragraph 4)

de·vour (di vour') *vt.* ⟦ME *devouren* < OFr *devorer* < L *devorare* < *de-*, intens. + *vorare*, to swallow whole: see VORACIOUS⟧ **1** to eat or eat up hungrily, greedily, or voraciously **2** to consume or destroy with devastating force **3** to take in greedily with the eyes, ears, or mind [the child *devours* fairy tales] **4** to absorb completely; engross [*devoured* by curiosity] **5** to swallow up; engulf —**de·vour'er** *n.*

forgo
(paragraph 2)

for·go (fôr gō') *vt.* **-·went', -·gone', -·go'ing** ⟦ME *forgon* < OE *forgan*: see FOR- & GO²⟧ **1** [Obs.] *a)* to go past *b)* to overlook; neglect **2** to do without; abstain from; give up —*SYN.* RELINQUISH —**for·go'er** *n.*

infinite
(paragraph 1)

in·fi·nite (in'fə nit) *adj.* ⟦ME < L *infinitus*: see IN-² & FINITE⟧ **1** lacking limits or bounds; extending beyond measure or comprehension: without beginning or end; endless **2** very great; vast; immense **3** *a) Math.* indefinitely large; greater than any finite number however large *b)* capable of being put into one-to-one correspondence with a part of itself [*infinite* set] —*n.* something infinite, as space or time —**the Infinite (Being)** God —**in'·fi·nitely** *adv.* —**in'·fi·nite·ness** *n.*

methodical
(paragraph 1)

me·thodi·cal (mə thäd'i kəl) *adj.* ⟦< LL *methodicus* < Gr *methodikos* + -AL⟧ characterized by method; orderly; systematic: also **me·thod'ic** —**me·thod'i·cally** *adv.* —**me·thod'i·cal·ness** *n.*

perimeter
(paragraph 2)

pe·rim·eter (pə rim'ə tər) *n.* ⟦L *perimetros* < Gr < *peri-*, around + *metron*, MEASURE⟧ **1** the outer boundary of a figure or area **2** the total length of this **3** an optical instrument for testing the scope of vision and the visual powers of various parts of the retina **4** *Mil.* a boundary strip where defenses are set up —*SYN.* CIRCUMFERENCE

rotation
(paragraph 8)

ro·ta·tion (rō tā'shən) *n.* ⟦L *rotatio*⟧ **1** a rotating or being rotated **2** the spinning motion around the axis of a celestial body: cf. REVOLUTION (sense 1a) **3** regular and recurring succession of changes [a *rotation* of duties] ☆**4** *Pool* a game in which the balls must be pocketed in the order of their numbers —**ro·ta'·tional** *adj.*

standardized
(paragraph 1)

stand·ard·ize (stan'dər dīz') *vt.* **-·ized', -·iz'·ing 1** to make standard or uniform; cause to be without variations or irregularities **2** to compare with, test by, or adjust to a standard —**stand'·ardi·za'·tion** *n.* —**stand'·ard·iz'er** *n.*

unique
(paragraph 1)

unique (yo͞o nēk') *adj.* ⟦Fr < L *unicus*, single < *unus*, ONE⟧ **1** one and only; single; sole [a *unique* specimen] **2** having no like or equal; unparalleled [a *unique* achievement] **3** highly unusual, extraordinary, rare, etc.: a common usage still objected to by some —**unique'·ly** *adv.* —**unique'·ness** *n.*

157

9A VOCABULARY
Choose the best answer.

___d___ 1. Something that is **standardized** is
    a. irregular.
    b. controlled by the government.
    c. open to personal interpretation.
    d. without variations.

___a___ 2. If you were to **forgo** something you desired, you would
    a. do without it, at least for a while.
    b. go ahead and try to get it.
    c. force yourself to save for it.
    d. borrow or rent it.

___c___ 3. If a number is **infinite,** it
    a. cannot be divided evenly.
    b. has a negative value.
    c. extends beyond measure.
    d. is limited in size.

___c___ 4. **Calamities** are also known as
    a. ex-Californians.
    b. telephone keypads.
    c. disasters.
    d. squid, cooked Italian style.

___b___ 5. To be **methodical** is to be
    a. careless.
    b. systematic.
    c. open-minded.
    d. a member of the Methodist Church.

___b___ 6. When people speak in **rotation,** they
    a. ramble and change the topic frequently.
    b. take turns talking in regular and recurring order.
    c. deliver memorized speeches.
    d. participate in public speaking contests.

___a___ 7. The **perimeter** of an object is its
    a. outer boundary.
    b. surface area.
    c. approximate volume.
    d. texture.

Name   Date

__d__ 8. To **devour** something is to
   a. travel around it.
   b. dedicate it to someone.
   c. leave it unopened.
   d. eat it hungrily.

__c__ 9. A **unique** experience is
   a. usual and ordinary.
   b. old-fashioned.
   c. rare or one of a kind.
   d. something one does by oneself.

9B   CENTRAL THEME AND MAIN IDEAS

Choose the answer.

__a__ 1. What is the central theme of "You Are How You Eat"?
   a. People eat ice cream and other foods in an infinite variety of ways.
   b. Ice cream can be eaten in five different ways.
   c. Scientific studies of how people eat are needed, but unfortunately they have not been done.
   d. People with peculiar ways of eating ice cream or other foods may be entirely normal in other respects.

__b__ 2. What is the main idea of paragraph 4?
   a. People should not eat ice cream during hot weather.
   b. People who eat ice cream cones slowly without dripping, even when the thermometer soars, irritate the author.
   c. People who can eat ice cream without dripping are irritating when they brag about it.
   d. When people eat ice cream cones properly, the ice cream remains as firm and rounded as it was in the scoop.

__d__ 3. What is the main idea of paragraph 9?
   a. All sandwich cookies are alike.
   b. The easiest sandwich cookies to eat are Oreos.
   c. Nutritionists claim that the proper way to eat a sandwich cookie is to split it in half and then eat one half at a time.
   d. A surprising number of people eat sandwich cookies by pulling the cookie apart and eating the plain side first.

9C   MAJOR DETAILS

Fill in the word or words that correctly complete each statement.

1. It is not strange to see a person walking along a _____street_____ eating an _____ice_____ _____cream_____ cone.

2. Some people use their tongues to _____push_____ the ice cream deep into the _____cone_____ .

3. Many people fight the _____temptation_____ to eat all the ice cream immediately.

4. People who throw away their empty ice cream cones should consider buying ice cream _____cups_____ instead of cones.

5. People who eat sundaes in layers are eating separate _____ingredients_____ , not sundaes.

6. There are _____three_____ main varieties of people who eat small individual _____chocolates_____ .

7. Most people eat peanuts and popcorn by the _____handful_____ .

8. People who eat peanuts and popcorn one piece at a time have iron _____discipline_____ .

9. Some people eat M&M's one _____color_____ at a time; others go from color to color in _____rotation_____ .

10. When given a plate of meat and vegetables, some people like to eat little bits of each food together, and others prefer to finish one _____thing_____ at a time.

Name   Date

9D INFERENCES
Choose the best answer.

___b___ 1. *Read the title again.* What does the title mean?
   a. What people eat shows how they were raised.
   b. How people eat can provide clues to their temperaments or personalities.
   c. Your health and sense of well-being are strongly affected by what you eat and how you eat it.
   d. Proper eating manners are essential for people who want to make a good impression on others.

___c___ 2. *Read paragraph 7 again.* Why does the author say that people who eat peanuts and popcorn one piece at a time "probably exercise every morning"?
   a. People who exercise regularly are usually trying to lose weight, so they eat small amounts of food.
   b. People who exercise and people who eat one peanut at a time are alike in not being able to have fun and enjoy life.
   c. People who limit their intake of high-calorie foods and who exercise regularly are alike in having much self-discipline.
   d. People who exercise think that eating one peanut or piece of popcorn at a time will strengthen their jaw and facial muscles.

___c___ 3. *Read paragraph 8 again.* Why do some people eat all M&M's of one color before starting another, while other people eat the colors in strict rotation?
   a. They believe they will digest the M&M's better if they follow one of these routines.
   b. The coating on some colors of M&M's melts faster than does the coating on others.
   c. They like to be able to structure even small aspects of their lives.
   d. As they eat the M&M's, they like to count the number of each color in each package.

9E CRITICAL READING: THE WRITER'S CRAFT
Choose the best answer.

___b___ 1. The author states her central theme only in
   a. the title and last paragraph.
   b. the title and first paragraph.
   c. the first and last paragraphs
   d. the title.

__b__ 2. To support her central theme, the author uses
   a. observations and statistics.
   b. observations, questions, quotations.
   c. questions and quotations.
   d. statistics, questions, quotations.

__i__ 3. Which of these words is *not* used by the author to show connections among ideas?
   a. "after this"   (paragraph 2)
   b. "on the other hand"   (3)
   c. "eventually"   (3)
   d. "then again"   (3)
   e. "first"   (5)
   f. "then"   (5)
   g. "finally"   (5)
   h. "of course"   (7)
   i. "among"   (8)

9F   READER RESPONSE: TO DISCUSS OR TO WRITE ABOUT

1. Many people have one set of table manners for eating with family and another set for more formal situations. What is your opinion of having dual standards? Explain your point of view.

2. Food is a central part of many official holidays, many types of family celebrations, many religious practices, and many other occasions. Other than to satisfy hunger, why do you think food is such a central part of most human cultures? Using specific examples, explain your answer.

3. Young children have to be taught table manners and then be reminded to use them. What do you think are the three most important table manners children should learn?

Name   Date

How Did You Do?   **9**   You Are How You Eat

SKILL (number of items)	Number Correct		Points for Each		Score
Vocabulary (9)	_____	×	1	=	_____
Central Theme and Main Ideas (3)	_____	×	5	=	_____
Major Details* (14)	_____	×	5	=	_____
Inferences (3)	_____	×	1	=	_____
Critical Reading: The Writer's Craft (3)	_____	×	1	=	_____

(Possible Total: 100) *Total*   _____

SPEED

Reading Time: _____ Reading Rate (page 397): _____ Words Per Minute

*Questions 1, 2, 6, and 9 in this exercise call for two separate answers. In computing your score, count each separate answer toward your number correct.

Flour Children

Lexine Alpert

(1) "Hey, Mister V., what are you doing dressed like that?" says a student as he enters the classroom at San Francisco's Mission High School. "I'm getting ready to deliver your baby," replies the sex education teacher, in surgical greens from cap to booties. "Do you have to take this thing so seriously?" asks another, laughing nervously as she watches her teacher bring out rubber gloves. "Yes, babies are a serious matter," he answers. As the students settle into their seats, Robert Valverde, who has been teaching sex education for four years—and "delivering babies" for three—raises his voice to convene the class.

(2) "Welcome to the nursery," he announces. "Please don't breathe on the babies. I just brought them from the hospital." The students' giggles quickly change to moans as Valverde delivers a "baby"—a five-pound sack of flour—to each student. "You must treat your baby as if it were real twenty-four hours a day for the next three weeks," he says. "It must be brought to every class. You cannot put the baby in your locker or your backpack. It must be carried like a baby, lovingly, and carefully in your arms. Students with jobs or other activities must find babysitters." To make sure the baby is being cared for at night and on weekends, Valverde calls his students at random. "If the baby is lost or broken, you must call a funeral parlor and find what it would cost to have a funeral," he says. The consequence is a new, heavier baby—a ten-pound flour sack.

(3) Valverde came up with the flour baby idea after hearing that some sex education classes assign students the care of an egg; he decided to try something more realistic. "A flour sack is heavier and more cumbersome—more like a real baby," Valverde says. To heighten the realism, he has the students dress their five-pound sacks in babies' clothes, complete with diaper, blanket, and bottle.

(4) "The primary goal is to teach responsibility," says Valverde. "I want those who can't do it to see that they can't, and to acknowledge that the students who can are doing something that is very difficult and embarrassing." After 36 classes and more than a thousand students, Valverde's project seems to be having the effect he wants. "I look at all the circumstantial evidence—the kids are talking to their parents in ways they never have before, and for the first time in their lives, they are forced to respond to an external environment. They have to fill out forms every day saying where they'll be that night and who's taking care of the baby. If their plans change I make them call me and say who's with the baby. They're forced to confront people's comments about their babies."

In "Baby Think It Over," a program designed to deter teen pregnancy, students learn parenting responsibility. Carrie takes a history test while holding a key in the baby's back to keep it from crying.

(5) Lupe Tiernan, vice-principal of the predominantly Hispanic and Asian inner-city high school, believes Valverde's class has helped to maintain the low number of teenage pregnancies at her school. "His students learn that having a baby is a novelty that wears off very quickly, and by three weeks, they no longer want any part of it," she says.

(6) At the beginning of the assignment, some students' parental instincts emerge right away. During the first week, sophomore Cylenna Terry took the rules so seriously that she was kicked out of her English class for refusing to take the baby off her lap and place it on the floor as instructed. "I said, 'No way am I putting my baby on the floor.'" Others, especially the boys, learn early that they can't cope with their new role. "I just couldn't carry the baby around," says Enrique Alday, 15. "At my age it was too embarrassing so I just threw it in my locker." He failed the class.

(7) By the second week, much of the novelty has worn off and the students begin to feel the babies are intruding on their lives. "Why does it have to be so heavy?" Cylenna Terry grumbles. "It's raining out—how am I supposed to carry this baby and open up my umbrella at the same time?" She has noticed other changes as well. "There's no way a boy is even going to look at me when I have this in my arms. No guys want to be involved with a girl who has a baby—they just stay clear."

(8) Rommel Perez misses baseball practice because he can't find a babysitter. Duane Broussard, who has helped care for his one-year-old nephew who lives in his household, learns new respect for how hard his mother and sister work at childcare. "At least this baby doesn't wake me in the middle of the night," he says. Maria Salinis says, "My boyfriend was always complaining about the sack and was feeling embarrassed about having it around. I told him, 'Imagine if it was a real baby.' It made us ask important questions of one another that we had never before considered."

(9) On the last day of the assignment, the temporary parents come to class dragging their feet. Valverde calls the students one by one to the front of the room to turn in their babies. Most, their paper skin now fragile from wear, are returned neatly swaddled in a clean blanket. But others have ended up broken and lying in the bottom of a trash bin; a half-dozen students wound up with ten-pound babies. The students' consensus is that babies have no place in their young lives. "I know that if I had a baby it would mess up my future and hold me down." "After this class, I don't want to have a baby. I couldn't handle it," says 15-year-old Erla Garcia. "It was only a sack of flour that didn't cry or scream, didn't need to be fed or put to sleep, and I still couldn't wait to get rid of it."

(1,004 words)

Here are some of the more difficult words in "Flour Children."

circumstantial
(paragraph 4)

cir·cum·stan·tial (sʉr′kəm stan′shəl) *adj.* **1** having to do with, or depending on, circumstances **2** not of primary importance; incidental **3** full or complete in detail **4** full of pomp or display; ceremonial —**cir′·cum·stan′·tially** *adv.*

confront
(paragraph 4)

con·front (kən frunt′) *vt.* [Fr *confronter* < ML *confrontare* < L *com-*, together + *frons*, forehead: see FRONT[1]] **1** to face; stand or meet face to face **2** to face or oppose boldly, defiantly, or antagonistically **3** to bring face to face (*with*) [to *confront* someone with the facts] **4** to set side by side to compare —**con·fron·ta·tion** (kän′ frən tā′shən) *n.* or **con·front′al** —**con′·fron·ta′·tion·al** *adj.* —**con′·fron·ta′·tion·ist** *n., adj.*

consensus
(paragraph 9)

con·sen·sus (kən sen′səs) *n.* [L < pp. of *consentire:* see fol.] **1** an opinion held by all or most **2** general agreement, esp. in opinion

consequence
(paragraph 2)

con·se·quence (kän′si kwens′, -kwəns) *n.* [OFr < L *consequentia* < *consequens,* prp. of *consequi,* to follow after < *com-*, with + *sequi,* to follow: see SEQUENT] **1** a result of an action, process, etc.; outcome; effect **2** a logical result or conclusion; inference **3** the relation of effect to cause **4** importance as a cause or influence [a matter of slight *consequence*] **5** importance in rank; influence [a person of *consequence*] —*SYN.* EFFECT, IMPORTANCE —**in consequence (of)** as a result (of) —**take the consequences** to accept the results of one's actions

convene
(paragraph 1)

con·vene (kən vēn′) *vi.* --vened′, --ven′·ing [ME *convenen* < OFr *convenir* < L *convenire* < *com-*, together + *venire,* to COME] to meet together, esp. for a common purpose —*vt.* **1** to cause to assemble, or meet together **2** to summon before a court of law —*SYN.* CALL —**con·ven′er** *n.*

cumbersome
(paragraph 3)

cum·ber·some (kum′bər səm) *adj.* hard to handle or deal with as because of size, weight, or many parts; burdensome; unwieldy; clumsy —*SYN.* HEAVY —**cum′·ber·somely** *adv.* —**cum′·ber·some·ness** *n.*

instincts
(paragraph 6)

in·stinct (in′stiŋkt′; *for adj.* in stiŋkt′, in′stiŋkt′) *n.* ⟦< L *instinctus,* pp. of *instinguere,* to impel, instigate < *in-,* in + *stinguere,* to prick: for IE base see STICK⟧ **1** (an) inborn tendency to behave in a way characteristic of a species; natural, unlearned, predictable response to stimuli [suckling is an *instinct* in mammals] **2** a natural or acquired tendency, aptitude, or talent; bent; knack; gift [an *instinct* for doing the right thing] **3** *Psychoanalysis* a primal psychic force or drive, as fear, love, or anger; specif., in Freudian analysis, either the life instinct (Eros) or the death instinct (Thanatos) —*adj.* filled or charged (*with*) [a look *instinct* with pity] —**in·stinc·tual** (in stiŋk′chōō əl) *adj.*

intruding
(paragraph 7)

in·trude (in trōōd′) *vt.* **·trud′ed, ·trud′ing** ⟦L *intrudere* < *in-,* in + *trudere,* to thrust, push: see THREAT⟧ **1** to push or force (something *in* or *upon*) **2** to force (oneself or one's thoughts) upon others without being asked or welcomed **3** *Geol.* to force (liquid magma, etc.) into or between solid rocks —*vi.* to intrude oneself —**in·trud′er** *n.*

SYN.—**intrude** implies the forcing of oneself or something upon another without invitation, permission, or welcome [to *intrude* upon another's privacy]; **obtrude** connotes even more strongly the distractive nature or the undesirability of the invasion [side issues keep *obtruding*]; **interlope** implies an intrusion upon the rights or privileges of another to the disadvantage or harm of the latter [the *interloping* merchants have ruined our trade]; **butt in** (or **into**) (at BUTT²) is a slang term implying intrusion in a meddling or officious way [stop *butting into* my business] See also TRESPASS

novelty
(paragraph 5)

nov·el·ty (näv′əl tē) *n., pl.* **·ties** ⟦ME *novelte* < OFr *noveleté* < LL *novellitas*⟧ **1** the quality of being novel; newness; freshness **2** something new, fresh, or unusual; change; innovation **3** a small, often cheap, cleverly made article, usually for play or adornment: *usually used in pl.* —*adj.* having characteristics that are new, unusual, atypical, etc. [a *novelty* tune]

predominantly
(paragraph 5)

pre·domi·nant (prē däm′ə nənt, pri-) *adj.* ⟦Fr *prédominant* < ML *predominans,* prp. of *predominari:* see PRE- & DOMINANT⟧ **1** having ascendancy, authority, or dominating influence over others; superior **2** most frequent, noticeable, etc.; prevailing; preponderant —*SYN.* DOMINANT —**pre·dom′i·nance** *n.* or **pre·dom′i·nancy,** *pl.* **·cies** —**pre·dom′i·nantly** *adv.*

swaddled
(paragraph 9)

swad·dle (swäd′l) *vt.* **·dled, ·dling** ⟦ME *swathlen,* prob. altered (infl. by *swathen,* to SWATHE¹) < *swethlen* < OE *swethel,* swaddling band, akin to *swathian,* to SWATHE¹⟧ **1** to wrap (a newborn baby) in swaddling clothes, a blanket, etc. **2** to bind in or as in bandages; swathe —*n.* ⟦ME *swathil* < OE *swethel:* see the *vt.*⟧ a cloth, bandage, etc. used for swaddling

10A   VOCABULARY

Using the vocabulary words on pages 167–168, fill in this crossword puzzle.

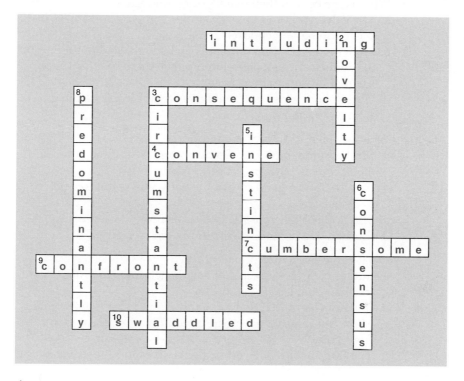

Across

1. forcing oneself on others
3. the logical result of an action
4. to call together
7. difficult to handle; heavy
9. to face or meet face to face
10. wrapped in long pieces of cloth

Down

2. something unusual
3. full or complete in detail
5. natural talents
6. opinion held by most people
8. most noticeably

10B   CENTRAL THEME AND MAIN IDEAS

Choose the best answer.

__a__ 1. What is the central theme of "Flour Children"?
  a. Mr. Valverde hopes to teach students the responsibility involved in having children.
  b. Students learn that taking care of a baby is a 24-hour-a-day job.
  c. Students learn that babies may cause them to miss out on planned events in their lives.
  d. High school girls learn that boys are not interested in girls who have babies.

__c__ 2. What is the main idea of paragraph 2?
  a. Mr. Valverde intends to check up on his students to make sure they take the project seriously.
  b. Failure to take good care of the baby will result in a new, heavier baby.
  c. The flour babies must be treated as if they were real babies.
  d. Students do not take their flour babies seriously.

__d__ 3. What is the main idea of paragraph 8?
  a. Students often missed after-school activities in order to care for their "babies."
  b. Students learn that they probably don't want to have babies.
  c. Many students were embarrassed at having to care for a flour baby.
  d. The flour babies affected students' lives in different ways.

10C   MAJOR DETAILS

Decide whether each detail is true (T), false (F), or not discussed (ND).

__T__ 1. Mr. Valverde takes his job teaching sex education very seriously.

__ND__ 2. For the first time students are not forced to respond to an external environment.

__T__ 3. Flour sacks instead of eggs are used because they more nearly resemble caring for an infant.

__ND__ 4. San Francisco's Mission High School Board requires this course of all students.

__ND__ 5. The students' parents have agreed to participate in the flour babies' care.

__T__ 6. Students were concerned about the embarrassment of carrying a flour baby.

Name   Date

__T__ 7. To make the babies seem more real, students must equip them with clothes, diapers, and bottles.

__ND__ 8. Students who communicate with their parents do well as flour baby parents.

10D INFERENCES

Choose the best answer.

__b__ 1. *Read paragraph 6 again.* By refusing to put her flour sack on the floor during English, Cylenna Terry is showing that
  a. she is afraid any damage would result in getting a larger baby.
  b. she has accepted the responsibility of a baby.
  c. she knows someone would tell Mr. Valverde.
  d. she is too embarrassed to let anyone see it on the floor.

__a__ 2. *Read paragraph 9 again.* "The temporary parents came to class dragging their feet" indicates that they were
  a. tired of playing this game.
  b. anxious to find out if they had passed.
  c. certain they did not want to have real babies.
  d. hesitant to part with their babies after all.

10E CRITICAL READING: FACT OR OPINION

Decide whether each statement, even if it quotes someone, contains a FACT or an OPINION.

OPINION 1. *From paragraph 1:* "Yes, babies are a serious matter [. . .]."

FACT 2. *From paragraph 4:* "The primary goal is to teach responsibility [. . .]."

OPINION 3. *From paragraph 5:* "[. . .] [the] class has helped to maintain the low number of teen pregnancies at her school."

FACT 4. *From paragraph 6:* "At my age, it was too embarrassing [. . .]."

OPINION 5. *From paragraph 7:* "No guys wanted to be involved with a girl who has a baby [. . .]."

FACT 6. *From paragraph 9:* "[. . .] babies have no place in their young lives."

10F CRITICAL READING: THE WRITER'S CRAFT

Choose the best answer.

__c__ 1. The author begins "Flour Children" with
    a. a satirical monologue.
    b. a comparison.
    c. a dramatic scene.
    d. constrasting opinions.

__b__ 2. To hold the reader's interest, the author
    a. alternates her opinions with those of the students.
    b. describes different student experiences.
    c. avoids the use of too many details.
    d. quotes authorities who are experts in the field of parenthood.

__c__ 3. In paragraphs 6–9, the author quotes the students in their own words instead of just describing what each did. She does this to
    a. demonstrate the regional accents used by various characters.
    b. keep the story as entertaining as possible.
    c. make the story seem vivid and real.
    d. create a suspenseful atmosphere.

__a__ 4. *Read paragraph 9 again.* If the expression "their paper skin now fragile from wear" were replaced by "their packaging torn," the revised passage would
    a. lose the connection with human babies.
    b. be much more dramatic.
    c. provide greater clarity.
    d. better illustrate the careless treatment of the flour sacks.

10G READER RESPONSE: TO DISCUSS OR TO WRITE ABOUT

1. If you were a high school student and had the option to register for a sex education class that required students to care for flour sack babies, would you enroll? Give specific reasons for your decision.

2. From a parent's point of view, do you think sex education and parenthood classes should be taught in the public schools? Explain your point of view.

3. From your experience, do you agree or disagree with the statement: "No guys wanted to be involved with a girl who has a baby" (paragraph 7). Do you think this attitude reflects these young men's roles as future fathers? Why?

    Name   Date

How Did You Do?   **10** Flour Children

SKILL (number of items)	Number Correct		Points for Each		Score
Vocabulary (11)	_____	×	2	=	_____
Central Theme and Main Ideas (3)	_____	×	4	=	_____
Major Details (8)	_____	×	4	=	_____
Inferences (2)	_____	×	4	=	_____
Critical Reading: Fact or Opinion (6)	_____	×	3	=	_____
Critical Reading: The Writer's Craft (4)	_____	×	2	=	_____

(Possible Total: 100) *Total* _____

SPEED

Reading Time: _____ Reading Rate (page 397): _____ Words Per Minute

Name   Date

The Magic Words Are "Will You Help Me?"

Michael Ryan

(1) I had been listening to Tom Harken's life story for almost an hour when the question that had formed in my mind suddenly emerged from his lips: "How did I get from there to here?" he said in a tone of real amazement. "How did that happen?" We all have been taught that America is a land where anyone can go from rags to riches, despite whatever obstacles fate may throw at us. But as I listened to Harken, 59, I understood for the first time just how many obstacles one human being can overcome—and just how far determination and courage can carry any one of us.

(2) The man across from me was a millionaire, the owner of eight franchises of the Casa Olé restaurant chain in Texas. His office is filled with mementos of his friendships with the great and famous, from members of Congress to Supreme Court Justices, from Henry Kissinger to Norman Vincent Peal. Yet, 48 years ago, this robust man was a sickly child. And, more than that, he had a secret he was too ashamed to tell anyone.

(3) "I grew up in Lakeview, Mich.," Harken told me. "I was a sick kid. I had tuberculosis. I developed polio. One day I was riding a bicycle; the next day I was in a hospital, in an iron lung." Just a few decades ago, polio was a terrifying disease that struck tens of thousands of children and adults. Many died or were paralyzed; some lived for months in iron lungs—huge, barrel-like machines that compressed and released lungs too weak to breathe for themselves. "I was in a room the size of a gymnasium, with 35 or 40 iron lungs," Harken recalled. "Imagine being in a hospital. It looks like you're never going to get out of the darned thing, and everybody's crying all around you. I was 11."

(4) It took more than a year of therapy for Tom to recover enough to go home. "I have one leg that's shorter than the other—that's the only evidence of the illness," he said. "The day I got out of that hospital was a great day. I still remember coming home with my mom and dad." But the great day soon turned sour, because Tom also had tuberculosis, and officials worried that he might still be contagious. "The next thing I knew, I was quarantined to one room in the house for a year," he said.

(5) Harken used to tell people his life went back to normal when this second nightmare ended. He went back to school, joined the Air Force and built up his successful business career. All that is true, but, until four years ago, the story Tom Harken told people was not his whole story. And sharing it would be the most difficult act of his life. "In 1992, I won the Horatio Alger Award," he told me. The award, given to men and women

who have overcome adversity to achieve greatness, has been awarded to such luminaries as Gen. Colin Powell, Maya Angelou and Bob Hope. Harken was thrilled—and humbled—to be chosen to receive it. "I got really emotional while I was dictating my acceptance speech, and I started wondering whether I should talk about it," he recalled. "I'd never talked about it. Melba knew, but nobody else." "It" was Tom Harken's long-held secret: For most of his life, he had been illiterate, unable to read even the simplest sentences, to order from printed menus or to fill out a form.

(6) The origin of the problems is easy to understand: After missing years of school, Tom returned to a classroom run by a teacher who ridiculed him. "He took me up to the board and said, 'Can you spell cat?'" Harken said, "I was nervous and shy, and he said again, 'Spell cat!' He was hollering at me. Then he made me sit down." That humiliation turned Tom off to reading—and school. With his parents' reluctant permission, he dropped out. Later, he enlisted in the Air Force, where he filled in multiple-choice tests at random, unable to read the questions. While he was serving in Oklahoma, Harken had two strokes of luck: He took an after-duty job in sales and learned that he had an aptitude for business. And he met the woman he still calls "Miss Melba," now his wife of 38 years. "I had to tell her that I couldn't read or write, because I needed her to fill out the marriage license," he recalled, emotion flooding his voice. But Melba saw something in this bright young man. "He was ambitious," she said. "And he was so smart. He was so exciting to talk to that I was never afraid he wouldn't succeed."

(7) Succeed he did—with help from Melba. When he moved to Beaumont, Tex., and developed a door-to-door vacuum-cleaner sales business, she would help him write up his order each night. "I have a good memory," he said. "I would memorize names and addresses, employers and credit information, and then Melba would write them down." Working together, they expanded into a recreational vehicle dealership and then into restaurant franchises. But the small humiliations were always there. "Whenever we went to a restaurant, I would order a cheeseburger," Harken said. "Everybody sells cheeseburgers. But one day I ordered a cheeseburger, and the waitress looked at me and said, 'What's the matter, can't you read? We don't make cheeseburgers.'"

(8) The Harkens had two sons, Tommy and Mark, both now grown and working in the family business. But Tom felt the sting of his illiteracy constantly as the boys were growing up. "They would crawl into my lap and ask me to read them something, like the Sunday comics," he said. "Melba would rescue me. She'd come over and say, 'Daddy's busy. I'll read that to you.'" A regular churchgoer, Harken recalled one occasion when he was attending Sunday school: "They passed the Scripture along, and everybody read a verse. I could feel my stomach tying itself in knots as it came closer to me, and I finally said, 'I have to go to the bathroom,' and I just left there and went home." He realized that he had to do something. He went to Melba for help. "She taught me word by word, over a course

Tom Harken learned to read with the help of his wife, "Miss Melba."

Brian Coats

of years," Harken told me. "I was hard to teach. I got very angry some-times." Harken worked his way through simple sentences to the point where he could read parts of the Bible aloud—as he did at the weddings of two of his employees. "That's still hard for me," he said, but Melba im-mediately cut him off. "You did it very well," she told him.

(9) When he was selected for the Horatio Alger Award, Harken thought about standing up in front of some of America's most important people and telling them that, until recently, he had been illiterate. Then he decided to do it. "I got teary-eyed," he told me. "Melba said I should do it and I should tell our two kids first." His sons were amazed by their father's story. "They were absolutely stunned," Harken recalled. But their reaction was nothing com-pared to the response of those attending the Horatio Alger awards ceremony in May 1992. They gave Harken a standing ovation. Colin Powell, the Rev. Robert Schuller and other dignitaries rushed to shake his hand.

(10) For many people, that triumphant evening would have been the end of a lifelong journey. For Harken, though, it was just a beginning. Since that night, he has given more than 300 speeches around the country, telling children and adults about the importance of literacy. After one speech, an 87-year-old woman approached him to say that she had just learned to read. "I couldn't read to my children or my grandchildren, but now I can read to my great-grandchildren," she told him. After another speech, an African-American man who was starting reading lessons told Harken that he had dispelled an onerous racist image: "He said that, before he heard me, he thought that only black people could be illiterate," Harken said. "He didn't know that illiteracy happens in every color."

(11) Harken's message is one he wants to get out to anyone who will listen: "I want people to know that they can go into any library and just say the magic words, 'Will you help me?' Just say those words, and someone will help you learn how to read. The Literacy Volunteers of America are everywhere, and they're ready to help. Everybody should know that." It

occurred to me that Tom Harken's whole life might have been changed if that one teacher had not ridiculed him. "Sure, it probably would have altered a lot of my life," Harken said. "But I'm not sure I'd want it altered. You never know your own strength until you've paid the price—and Miss Melba and I have paid the price."

(1,396 words)

Vocabulary List

Here are some of the more difficult words in "The Magic Words Are 'Will You Help Me?'"

adversity
(paragraph 5)

ad·ver·si·ty (ad vʉr′sə tē, əd-) *n.* 〚ME < OFr *adversité, aversite* < L *adversitas < adversus*, prec.〛 **1** a state of wretchedness or misfortune; poverty and trouble **2** *pl.* **-ties** an instance of misfortune; calamity

aptitude
(paragraph 6)

ap·ti·tude (ap′tə tōōd′, -tyōōd′) *n.* 〚ME < LL *aptitudo* < L *aptus*: see APT[1]〛 **1** the quality of being apt or appropriate; fitness **2** a natural tendency or inclination **3** a natural ability or talent **4** quickness to learn or understand *—SYN.* TALENT

dispelled
(paragraph 10)

dis·pel (di spel′) *vt.* **··pelled′, ··pel′·ling** 〚ME *dispellen* < L *dispellere* < *dis-*, apart + *pellere*, to drive: see FELT〛 to scatter and drive away; cause to vanish; disperse *—SYN.* SCATTER

franchises
(paragraph 2)

fran·chise (fran′chīz′) *n.* 〚ME < OFr < *franc*, free: see FRANK[1]〛 **1** [Archaic] freedom from some restriction, servitude, etc. **2** any special right, privilege, or exemption granted by the government, as to be a corporation, operate a public utility, etc. **3** the right to vote; suffrage: usually preceded by *the* **4** *a)* the right to market a product or provide a service, often exclusive for a specified area, as granted by a manufacturer or company *b)* a business granted such a right ☆**5** *a)* the right to own a member team as granted by a league in certain professional sports *b)* such a member team *—vt.* **··chised′, ··chis′·ing** to grant a franchise to *—adj.* designating a player on a professional team who is regarded as being essential to that team's success

illiterate
(paragraph 5)

il·lit·er·ate (i lit′ər it) *adj.* 〚L *illiteratus*, unlettered: see IN-[2] & LITERATE〛 **1** ignorant; uneducated; esp., not knowing how to read or write **2** having or showing limited knowledge, experience, or culture, esp. in some particular field *[musically illiterate]* **3** violating accepted usage in language *[an illiterate sentence]* *—n.* an illiterate person; esp., a person who does not know how to read or write *—SYN.* IGNORANT *—il·lit′·er·ately adv.*

literacy
(paragraph 10)

lit·era·cy (lit′ər ə sē) *n.* the state or quality of being literate; specif., *a)* ability to read and write *b)* knowledgeability or capability *[computer literacy]*

178

obstacles
(paragraph 1)

ob·sta·cle (äb′stə kəl) *n.* [[OFr < L *obstaculum,* obstacle < *obstare,* to withstand < *ob-* (see OB-) + *stare,* to STAND]] anything that gets in the way or hinders; impediment; obstruction; hindrance

SYN.—**obstacle** is used of anything which literally or figuratively stands in the way of one's progress /her father's opposition remained their only *obstacle/*; **impediment** applies to anything that delays or retards progress by interfering with the normal action /a speech *impediment/*; **obstruction** refers to anything that blocks progress or some activity as if by stopping up a passage /your interference is an *obstruction* of justice/*; **hindrance** applies to anything that thwarts progress by holding back or delaying /lack of supplies is the greatest *hindrance* to my experiment/*; **barrier** applies to any apparently insurmountable obstacle that prevents progress or keeps separate and apart /language differences are often a *barrier* to understanding/

onerous
(paragraph 10)

on·er·ous (än′ər əs, ōn′-) *adj.* [[ME < MFr *onereus* < L *onerosus* < *onus,* a load: see ONUS]] **1** burdensome; laborious **2** *Law* involving a legal obligation that equals or exceeds the benefits /*onerous* lease/ —**on′·er·ous·ly** *adv.* —**on′·er·ous·ness** *n.*

SYN.—**onerous** applies to that which is laborious or troublesome, often because of its annoying or tedious character /the *onerous* task of taking inventory/*; **burdensome** applies to that which is wearisome or oppressive to the mind or spirit as well as to the body /*burdensome* responsibilities/*; **oppressive** stresses the overbearing cruelty of the person or thing that inflicts hardship, or emphasizes the severity of the hardship itself /*oppressive* weather, an *oppressive* king/*; **exacting** suggests the making of great demands on the attention, skill, care, etc. /an *exacting* supervisor, *exacting* work/

quarantined
(paragraph 4)

quar·an·tine (kwôr′ən tēn, kwär′-) *n.* [[It *quarantina,* lit., space of forty days < *quaranta,* forty < L *quadraginta* < base of *quattuor,* FOUR]] **1** *a)* the period, orig. 40 days, during which an arriving vessel suspected of carrying contagious disease is detained in port in strict isolation *b)* the place where such a vessel is stationed **2** any isolation or restriction on travel or passage imposed to keep contagious diseases, insect pests, etc. from spreading **3** the state of being quarantined **4** a place where persons, animals, or plants having contagious diseases, insect pests, etc. are kept in isolation, or beyond which they may not travel **5** any period of seclusion, social ostracism, etc. —*vt.* **-tined′, -tin′·ing 1** to place under quarantine **2** to isolate politically, commercially, socially, etc. —**quar′·an·tin′·able** *adj.*

reluctant
(paragraph 6)

re·luc·tant (-tənt) *adj.* [[L *reluctans,* prp. of *reluctari,* to resist < *re-,* against + *luctari,* to struggle: see LOCK¹]] **1** opposed in mind (*to* do something); unwilling; disinclined **2** marked by unwillingness /a *reluctant* answer/ **3** [Rare] struggling against; resisting; opposing —**re·luc′·tantly** *adv.*

robust
(paragraph 2)

ro·bust (rō bust′, rō′bust′) *adj.* [[L *robustus,* oaken, hard, strong < *robur,* hard variety of oak, hardness, strength, earlier *robus,* prob. akin to *ruber,* RED]] **1** *a)* strong and healthy; full of vigor; hardy *b)* strongly built or based; muscular or sturdy **2** suited to or requiring physical strength or stamina /*robust* work/ **3** rough; coarse; boisterous **4** full and rich, as in flavor /a *robust* port wine/ —**ro·bust′ly** *adv.* —**ro·bust′·ness** *n.*

11A VOCABULARY

Using the vocabulary words listed on pages 178–179, fill in the blanks.

1. At the age of four, Tamika showed an ____aptitude____ for playing the drums.

2. Mom was ____reluctant____ to let Quassim play ice hockey because his temperature was 100 degrees.

3. When my sister and I received an inheritance from our grandmother, we invested the money in a pizza ____franchise____ .

4. The ____robust____ appearance of that 70-year-old woman results from years of serious exercise.

5. The greatest ____adversity____ Dat Pham had to overcome as a college student was his deafness.

6. When I returned from overseas with my dog Hershey, she was ____quarantined____ to make sure she had not picked up a contagious disease.

7. The cadets had to overcome many ____obstacles____ in their outdoor survival training.

8. The Dallas ____Literacy____ Council uses volunteers to help people of all ages learn to read.

9. Standing up and speaking in front of a class can be an ____onerous____ burden for some students.

10. The Queen's appearance at the balcony window ____dispelled____ the rumor that she was hospitalized.

11. People who have almost never gone to school are often ____illiterate____ .

Name   Date

11B CENTRAL THEME AND MAIN IDEAS

Choose the best answer.

__c__ 1. What is the central theme of "The Magic Words Are 'Will You Help Me?' "
  a. Tom Harken's being belittled by a teacher drove him to drop out of school.
  b. Tom Harken's story shows that being able to read is not essential to becoming a successful businessperson.
  c. Tom Harken spent years covering up a secret shame until he finally asked for help.
  d. Tom Harken's success in business is the result of his wife's support and hard work.

__d__ 2. What is the main idea of paragraph 5?
  a. Tom Harken's life returned to normal when he was well enough to attend school.
  b. The Horatio Alger Award recognized that Tom Harken overcame adversity to become successful.
  c. Only Melba Harken knew that her husband could neither read nor write.
  d. In his acceptance speech at the awards ceremony, Tom Harken planned to reveal the incredible adversity he had endured all his life.

__a__ 3. What is the main idea of paragraph 11?
  a. Help in learning to read is available to anyone who asks.
  b. Tom Harken's life would have been different if a teacher had not embarrassed him.
  c. The Literacy Volunteers of America helps people learn to read.
  d. Tom Harken and his wife suffered embarrassment because he could not read.

11C MAJOR DETAILS

Decide whether each detail listed here is MAJOR or MINOR based on the context of the reading selection.

MINOR 1. Tom Harken grew up in Lakeview, Michigan.

MAJOR 2. As a child, Tom Harken had polio.

MINOR 3. Tom Harken has one leg that is shorter than the other.

MAJOR 4. Tom Harken ordered a cheeseburger every time he went to a restaurant.

MAJOR 5. Tom Harken felt humiliated at not being able to spell "cat."

MINOR   6. Tom and Melba Harken have been married 38 years.

MINOR   7. Tom Harken served in the U.S. Air Force.

MAJOR   8. Tom Harken had a good memory.

MINOR   9. Tom Harken's sons, Tommy and Mark, work in the family business.

MAJOR 10. Tom Harken asked his wife, Melba, to teach him to read.

11D   INFERENCES

Choose the best answer.

__d__   1. *Reread paragraph 5.* Tom Harken dictated his acceptance speech because
   a. it gave his secretary something to do.
   b. it took less time than writing one.
   c. he liked to hear himself talk.
   d. he found writing a difficult activity.

__a__   2. *Reread paragraph 6.* The teacher embarrassed Tom Harken because the teacher
   a. hoped embarrassment would force the boy to answer a question.
   b. thought embarrassment would make the boy a better speller.
   c. felt embarrassment would help the boy overcome his shyness.
   d. used embarrassment to discipline unruly students.

__c__   3. *Reread paragraph 8.* Tom Harken felt he was "difficult to teach" because
   a. he did not study.
   b. his wife was not a trained teacher.
   c. he was impatient with his progress.
   d. he could not concentrate on anything for long.

11E   CRITICAL READING: FACT OR OPINION

Decide whether each statement contains a FACT or an OPINION.

OPINION 1. *From paragraph 1:* "America is a land where anyone can go from rags to riches [. . .]."

FACT 2. *From paragraph 3:* Many people either died or were paralyzed from polio.

FACT 3. *From paragraph 5:* Before learning to read, Tom Harken spoke to no one but his wife about his illiteracy.

FACT 4. *From paragraph 6:* Tom Harken learned that he had an aptitude for business.

FACT 5. *From paragraph 8:* Reading the Bible aloud at the wedding of some of his employees was difficult for Tom Harken.

FACT 6. *From paragraph 10:* Since his acceptance speech for the Alger Award, Tom Harken has spoken many times on the topic "Illiteracy."

OPINION 7. *From paragraph 11:* The words "will you help me" are magic.

OPINION 8. *From paragraph 11:* Anyone can get help learning to read by contacting the Literacy Volunteers of America.

11F CRITICAL READING: THE WRITER'S CRAFT

Choose the best answer.

__b__ 1. Read the title again. The question "Will You Help Me?" suggests
   a. Tom Harken's plea as a sickly child to his doctors.
   b. Tom Harken's suggested words for illiterate people to use in seeking help.
   c. Tom Harken's response to the teacher who ridiculed him.
   d. Tom Harken's reply to his wife when they applied for a marriage license.

__d__ 2. The author states his central theme in
   a. the title.
   b. paragraph 8.
   c. paragraph 11.
   d. all of the above.

__a__ 3. *Reread paragraph 11.* What did Tom Harken mean by the expression ". . . have paid the price"? He
   a. suffered many humiliations.
   b. lost money in business deals.
   c. paid the remaining balance of his doctor bills.
   d. contributed money to literacy programs.

11G READER RESPONSE: TO DISCUSS OR TO WRITE ABOUT

1. Have you or someone you know or have heard about ever felt humiliated privately or publicly by an incident in college, at work, or in a social setting? Being as specific as you can, explain what happened.

2. Melba Harken thought her husband, Tom, "was so smart" even though he could not read or write. Do you think someone can be smart without those skills? Using a specific experience you know about, explain why you think this is so.

3. Would you ask someone for help in learning to read if you were an adult who could not read a book, the mail, street signs, traffic directions, package labels, billboard advertisements, and many other things? Explain your reasons.

How Did You Do?   11 The Magic Words Are "Will You Help Me?"

SKILL (number of items)	Number Correct		Points for Each		Score
Vocabulary (11)	_____	×	2	=	_____
Central Theme and Main Ideas (3)	_____	×	6	=	_____
Major Details (10)	_____	×	4	=	_____
Inferences (3)	_____	×	2	=	_____
Critical Reading: Fact or Opinion (8)	_____	×	1	=	_____
Critical Reading: The Writer's Craft (3)	_____	×	2	=	_____

(Possible Total: 100) *Total*   _____

SPEED

Reading Time: _____ Reading Rate (page 397): _____ Words Per Minute

---

Name   Date

Selection 12

Mute in an English-Only World

Chang-rae Lee

(1) When I read of the trouble in Palisades Park, New Jersey, over the proliferation of Korean-language signs along its main commercial strip, I unexpectedly sympathized with the frustrations, resentments, and fears of the longtime residents. They clearly felt alienated and even unwelcome in a vital part of their community. The town, like seven others in New Jersey, has passed laws requiring that half of any commercial sign in a foreign language be in English. Now I certainly would never tolerate any exclusionary ideas about who could rightfully settle and belong in the town. But having been raised in a Korean immigrant family, I saw every day the exacting price and power of language, especially with my mother, who was an outsider in an English-only world.

(2) In the first years we lived in America, my mother could speak only the most basic English, and she often encountered great difficulty whenever she went out. We lived in New Rochelle, New York, in the early 1970's, and most of the local businesses were run by the descendants of immigrants who, generations ago, had come to the suburbs from New York City. Proudly dotting Main Street and North Avenue were Italian pastry and cheese shops, Jewish tailors and cleaners, and Polish and German butchers and bakers. If my mother's marketing couldn't wait until the weekend, when my father had free time, she would often hold off until I came home from school to buy the groceries. Though I was only six or seven years old, she insisted that I go out shopping with her and my younger sister. I mostly loathed the task, partly because it meant I couldn't spend the afternoon playing catch with my friends but also because I knew our errands would inevitably lead to an awkward scene, and that I would have to speak up to help my mother.

(3) I was just learning the language myself, but I was a quick study, as children are with new tongues. I had spent kindergarten in almost complete silence, hearing only the high nasality of my teacher and comprehending little but the cranky wails and cries of my classmates. But soon, seemingly mere months later, I had already become a terrible ham and mimic, and I would crack up my father with impressions of teachers, his friends, and even himself. My mother scolded me for aping his speech, and the one time I attempted to make light of hers I rated a roundhouse smack on my bottom.

(4) For her, the English language was not very funny. It usually meant trouble and a good dose of shame, and sometimes real hurt. Although she had a good reading knowledge of the language from university classes in South Korea, she had never practiced actual conversation. So, in America

Eight towns in New Jersey have passed laws that half of any commercial sign in a foreign language be in English, unlike these Korean-only signs in Los Angeles, California.

© J. Nordell/The Image Works

she used English flashcards and phrase books and watched television with us kids. And she faithfully carried a pocket workbook illustrated with stick-figure people and compound sentences to be filled in. But none of it seemed to do her much good. Staying mostly at home to care for us, she didn't have many chances to try out sundry words and phrases. When she did, say, at the window of the post office, her readied speech would stall, freeze, sometimes altogether collapse.

(5) One day was unusually harrowing. We ventured downtown in the new Ford Country Squire my father had bought her, an enormous station wagon that seemed as long—and deft—as an ocean liner. We were shopping for a special meal for guests visiting that weekend, and my mother had heard that a particular butcher carried fresh oxtails, which she needed for a traditional soup. We'd never been inside the shop, but my mother would pause before its window, which was always lined with whole hams, crown roasts, and ropes of plump handmade sausages. She greatly esteemed the bounty with her eyes, and my sister and I did also, but despite our desirous cries she'd turn us away and instead buy the packaged links at the Finast supermarket, where she felt comfortable looking them

over and could easily spot the price. And, of course, not have to talk. But that day she was resolved. The butcher store was crowded, and as we stepped inside the door jingled a welcome. No one seemed to notice. We waited for some time, and people who entered after us were now being served. Finally, an old woman nudged my mother and waved a little ticket, which we hadn't taken. We patiently waited again, until one of the beefy men behind the glass display hollered our number. My mother pulled us forward and began searching the cases, but oxtails were nowhere to be found. The man, his big arms crossed, sharply said, "Come on, lady, whaddya want?" The butcher looked as if my mother had put something sour in his mouth, and he glanced back at the lighted board and called the next number.

(6) Before I knew it, she had rushed us outside and back in the wagon, which she had double-parked because of the crowd. She was furious, almost vibrating with fear and grief, and I could see she was about to cry. She wanted to go back inside but now the driver of the car we were blocking wanted to pull out. She was shooing us away. My mother, who had just earned her driver's license, started furiously working the pedals. But in her haste she must have flooded the engine, for it wouldn't turn over. The driver started honking and then another car began honking as well, and soon it seemed the entire street was shrieking at us.

(7) In the following years, my mother grew steadily more comfortable with English. In Korean, she could be fiery, stern, deeply funny and ironic; in English just slightly less so. If she was never quite fluent, she gained enough confidence to make herself clearly known to anyone, and particularly to me.

(8) Five years ago, she died of cancer, and some months after we buried her I found myself in the driveway of my father's house, washing her sedan. I liked taking care of her things; it made me feel close to her. While I was cleaning out the glove compartment, I found her pocket English workbook, the one with the silly illustrations. I had not seen it in nearly twenty years. The yellowed pages were brittle and dog-eared. She had fashioned a plain-paper wrapping for it, and I wondered whether she meant to protect the book or hide it.

(9) I doubt that she would have appreciated doing the family shopping on the new Broad Avenue of Palisades Park. But I like to think, too, that she would have understood those who now complain about the Korean-only signs. I wonder what these same people would have done if they had seen my mother studying her English workbook—or lost in a store. Would they have nodded gently at her? Would they have lent a kind word?

(1,775 words)

Vocabulary List

Here are some of the more difficult words in "Mute in an English-Only World."

alienated
(paragraph 1)

alien·ate (āl′yən āt′, āl′ē ən-) *vt.* --at′ed, --at′ing [[< L *alienatus*, pp. of *alienare* < *alius*, other: see ELSE]] **1** to transfer the ownership of (property) to another **2** to make unfriendly; estrange [his behavior *alienated* his friends] **3** to cause to be withdrawn or detached, as from one's society **4** to cause a transference of (affection) — **al′iena′·tor** *n.*

aping
(paragraph 3)

ape (āp) *n.* [[ME < OE *apa*; akin to Ger *affe* < Gmc **apan*, prob. < OSlav *opica*]] **1** any gibbon or great ape **2** loosely, any Old or New World monkey **3** a person who imitates; mimic **4** a person who is uncouth, gross, clumsy, etc. —*vt.* **aped, ap′·ing** to imitate or mimic —*SYN.* IMITATE —**go ape** [Slang] to become mad; also, to become wildly enthusiastic —**ape′·like′** *adj.* —**ap′er** *n.*

bounty
(paragraph 5)

bounty (-tē) *n., pl.* -ties [[ME *bounte* < OFr *bonte* < L *bonitas*, goodness < *bonus*, good: see BONUS]] **1** generosity in giving **2** something given freely; generous gift **3** a reward, premium, or allowance, esp. one given by a government for killing certain harmful animals, raising certain crops, etc. —*SYN.* BONUS

deft
(paragraph 5)

deft (deft) *adj.* [[ME *defte, dafte*: see DAFT]] skillful in a quick, sure, and easy way; dexterous —*SYN.* DEXTEROUS —**deft′ly** *adv.* —**deft′· ness** *n.*

descendants
(paragraph 2)

de·scend·ant (dē sen′dənt, di-) *adj.* [[ME *descendaunt* < OFr *descendant* < L *descendens*, prp. of *descendere*: see prec.]] descending: also **de·scend′·ent** —*n.* **1** a person who is an offspring, however remote, of a certain ancestor, family, group, etc. **2** something that derives from an earlier form

exacting
(paragraph 1)

ex·act·ing (eg zak′tiŋ, ig-) *adj.* **1** making severe or excessive demands; not easily satisfied; strict [an *exacting* teacher] **2** demanding great care, patience, effort, etc.; arduous [an *exacting* job] —*SYN.* ONEROUS —**ex·act′·ingly** *adv.*

harrowing
(paragraph 5)

har·row[1] (har′ō) *n.* [[ME *harwe* < ? OE **hearwa*: akin to ON *harfr* < IE **(s)kerp-*: see HARVEST]] a frame with spikes or sharp-edged disks, drawn by a horse or tractor and used for breaking up and leveling plowed ground, covering seeds, rooting up weeds, etc. —*vt.* **1** to draw a harrow over (land) **2** to cause mental distress to; torment; vex —*vi.* to take harrowing [ground that *harrows* well] —**har′· rower** *n.* —**har′·row·ing** *adj.* — **har′·row·ingly** *adv.*

DISK HARROW

loathed
(paragraph 2)

loathe (lōth) *vt.* **loathed, loath′·ing** [[ME *lothen* < OE *lathian*, to be hateful < base of *lath*: see prec.]] to feel intense dislike, disgust, or hatred for; abhor; detest —*SYN.* HATE —**loath′er** *n.*

proliferation
(paragraph 1)

pro·lif·er·ate (prō lif′ə rāt′, prə-) *vt.* --at′ed, --at′ing [[back-form. < *proliferation* < Fr *prolifèration* < *prolifère*, PROLIFEROUS + -ATION]] **1** to reproduce (new parts) in quick succession **2** to produce or create in profusion —*vi.* **1** to grow by multiplying new parts, as by budding, in quick succession **2** to multiply rapidly; increase profusely —**pro·lif′·era′·tion** *n.*

resolved
(paragraph 5)

re·solved (ri zälvd′, -zôlvd′) *adj.* firm and fixed in purpose; determined; resolute —**re·solv′·edly** (-zäl′vid lē, -zôl′-) *adv.*

sundry
(paragraph 4)

sun·dry (sun′drē) *adj.* ⟦ME *sundri* < OE *syndrig*, separate < *sundor*, apart: see SUNDER & -Y²⟧ various; miscellaneous; divers *[sundry* items of clothing*]* —**pron.** *[with pl. v.]* sundry persons or things: used mainly in the phrase **all and sundry**, everybody; one and all

wails
(paragraph 3)

wail (wāl) *vi.* ⟦ME *wailen* < ON *væla*, to lament < *væ*, WOE⟧ **1** to express grief or pain by long, loud cries **2** to make a plaintive, sad, crying sound *[the wind wailing* in the trees*]* **3** [Slang] *Jazz* to play in an intense or inspired manner —**vt.** [Archaic] **1** to lament; mourn *[to wail* someone's death*]* **2** to cry out in mourning or lamentation —**n.** **1** a long, pitiful cry of grief and pain **2** a sound like this **3** the act of wailing —**SYN.** CRY —**wail′er n.**

12A VOCABULARY

Choose the best answer.

__c__ 1. An **alienated** person feels
    a. friendly.
    b. happy.
    c. withdrawn.
    d. confident.

__d__ 2. **Aping** someone else's actions means
    a. accepting.
    b. ridiculing.
    c. changing.
    d. imitating.

__a__ 3. A **bounty** is
    a. generous.
    b. small.
    c. level.
    d. inappropriate.

__a__ 4. A surgeon needs **deft** hands, hands that are
    a. skillful.
    b. germ free.
    c. smooth.
    d. small.

b   5. A **descendant** is a person who is a(n) _____ of a certain
     ancestor, family, or group.
     a. conspirator
     b. offspring
     c. deadbeat
     d. advocate

a   6. The word **exacting** is closest in meaning to
     a. demanding.
     b. examining.
     c. offending.
     d. increasing.

b   7. A **harrowing** experience is one that causes
     a. mischief.
     b. distress.
     c. happiness
     d. inconvenience.

d   8. To be **loathed** is to be
     a. lost.
     b. liked.
     c. envied.
     d. hated.

c   9. A **proliferation** of signs suggests a(n)
     a. decrease.
     b. absence.
     c. increase.
     d. assortment.

a   10. Someone who is **resolved** to enter a store is
     a. determined.
     b. ready
     c. prepared.
     d. reluctant.

c   11. **Sundry** as used in this essay means
     a. superb.
     b. selective.
     c. various.
     d. specific.

Name   Date

___d___ 12. The **wail** of a grief-stricken person is best described as (a)

       a. soothing sound.

       b. whisper.

       c. lively chatter.

       d. high-pitched cry.

12B CENTRAL THEME AND MAIN IDEAS

Choose the best answer.

___b___ 1. Another title for this selection could be

       a. Shopping in Palisades, New Jersey

       b. A Mother's Difficulty with English

       c. Preserving English as a National Language

       d. Role Reversal in Immigrant Families

___c___ 2. The main idea of paragraph 2 is

       a. As a child, Chang-rae Lee lived in New Rochelle, New York.

       b. A wide variety of shops dotted Main Street and North Avenue.

       c. Change-rae Lee's mother had difficulty speaking English when she shopped.

       d. Chang-rae Lee and his sister sometimes accompanied their mother on shopping trips.

___d___ 3. The main idea of paragraph 5 is

       a. Chang-rae Lee's mother drove downtown in the family's new Ford station wagon to shop.

       b. Chang-rae Lee's mother shopped at Finast supermarket because she could buy packaged meat.

       c. One butcher shop carried a wide selection of meat, including hams, roasts, and sausages.

       d. Shopping for oxtails in a butcher shop resulted in an upsetting experience for Chang-rae Lee's mother.

12C MAJOR DETAILS

Decide whether each detail is true (T), false (F), or not discussed (ND).

___T___ 1. Eight towns in New Jersey passed laws requiring that half of any commercial sign in a foreign language be in English.

___F___ 2. Chang-rae Lee's family was from Japan.

___T___ 3. Chang-rae Lee did not like shopping with his mother.

___F___ 4. Change-rae Lee had difficulty learning English when he started school.

F 5. Most businesses in New Rochelle were run by descendants of Asian immigrants.

T 6. Chang-rae Lee's mother disapproved of Lee's making fun of his father's English.

ND 7. Chang-rae Lee's mother had taken only basic English courses at the university in South Korea.

T 8. Change-rae Lee's mother had a better command of reading English than speaking it.

12D   INFERENCES

Decide whether each statement below can be inferred (YES) or cannot be inferred (NO) from the reading selection.

NO 1. In the early 1970's, Chang-rae Lee's family was the only Korean family in New Rochelle.

NO 2. Chang-rae Lee's father resented having to give up his free time to shop with his wife.

YES 3. Chang-rae Lee's mother watched children's cartoons on television to help her learn English.

NO 4. Chang-rae Lee's mother had a job outside the home.

YES 5. The butcher could not speak Korean.

NO 6. Chang-rae Lee's mother knew it was illegal to double-park outside the butcher shop.

12E   CRITICAL READING: FACT OR OPINION

Decide whether each statement, even if it quotes someone, contains a FACT or an OPINION.

FACT 1. *From paragraph 1:* "But having been raised in a Korean immigrant family, I saw every day the exacting price and power of language […]."

FACT 2. *From paragraph 4:* "For her, the English language was not very funny."

OPINION 3. *From paragraph 6:* "But in her haste she must have flooded the engine, for it wouldn't turn over."

FACT 4. *From paragraph 8:* "I liked taking care of her things; it made me feel close to her."

Name   Date

OPINION 5. From paragraph 9: "I doubt that she would have appreciated doing the family shopping on the new Broad Avenue of Palisades Park."

12F CRITICAL READING: THE WRITER'S CRAFT
Choose the best answer.

__c__ 1. The story is told from the viewpoint of the
a. mother.
b. sister.
c. author.
d. father.

__a__ 2. The overall tone of "Mute in an English-Only World" is
a. sad but enlightening.
b. bitterness and desire for revenge.
c. confusion but victory.
d. hatred and rage.

__d__ 3. *Read paragraph 9 again.* The author concludes the paragraph with a
a. quotation from his mother.
b. summary.
c. warning to immigrants.
d. speculation to think about.

12G READER RESPONSE: TO DISCUSS OR TO WRITE ABOUT

1. The United States is a country of immigrants. Europeans began to arrive in the United States in the seventeenth century. Immigrants are still coming to the United States. Why do so many people resent the recent influx of immigrants to the United States? Be specific with your reasons.

2. Should the United States Congress pass a law to make English the "official" language of the United States? What would be the advantages of this law be? The disadvantages?

3. Lee mentions that many of the businesses in his neighborhood were run by descendants of immigrants, many of whom had parents and grandparents who had struggled with English. Why do you think the butcher was so hateful and irritated with Lee's mother when she did not answer his question? Did Lee's mother have any other choice but to run from the store? Have you ever been treated rudely by a salesperson? If so, explain how you reacted.

Name   Date

How Did You Do?   12   Mute in an English-Only World

SKILL (number of items)	Number Correct		Points for Each		Score
Vocabulary (12)	_____	×	2	=	_____
Central Theme and Main Ideas (3)	_____	×	4	=	_____
Major Details (8)	_____	×	2	=	_____
Inferences (6)	_____	×	4	=	_____
Critical Reading: Fact or Opinion (5)	_____	×	3	=	_____
Critical Reading: The Writer's Craft (3)	_____	×	3	=	_____

(Possible Total: 100) *Total* _____

SPEED

Reading Time: _____ Reading Rate (page 397): _____ Words Per Minute

Name   Date

▪ Part 4 ▪

Thinking: Getting Started

A s you get ready to read, remain conscious of the fact that your mind must participate actively during reading. Use the visuals and accompanying questions on the next three pages to begin engaging with the topics in Part 4 of this book. Turn also to each reading selection in Part 4 and *survey* it by looking at its title and its first and last paragraphs. Predict what the selection will be about. Your prediction might be off the mark—especially until you get more experienced at making predictions. Still, making a prediction focuses your mind usefully on what you will be reading.

After you *survey,* ask *questions.* This technique is explained on page 31. You need only ask the questions, not answer them. Later, when you read with questions in mind, the answers will often seem to "jump out" from the page as you come across them. The purpose of asking questions, then, is to gear up your mind so that it actively confronts new information.

"I used to think it was cruel to keep a dog in the city, but Homer's made a remarkable adjustment."

What animals might people expect to "adjust" happily to mostly indoor living with humans? (See "Out of Their Element.")

In what ways are twins born equal to each other, and in what ways do they differ? (See "Genes and Behavior: A Twin Legacy.")

What are some of the reasons that all children as they grow up should learn not only academic subjects but also practical subjects such as carpentry, electricity basics, and cooking? (See "Every Kid Needs Manual Art.")

Art Director: Derek Norman & William Barre. Writer: William Barre and Derek Norman. Courtesy Illinois Council Against Hand Gun Violence.

What does "like a hole in the head" mean? Do you think that banning bullets would solve the problem of gun abuse? (See "Richard Cory, All Over Again.")

Reproduced courtesy of the Norman Rockwell Family Trust.

In what specific ways can parents share in both the joys and the responsibilities of raising children? (See "Escaping the Daily Grind for Life as a House Father.")

More on next page . . .

Artists: Tom Feelings. Source: Juneteenth.com.

What June celebration, besides Father's Day and Flag Day, is increasing in popularity? (See "Forty Acres and a Holiday.")

Genes and Behavior: A Twin Legacy

Constance Holden

(1) Biology may not be destiny, but genes apparently have a far greater influence on human behavior than is commonly thought. Similarities ranging from phobias to hobbies to bodily gestures are being found in pairs of twins separated at birth. Many of these behaviors are "things you would never think of looking at if you were going to study the genetics of behavior," says psychologist Thomas J. Bouchard, Jr., director of the Minnesota Center for Twin and Adoption Research at the University of Minnesota.

(2) Bouchard reports that so far, exhaustive psychological tests and questionnaires have been completed with approximately 50 pairs of identical twins reared apart, 25 pairs of fraternal twins reared apart and comparison groups of twins reared together. "We were amazed at the similarity in posture and expressive style," says Bouchard. "It's probably the feature of the study that's grabbed us the most." Twins tend to have similar mannerisms, gestures, speed and tempo in talking, habits, and jokes.

(3) Many of the twins dressed in similar fashion—one male pair who had never previously met arrived in England sporting identical beards, haircuts, wire-rimmed glasses and shirts. (Their photo shows them both with thumbs hooked into their pants tops.) One pair had practically the same items in their toilet cases, including the same brand of cologne and a Swedish brand of toothpaste.

(4) Although many of the separated pairs had differing types of jobs and educational levels, the investigators are finding repeated similarities in hobbies and interests—one pair were both volunteer firefighters, one pair were deputy sheriffs, a male pair had similar workshops in their basements and a female pair had strikingly similar kitchen arrangements. In one case, two women from different social classes, one of whom was a pharmacological technician and the other a bookkeeper and a high school dropout, had results on their vocational-interest tests that were "remarkably similar."

(5) Bouchard doesn't have enough information on abnormal behavior or psychopathology to make generalizations, but he has found repeated similarities. One pair of women were both very superstitious; another pair would burst into tears at the drop of a hat, and questioning revealed that both had done so since childhood. "They were on a talk show together and both started crying in response to one of the questions," says Bouchard. A third pair had the same fears and phobias. Both were afraid of water and had adopted the same coping strategy: backing into the ocean up to their knees. Bouchard took

Because identical twins look alike, are their personalities usually alike?

them to a shopping center one day, driving up a long, winding parking ramp to let them off. He later learned that they were both so frightened by the drive they sat on a bench for two hours to collect themselves.

(6) The most striking example of common psychopathology, however, came from a pair of fraternal twins reared apart. One had been reared by his own (poor) family; the other had been adopted into a "good solid upper-middle-class family." Both are now considered to be antisocial personalities, suffering from lack of impulse control, and both have criminal histories. Although fraternal twins share, on average, 50 percent of their genes, Bouchard suggests that the overlap is probably considerably more with this pair.

(7) Another eerie congruence that occurred in the absence of identical genes was observed in the case of two identical-twin women reared apart. Each has a son who has won a statewide mathematics contest, one in Wyoming, one in Texas.

(8) Personality similarities between the identical twins reared apart are almost as pervasive as they are with identical twins reared together, according to the results of a test developed by University of Minnesota psychologist Auke Tellegen. His personality questionnaire contains scales such as "social closeness," "harm avoidance" and "well-being." The researchers were especially surprised to find that "traditionalism"—a trait implying conservatism and respect for authority—can be inherited. In fact, says Bouchard, his and other studies have found about 11 personality traits that appear to have significant genetic input.

(9) Overall, the emerging findings of the Minnesota study constitute a powerful rebuttal to those who maintain that environmental influences are the primary shaping forces of personality. The textbooks are going to have to be rewritten, Bouchard predicts.

(694 words)

Here are some of the more difficult words in "Genes and Behavior: A Twin Legacy."

congruence
(paragraph 7)

con·gru·ence (käŋ'grōō əns, kän'-; kən grōō'əns) *n.* 〖ME < L *congruentia:* see fol.〗 **1** the state or quality of being in agreement; correspondence; harmony **2** *Geom.* the property of a plane or solid figure whereby it coincides with another plane or solid figure after it is moved, rotated, or flipped over **3** *Math.* the relation between two integers each of which, when divided by a third (called the *modulus*), leaves the same remainder Also **con'·gru·ency**

conservatism
(paragraph 8)

con·serva·tism (kən sur'və tiz'əm) *n.* the principles and practices of a conservative person or party; tendency to oppose change in institutions and methods
con·serva·tive (kən sur'və tiv) *adj.* 〖OFr *conservatif* < LL *conservativus*〗 **1** conserving or tending to conserve; preservative **2** tending to preserve established traditions or institutions and to resist or oppose any changes in these *[conservative* politics, *conservative* art*]* **3** of or characteristic of a conservative **4** [C-] designating or of the major political party of Great Britain or the similar one in Canada that is characterized by conservative positions on social and economic issues ☆**5** moderate; cautious; safe *[a conservative* estimate*]* **6** [C-] *Judaism* designating or of a movement that accepts traditional forms and religious ritual that have been adapted to modern life with moderation and flexibility —*n.* **1** [Archaic] a preservative **2** a conservative person **3** [C-] a member of the Conservative Party of Great Britain or of the Progressive Conservative Party of Canada —**con·serv'a·tively** *adv.* —**con·serv'·a·tive·ness** *n.*

destiny
(paragraph 1)

des·tiny (des'tə nē) *n., pl.* **-nies** 〖ME *destine* < OFr *destinee,* fem. pp. of *destiner:* see prec.〗 **1** the seemingly inevitable or necessary succession of events **2** what will necessarily happen to any person or thing; (one's) fate **3** that which determines events: said of either a supernatural agency or necessity —*SYN.* FATE

fraternal twins
(paragraph 2)

fra·ter·nal (frə tur'nəl) *adj.* 〖ME < ML *fraternalis* < L *fraternus,* brotherly < *frater,* BROTHER〗 **1** of or characteristic of a brother or brothers; brotherly **2** of or like a fraternal order or a fraternity **3** designating twins, of either the same or different sexes, developed from separately fertilized ova and thus having hereditary characteristics not necessarily the same: cf. IDENTICAL (sense 3) —**fra·ter'·nal·ism'** *n.* —**fra·ter'·nally** *adv.*

genes
(paragraph 1)

☆**gene** (jēn) *n.* 〖< Ger *gen,* short for *pangen* (< *pan-,* PAN- + *-gen,* -GEN, after PANGENESIS)〗 *Genetics* any of the units occurring at specific points on the chromosomes, by which hereditary characters are transmitted and determined: each is regarded as a particular state of organization of the chromatin in the chromosome, consisting primarily of DNA and protein: see DOMINANT, RECESSIVE, MENDEL'S LAWS

genetics
(paragraph 1)

ge·net·ics (jə net'iks) *n.* 〖GENET(IC) + -ICS〗 **1** the branch of biology that deals with heredity and variation in similar or related animals and plants **2** the genetic features or constitution of an individual, group, or kind

identical twins
(paragraph 2)

iden·ti·cal (ī den'ti kəl) *adj.* 〖prec. + -AL〗 **1** the very same **2** exactly alike or equal: often followed by *with* or *to* **3** designating twins, always of the same sex, developed from a single fertilized ovum and very much alike in physical appearance: cf. FRATERNAL (sense 3) —*SYN.* SAME —**iden'·ti·cally** *adv.*

pervasive
(paragraph 8)

per·va·sive (pər vā'siv) *adj.* tending to pervade or spread throughout —**per·va'·sively** *adv.* —**per·va'·sive·ness** *n.*

phobias
(paragraph 1)

pho·bia (fō'bē ə, fō'byə) *n.* 〖ModL < Gr *phobos,* fear: see prec.〗 an irrational, excessive, and persistent fear of some particular thing or situation

Vocabulary List

psychopathology
(paragraph 5)

psycho·pa·thol·ogy (sī′kō pə thäl′ə jē) *n.* ⟦PSYCHO- + PATHOLOGY⟧ **1** the science dealing with the causes and development of mental disorders **2** psychological malfunctioning, as in a mental disorder —**psy′cho·path′o·log′i·cal** (-path′ə läj′i kəl) *adj.* —**psy′cho·pa·thol′o·gist** *n.*

rebuttal
(paragraph 9)

re·but (ri but′) *vt.* --**but′·ted**, --**but′·ting** ⟦ME *rebuten* < Anglo-Fr *reboter* < OFr *rebuter* < *re-*, back + *buter*, to thrust, push: see BUTT²⟧ **1** to contradict, refute, or oppose, esp. in a formal manner by argument, proof, etc., as in a debate **2** [Obs.] to force back; repel —*vi.* to provide opposing arguments —*SYN.* DISPROVE —**re·but′·table** *adj.*
re·but·tal (-but′'l) *n.* a rebutting, esp. in law

vocational
(paragraph 4)

vo·ca·tional (-shə nəl) *adj.* **1** of a vocation, trade, occupation, etc. ☆**2** designating or of education, training, a school, etc. intended to prepare one for an occupation, sometimes specif. in a trade —**vo·ca′·tion·al·ism′** *n.* —**vo·ca′·tion·al·ly** *adv.*

13A   VOCABULARY
Using the vocabulary words listed on pages 201–202, fill in the blanks.

1. Police statistics show that there is ____congruence____ between the amount of drug use and the number of burglaries in any neighborhood.

2. Specific areas of the brain control specific behaviors, and as scientists' knowledge of such connections improves, methods may be developed to repair damaged or misformed parts of the brain and cure some kinds of __psychopathology__ .

3. Although some people believe that fate controls their lives, polls indicate that on the average, Americans believe that they control their own ____destiny____ .

4. ____Genetics____ is the study of heredity in animals and plants, including how ____genes____ transmit various characteristics.

5. Students who plan to learn a trade choose to attend a ____vocational____ school.

6. People with excessive and persistent fears ought to seek professional counseling before ____phobias____ destroy their lives.

7. Expressions based on sports are ____pervasive____ in our society; even people who have never seen a basketball game may speak of being "fouled" by an unfair competitor.

Name   Date

8. Most people think of twins as looking absolutely alike; actually, such complete resemblance is typical only of ____identical____ _____twins_____ , and __fraternal twins__ often look very different from one another.

9. The __conservatism__ of candidates who call for a return to the "good old days" is appealing to voters who are uncomfortable with rapid progress.

10. The band members compiled a list of songs with social messages as a _____rebuttal_____ to charges that rock music encourages irresponsible behavior.

13B CENTRAL THEME AND MAIN IDEAS

Choose the best answer.

__c__ 1. What is the central theme of "Genes and Behavior: A Twin Legacy"?
   a. Extensive psychological tests and questionnaires have been completed by numbers of identical and fraternal twins.
   b. Carefully controlled studies show that many identical as well as fraternal twins, even when they are reared apart, tend to dress in similar fashion.
   c. Studies of twins, both identical and fraternal, provide evidence for the theory that genes have a greater influence on human behavior than is commonly thought.
   d. Thorough research about both identical and fraternal twins reveals that even if they are raised apart, they generally share the same phobias, hobbies, and gestures.

__a__ 2. What is the main idea of paragraph 2?
   a. Bouchard has studied fraternal and identical twins, some reared apart and some reared together.
   b. Bouchard has studied only identical twins, some reared apart and some together.
   c. Bouchard has studied only fraternal twins, some reared apart and some together.
   d. Bouchard has studied fraternal and identical twins, all of whom were raised apart.

__d__ 3. What is the main idea of paragraph 5?
   a. Research shows that abnormal behavior in separated, identical twins is rare.
   b. Studies reveal that female identical twins are more likely than male identical twins to develop fears and phobias.
   c. Fear of long, winding ramps seems to be genetically determined, according to the research of Dr. Bouchard.
   d. Researchers have not found enough examples of abnormal behavior in separated identical twins to be certain that a pattern exists.

13C   MAJOR DETAILS

Decide whether each detail is true (T), false (F), or not discussed (ND).

__T__ 1. Thomas J. Bouchard is the director of the Minnesota Center for Twin and Adoption Research.

__F__ 2. The behavior of separated twins is being compared with the behavior of a group of 25 pairs of twins raised together.

__T__ 3. Even though many of the separated twins have different jobs, they often share the same hobbies and interests.

__F__ 4. One pair of identical twins who burst into tears easily both cried when asked to appear on a talk show.

__ND__ 5. Twins who are afraid of water are usually also afraid of the dark and of animals.

__T__ 6. One set of separated fraternal twins both had antisocial personalities and grew up to be criminals.

__F__ 7. A woman's twin sons won mathematics competitions in Wyoming and Texas.

__ND__ 8. Social closeness is essential for happiness in humans.

__F__ 9. Environmental influences are the most important shapers of personality.

__F__ 10. Genes determine almost all personality traits.

Name   Date

13D INFERENCES

Choose the best answer.

__c__ 1. *Read paragraph 1 again.* What does the author mean by "Biology may not be destiny"?
   a. Most psychologists believe that biology controls people's destinies.
   b. Most psychologists believe that biology does not control people's destinies.
   c. The debate over whether biology or environment controls people's destinies has been going on for a long time.
   d. The author is not sure whether biology is destiny, so she is showing that she does not support the conclusions of Bouchard's study.

__c__ 2. *Read paragraph 1 again.* Why does Bouchard say these behaviors are "things you would never think of looking at if you were going to study the genetics of behavior"?
   a. These behaviors seemed too unimportant for scientists to observe.
   b. These behaviors seemed too intimate to allow scientists to observe them.
   c. Psychologists assumed these relatively external characteristics could not be biologically based.
   d. Psychologists assumed that the causes of these behaviors were too complicated for current methods of observation.

__a__ 3. *Read paragraph 5 again.* Why does Bouchard need more information before he can make generalizations?
   a. He has not yet found a strong pattern of particular kinds of abnormal behavior among separated identical twins.
   b. The government says researchers must have ten examples before they can make a generalization about a psychological issue.
   c. He is afraid of being sued if he makes a statement that might later be shown to be inaccurate.
   d. He does not want to embarrass the people in the small group he has studied, and so he is looking for additional, anonymous twins to study.

Name   Date

13E CRITICAL READING: THE WRITER'S CRAFT

Choose the best answer.

___d___ 1. To make her point, the author uses all of these devices *except*
  a. quotations from experts.
  b. detailed examples.
  c. anecdotes.
  d. definitions of key terms.

___b___ 2. The author shows connections between her ideas with all of these words *except*
  a. "but"   (paragraph 1)
  b. "so far"   (2)
  c. "in one case"   (4)
  d. "but"   (5)
  e. "one . . . another" (5)
  f. "however"   (6)
  g. "one . . . the other" (6)
  h. "in fact"   (8)
  i. "overall"   (9)

___d___ 3. The author ends her essay with
  a. a quotation from the Minnesota study.
  b. a summary.
  c. a detailed analysis of an opposing opinion.
  d. reference to an authority.

13F READER RESPONSE: TO DISCUSS OR TO WRITE ABOUT

1. Should parents of twins encourage them to dress and act differently or alike? Using specific examples, explain your point of view.

2. Twins occur about once in every 89 births. What are the advantages or disadvantages to having twins? Be specific with your reasons.

3. Sometimes fertility drugs are used by women to increase the possibility of pregnancy. Women who use these drugs sometimes have multiple births—four or more children. How do you feel about this? Are these women violating the Law of Nature? Give specific reasons to support your point of view.

Name   Date

How Did You Do?

13 Genes and Behavior:
A Twin Legacy

SKILL *(number of items)*	Number Correct		Points for Each		Score
Vocabulary* (12)	_____	×	3	=	_____
Central Theme and Main Ideas (3)	_____	×	5	=	_____
Major Details (10)	_____	×	4	=	_____
Inferences (3)	_____	×	2	=	_____
Critical Reading: The Writer's Craft (3)	_____	×	1	=	_____

(Possible Total: 100) *Total* _____

SPEED

Reading Time: _____ Reading Rate (page 397): _____ Words Per Minute

*Questions 4 and 8 in this exercise call for two separate answers each. In computing your score, count each separate answer toward your number correct.

Name _____   Date _____   207

Every Kid Needs Some Manual Arts

William Raspberry

(1) Suppose my evening's TV-watching was interrupted by the sound of an electric saw. My first thought would be that some burglar was testing my power tools before making off with them; the second, that my 15-year-old son was about to do himself serious injury. (It would not enter my head that my daughters might be the source of the noise.)

(2) That dismaying thought summarizes for me one of the things that I think has gone wrong with the way we do school. I was using my father's tools—handsaws, power saws, drill presses, miter boxes—long before I was the age my son is now. Neither my father nor I thought I would ever do woodwork for a living. Fooling around with tools was just something boys did. More to the point, it was something the boys—at least at my small-town Mississippi school—were taught to do.

(3) Today's youngsters, except for those deemed slow enough to be consigned to shop class, are unlikely to be taught even how to make a shoeshine box or replace a frayed lamp cord. My prep school children are innocent of any such household skills and uninterested in acquiring them. But it isn't just prep school children who are deprived of the chance to learn rudimentary manual skills. Probably most academically gifted youngsters are hustled into "academic" tracks whose focus is almost entirely on courses that will help them to get into college. One result is that those who don't go on to college are likely to leave high school unable to earn a decent living. It's a mistake, and not just for the boys. A small part of the reason is cost. Shop classes large enough to accommodate all the children at a school take too much space and too much money. But a larger part is our either/or mentality with regard to academic and manual training. Smart kids do books; dumb kids do tools.

(4) It is a dichotomy we would do well to abandon, for at least three reasons. The first is that a lot of reasonably bright youngsters whose special gifts are in the manual arts are denied the chance to excel at what they do best. One result is that they lose interest in school and drop out. The second, given the large number of young people whose formal education ends with high school, is that we are turning out high school graduates who have learned very little beyond reading, writing and basic math that will help them to land a decent job—as apprentice carpenters or masons or electricians, for instance. Lately, our attention has been focused on the Year 2000, by which time, we are told, a college degree will be the basic job credential. Even today, we are led to believe, college training is a virtual necessity for decently paid work. Our schools are organized on that assumption.

A Youth Construction Initiative Program in New York teaches students the trades. Jessica Stanek (bottom) hands a tray of drywall compound to Kenia Chanelo.

(5) But, as anybody who has had the bad luck to need a plumber or an electrician knows, it isn't true. How might we do it differently? For one thing, every large public high school ought to have mandatory courses in such things as simple carpentry, sewing, typing, mechanics, electricity/electronics and upholstery, with students free to choose a course or two of special interest. Those who discover latent skills (or interest) as a result of these mandatory classes would have the option of "majoring" in them, while, at the same time, earning their college-entry credentials. Thus, the student who leaves school after high school might easily find work as, say, an assistant to the manager of an apartment or small office building, with a clear path to a well-paid profession. The student who goes on to college might earn some extra income by performing such things as word-processing or painting or repair. And all students—dropouts, high school graduates and PhD's alike—could save themselves a good piece of cash by knowing how to do some things for themselves.

(6) Nor is it just the boys I have in mind. We are forever talking about the increase in the number of female-headed households, particularly among ethnic minorities. It is a problem, no doubt about it. But wouldn't these single mothers be a good deal better off if they knew how to free a sticking door, replace the ball on a toilet, change a faucet washer, build a bookcase or fix a lamp? We are placing so much emphasis on college that we neglect to give our youngsters a chance at a noncollege career—by teaching them the things that all of us ought to know.

(773 words)

Here are some of the more difficult words in "Every Kid Needs Some Manual Arts."

apprentice
(paragraph 4)

ap·pren·tice (ə pren′tis) *n.* [[ME *aprentis* < OFr *aprentiz* < *apren-dre*, learn < L *apprehendere*, APPREHEND]] **1** a person under legal agreement to work a specified length of time for a master crafts-man in a craft or trade in return for instruction and, formerly, support **2** a person who is acquiring a trade, craft, or skill under specified conditions, usually as a member of a labor union **3** any learner or beginner; novice —*vt.* **-ticed, -tic·ing** to place or accept as an apprentice —**ap·pren′·tice·ship′** *n.*

consigned
(paragraph 3)

con·sign (kən sīn′) *vt.* [[L *consignare,* to seal, register < *com-,* together + *signare,* to sign, mark < *signum,* SIGN]] **1** to hand over; give up or deliver [*consigned* to jail] **2** to put in the care of another; entrust [*consign* the orphan to her uncle's care] **3** to assign to an undesirable position or place; relegate [*consigned* to oblivion] **4** to send or deliver, as goods to be sold —*vi.* [Obs.] to agree or submit —*SYN.* COMMIT —**con·sign′·able** *adj.* —**con·sig·na·tion** (kän′sig nā′ shən) *n.*

credential
(paragraph 4)

cre·den·tial (kri den′shəl) *adj.* [[ME *credencial* < ML *credentialis:* see CREDENCE]] [Rare] entitling to credit, confidence, etc.; accredit-ing —*n.* [*usually pl.*] **1** anything giving evidence that someone is entitled to or deserving of credit, confidence, etc. **2** a document that serves as official proof of a person's position, authority, etc.; specif., LETTERS OF CREDENCE —*vt.* **-tialed, -tial·ing** to furnish with credentials

deemed
(paragraph 3)

deem (dēm) *vt., vi.* [[ME *deman* < OE *deman,* to judge, decree < base of *dom,* DOOM[1]]] to think, believe, or judge

dichotomy
(paragraph 4)

di·chot·o·my (-mē) *n., pl.* **-mies** [[Gr *dichotomia:* see DICHO- & -TOMY]] **1** division into two parts, groups, or classes, esp. when these are sharply distinguished or opposed **2** *Astron.* the appear-ance of the moon or of a planet when half of the surface facing the earth is illuminated **3** *Biol.* a dividing or branching into two equal parts, esp. when repeated —**di·chot′o·mous** (-məs) *adj.* —**di·chot′o·mously** *adv.*

latent
(paragraph 5)

la·tent (lāt″nt) *adj.* [[L *latens,* prp. of *latere,* to lie hidden, lurk < IE *lāidh-* < base *lā-,* to be hidden > ON *lōmr,* deception, Gr *lēthē,* forgetfulness, *lanthanein,* to be hidden]] **1** present but invisible or inactive; lying hidden and undeveloped within a person or thing, as a quality or power **2** *Biol.* dormant but capable of normal develop-ment under the best conditions: said of buds, spores, cocoons, etc. **3** *Psychol.* unconsciously but not actively so [a *latent* homosexual] —*n.* a fingerprint found on an object as at the scene of a crime — **la′·tency** *n.* —**la′·tently** *adv.*

SYN.—**latent** applies to that which exists but is as yet concealed or unrevealed [his *latent* ability]; **potential** applies to that which exists in an undeveloped state but which can be brought to development in the normal course of events [a *potential* concert pianist]; **dormant** suggests a lack of visible activity, as of some-thing asleep [a *dormant* volcano]; **quiescent** implies a stopping of activity, usually only temporarily [the raging sea had become *quiescent*] —*ANT.* active, actual, operative

rudimentary
(paragraph 3)

ru·di·men·tary (rōō′də men′tər ē, -men′trē) *adj.* of, or having the nature of, a rudiment or rudiments; specif., *a)* elementary *b)* incompletely or imperfectly developed *c)* vestigial: sometimes **ru′·di·men′·tal** —**ru·di·men·tari·ly** (rōō′də men ter′ə lē, -men′tər ə lē) *adv.* —**ru′·di·men′·ta·ri·ness** *n.*

virtual
(paragraph 4)

vir·tual (vər′chōō əl) *adj.* [[ME *vertual* < ML *virtualis* < L *virtus,* strength, VIRTUE]] **1** being such practically or in effect, although not in actual fact or name [a *virtual* impossibility] **2** *Comput. a)* designating or of a kind of MEMORY (sense 8*b*) that makes use of disk space to supplement main memory while large programs are being executed *b)* of, pertaining to, or taking place in cyberspace or in virtual reality [a *virtual* business conference] —**vir·tu·al′·ity** (-al′ə tē) *n.*

14A VOCABULARY

Using the vocabulary words listed on page 211, fill in this crossword puzzle.

Across

3. elementary
6. undeveloped
7. a beginner
8. judged

Down

1. almost certain
2. an estimate of a person's authority
4. division into groups
5. handed over

Name   Date

14B CENTRAL THEME AND MAIN IDEAS
Choose the best answer.

__b__ 1. What is the central theme of "Every Kid Needs Some Manual Arts"?
    a. Schools are not preparing students for the workforce.
    b. All students should be required to take courses that demand use of their hands.
    c. Parents should encourage their children to take manual arts courses.
    d. William Raspberry's children are enrolled in academic courses.

__c__ 2. What is the main idea of paragraph 3?
    a. In a shop class, students learn how to make a shoeshine box or replace a lamp cord.
    b. William Raspberry's children, like other prep school children, are not interested in manual arts courses.
    c. Well-educated students need to take both academic courses and manual arts courses.
    d. Students who do not plan to attend college should be required to enroll in manual arts courses.

14C MAJOR DETAILS
Decide whether each detail is true (T), false (F), or not discussed (ND).

__T__ 1. William Raspberry learned to use power tools when he was a boy.

__T__ 2. William Raspberry's children are not interested in learning to do simple household repairs.

__F__ 3. William Raspberry's father thought his son's use of power tools meant the son would do woodworking for a living.

__ND__ 4. All Mississippi schools required boys to take shop classes when William Raspberry was a boy.

__F__ 5. Cost and space are the only reasons that students are not required to take manual arts courses.

__T__ 6. Manual arts courses include courses such as typing and sewing.

__T__ 7. The number of female-headed households is on the increase among ethnic minorities.

__ND__ 8. William Raspberry has a woodwork shop at his home.

14D INFERENCES
Decide whether each statement below can be inferred (YES) or cannot be inferred (NO) from the reading selection.

NO 1. William Raspberry's father was a shop teacher.

NO 2. A college degree is necessary for a well-paid job.

YES 3. William Raspberry wishes his daughters could do simple manual household jobs.

NO 4. People who call a plumber will bring bad luck to their lives.

NO 5. William Raspberry believes all male students should take manual arts courses in cooking and sewing.

YES 6. William Raspberry would like today's schools organized the way they were when he was a boy.

14E CRITICAL READING: FACT OR OPINION
Decide whether each statement, even if it quotes someone, contains a FACT or an OPINION.

OPINION 1. *From paragraph 2:* "Fooling around with tools was just something boys did."

OPINION 2. *From paragraph 3:* "Smart kids do books; dumb kids do tools."

FACT 3. *From paragraph 3:* Most "academic" track programs do not include manual arts courses.

FACT 4. *From paragraph 4:* A large number of high school students end their formal education after high school graduation.

OPINION 5. *From paragraph 6:* "We are placing so much emphasis on college that we neglect to give our youngsters a chance at a noncollege career [. . .]."

14F CRITICAL READING: THE WRITER'S CRAFT
Choose the best answer.

d 1. To get the reader's interest, the author begins by
   a. talking about his sons and daughters.
   b. focusing on a topic that appeals mostly to males.
   c. using an example to shock readers.
   d. describing an imaginary situation.

Name   Date

__a__ 2. *Reread the last sentence in paragraph 3.* It is an effective conclusion to the paragraph because the sentence does all of the following *except*
   a. conveys a gentle tone.
   b. repeats the word "kids" to enhance its impact.
   c. uses the antonyms "smart" and "dumb" for balance.
   d. uses a semicolon to emphasize the connection between the two short sentences.

__c__ 3. Which of these words is *not* used by the author to show connection among ideas?
   a. "more to the point" (paragraph 2)
   b. "but" (3)
   c. "probably" (3)
   d. "first" (4)
   e. "second" (4)
   f. "thus" (5)
   g. "nor" (6)

14G   READER RESPONSE: TO DISCUSS OR TO WRITE ABOUT

1. Do you agree or disagree with the following statement: "Smart kids do books; dumb kids do tools"? Defend your position with specific reasons and examples.

2. Do you agree with William Raspberry's idea that all schools should require manual arts courses? Explain your point of view, being as specific as possible.

3. William Raspberry mentions that the lack of manual arts courses in all schools is one example of what is wrong with schools today. Do you think high schools today are doing a better or worse job in preparing students for life than when you or your parents were in high school?

How Did You Do? **14** Every Kid Needs Some Manual Arts

SKILL *(number of items)*	Number Correct		Points for Each		Score
Vocabulary (8)	_____	×	2	=	_____
Central Theme and Main Ideas (2)	_____	×	6	=	_____
Major Details (8)	_____	×	5	=	_____
Inferences (6)	_____	×	3	=	_____
Critical Reading: Fact or Opinion (5)	_____	×	1	=	_____
Critical Reading: The Writer's Craft (3)	_____	×	3	=	_____

(Possible Total: 100) *Total* _____

SPEED

Reading Time: _____ Reading Rate (page 397): _____ Words Per Minute

Name   Date

Richard Cory, All Over Again

Roy Meador

(1) The same as the rest of us, my friend wanted to be somebody. To make his mark in the world. To have his life count. At the end, he did make his mark in headlines: *Deaths Called Murder-Suicide. Son Finds Bodies.*

(2) Carl L. Stinedurf was a good friend. We often lunched together, and our conversations ranged from politics to literature. Carl enjoyed ideas. He knew how to laugh. Face-to-face, most people used his middle name, Larry. But the waitress called him "Frank" because he preferred Sinatra's old records to new stuff. Carl often talked enthusiastically about his family, his son at the university, his daughter in high school. He mentioned his wife, Norma, with special pride. In her 30's, with his help she had finished college and begun teaching. Carl was delighted with his family's accomplishments. But underneath, well-masked, there must have been agonizing terror. Carl carried his pain in silence.

(3) My friend worked as an estimator and customer representative for a large printing firm. He was gentle, always soft-spoken, exceptionally conscientious. When I gave him work to do for my company, I knew it would be finished with care.

(4) Carl tended toward the liberal. He thought more of people than of profits. He deplored cruelty. I considered him one of those who patiently keep what we call civilization humming along after its fashion.

(5) There was just one anomaly I never understood. Carl's hobby was guns. He kept a loaded .38 in his bedroom. There were handguns and rifles throughout his home. Carl used them for target shooting and hunting. A fellow hunter said Carl was an expert marksman, that when he fired at game he made certain of his shot so the animal wouldn't suffer.

(6) I couldn't appreciate the gun side of my friend's character. I guess I had seen too much of the gun religion in the Korean war. Carl and I disagreed about guns. He would vote for George McGovern and simultaneously support every argument of the National Rifle Association and the gun lobbies. Yet because he was a peaceful, compassionate man, I considered him one of those who could be trusted to own and use guns responsibly.

(7) I saw Carl on that last Friday afternoon. We talked about a printing job. He was cheerful, and I think he was already on the other side of his decision. He finished his work that day like someone going on vacation. Like someone not expecting to return on Monday.

(8) We had a relaxed talk. Later I learned of the misery he had concealed. "He saw customers and kept control," his employer told me.

"When the customer left, he often went in the restroom and vomited. Family trouble."

(9) The virus of restlessness. Norma, after 23 years, with a new career and new friends, wanted to leave. She needed to seek that popular, elusive goal, "more out of life." But Carl was an old-fashioned man captive in a time of new fashions. He couldn't handle this threat to the family. He sought medical advice, but every answer seemed to require letting Norma go, with the frail hope she might come back. Carl couldn't live with the uncertainty.

(10) It rained that Friday night. Carl went home and in their bedroom he put two bullets through his wife's head, one through his own. He used a .357 magnum handgun. One of Carl's friends told me this proved it was carefully planned. The .357 magnum meant Carl didn't want Norma to suffer. That friend and others were reluctant to credit guns as factors in the event. "Guns are simply tidier than axes," said one. But Carl was a sensitive, orderly man. I doubt he could ever have done the job with less efficient, messier weapons. It had to be over in a moment. So he used the mercy weapon, the no-pain gun, the .357 magnum. It was handy in a house of guns.

(11) Endless postmortems began among those who knew Carl and Norma. Why in his torment couldn't he wait? Why couldn't he give time a chance? Why?

(12) No one I listened to blamed the guns, questioned their proximity, their easy availability. It will probably be a long time before Carl's small estate is settled for the son who found the bodies, for the daughter in high school. I suppose his guns eventually will be sold and redistributed, including the .357 magnum. Guns are made from enduring metal. They outlive their owners. They go on about their business.

(13) News accounts carried the standard facts: Description of Carl's hobby. His age, 39. The comment of a neighbor that Carl and Norma were "very nice." Details of the funeral. There was no indication whether or not gun clubs and the National Rifle Association sent flowers, or assistance for the survivors.

(14) The irony department: Carl learned enthusiasm for guns as an adult. His teacher later abandoned guns in favor of photography.

(15) I'll miss Carl very much. His last day was Edwin Arlington Robinson's poem translated into tragic fact. "And Richard Cory, one calm summer night,/Went home and put a bullet through his head." Richard Cory wasn't the sort to use an ice pick. The same with Carl. Only a gun.

(16) Damn those guns.

(950 words)

Richard Cory

EDWIN ARLINGTON ROBINSON

Whenever Richard Cory went down town,
We people on the pavement looked at him:
He was a gentleman from sole to crown,
Clean favored, and imperially slim.

And he was always quietly arrayed,
And he was always human when he talked;
But still he fluttered pulses when he said,
"Good-morning," and he glittered when he walked.

And he was rich—yes, richer than a king—
And admirably schooled in every grace:
In fine,* we thought that he was everything
To make us wish that we were in his place.

So on we worked, and waited for the light,
And went without the meat, and cursed the bread;
And Richard Cory, one calm summer night,
Went home and put a bullet through his head.

*In short

Vocabulary List

Here are some of the more difficult words in "Richard Cory, All Over Again."

agonizing
(paragraph 2)

ago·nize (ag′ə nīz′) *vi.* ··nized′, ··niz′·ing ⟦LL *agonizare* < Gr *agōnizesthai*, to contend for a prize < *agōn*, AGON⟧ **1** to make convulsive efforts; struggle **2** to be in agony or great pain; feel anguish —*vt.* to cause great pain to; torture —**ag′o·niz′·ing** *adj.* —**ag′o·niz′·ingly** *adv.*

anomaly
(paragraph 5)

anoma·ly (ə näm′ə lē) *n., pl.* ··lies ⟦L *anomalia* < Gr *anōmalia*, inequality: see prec.⟧ **1** departure from the regular arrangement, general rule, or usual method; abnormality **2** anything anomalous **3** *Astron.* a measurement used for any orbiting body, as a planet's angular distance around its orbit from its perihelion, taken as if viewed from the sun

compassionate
(paragraph 6)

com·pas·sion·ate (-it; *for v.*, -āt′) *adj.* feeling or showing compassion; sympathizing deeply; pitying —*vt.* ··at·ed, ··at·ing to pity — *SYN.* TENDER[1] —**com·pas′·sion·ately** *adv.*

conscientious
(paragraph 3)

con·sci·en·tious (kän′shē en′shəs) *adj.* ⟦Fr *conscientieux* < ML *conscientiosus:* see CONSCIENCE & -OUS⟧ **1** governed by, or made or done according to, what one knows is right; scrupulous; honest **2** showing care and precision; painstaking —**con′·sci·en′·tiously** *adv.* —**con′·sci·en′·tious·ness** *n.*

deplored
(paragraph 4)

de·plore (dē plôr′, di-) *vt.* ··plored′, ··plor′·ing ⟦Fr *déplorer* < L *deplorare* < *de-*, intens. + *plorare*, to weep⟧ **1** to be regretful or sorry about; lament **2** to regard as unfortunate or wretched **3** to condemn as wrong; disapprove of —**de·plor′er** *n.*

elusive
(paragraph 9)

elu·sive (ē lōō′siv, i-) *adj.* ⟦< L *elusus* (see prec.) + -IVE⟧ **1** tending to elude **2** hard to grasp or retain mentally; baffling Also [Rare] **elu′·sory** (-sə rē) —**elu′·sively** *adv.* —**elu′·sive·ness** *n.*

irony
(paragraph 14)

irony[1] (ī′rə nē, ī′ər nē) *n., pl.* ··nies ⟦Fr *ironie* < L *ironia* < Gr *eirōneia* < *eirōn*, dissembler in speech < *eirein*, to speak < IE base **wer-*, to speak > WORD⟧ **1** *a*) a method of humorous or subtly sarcastic expression in which the intended meaning of the words is the direct opposite of their usual sense *[the irony* of calling a stupid plan "clever"*] b*) an instance of this **2** the contrast, as in a play, between what a character thinks the truth is, as revealed in a speech or action, and what an audience or reader knows the truth to be: often **dramatic irony 3** a combination of circumstances or a result that is the opposite of what is or might be expected or considered appropriate *[an irony* that the firehouse burned*] 4 a*) a cool, detached attitude of mind, characterized by recognition of the incongruities and complexities of experience *b*) the expression of such an attitude in a literary work **5** the feigning of ignorance in argument: often called **Socratic irony** (after Socrates' use of this tactic in Plato's *Dialogues*) —*SYN.* WIT[1]

220

lobbies
(paragraph 6)

lobby (läb′ē) *n.*, *pl.* **-bies** 〚LL *lobia*: see LODGE〛 **1** a hall or large anteroom, as a waiting room or vestibule of an apartment house, hotel, theater, etc. **2** a large hall adjacent to the assembly hall of a legislature and open to the public ☆**3** a group of lobbyists representing the same special interest [the oil *lobby*] —☆*vi.* **-bied, -by·ing** 〚after the practice of meeting with legislators in the LOBBY (*n.* 2)〛 **1** to act as a lobbyist **2** to attempt to influence a public official in favor of something: often with *for* —☆*vt.* **1** to attempt to influence (a public official) by acting as a lobbyist **2** to attempt to influence the passage of (a measure) by acting as a lobbyist
☆**lob·by·ist** (-ist) *n.* a person, acting for a special interest group, who tries to influence the introduction of or voting on legislation or the decisions of government administrators —**lob′·by·ism′** *n.*

postmortems
(paragraph 11)

post·mor·tem (pōst′môr′təm) *adj.* 〚L, lit., after death〛 **1** happening, done, or made after death **2** having to do with a post-mortem examination —*n.* **1** *short for* POSTMORTEM EXAMINATION **2** a detailed examination or evaluation of some event just ended Also written **post-mortem**

proximity
(paragraph 12)

prox·im·ity (präk sim′ə tē) *n.* 〚MFr *proximité* < L *proximitas* < *proximus*: see prec.〛 the state or quality of being near; nearness in space, time, etc.

Vocabulary List

15A VOCABULARY

From the context of "Richard Cory, All Over Again," explain the meaning of each of the vocabulary words shown in boldface below.

1. *From paragraph 2:* But underneath, well-masked, there must have been **agonizing** terror.

   greatly painful

2. *From paragraph 3:* He was gentle, always soft-spoken, exceptionally **conscientious.**

   careful and precise; knowing what is right

3. *From paragraph 4:* He **deplored** cruelty.

   was regretful or sorry about

4. *From paragraph 5:* There was just one **anomaly** I never understood. Carl's hobby was guns.

   abnormality

   _____

5. *From paragraph 6:* He would vote for George McGovern and simultaneously support every argument of the National Rifle Association and the gun **lobbies.**

   groups that try to influence legislators to support their interests

   _____

6. *From paragraph 6:* Yet because he was a peaceful, **compassionate** man, I considered him one of those who could be trusted to own and use guns responsibly.

   tender

   _____

7. *From paragraph 9:* She needed to seek that popular, **elusive** goal, "more out of life."

   baffling and hard to grasp

   _____

8. *From paragraph 11:* Endless **postmortems** began among those who knew Carl and Norma.

   evaluations after death

   _____

9. *From paragraph 12:* No one I listened to blamed the guns, questioned their **proximity,** their easy availability.

   being so near

   _____

10. *From paragraph 14:* The **irony** department: Carl learned enthusiasm for guns as an adult. His teacher later abandoned guns in favor of photography.

    opposite of what might be expected

    _____

Name   Date

15B CENTRAL THEME AND MAIN IMAGES
Follow the directions for each item below.

1. There are two central themes in "Richard Cory, All Over Again." One central theme is about Carl L. Stinedurf. The second central theme is about guns. Explain each central theme.

   a. *About Carl L. Stinedurf:* ___He seemed to be happy and proud___ ___of his family, but underneath he was so miserable about hid-___ ___den family problems that he killed his wife and himself.___

   b. *About guns:* ___Probably if guns had not been so easily available___ ___to Carl, the murder and suicide would not have happened.___

2. In Edwin Arlington Robinson's poem "Richard Cory," there are two images. One image is a picture of Richard Cory. The second image is a picture of the people telling the story. Describe each image.

   a. *Of Richard Cory:* ___He was a gentleman, rich, attractive, and en-___ ___vied. One day, he committed suicide.___

   b. *Of the people telling the story:* ___They were hard-working, poor,___ ___hungry people who wished they were Richard Cory—until he___ ___killed himself.___

15C MAJOR DETAILS
Decide whether each detail is MAJOR or MINOR based on the context of the reading selection.

MAJOR 1. Carl L. Stinedurf was a good friend of Roy Meador.

MINOR 2. The waitress called Carl "Frank."

MAJOR 3. Carl often talked enthusiastically about his family.

MAJOR 4. Carl's wife, Norma, had recently finished college and had begun to teach.

MAJOR 5. Underneath Carl's delight, there must have been a well-masked agonizing terror.

MINOR 6. Carl worked as a printing estimator and a customer representative.

Name	Date	

MAJOR   7. Carl was gentle, soft-spoken, and hated cruelty.

MAJOR   8. Carl's hobby was guns.

MINOR   9. The .38 that Carl kept in his bedroom was loaded.

MAJOR 10. Norma, after 23 years of marriage, wanted to leave Carl.

MAJOR 11. Carl went home and put two bullets through his wife's head and one through his own.

MAJOR 12. Roy Meador feels that Carl would not have been able to kill if he had had to use a messy weapon such as an ice pick.

MINOR 13. Roy Meador did not know if gun clubs and the National Rifle Association sent flowers to the funeral.

15D INFERENCES

Choose the best answer.

__a__ 1. *Read paragraph 6 again.* George McGovern, the 1972 Democratic presidential candidate, ran against Richard Nixon. McGovern's liberal views included being in favor of strong gun-control legislation. Why did Carl vote for McGovern?
   a. Carl was a liberal.
   b. Carl was anti-Nixon.
   c. Carl was influenced by Roy Meador.
   d. Carl wanted to impress his wife.

__c__ 2. *Read paragraph 7 again.* Carl was cheerful on that last Friday afternoon because he
   a. was looking forward to a weekend with his guns.
   b. enjoyed his lunches with Roy.
   c. had made up his mind and the uncertainty was now over.
   d. was going to see his beloved wife soon.

__d__ 3. *Read paragraph 10 again.* The .357 magnum is considered "the mercy weapon, the no-pain gun" because
   a. it is very well made.
   b. it wounds but does not kill.
   c. it is not a real gun.
   d. it kills instantly.

Name   Date

___c___ 4. *Read paragraph 13 again.* The gun clubs or the National Rifle Association might have sent flowers or assistance for the survivors because
   a. they had a humane concern for the survivors of people killed by guns or rifles.
   b. they hoped to receive contributions from the survivors and their friends to help support their efforts to get gun control laws passed.
   c. they wanted to lessen the chance that the survivors and the media would start another outcry for gun control laws.
   d. Carl was an active member of their groups, and they wanted to pay their respects.

15E CRITICAL READING: THE WRITER'S CRAFT
Choose the best answer.

___b___ 1. In paragraph 9 the image "virus of restlessness" is contained in the words
   a. "Carl was an old-fashioned man."
   b. ". . . to seek that popular, elusive goal, 'more out of life.'"
   c. ". . . this threat to the family."
   d. "He sought medical advice."

___d___ 2. In paragraph 15 the author quotes from Edwin Arlington Robinson's poem "Richard Cory" because Roy Meador wants to
   a. show he knows how to translate.
   b. urge people to improve themselves by reading poetry.
   c. describe how much he liked Carl.
   d. illustrate that themes recur often, in life as well as in literature.

___d___ 3. *Read the poem again.* Why does Roy Meador call his essay "Richard Cory, All Over Again"?
   a. Both Richard and Carl were wealthy.
   b. Both Richard and Carl were married.
   c. Both Richard and Carl were envied by everyone.
   d. Both Richard and Carl, though seemingly happy, committed suicide.

___b___ 4. Why does the author of the poem wait until his last two lines to reveal what happened to Richard Cory?
   a. He probably could not have worked out his end-of-line rhymes any other way.
   b. He wanted to dramatize the suddenness of the suicide.
   c. He wanted to write about Richard Cory's life, not his death.
   d. He did not want to horrify his readers with too many details about the death.

15F READER RESPONSE: TO DISCUSS OR TO WRITE ABOUT

1. In your opinion, if guns had not been available to Carl, would he have killed his wife and committed suicide? Explain.

2. What would be the effect on society if everyone started to carry guns or other lethal weapons? Using specific examples, explain your point of view fully.

3. If Norma had been content to be a housewife and stay at home, she probably would still be alive. Instead, she grew restless with her job as a homemaker, returned to school, made new friends, and found a job as a teacher. What is your opinion of Norma's wanting to leave her husband so that she could get "more out of life"? Explain.

How Did You Do? 15 Richard Cory, All Over Again

SKILL (number of items)	Number Correct		Points for Each		Score
Vocabulary (10)	_____	×	2	=	_____
Central Theme and Main Ideas* (4)	_____	×	5	=	_____
Major Details (13)	_____	×	4	=	_____
Inferences (4)	_____	×	1	=	_____
Critical Reading: The Writer's Craft (4)	_____	×	1	=	_____

(Possible Total: 100) *Total* _____

SPEED

Reading Time: _____ Reading Rate (page 398): _____ Words Per Minute

*Both questions in this exercise call for two separate answers each. In computing your score, count each separate answer toward your number correct.

Escaping the Daily Grind for Life as a House Father

Rick Greenberg

(1) "You on vacation?" my neighbor asked.

(2) My 15-month-old son and I were passing her yard on our daily hike through the neighborhood. It was a weekday afternoon and I was the only working-age male in sight.

(3) "I'm uh . . . working out of my house now," I told her.

(4) Thus was born my favorite euphemism for house fatherhood, one of those new lifestyle occupations that is never merely mentioned. Explained, yes. Defended. Even rhapsodized about. I was tongue-tied then, but no longer. People are curious and I've learned to oblige.

(5) I joined up earlier this year when I quit my job—a dead-end, ulcer-producing affair that had dragged on interminably. I left to be with my son until something better came along. And if nothing did, I'd be with him indefinitely.

(6) This was no simple transition. I had never known a house father, never met one. I'd only read about them. They were another news magazine trend. Being a traditionalist, I never dreamed I'd take the plunge.

(7) But as the job got worse, I gave it serious thought. And more thought. And in the end, I still felt ambivalent. This was a radical change that seemed to carry as many drawbacks as benefits. My dislike for work finally pushed me over the edge. That, and the fact that we had enough money to get by.

(8) Escaping the treadmill was a bold stroke. I had shattered my lethargy and stopped whining, and for that I was proud.

(9) Some friends said they were envious. Of course they weren't quitting one job without one waiting—the ultimate in middle-class taboos. That ran through my mind as I triumphantly, and without notice, tossed the letter of resignation on my boss's desk. Then I walked away wobbly-kneed.

(10) The initial trauma of quitting, however, was mitigated by my eagerness to raise our son. Mine was the classic father's lament: I felt excluded. I had become "the man who got home after dark," that other person besides Mama. It hurt when I couldn't quiet his crying.

(11) I sensed that staying home would be therapeutic. The chronic competitiveness and aggressiveness that had served me well as a daily journalist would subside. Something better would emerge, something less obnoxious. My ulcer would heal. Instead of beating deadlines, I'd be doing something important for a change. This was heresy coming from a newspaper gypsy, but it rang true.

(12) There was unease, too. I'd be adrift, stripped of the home-office-home routine that had defined my existence for more than a decade. No more earning a living. No benchmarks. Time would be seamless. Would Friday afternoons feel the same?

(13) The newness of it was scary.

(14) Until my resignation, my wife and I typified today's baby-boomer couples, the want-it-all generation. We had two salaries, a full-time nanny and guilt pangs over practicing parenthood by proxy.

(15) Now, my wife brings home the paychecks, the office problems and thanks for good work on the domestic front. With me at home, her work hours are more flexible. Nanny-less, I change diapers, prepare meals and do all the rest. And I wonder what comes next.

(16) What if I don't find another job? My field is tight. At 34, I'm not getting any more marketable and being out of work doesn't help.

(17) As my father asked incredulously: "Is this going to be what you do?"

(18) Perhaps. I don't know. I wonder myself. It's even more baffling to my father, the veteran of a long and traditional 9-to-5 career. For most of it, my mother stayed home. My father doesn't believe in trends. All he knows is that his only son—with whom he shares so many traits—has violated the natural order of men providing and women raising children. In his view, I've shown weakness and immaturity by succumbing to a bad job.

(19) But he's trying to understand, and I think he will.

(20) I'm trying to understand it myself. House fatherhood has been humbling, rewarding and unnerving.

(21) "It's different," I tell friends. "Different."

(22) Imagine never having to leave home for the office in the morning. That's how different. No dress-up, no commute. Just tumble out of bed and you're there. House fathering is not for claustrophobics.

(23) I find myself enjoying early morning shopping. My son and I arrive right after the supermarket opens. The place is almost empty. For the next hour we glide dreamily, cruising the aisles to a Muzak accompaniment. This is my idyll. My son likes it, too; he's fascinated by the spectacle.

(24) Housekeeping still doesn't seem like work, and that's by design. I've mastered the art of doing just enough chores to get by. This leaves me enough free time. Time to read and write and daydream. Time with my son. Time to think about the structure.

(25) So much time, and so little traditional structure, that the days sometimes blur together. I remember on Sunday nights literally dreading the approaching work week, the grind. Today, the close of the weekend still triggers a shiver of apprehension; I now face the prospect of a week without tangible accomplishments, a void.

(26) On our hikes to the playground, I can feel my old identity fading. All around are people with a mission, a sense of purpose. Workers. And then, there's the rest of us—the stroller and backpack contingent. The

moms, the nannies, and me. I wonder if I've crossed over a line never to return.

(27) Still, the ulcer seems to be healing. I take pride in laying out a good dinner for the family and in pampering my wife after a tough day at the office. I love reading to my son. Running errands isn't even so bad. A lot of what had been drudgery or trivia is taking on new meaning; maybe I'm mellowing.

(28) Which is ironic. To be a truly committed and effective at-home parent, there must be this change—a softening, a contentment with small pleasures, the outwardly mundane. This is a time of reduced demands and lowered expectations. Progress is gradual, often agonizingly so. Patience is essential. Ambition and competitiveness are anathema. Yet eliminating these last two qualities—losing the edge—could ruin my chances of resurrecting my career. I can't have it both ways.

(29) The conflict has yet to be resolved. And it won't be unless I make a firm commitment and choose one lifestyle over the other. I'm not yet ready for that decision.

(30) In the meantime, a wonderful change is taking place in our home. Amid all the uncertainties, my son and I have gotten to know each other. He can't put a phrase together, but he confides in me. It can be nothing more than a grin or a devilish look. He tries new words on me, new shtick. We roll around a lot; we crack each other up. I'm no longer the third wheel, the man who gets home after dark. Now, I'm as much a part of his life as his mother is. I, too, can stop his crying. So far, that has made the experiment worthwhile.

(1,197 words)

Here are some of the more difficult words In "Escaping the Daily Grind for Life as a House Father."

ambivalent
(paragraph 7)

am·biva·lence (am biv′ə ləns) *n.* ⟦AMBI- + VALENCE⟧ simultaneous conflicting feelings toward a person or thing, as love and hate: also [Chiefly Brit.] **am·biv′a·lency** —**am·biv′a·lent** *adj.* —**am·biv′a·lently** *adv.*

anathema
(paragraph 28)

anath·ema (ə nath′ə mə) *n., pl.* ··**mas** ⟦LL(Ec) < Gr, thing devoted to evil; previously, anything devoted < *anatithenai*, to dedicate < *ana-*, up + *tithenai*, to place: see DO¹⟧ **1** a thing or person accursed or damned **2** a thing or person greatly detested **3** *a*) a solemn ecclesiastical condemnation of a teaching judged to be gravely opposed to accepted church doctrine, or of the originators or supporters of such a teaching *b*) the excommunication often accompanying or following this condemnation —*adj.* **1** greatly detested **2** viewed as accursed or damned **3** subjected to an ecclesiastical anathema

claustrophobics
(paragraph 22)

claustro·pho·bia (klôs′trə fō′bē ə) *n.* ⟦< L *claustrum* (see CLOISTER) + -PHOBIA⟧ an abnormal fear of being in an enclosed or confined place —**claus′tro·pho′·bic** *adj.*

Vocabulary List

229

Vocabulary List

contingent
(paragraph 26)

con·tin·gent (kən tin′jənt) *adj.* [L *contingens,* prp. of *contingere,* to touch: see CONTACT] **1** [Obs.] touching; tangential **2** that may or may not happen; possible **3** happening by chance; accidental; fortuitous **4** unpredictable because dependent on chance **5** dependent (*on* or *upon* something uncertain); conditional **6** *Logic* true only under certain conditions or in certain contexts; not always or necessarily true **7** *Philos.* not subject to determinism; free —*n.* **1** [Now Rare] an accidental or chance happening **2** a share or quota, as of troops, laborers, delegates, etc. **3** a group forming part of a larger group —con·tin′gent·ly *adv.*

euphemism
(paragraph 4)

eu·phe·mism (yōō′fə miz′əm) *n.* [Gr *euphēmismos* < *euphēmizein,* to use words of good omen < *euphēmos,* of good sound or omen < *eu-* (see EU-) + *phēmē,* voice < *phanai,* to say: see BAN[1]] **1** the use of a word or phrase that is less expressive or direct but considered less distasteful, less offensive, etc. than another **2** a word or phrase so substituted (Ex.: *remains* for *corpse*) —eu′·phe·mist *n.* —eu′·phe·mis′·tic *adj.* or eu′·phe·mis′·ti·cal —eu′·phe·mis′·ti·cally *adv.*

heresy
(paragraph 11)

her·esy (her′ə sē) *n., pl.* -sies [ME *heresie* < OFr < L *haeresis,* school of thought, sect, in LL(Ec), heresy < Gr *hairesis,* a taking, selection, school, sect, in LGr(Ec), heresy < *hairein,* to take] **1** *a*) a religious belief opposed to the orthodox doctrines of a church; esp., such a belief specifically denounced by the church *b*) the rejection of a belief that is a part of church dogma **2** any opinion (in philosophy, politics, etc.) opposed to official or established views or doctrines **3** the holding of any such belief or opinion

idyll
(paragraph 23)

idyll or idyl (īd′′l; *Brit* id′′l) *n.* [L *idyllium* < Gr *eidyllion,* dim. of *eidos,* a form, figure, image: see -OID] **1** a short poem or prose work describing a simple, peaceful scene of rural or pastoral life **2** a scene or incident suitable for such a work **3** a narrative poem somewhat like a short epic [Tennyson's *"Idylls* of the King"] **4** *Music* a simple, pastoral composition

lethargy
(paragraph 8)

leth·argy (leth′ər jē) *n.* [ME *litarge* < OFr < LL *lethargia* < Gr *lēthargia* < *lēthargos,* forgetful < *lēthē* (see LETHE) + *argos,* idle < *a-,* not + *ergon,* WORK] **1** a condition of abnormal drowsiness or torpor **2** a great lack of energy; sluggishness, dullness, apathy, etc.

mitigated
(paragraph 10)

miti·gate (mit′ə gāt′) *vt., vi.* -·gat·ed, -·gat·ing [ME *mitigaten* < L *mitigatus,* pp. of *mitigare,* to make mild, soft, or tender < *mitis,* soft (see MIGNON) + *agere,* to drive: see ACT[1]] **1** to make or become milder, less severe, less rigorous, or less painful; moderate **2** [< confusion with MILITATE] to operate or work (*against*): generally considered a loose or erroneous usage —*SYN.* RELIEVE —mit′i·gable (-i gə bəl) *adj.* —mit′i·ga′·tion *n.* —mit′i·ga′·tive *adj.* —mit′i·ga′·tor *n.* —mit′i·ga·to′ry (-gə tôr′ē) *adj.*

mundane
(paragraph 28)

mun·dane (mun′dān′, mun dān′) *adj.* [LME *mondeyne* < OFr *mondain* < LL *mundanus* < L *mundus,* world (in LL(Ec), the secular world, as opposed to the church)] **1** of the world; esp., worldly, as distinguished from heavenly, spiritual, etc. **2** commonplace, everyday, ordinary, etc. —*SYN.* EARTHLY —mun′·dane′ly *adv.* —mun′·dan′·ity (-dan′ə tē) *n., pl.* -·ties

proxy
(paragraph 14)

proxy (präk′sē) *n., pl.* prox′·ies [ME *prokecie,* contr. < *procuracie,* the function of a procurator, ult. < L *procuratio*] **1** the agency or function of a deputy **2** the authority to act for another **3** a document empowering a person to act for another, as in voting at a stockholders' meeting **4** a person empowered to act for another —*SYN.* AGENT

rhapsodized
(paragraph 4)

rhap·so·dize (-dīz′) *vi.* -·dized′, -·diz′·ing **1** to speak or write in an extravagantly enthusiastic manner **2** to recite or write rhapsodies —*vt.* to recite or utter as a rhapsody
rhap·sody (rap′sə dē) *n., pl.* -·dies [Fr *r(h)apsodie* < L *rhapsodia* < Gr *rhapsōidia* < *rhapsōidos,* one who strings songs together, reciter of epic poetry < *rhaptein,* to stitch together (< IE **werp-, *wrep-,* extension of base **wer-,* to turn, bend > WORM, WRAP, RAVEL) + *ōidē,* song: see ODE] **1** in ancient Greece, a part of an epic poem suitable for a single recitation **2** any ecstatic or extravagantly enthusiastic utterance in speech or writing **3** great delight;

shtick
(paragraph 30)

☆shtick (shtik) *n.* [< E Yiddish *shtik,* pl., pranks, interpreted as sing. < *shtik,* lit., piece < MHG *stücke*] [Slang] **1** a comic scene or piece of business, as in a vaudeville act **2** an attention-getting device **3** a special trait, talent, etc. Also sp. shtik

taboos
(paragraph 9)

ta·boo (tə bōō′, ta-) ***n., pl.*** **-·boos′** ⟦< a Polynesian language: cf. Tongan, Samoan, Maori, etc. *tapu*⟧ **1** *a*) among some Polynesian peoples, a sacred prohibition put upon certain people, things, or acts which makes them untouchable, unmentionable, etc. *b*) the highly developed system or practice of such prohibitions **2** *a*) any social prohibition or restriction that results from convention or tradition *b*) *Linguis.* the substitution of one word or phrase for another because of such restriction —***adj.*** **1** sacred and prohibited by taboo **2** restricted by taboo: said of people **3** prohibited or forbidden by tradition, convention, etc. —***vt.*** **-booed′, -boo′·ing 1** to put under taboo **2** to prohibit or forbid because of tradition, convention, etc.

therapeutic
(paragraph 11)

thera·peu·tic (ther′ə pyōōt′ik) ***adj.*** ⟦MqdL *therapeuticus* < Gr *therapeutikos* < *therapeutēs*, attendant, servant, one who treats medically < *therapeuein*, to nurse, treat medically⟧ **1** *a*) serving to cure or heal; curative *b*) serving to preserve health *[therapeutic abortion]* **2** of therapeutics Also **ther′a·peu′·ti·cal** —**ther′a·peu′·ti·cally *adv.***

16A   VOCABULARY

From the context of "Escaping the Daily Grind for Life as a House Father," explain the meaning of each of the vocabulary words shown in boldface below.

1. *From paragraph 4:* Thus was born my favorite **euphemism** for house fatherhood [. . .].

   less offensive expression

2. *From paragraph 4:* "Explained, yes. Defended. Even **rhapsodized** about."

   enthusiastically spoken

3. *From paragraph 7:* "And in the end, I still felt **ambivalent.**"

   conflicting feelings

4. *From paragraph 8:* "I had shattered my **lethargy** and stopped whining, and for that I was proud."

   lack of energy

5. *From paragraph 9:* "[. . .] the ultimate in middle-class **taboos.**"

   social restrictions

6. *From paragraph 10:* "The initial trauma of quitting, however, was **mitigated** by my eagerness to raise our son."

   made less severe

7. *From paragraph 11:* "I sensed that staying home would be **therapeutic**."

   healing

8. *From paragraph 11:* "This was **heresy** [. . .]."

   the rejection of a particular belief

9. *From paragraph 14:* "We had two salaries, a full-time nanny and guilt pangs over practicing parenthood by **proxy**."

   authorizing someone else to do the parenting

10. *From paragraph 22:* "House fathering is not for **claustrophobics**."

    people with an abnormal fear of being enclosed

11. *From paragraph 23:* "This is my **idyll**."

    peaceful scene of life

12. *From paragraph 26:* "[. . .] the stroller and backpack **contingent**."

    group

13. *From paragraph 28:* "[. . .] a softening, a contentment with small pleasures, the outwardly **mundane**."

    commonplace

14. *From paragraph 28:* "Ambition and competitiveness are **anathema**."

    detested

Name   Date

15. *From paragraph 30:* "He tries new words on me, new **shtick**."

comic expression

16B   CENTRAL THEME AND MAIN IDEAS

Choose the best answer.

__b__ 1. What is the central theme of "Escaping the Daily Grind for Life as a House Father"?
  a. More fathers should quit work to take care of their children.
  b. One man finds that raising a child can be as fulfilling an occupation as a traditional career.
  c. The author discovers that he is better at being a house father than at being a journalist.
  d. House fathering is a new occupation for fathers suffering from stress and job burnout.

2. In your own words, give the main idea of paragraph 18.

Older traditional parents view changes in traditional

male and female roles as a violation of the natural order.

3. In your own words, give the main idea of paragraph 28.

The change the author sees as a new effective at-home parent is a

softening—a release of workplace competitiveness and aggression.

__d__ 4. What is the main idea of paragraph 30?
  a. The author and his son enjoy spending quality time with each other.
  b. Radical lifestyle change is often beneficial for parents experiencing child-rearing stress.
  c. Children adapt well to changes in their lifestyles.
  d. The author has succeeded in getting to know his son as well as his mother does.

16C   MAJOR DETAILS

Decide whether each detail is MAJOR or MINOR based on the context of the reading selection.

MINOR 1. Some friends were envious about the author's lifestyle change.

MAJOR 2. The author was willing to be with his son until a better job came along, or indefinitely.

MAJOR 3. Because of his intense dislike of his job, the author felt that staying home with his son would be therapeutic.

MAJOR 4. The author usually got home from work too late to spend much time with his son.

MINOR 5. The author and his wife had a nanny.

MAJOR 6. The author felt excluded from the child-raising process.

MINOR 7. The author takes his son grocery shopping.

MINOR 8. The author was a daily journalist.

MAJOR 9. Now the author can stop his son's crying, too.

16D INFERENCES
Choose the right answer.

__b__ 1. *Read paragraph 4 again.* The author was tongue-tied because
 a. he thought his neighbor was too nosy.
 b. he was embarrassed to admit his new lifestyle.
 c. he did not want to explain in front of his son.
 d. he thought his wife should explain the situation.

__c__ 2. *Read paragraph 9 again.* Why did the author walk away from his boss's desk with wobbly knees?
 a. He was worried about his boss's reaction.
 b. He was shy about quitting his job.
 c. He was nervous about quitting his job.
 d. He did not think he would be good at house fathering.

__c__ 3. *Read paragraph 10 again.* Why does the author describe himself as "the man who got home after dark"?
 a. The author is making a sarcastic reference to the time he returns home from work.
 b. The author prefers not to use his real name in the article.
 c. Because of the author's work schedule, the son does not know his father nearly as well as he knows his mother.
 d. The author is making a social remark about the long hours he works.

__b__ 4. *Read paragraph 15 again.* The author's remark "And I wonder what comes next" suggests that he
 a. is hesitant about the change in his domestic responsibilities.
 b. is eager for the challenge of new experiences.
 c. resents the lowered expectations of house fathering.
 d. does not feel confident about the future.

Name   Date

___a___ 5. *Read paragraph 22 again.* House fathering is not for claustrophobics because claustrophobics
   a. would find staying at home every day too confining.
   b. enjoy working in small, confined areas.
   c. need to go to work every day in order to feel productive.
   d. feel the need to work with many people in a controlled setting.

___d___ 6. *Read paragraph 26 again.* "And then there's the rest of us" implies that the author
   a. is longing for his old job and sense of identity.
   b. views child care as a pastime requiring few skills or expertise.
   c. now identifies with a group of people who are not qualified for any other occupation.
   d. sees himself as part of a group having no particular mission or sense of purpose.

16E CRITICAL READING: FACT OR OPINION

Decide whether each statement, even if it quotes someone, contains a FACT or an OPINION.

OPINION 1. *From paragraph 7:* "This was a radical change that seemed to carry as many drawbacks as benefits."

FACT 2. *From paragraph 9:* "Some friends said they were envious."

FACT 3. *From paragraph 10:* "It hurt when I couldn't quiet his crying."

FACT 4. *From paragraph 11:* "Something better would emerge, something less obnoxious."

OPINION 5. *From paragraph 15:* "With me at home, her work hours are more flexible."

16F CRITICAL READING: THE WRITER'S CRAFT
Choose the best answer.

___c___ 1. The use of short sentences and often one-sentence paragraphs is customary in newspaper reporting. The presence of that style in this selection indicates that the author
   a. is concerned with the difficulty level of the selection.
   b. is unfamiliar with a more sophisticated method of composition.
   c. is writing as he has been trained to do as a daily journalist.
   d. is writing in a style indicative of his subject matter.

__a__ 2. The author's tone in paragraph 30 is
   a. proud and optimistic.
   b. conceited yet enthusiastic.
   c. bewildered but hopeful.
   d. exasperated but fascinated.

16G   READER RESPONSE: TO DISCUSS OR TO WRITE ABOUT

1. If you are a male, explain how you would feel about becoming a house father, one who stays at home to raise your child(ren) while your wife works outside the home. If you are a female, explain how you would feel about working outside the home while your husband stayed at home and cared for your child(ren).

2. Do you believe that raising a child can be as fulfilling an occupation as a traditional career? Explain.

3. In order to meet their financial obligations, in many families both the husband and the wife often work outside the home and leave their child(ren) in day care centers. What effects do you think this has on the children—emotionally, educationally, and socially? Use specific examples to support your point of view.

How Did You Do?   16   Escaping the Daily Grind for Life as a House Father

SKILL (number of items)	Number Correct		Points for Each		Score
Vocabulary (15)	_____	×	2	=	_____
Central Theme and Main Ideas (4)	_____	×	4	=	_____
Major Details (9)	_____	×	2	=	_____
Inferences (6)	_____	×	3	=	_____
Critical Reading: Fact or Opinion (5)	_____	×	2	=	_____
Critical Reading: The Writer's Craft (2)	_____	×	4	=	_____

(Possible Total: 100) *Total* _____

SPEED

Reading Time: _____ Reading Rate (page 398): _____ Words Per Minute

Name   Date

Selection 17

Forty Acres and a Holiday

Lisa Jones

(1) There are three legends told of how enslaved Africans in the Texas territory came to know of their freedom, and why the word didn't get to them until two months after the Civil War ended, which was a good two and half years after Lincoln's Emancipation Proclamation. Or, to make it plain, rather late. One legend says the messenger, a black Union soldier, was murdered. Another says he arrived, but had been delayed by mule travel. (A variation on this is that he had stopped to get married.) The third and favored is that the news was withheld by white landowners so they could bleed one last crop from slave labor. What is held as fact is that June nineteenth—the day that federal troops rode into Galveston with orders to release those kept as slaves—has been celebrated for 127 years, in Texas and beyond, as Emancipation Day, as Jubilation day, as Juneteenth. The day the last ones heard.

(2) Juneteenth, the name, is one of those fab African-Americanisms, functional, rhythmic, at once concise and not too concise. It fuses the month of June with the number nineteen, and alludes to the fact that the holiday was held in adjoining states on different days of the month as folks got the word. Early emancipation rituals were not exclusive to Texas (South Carolina and Mississippi's fall in May)—or to the South. What may have been the first emancipation ceremony was held in New York as early as 1808 to mark the legal cessation of the slave trade.

(3) No state comes close to Juneteenth in Texas, the black folks' Fourth of July, with its parades, feasting, pageants, and preachifying. Emancipation day organizations in Texas date back to the turn of the century. The most powerful image from the early days must have been former slaves themselves, who, according to tradition, marched together at the end of parade lines. By the 1950s Juneteenth Day came to be linked with, not freedom from slavery, but segregation. On Juneteenth, Texas's Jim Crow cities would allow blacks to be citizens for twelve hours a year by granting them entry into whites-only parks and zoos. With the passage of civil rights legislation in the sixties, refined black Texans abandoned Juneteenth to their country cousins and took to celebrating Independence Day in July along with their white brethren.

(4) A Juneteenth renaissance has been gathering steam since the mid eighties, spurred by the Afrocentricity crusade. Beyond being a hootenanny for black Texas (the condescending folksy portrait favored by the local press), it's become a holiday eagerly adopted nationwide by African Americans in search of cultural signposts. Not to mention one that offers, as is required these days, a dramatic tube-and-T-shirt-friendly sound bite

Miss Juneteenth, Deneka Dove, waves to parade watchers on June 19, 2001, in Austin, Texas.

© AP/World Wide Photos

of black history. The J-Day momentum is due in large part to the efforts of a man you might call Daddy Juneteenth, state representative Al Edwards from Houston. Edwards sponsored the bill that made Juneteenth an official Texas holiday thirteen years ago, a feat in a state that still closes banks for Confederate Heroes Day. Juneteenth U.S.A., Edwards's organization, tracks J-Day rites across the county and is fundraising for a national educational headquarters. To Edwards the holiday has tremendous secular and sacred promise. He sees it as an economic vehicle for African Americans, as well as a day that should be observed with almost holy remembrance: "The Jews say if they ever forget their history, may their tongues cleave to the roof of their mouth. . . . Let the same happen to us."

(5) You can find Juneteenth rituals in all regions of the country now. States like California, where Texans migrated en masse, have held Juneteenth festivities for decades. The New York area's largest is in Buffalo, tapping into upstate's rich history of antislavery activity. Wisconsin counts at least five, including Milwaukee's, where Juneteenth has been celebrated since 1971 and is the best attended single-day cultural event in the state. Far from being family picnics, these festivals sometimes last for days, made possible by the legwork of community groups, city cooperation, and private sector donations. Juneteenth in Minneapolis, now

in its seventh year, is building a rep as one of the most progressive and trend setting J-Day celebrations in the Texas diaspora. What began as a poetry reading in a church basement is now two weeks of programming, including a film festival and an Underground Railroad reenactment. At these celebrations old world often knocks against new world, when Miss Juneteenth pageants (inherited from towns like Brenham, Texas, which crowns a "Goddess of Liberty") share the stage with Afro-chic street fairs ablaze in faux kente.

(6) There are those who think Juneteenth is an embarrassment. That the holiday tells more of our ignorance and subjugation than of an inheritance that predates slavery in the Americas. Or that it's "too black" because it promotes a separate but not equal Fourth of July, or "not black enough" as it's often funded by white purses. And of course that it's far too symbolic and doesn't solve anything. What does a Juneteenth celebration mean anyway when the Freedman's Bureau never gave us our forty acres and a mule? (Not thrilled about news of the state holiday, one former Texas legislator had this to say: "Dancing up and down the streets, drinking red soda water, eating watermelons . . . I grew out of that.") But Juneteenth critics haven't put a dent in the holiday's grass-roots popularity.

(7) Folks are hungrier than ever for rituals that enshrine our identity as hyphen Americans. Kwanzaa's metamorphosis in the last few years speaks to this need. And merchandising opportunities are never far behind: Evolving in two short decades from cultural nationalist position paper to mainstream ethnic festival profiled in the *Times*'s Living Section. Kwanzaa has spawned its own designer cookbook and Santa surrogate, Father Kwanzaa. Now Juneteenth spreads like spring fever. Also gaining steam are rites of passage ceremonies for young men and women that are based on ancient African models and seek to address modern urban ills. (The National Rites of Passage Organization held its fifth annual conference this year.) And spotted last year in *Sage: A Scholarly Journal on Black Women*: plans for a Middle Passage memorial holiday that would fall near Thanksgiving.

(8) Buried in their shopping ethos, we tend to forget holidays were once holy days that once defined us in more profound ways than what Nintendo jumbo pack we got for Christmas. Michael Chaney, an arts activist in Minneapolis, believes that Juneteenth rituals could be more than acts of racial communion; they could have a role in redefining America: "We have to realize our own role as historians. We need to ascribe our treasures and offer them to the world. Juneteenth should be a day for all Americans to get in touch with the Africanism within."

(9) Juneteenth does have great possibilities as a new American holiday. Along with reuniting blood relatives, the families that emancipated slaves made embraced family beyond kin, family as community. In this tradition, modern Juneteenth doesn't circumscribe any Dick-and-Jane paean to the nuclear family. You can be a single parent, gay, from D.C. or Ann Arbor; it's a history that includes you. You can read the Emancipation Proclamation

out loud or drink some red soda water if you damn please. Or just take a moment out of your day to think about all the folks that laid down nothing less than their lives so that you could see the twentieth century.

(1,235 words)

Vocabulary List

Here are some of the more difficult words in "Forty Acres and a Holiday."

cessation
(paragraph 2)

ces·sa·tion (se sā′shən) *n.* [L *cessatio* < pp. of *cessare*, CEASE] a ceasing, or stopping, either forever or for some time

Diaspora
(paragraph 5)

Di·as·po·ra (dī as′pə rə) *n.* [Gr *diaspora*, a scattering < *diasperein*, to scatter < *dia-*, across + *speirein*, to sow: see SPORE] **1** *a*) the dispersion of the Jews after the Babylonian Exile *b*) the Jews thus dispersed *c*) the places where they settled **2** [d-] any scattering of people with a common origin, background, beliefs, etc.

emancipation
(paragraph 1)

eman·ci·pate (ē man′sə pāt′, i-) *vt.* ··pat′ed, ··pat′ing [< L *emancipatus*, pp. of *emancipare* < *e-*, out + *mancipare*, to deliver up or make over as property < *manceps*, purchaser < *manus*, the hand (see MANUAL) + *capere*, to take (see HAVE)] **1** to set free (a slave, etc.); release from bondage, servitude, or serfdom **2** to free from restraint or control, as of social convention **3** *Law* to release (a child) from parental control and supervision —*SYN.* FREE —**eman′·ci·pa′·tion** *n.* —**eman′·ci·pa′·tive** *adj.* or **eman′·ci·pa·to′ry** (-pe tôr′ē) —**eman′·ci·pa′·tor** *n.*

ethos
(paragraph 8)

ethos (ē′thäs′) *n.* [Gr *ēthos*, disposition, character: see ETHICAL] the characteristic and distinguishing attitudes, habits, beliefs, etc. of an individual or of a group

hootenanny
(paragraph 4)

☆**hooten·anny** (ho͞ot′′n an′ē) *n.*, *pl.* ··nies [orig. in sense of "dingus," "thingamajig"; a fanciful coinage] a meeting of folk singers, as for public entertainment

Jim Crow
(paragraph 3)

☆**Jim Crow** [name of an early black minstrel song] [*also* j- c-] [Informal] traditional discrimination against or segregation of blacks, esp. in the U.S. —**Jim′-Crow′** *vt.*, *adj.* —**Jim Crow′·ism′**

metamorphosis
(paragraph 7)

meta·mor·pho·sis (-môr′fə sis, -môr fō′sis) *n.*, *pl.* ··ses′ (-sēz′) [L < Gr *metamorphōsis* < *metamorphoun*, to transform, transfigure < *meta*, over (see META-) + *morphē*, form, shape] **1** *a*) change of form, shape, structure, or substance; transformation, as, in myths, by magic or sorcery *b*) the form resulting from such change **2** a marked or complete change of character, appearance, condition, etc. **3** *Biol.* a change in form, structure, or function as a result of development; specif., the physical transformation, more or less sudden, undergone by various animals during development after the embryonic state, as of the larva of an insect to the pupa and the pupa to the adult, or of the tadpole to the frog **4** *Med.* a pathological change of form of some tissues

paean
(paragraph 9)

paean (pē′ən) *n.* [L < Gr *paian*, hymn < *Paian*, the healing one, epithet of Apollo < *paiein*, to strike, touch < ? IE base *pēu-* > PAVE] **1** in ancient Greece, a hymn of thanksgiving to the gods, esp. to Apollo **2** a song of joy, triumph, praise, etc.

240

renaissance
(paragraph 4)

ren·ais·sance (ren′ə säns′, -zäns′; ren′ə säns′, -zäns′; *chiefly Brit* ri nā′səns) *n.* ⟦Fr < *renaître*, to be born anew < OFr *renestre* < *re-* + VL **nascere*, for L *nasci*, to be born: see GENUS⟧ **1** a new birth; rebirth; renascence **2** *a)* [R-] the style and forms of art, literature, architecture, etc. of the Renaissance *b)* [*often* R-] any revival of art, literature, or learning similar to the Renaissance —*adj.* [R-] **1** of, characteristic of, or in the style of the Renaissance **2** designating or of a style of architecture developed in Italy and western Europe between 1400 and 1600, characterized by the revival and adaptation of classical orders and design —**the Renaissance 1** the great revival of art, literature, and learning in Europe in the 14th, 15th, and 16th cent., based on classical sources: it began in Italy and spread gradually to other countries and marked the transition from the medieval world to the modern **2** the period of this revival

rituals
(paragraph 2)

ritu·al (rich′o͞o əl) *adj.* ⟦L *ritualis*⟧ of, having the nature of, or done as a rite or rites *[ritual dances]* —*n.* **1** a set form or system of rites, religious or otherwise **2** the observance of set forms or rites, as in public worship **3** a book containing rites or ceremonial forms **4** a practice, service, or procedure done as a rite, especially at regular intervals **5** ritual acts or procedures collectively —*SYN.* CEREMONY —**rit′u·ally** *adv.*

secular
(paragraph 4)

secu·lar (sek′yə lər) *adj.* ⟦ME *seculer* < OFr < LL(Ec) *saecularis*, worldly, profane, heathen < L, of an age < *saeculum*, an age, generation < IE **seitlo-* < base **sei-*, to scatter, SOW²⟧ **1** *a)* of or relating to worldly things as distinguished from things relating to church and religion; not sacred or religious; temporal; worldly *[secular* music, *secular* schools*] b)* of or marked by secularism; secularistic **2** ordained for a diocese **3** *a)* coming or happening only once in an age or century *b)* lasting for an age or ages; continuing for a long time or from age to age —*n.* **1** a cleric ordained for a diocese **2** a person not a cleric; layman —**sec′u·larly** *adv.*

subjugation
(paragraph 6)

sub·ju·gate (sub′jə gāt′) *vt.* --gat′ed, --gat′ing ⟦ME *subiugaten* < L *subjugatus*, pp. of *subjugare*, to bring under the yoke < *sub-*, under + *jugum*, YOKE⟧ **1** to bring under control or subjection; conquer **2** to cause to become subservient; subdue —*SYN.* CONQUER —**sub′·ju·ga′·tion** *n.* —**sub′·ju·ga′·tor** *n.*

17A VOCABULARY
Choose the best answer.

__d__ 1. The **cessation** of the slave trade meant it was
   a. discussed.
   b. celebrated.
   c. approved.
   d. stopped.

__c__ 2. Lincoln's **Emancipation** Proclamation concerned the slaves'
   a. capture.
   b. disobedience.
   c. freedom.
   d. duties.

__b__ 3. A **hootenanny** involves a gathering of
   a. marchers.
   b. singers.
   c. dancers.
   d. demonstrators.

Name   Date

    a   4. **Subjugation** of a people indicates that the group has been
        a. conquered.
        b. honored.
        c. released.
        d. subdivided.

    c   5. A **paean** is a song of
        a. love.
        b. hate.
        c. joy.
        d. sadness.

    d   6. **Secular** refers to things that are
        a. religious.
        b. secretive.
        c. expensive.
        d. worldly.

    b   7. **Diaspora** is a word used to refer to people who have
        a. rebelled.
        b. scattered.
        c. assembled.
        d. disappeared.

    a   8. **Rituals** are ceremonies that involve
        a. a set form.
        b. a debate.
        c. a rehearsal.
        d. candlesticks.

    a   9. **Ethos** as used in this essay means
        a. habit.
        b. purpose.
        c. bargain.
        d. celebration.

    c   10. **Jim Crow** is a term used to refer to the policy of
        a. integration.
        b. migration.
        c. segregation.
        d. compensation.

    b   11. **Renaissance** as used in this essay means
        a. festival.
        b. revival.
        c. holiday.
        d. revolt.

Name   Date

___d___ 12. A **metamorphosis** occurs when something undergoes a noticeable
    a. destruction.
    b. control.
    c. restoration.
    d. change.

17B   CENTRAL THEME AND MAIN IDEAS

Choose the best answer.

___c___ 1. What is the central theme of "Forty Acres and a Holiday"?
    a. Lincoln's Emancipation Proclamation freed the slaves in territories still at war with the Union.
    b. Juneteenth gets its name from a combination of June and the number nineteen.
    c. Celebrated for over one hundred years, Juneteenth has increased in popularity as an American holiday to acknowledge the freeing of the slaves.
    d. Juneteenth is the oldest known celebration of the ending of slavery.

___d___ 2. What is the main idea of paragraph 1?
    a. Texas, as well as other states, has celebrated June nineteenth for over 127 years in recognition of the Emancipation Proclamation.
    b. President Abraham Lincoln issued the Emancipation Proclamation during the Civil War to free the slaves.
    c. Federal troops arrived in Galveston, Texas, on June 19 to free those slaves still in bondage.
    d. Three legends have been passed down to explain why Lincoln's Emancipation Proclamation failed to reach Texas until two and a half years after its issue.

___b___ 3. What is the main idea of paragraph 6?
    a. The Freedmen's Bureau did not give forty acres and a mule to the freed slaves.
    b. There are those who think Juneteenth is an embarrassment.
    c. Juneteenth is a state holiday in Texas.
    d. One of the most vocal critics of the Juneteenth holiday is a former Texas state legislator.

17C MAJOR DETAILS

Decide whether each detail is MAJOR or MINOR based on the context of the reading selection.

MINOR 1. The black Union soldier was late bringing news of the Emancipation Proclamation to Texas because he stopped en route to marry.

MAJOR 2. Federal troops arrived in Galveston on June 19 with the news that the slaves were freed.

MINOR 3. South Carolina and Mississippi celebrate the freeing of the slaves in May.

MAJOR 4. In the 1950s, Juneteenth Day came to be linked with segregation, not slavery.

MINOR 5. One way African Americans in Texas celebrate Juneteenth is with a hootenanny.

MAJOR 6. Texas state representative Al Edwards sponsored a bill that made Juneteenth an official state holiday in 1980.

MINOR 7. A Miss Juneteenth pageant is part of the Juneteenth celebration in Texas.

17D INFERENCES

Choose the best answer.

___c___ 1. *Read paragraph 3 again.* In the early parade, the former slaves marched at the end of parade lines because
   a. they were too weak to keep the fast pace of the younger participants.
   b. the spectators wanted to see the dancers, musicians, floats, and honored guests first.
   c. their presence served as a lasting reminder to the onlookers of the significance of the celebration.
   d. they could not afford to buy showier clothes expected to be worn by parade participants.

___d___ 2. *Read paragraph 5 again.* Why are two of the largest celebrations now in Milwaukee and Minneapolis?
   a. These cities now have a black majority population.
   b. Attendees prefer to celebrate in the cooler climate of Wisconsin and Minnesota.
   c. Employers, both state and private, give employees the day off.
   d. These cities have sound financial backing and support to offer a wide range of activities.

Name   Date

_d_ 3. In paragraph 5, the "faux kente" seen at the Afro-chic street fairs
is popular for all of these reasons *except*
a. it is traditional African dress.
b. it reminds African Americans of their ancestry.
c. it is brightly-colored material.
d. it is inexpensive and comfortable.

_b_ 4. In paragraph 7, the word *hyphen* in the phrase "hyphen Americans" suggests any people who seek to
a. hide their ethnic identity.
b. emphasize their ethnic identity.
c. recognize their ethnic language.
d. promote their ethnic holidays.

17E   CRITICAL READING: FACT OR OPINION

Decide whether each statement, even if it quotes someone, contains a FACT or an OPINION.

OPINION 1. *From paragraph 2:* "Juneteenth, the name, is one of those fab African-Americanisms, functional, rhythmic, at once concise and not too concise."

OPINION 2. *From paragraph 3:* "No state comes close to Juneteenth in Texas, the black folks' Fourth of July, with its parades, feasting, pageants, and preachifying."

FACT 3. *From paragraph 4:* "To Edwards the holiday has tremendous secular and sacred promise."

FACT 4. *From paragraph 5:* "What began as a poetry reading in a church basement is now two weeks of programming, including a film festival and an Underground Railroad reenactment."

FACT 5. *From paragraph 6:* "Dancing up and down the streets, drinking red soda water, eating watermelons [. . .] I grew out of that."

FACT 6. *From paragraph 7:* "Kwanzaa has spawned its own designer cookbook and Santa surrogate, Father Kwanzaa."

17F   CRITICAL READING: THE WRITER'S CRAFT

Choose the best answer.

__c__ 1. Why did the author begin by recounting the legends of how slaves in Texas learned of their freedom?
  a. To give the reader confidence that the author researched her topic well
  b. To prove that no one knows for certain the reason that the news was so long in reaching Texas
  c. To prove that a legend is more likely to be remembered than the actual fact of the federal troops' arrival
  d. To conceal the truth that there were not enough Union troops in Texas to enforce the Emancipation Proclamation

__b__ 2. The overall tone of "Forty Acres and a Holiday" is
  a. suspicious and unforgiving.
  b. informative and inspiring.
  c. annoyed and gloomy.
  d. prejudiced and hostile.

17G   READER RESPONSE: TO DISCUSS OR TO WRITE ABOUT

1. On June 19, 1865, Major General Gordon Granger arrived in Galveston, Texas, with the news that the Civil War had ended and that the slaves were free. Describe what you think may have been the reactions to this news from the standpoint of the former masters or the former slaves. Was it shock? Jubilation? Why did many of the free men and women leave Texas and head north? What social, educational, and/or economic challenges would they have faced?

2. The spot where General Granger read General Order Number 3, which announced the repeal of slavery, was at the corner of 22nd and Strand in Galveston. There is no marker there as yet to commemorate this date and event. Assume the local historical society has asked you to create a marker for this location. What would the marker say?

3. Every ethnic group has certain traditions or celebrations that it recognizes and observes. Describe one that either you or your family participates in. Does it relate to a specific event in history? Is it participated in by people of other races? Does it involve special outdoor activities, food, ceremonies, contests, parades, speeches, or gifts? Be specific as to how you observe this tradition or celebration.

Name   Date

How Did You Do?　　　**17**　Forty Acres and a Holiday

SKILL *(number of items)*	Number Correct		Points for Each		Score
Vocabulary (12)	_____	×	2	=	_____
Central Theme and Main Ideas (3)	_____	×	5	=	_____
Major Details (7)	_____	×	3	=	_____
Inferences (4)	_____	×	4	=	_____
Critical Reading: Fact or Opinion (6)	_____	×	3	=	_____
Critical Reading: The Writer's Craft (2)	_____	×	3	=	_____

(Possible Total: 100) *Total*　_____

SPEED

Reading Time: _____ Reading Rate (page 398): _____ Words Per Minute

---

Name　　　　　　　　　　　Date　　　　　　　247

Selection 18

Out of Their Element

Bob Akin

(1) The oil field was the world, and Houston in the late '70s was just the place for a new college graduate. After finding work downtown, I searched for housing that was close and cheap. Just south of Richmond on Mandell, I stood before a somewhat disjointed, three-story red-brick house hiding behind two enormous sycamores. A three-story house was an oddity in the neighborhood, or anywhere in Houston, and it had a loosely hung-together look as though the architect could not quite make the pieces fit. I walked down the driveway on the right to the back, where two buildings of garage apartments filled the lot.

(2) Annie was a compact, gray-haired woman whose carriage belied a strength acquired from many years of work. She mounted the hall stairs and opened a door to the left to show me a small, modest one-bedroom apartment. "I clean on Tuesdays and Fridays. Just leave the trash outside in the hall," she said. I liked the soft resonance in her voice. She took my check and gave me the key.

(3) Downtown Houston was a panorama of sleek banks, stores and oil companies. Everywhere, the glossy opulence of new steel and glass testified to the city's wealth. I chatted with the clerks at Foley's and the counterman at James' Coney Island, but I was aware that they were really too busy to visit. Surrounded by people, I knew virtually no one. When sunset turned the streets into great purple canyons, I felt an acute pang for my old small-town university neighborhood. There, we swapped news on front porches in the evenings, knew everybody who lived around us and dropped by to visit without calling, except on Sunday mornings. Familiarity so long taken for granted was now a precious commodity that I lacked. I reminded myself that meeting new people and making friends took time, but the feelings of isolation and aloneness would sometimes nag at me like bad children. My head understood that new characters in the common story were out there, but my voice had not yet found a kindred spirit to talk to.

(4) Mellow fall turned to frosty winter that year. I came home one damp, fog-glazed night to find a badly rumpled *People* magazine outside my door. After dinner, I thumbed through it absently while Fleetwood Mac kept me company. The articles were dull until I came across one about an older couple who kept a pet gorilla in their house. They had acquired him in South Africa, having spent some 30 years there as missionaries. The great ape was orphaned while still an infant. They adopted him and, unable to part with their surrogate child, brought him back to the United States. A gorilla in the house was an exotic and ridiculous idea that intrigued me. Like a lightning bolt, the faces in the picture on the page leapt

This gorilla is what Hugo looked like.

Bruce Coleman, Inc.

out at me. Annie and her husband, Charlie, glowed with their proud adoptee, Hugo. Surely there was some mistake. Yet the article clearly identified the couple, the neighborhood and the city. A 500-pound, fully grown male jungle gorilla was living not 30 feet from my doorstep. I was delirious with amazement.

(5) I raced down the stairs but slowed to a creep at the back door to the house. No lights reflected from the windows. Circling the house like a thief, I peered for a clue to its primordial resident. Visions from *Murders in the Rue Morgue* danced on the porch roofs and gables. With a seminaked beauty slung over his shoulder, Hugo arced the rooftops like the champion in a silent movie. My straining ears heard only the muted night, wet rubber on asphalt. Daylight would come before my curiosity could be satisfied.

(6) Annie's smile was practiced and indulgent. The acrobats in my stomach were doing somersaults as the anticipation of a new first experience made me giddy. Bright February sun made the house's interiors seem old, dark and faded. Where does one keep a gorilla in the house?

(7) Annie led me through two short hall-ways into their living room. "He's quite intelligent, really. About the same as a 4 to 5-year-old child. When he first sees you, he'll make an awful rumpus, but you mustn't let on that you're afraid. If you do, he'll never stop. Just stand quietly, and in a few minutes he'll come to the window to get a good look at you." My heart felt like the congas that Hugo must have heard when he was growing up. We crossed the room to a window set in the far end of a wall facing the rear of the house. Through the window I saw a large, wide room made of concrete with steel bars to the left. Severed tree trunks, a few boulders and hanging ropes filled the space. A tire swing on a hemp-style cable hung from the ceiling. At the far end, Hugo sat playing with a small object that I could not see. When Annie spoke to him, his great head swung around sharply, and for a moment he froze, cutting his eyes straight at me. He rose slowly and then charged toward the window at full speed, slamming into it with a thunderous sound. He bellowed with rage, pounded his chest and threw himself around the caged room, smashing into everything in his path. He attacked the window again to roar and beat the bars. I was fairly shocked in place and too riveted to move or speak. He leapt on the steel bars to the left and rocketed himself back and forth, screaming his displeasure. He jumped to the ledges on the right wall, up and down, over and over, beating the walls and floor with his fists, his arms, his whole body. Hugo rammed the window again, those fierce explosive eyes piercing through me. Then he stopped.

(8) Hugo backed away from the window to the center of the room, where he circled slowly and dropped to all fours, his roadwide back a perfect horizontal to the ground. He crept to the window and, swaying his head ever so slightly, examined me with cool interest. Those enormous shining black eyes regarded me with what seemed like amusement, as though I was the object of curiosity. As we stared at each other, I could see reflected in his eyes some fixtures in the room, the old chair and standing brass lamp next to me, and finally, an outline image of myself. Hugo became so still that it was almost like looking into an ebony mirror. What did he see? What pictures and sounds coursed through his childlike consciousness? For an undefined moment, the bars, the window, the room and all around me were swept away, and I was the entity out of place in the gray-green twilight of his rain forest, a world without mechanism or man. Hugo's delicate breathing and primal scent were thick on my skin. His quixotic smile held me transfixed.

(9) Annie's returning voice made me realize that she had not been there for some time. "His favorite foods are spaghetti, ice cream and potato chips. He's particularly fond of bright, shiny things that move or make noise. I think he likes you," Annie said, busying herself around the room while I slowly came back to my senses. "We used to go inside the cage to play with him but not anymore. The last time Charlie went in, it took a whole day for him to get out. Hugo didn't want to let him go. Lonely, you know. We finally distracted him with Charlie's watch. He still has it in

there." Hugo and I wondered at each other a bit longer, and then I left; it was Hugo's dinnertime.

(10) Hugo visited my consciousness often in the following days and weeks; he would peer out at me from the low branches of ancient magnolias, look over my shoulder at the coffee machine in the office or widen his eyes from behind the banana display at Weingarten's. Annie invited me into the hall that ran parallel to Hugo's room. "You mustn't get close enough for him to touch you. He's liable to take your arm and not want to let go." "How old is he?" I asked. "About 17, middle-aged for a gorilla."

(11) In Hugo's room I saw items I had not noticed before: pillows, quilts, blankets, and a storehouse of toys and stuffed animals. The pallet where he slept looked thick and comfortable. Candy bar wrappers and a potato chip bag peeked out from under a large grinning Snoopy Dog. "Do you think you will ever get another ape for Hugo, a friend, or maybe a mate?" "Heavens no. He costs a fortune to feed as it is. Besides, there really isn't room." "Will Hugo ever return to the wild? I mean, do you ever plan to go back to Africa?" Annie's voice was gentle and patient. "Hugo couldn't survive in the wild. We have always taken care of him. Our other children here come and go, but Hugo stays. He's happy here."

(12) An odd assortment of people, as seemingly disjointed as the house itself, lived in Annie's and Charlie's rooms. A neighbor had told me that they were mostly foster children or transients who were fighting addiction, criminal records or mental illness. It came as no surprise. Annie and Charlie were childless. Being their child had doomed Hugo to a lifetime of imprisonment.

(13) Hugo crept to the bars like a timid child. Less than five feet from me, he arched his head up and sniffed the air. He gently curled his mammoth hands around the bars and eyed me while rocking his head. He cocked that massive skull to one side as coyly as a debutante. I smiled. The sense of his presence awed one, like the roar of Niagara Falls or a star-riddled summer night. His movement was small and precise, a ballet dancer possessed of delicately cathartic destruction. He settled on the floor to groom his fur with patient fingers, an invitation for me to come closer. The pull to touch that luminous giant was fearsome and magnetic. Finished with her chores, Annie called me to follow her back into the living room.

(14) A rainy Tuesday afternoon found me sitting outside Hugo's room watching him watch me. A great, fine figure of his species, in the wild he would have possessed a harem of females. But there would be no offspring, no son of Hugo to reflect his image back to him. My sense of isolation dwindled in the shadow of his life.

(15) I would visit Hugo several times, but as weeks turned into months, my new city life demanded more and more attention. Dates, business dinners and Astros games with new buddies took the place of long evening walks and time with Hugo.

(16) My solitary walls had melted, but he was still alone. He did not seem unhappy, yet I wondered if Annie and Charlie felt that the price he

had paid was worth it to them. For a while, Hugo gave me something above an awareness of the value of freedom—a sublime sense of choice.

(17) Heavy rains came with spring, and one wet day I met Annie sweeping damp leaves from the driveway. Hugo had come down with pneumonia during the last torrential flooding. An elderly veterinarian had shot Hugo with a pellet of antibiotics from outside the bars of his room. Much sicker than even Annie and Charlie had realized, Hugo had gone to sleep, never to wake up.

(18) Enough years have passed that every picture or mention of monkeys, apes, orangutans or gorillas does not conjure up Hugo's ghost. Yet sometimes he comes at odd moments, like an old friend who just dropped by to look into my face and see how I am doing. I remember Hugo's scent, his size, his gentle childlike movement and some intangible conundrum. What fascinated me most even then were Hugo's eyes. They still do.

(2,008 words)

Here are some of the more difficult words in "Out of Their Element."

carriage
(paragraph 2)

car·riage (kar′ij; *for 2, usually* kar′ē ij′) *n.* ⟦ME *cariage*, baggage, transport < Anglo-Fr, cart, carriage < *carier*, CARRY⟧ **1** the act of carrying; transportation **2** the cost of carrying; transportation charge **3** [Archaic] *a*) management or handling *b*) conduct; behavior **4** manner of carrying the head and body; posture; bearing **5** *a*) a four-wheeled passenger vehicle, usually horse-drawn and often private *b*) *short for* BABY CARRIAGE **6** [Brit.] a railroad passenger car **7** a wheeled frame or support for something heavy [a gun *carriage*] **8** a moving part (of a machine) for supporting and shifting something [the *carriage* of a typewriter] —*SYN.* BEARING

commodity
(paragraph 3)

com·mod·i·ty (kə mäd′ə tē) *n., pl.* **-ties** ⟦ME & OFr *commodite*, benefit, profit < L *commoditas*, fitness, adaptation < *commodus*: see COMMODE⟧ **1** any useful thing **2** anything bought and sold; any article of commerce **3** [*pl.*] basic items or staple products, as of agriculture or mining **4** [Archaic] personal advantage

conundrum
(paragraph 18)

co·nun·drum (kə nun′drəm) *n.* ⟦16th-c. Oxford University l. slang for pedant, whim, etc.; early sp. *quonundrum*⟧ **1** a riddle whose answer contains a pun (Ex.: "What's the difference between a jeweler and a jailer?" "One sells watches and the other watches cells.") **2** any puzzling question or problem —*SYN.* MYSTERY[1]

doomed
(paragraph 12)

doom[1] (do̅o̅m) *n.* ⟦ME & OE *dom*, lit., what is laid down, decree, akin to Goth *doms*, judgment < IE base **dhē-*: see DO[1]⟧ **1** [Historical] a statute; decree **2** a judgment; esp., a sentence of condemnation **3** destiny; fate **4** tragic fate; ruin or death **5** Judgment Day —*vt.* **1** to pronounce judgment on; condemn; sentence **2** to destine to a tragic fate **3** to ordain as a penalty —*SYN.* FATE

entity
(paragraph 8)

en·ti·ty (en′tə tē) *n., pl.* **-ties** ⟦< Fr *entité* or ML *entitas* < L *ens* (gen. *entis*), prp. of *esse*, to be: see IS[1]⟧ **1** being; existence **2** a thing that has definite, individual existence outside or within the mind; anything real in itself

luminous
(paragraph 13)

lu·mi·nous (lo̅o̅′mə nəs) *adj.* ⟦ME < L *luminosus* < *lumen*, LIGHT[1]⟧ **1** giving off light; shining; bright **2** filled with light; illuminated **3** glowing in the dark, as paint with a phosphor in it **4** clear; readily understood **5** intellectually brilliant —*SYN.* BRIGHT —**lu′·mi·nous·ly** *adv.* —**lu′·mi·nous·ness** *n.*

Vocabulary List

Vocabulary List

missionaries
(paragraph 4)

mis·sion·ary (-er'ē) *adj.* ⟦ModL (Ec) *missionarius*⟧ of or characteristic of missions or missionaries, esp. religious ones —*n., pl.* -**ar·ies** a person sent on a mission, esp. on a religious mission: also **mis'·sioner** (-ər)

opulence
(paragraph 3)

opu·lent (äp'yōō lənt, -yə-) *adj.* ⟦L *opulentus* or *opulens* < *ops*: see OPUS⟧ 1 very wealthy or rich 2 characterized by abundance or profusion; luxuriant —*SYN.* RICH —**op'u·lence** *n.* or **op'u·lency** — **op'u·lently** *adv.*

pang
(paragraph 3)

pang (paŋ) *n.* ⟦< ? LME *pronge*: see PRONG⟧ a sudden, sharp, and brief pain, physical or emotional; spasm of distress

panorama
(paragraph 3)

pano·rama (pan'ə ram'ə, -rä'mə) *n.* ⟦coined (*c.* 1789) by Robert Barker (1739-1806), Scot artist < PAN- + Gr *horama*, a view < *horan*, to see < IE base *wer-*, to heed > WARD, GUARD⟧ 1 *a*) a picture or series of pictures of a landscape, historical event, etc., presented on a continuous surface encircling the spectator; cyclorama *b*) a picture unrolled before the spectator in such a way as to give the impression of a continuous view 2 an unlimited view in all directions 3 a comprehensive survey of a subject 4 a continuous series of scenes or events; constantly changing scene —**pan'o·ram'ic** *adj.* —**pan'o·ram'i·cally** *adv.*

primordial
(paragraph 5)

pri·mor·dial (prī môr'dē əl) *adj.* ⟦ME < LL *primordialis* < L *primordium*, the beginning < *primus*, first (see PRIME) + *ordiri*, to begin (see ORDER)⟧ 1 first in time; existing at or from the beginning; primitive; primeval 2 not derivative; fundamental; original 3 *Biol.* earliest formed in the development of an organism, organ, structure, etc.; primitive —**pri·mor'·di·ally** *adv.*

quixotic
(paragraph 8)

quix·otic (kwik sät'ik) *adj.* 1 [*often* Q-] of or like Don Quixote 2 extravagantly chivalrous or foolishly idealistic; visionary; impractical or impracticable: also **quix·ot'i·cal** —**quix·ot'i·cally** *adv.*

rumpus
(paragraph 7)

rum·pus (rum'pəs) *n.* ⟦< ?⟧ [Informal] an uproar or commotion

sublime
(paragraph 16)

sub·lime (sə blīm') *adj.* ⟦L *sublimus* < *sub-*, up to + *limen*, lintel (hence, orig. up to the lintel): see LIMEN⟧ 1 noble; exalted; majestic 2 inspiring awe or admiration through grandeur, beauty, etc. 3 [Informal] outstandingly or supremely such [a man of *sublime* taste] 4 [Archaic] *a*) elated; joyful *b*) proud; lofty; haughty *c*) upraised; aloft —*vt.* -**limed'**, -**lim'·ing** ⟦ME *sublimen* < MFr *sublimer* < ML *sublimare* < L, to lift high < the adj.⟧ 1 to make sublime 2 SUBLIMATE (*vt.* 1) —*vi.* SUBLIMATE —**the sublime** sublime quality; sublimity —**sub·lime'ly** *adv.* —**sub·lime'·ness** *n.*

surrogate
(paragraph 4)

sur·ro·gate (sur'ə git, -gāt'; *for v.*, -gāt') *n.* ⟦L *surrogatus*, pp. of *surrogare*, to elect in place of another, substitute < *sub-* (see SUB-) + *rogare*, to ask: see ROGATION⟧ 1 a deputy or substitute ☆2 in some states, probate court, or a judge of this court 3 *Psychiatry* a substitute figure, esp. a person of some authority, who replaces a father or mother in one's feelings 4 a woman who, by prior agreement, becomes pregnant and bears a child for another woman, who will raise the child as its mother —*adj.* of or acting as a surrogate —*vt.* -**gat'ed**, -**gat'·ing** to put in another's place as a substitute or deputy

18A VOCABULARY

Using the dictionary entries on pages 253–254, fill in the blanks.

1. As he walked down the hospital corridor, his _____carriage_____ was that of a man in his 80s, not his 60s.

2. From the 110th floor of the Sears Tower in Chicago, people can see a _____panorama_____ of stores, hotels, restaurants, and office buildings.

3. As I drove through Chickasaw Gardens and saw the expensive cars in the driveways, I became aware of the neighborhood's _____opulence_____ .

4. The first time eight-year-old Meg slept over at a friend's home, she felt a _____pang_____ of homesickness.

5. When the electricity went off at night, the one _____commodity_____ I did not have was a flashlight.

6. The first Sunday of each month, the minister asks every church member to contribute two dollars to help support _____missionaries_____ in foreign countries.

7. After we bought the puppy, we put a stuffed sock to serve as a _____surrogate_____ mother in her cardboard box.

8. H. G. Wells wrote, " _____Primordial_____ man could have had little or no tradition before the development of speech."

9. My parents told my friends and me to play in the basement, so they would not hear the _____rumpus_____ we made.

10. In her grief, she had come to question her _____entity_____ .

11. In some New York restaurants, waiters exhibit _____quixotic_____ behavior by giving two menus: one with prices to the males and another without prices to their female companions.

12. Passengers aboard the *Titanic* were _____doomed_____ to a watery grave after the ship hit an iceberg.

13. As they drove along the beautiful Blue Ridge Parkway in Virginia, they found the view of the mountains _____ sublime _____ .

14. Many stars are more _____ luminous _____ than our sun.

15. A _____ conundrum _____ is a riddle whose answer involves a play on words, as in "When is a door, not a door? When it is 'ajar.'"

18B CENTRAL THEME AND MAIN IDEAS

Choose the best answer.

__b__ 1. What is the central theme of "Out of Their Element"?
   a. Annie and Charlie adopted a gorilla that had been orphaned in Africa.
   b. Hugo was intended to reside in the animal world, not the human world.
   c. Annie and Charlie's home was open to anyone without a place to live—even a gorilla.
   d. A gorilla makes a fascinating pet.

__b__ 2. What is the main idea of paragraph 3?
   a. Downtown Houston was a modern city with banks, stores, and oil companies.
   b. Raised in a small town, the author felt a sense of loneliness in a large city like Houston.
   c. Living in a small town is better than living in a large city.
   d. After moving to Houston, the author had difficulty making friends at first.

18C MAJOR DETAILS

Decide whether each detail is MAJOR or MINOR based on the context of the reading selection.

MINOR 1. Bob Akin was a recent college graduate.

MINOR 2. Annie cleaned the apartment on Tuesdays and Fridays.

MAJOR 3. Annie and Charlie were missionaries in Africa.

MAJOR 4. Bob Akin read in *People* magazine about a couple who kept a gorilla in their house.

MAJOR 5. Hugo's cage contained severed tree trunks, some boulders, hanging ropes, and a tire on a cable.

Name   Date

MAJOR 6. Upon seeing Bob Akin the first time, the gorilla bellowed with rage, pounded his chest, and leapt from one side of the cage to the other.

MINOR 7. Hugo's favorite foods were spaghetti, ice cream, and potato chips.

MAJOR 8. Hugo was seventeen years old.

MAJOR 9. Hugo would never have another gorilla for a friend or a mate.

MAJOR 10. Annie and Charlie were childless.

MAJOR 11. Hugo came down with pneumonia a few months after Bob Akin had met him.

MINOR 12. A veterinarian used a gun to shoot antibiotics into Hugo.

18D INFERENCES

Decide whether each statement below can be inferred (YES) or cannot be inferred (NO) from the reading selection.

NO 1. Bob Akin searched for housing near his work downtown because he did not own a car.

NO 2. In the early evenings, Bob Akin felt especially alone and longed to return to being a college student.

YES 3. Foley's, James' Coney Island, and Weingarten's were stores in Houston.

NO 4. Fleetwood Mac rented an apartment next door to Bob Akin.

YES 5. The window through which Bob Akin viewed Hugo had no glass.

YES 6. Although Hugo was powerful and strong, his movements and behavior at times appeared innocent and gentle to Bob Akin.

NO 7. If Bob Akin had gotten close enough for Hugo to touch him, Hugo would have bitten Akin's arm.

YES 8. Bob Akin believed Annie and Charlie should not have brought Hugo back from Africa and caged him in a private home.

NO 9. Torrential rains caused Hugo to develop pneumonia.

YES 10. Annie and Charlie treated Hugo as if he might have been their child.

18E CRITICAL READING: FACT OR OPINION
Decide whether each statement, even if it quotes someone, contains a FACT or an OPINION.

OPINION 1. *From paragraph 1:* Houston in the late 1970s was an ideal location for a recent college graduate.

FACT 2. *From paragraph 4:* The magazine article identified the couple, the neighborhood, and the city where the 500-pound gorilla lived.

OPINION 3. *From paragraph 7:* "He's quite intelligent, really. About the same as a 4 to 5-year-old child."

FACT 4. *From paragraph 8:* Bob Akin could see reflected in Hugo's eyes some fixtures in the room, the old chair, and an outline image of himself.

OPINION 5. *From paragraph 9:* "I think he likes you, [. . .]."

FACT 6. *From paragraph 11:* Feeding Hugo was expensive for Annie.

OPINION 7. *From paragraph 11:* "Hugo couldn't survive in the wild. [. . .] He's happy here."

FACT 8. *From paragraph 15:* Bob Akin's dates, business matters, and Astros games with new friends took the place of long evening walks and time with Hugo.

18F CRITICAL READING: THE WRITER'S CRAFT
Choose the best answer.

__a__ 1. In order to develop the topic, Bob Akin uses the following method:
a. tells a story
b. gives a fact
c. tells a joke
d. gives a definition

__b__ 2. *Read paragraph 8 again.* Identify the senses used.
a. sight, sound, taste
b. sight, sound, smell
c. sound, smell
d. smell, sight

Name   Date

___d___ 3. *Read paragraph 5 again.* What would the reader miss if "muted night, wet rubber asphalt" were replaced by the phrase "no sounds except tires hitting wet streets"?
   a. Suspense of the event; visual and auditory impact
   b. Visual and auditory impact; descriptive language
   c. Suspense of the event; descriptive language
   d. Suspense of the event; visual and auditory impact; descriptive language

___d___ 4. In the title, "Out of Their Element," the pronoun *their* refers to
   a. Annie, Charlie, and Hugo.
   b. Bob Akin, Annie, and Charlie.
   c. Hugo and Bob Akin.
   d. Hugo, Bob Akin, and Annie and Charlie.

18G   READER RESPONSE: TO DISCUSS OR WRITE ABOUT

1. Do you think Annie and Charlie were cruel to keep Hugo imprisoned in their house? If so, how do you justify people's keeping pets in their homes—a cat, dog, or bird? Are domesticated animals better off set free or kept as pets? Defend your position with specific reasons.

2. A zoo is viewed by many people as a prison for animals, birds, and reptiles. Although the animals are placed in roomy pens, cages, or tanks, their freedom is still limited. Assume you are the voice for an animal in the zoo. Plead your argument for or against being set free.

3. Loneliness, according to psychologists, is a major social problem in the United States. Have you ever experienced loneliness when moving to a new neighborhood, taking a new job, attending social functions, or any other situation? Describe the situation, how you felt, and what you did to try to deal with the loneliness.

How Did You Do?   18 Out of Their Element

SKILL (number of items)	Number Correct		Points for Each		Score
Vocabulary (15)	_____	×	2	=	_____
Central Theme and Main Ideas (2)	_____	×	5	=	_____
Major Details (12)	_____	×	2	=	_____
Inferences (10)	_____	×	2	=	_____
Critical Reading: Fact or Opinion (8)	_____	×	1	=	_____
Critical Reading: The Writer's Craft (4)	_____	×	2	=	_____

(Possible Total: 100) *Total* _____

SPEED

Reading Time: _____ Reading Rate (page 398): _____ Words Per Minute

Name   Date

▪ Part 5 ▪

Thinking: Getting Started

A̲s you read the selections in Part 5, keep in mind that reading takes place at three levels: *on the line, between the lines, and beyond the lines*. The reading selections in Part 5 particularly challenge you to move with more confidence into reading *between the lines and beyond the lines*. As you attend to the stated material (what is *on the line*) also be alert for the logical conclusions that can be drawn from the material (what is *between the lines*). What is not stated is often as important as what is stated.

When you read *between the lines and beyond the lines*, you experience most dramatically the interplay between what your eyes see and your mind thinks about. First, use the visuals and accompanying questions on the next three pages to access your prior knowledge. Next, survey and ask questions. Then as you read, be aware that the material *between the lines and beyond the lines* will round out your understanding of a reading selection. Work particularly closely with the exercises on inferences, critical reading, and reader response that follow each reading selection.

Joseph Sohm/Chromosch/Unicorn Stock Photos.

*What motivates people to donate their time and energies to help to better the world? (See "Restored to the Sea.")
How important is a young person's determination in making a dream come true? (See "She Made Her Dream
Come True.")*

If they
think they can,
they can.

© Tom Stack & Associates/Dick Pietrzyk.

*How can teachers help students become more
confident and "think they can"? (See "I
Became Her Target.")*

Immigrants who don't learn English can really clean up in America.

Who cares if immigrants don't learn the language of equal opportunity? Not the politicians who have forgotten what makes this great melting pot work. Not the self-described advocates for immigrants who put their own political agendas ahead of real advancement for non-English speaking citizens. But we're U.S. ENGLISH and we do. With over 1.4 million members, we're the largest non-partisan organization working to promote English as the common language. Because how can we expect our newest residents to work hard for the American dream if we don't communicate that the price of advancement is understanding and speaking English. To join our efforts, visit our web site at www.us-english.org. Or call 1-800-US ENGLISH.

U.S. ENGLISH

Courtesy of U.S. ENGLISH, Inc.

Is knowing the local language all that's needed for an immigrant to be successful? (See "From In Search of Bernabé.")

More on next page . . .

How does witnessing an execution affect some people? (See "Death Penalty Victims.")

"Are we to understand, then, that you would have no scruples about imposing the death penalty?"

"He likes to say we're a team, but really he's the coach and *I'm* the team."

Why do many married women today keep their unmarried name or hyphenate their unmarried name with their husband's last name? (See "Should a Wife Keep Her Name?")

Death Penalty Victims

Bob Herbert

(1) Leighanne Gideon was twenty-six when she witnessed an execution for the first time. Ms. Gideon is a reporter for *The Huntsville Item* in Texas, and part of her job has been to cover executions. Nowhere in the Western world is the death penalty applied as frequently as in Texas. Ms. Gideon has watched as fifty-two prisoners were put to death.

(2) In a documentary to be broadcast today on National Public Radio's "All Things Considered," Ms. Gideon says: "I've walked out of the death chamber numb and my legs feeling like rubber sometimes, my head not really feeling like it's attached to my shoulders. I've been told it's perfectly normal—everyone feels it—and after awhile that numb feeling goes away. And indeed it does." But other things linger. "You will never hear another sound," Ms. Gideon says, "like a mother wailing whenever she is watching her son be executed. There's no other sound like it. It is just this horrendous wail and you can't get away from it. . . . That wail surrounds the room. It's definitely something you won't ever forget."

(3) Not much attention has been given to the emotional price paid by the men and women who participate in—or witness— the fearful business of executing their fellow beings. The documentary, titled "Witness to an Execution," is narrated by Jim Willett, the warden at the unit that houses the execution chamber in Huntsville, where all of the Texas executions take place. "Sometimes I wonder," Mr. Willett says, "whether people really understand what goes on down here, and the effect it has on us."

(4) Fred Allen was a guard whose job was to help strap prisoners on the gurneys on which they would be killed. He participated in 130 executions and then had a breakdown, which he describes in the documentary. I called him at his home in Texas. He is still shaken. "There were so many," he said, his voice halting and at times trembling. "A lot of this stuff I just want to try to forget. But my main concern is the individuals who are still in the process. I want people to understand what they're going through. Because I don't want what happened to me to happen to them."

(5) Everyone understands that the condemned prisoners have been convicted of murder. No one wants to free them. But this relentless bombardment of state-sanctioned homicide is another matter entirely. It is almost impossible for staff members and others in the death chamber to ignore the reality of the prisoners as physically healthy human beings—men and (infrequently) women who walk, talk, laugh, cry and sometimes pray. Killing them is not easy. "It's kind of hard to explain what you actually feel when you talk to a man, and you kind of get to know that person," says

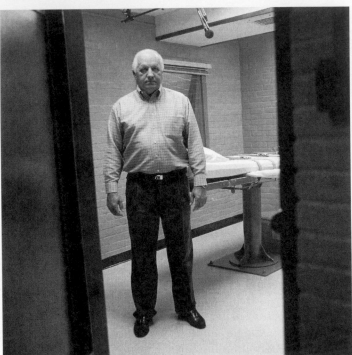

Warden Jim Willett stands in the death chamber at the Huntsville prison in Texas.

© Andrew Lichtenstein/Aurora

Kenneth Dean, a major in the Huntsville corrections unit. "And then you walk him out of a cell and you take him in there to the chamber and tie him down and then a few minutes later he's gone." Jim Brazzil, a chaplain in the unit, recalls a prisoner who began to sing as his final moment approached: "He made his final statement and then after the warden gave the signal, he started singing 'Silent Night.' And he got to the point, 'Round yon virgin, mother and child,' and just as he got 'child' out, was the last word."

(6) David Isay, who co-produced the documentary with Stacy Abramson, said: "It is certainly chilling to hear the process of what goes on, the ritual of the execution. The folks who do these executions are just regular, sensitive people who are doing it because it's their job. And it has an enormous impact on some of them." The Rev. Carroll Pickett, a chaplain who was present for ninety-five executions in Huntsville before he retired in 1995, told me in a telephone conversation that symptoms of some kind of distress were common among those who participated in the executions. "Sure," he said. "It affects you. It affects anybody." I asked how it had affected him. "Well," he said, "I think it was a contributing factor to a triple bypass I had about eighteen months later. Just all of the stress, you know? I have to say that when I retired I probably had had as much as I could take." I asked Fred Allen, who suffered the breakdown, if his view on the death penalty had changed. "Yes," he said. Then after a long pause, he said, "There's nothing wrong with an individual spending the rest of his life in prison."

(763 words)

Here are some of the more difficult words in "Death Penalty Victims."

bombardment
(paragraph 5)

bom·bard (bäm bärd´; *for n.* bäm´bärd´) *vt.* 〖Fr *bombarder* < *bombarde*, mortar < *bombe*, BOMB〗 **1** to attack with or as with artillery or bombs **2** to keep attacking or pressing with questions, suggestions, etc. **3** to direct a stream of particles at (atomic nuclei) to produce nuclear transmutations —*n.* the earliest type of cannon, originally for hurling stones —*SYN.* ATTACK —**bom·bard´·ment** *n.*

chaplain
(paragraph 5)

chap·lain (chap´lən) *n.* 〖ME *chapelain* < OFr < ML *capellanus*, orig., custodian of St. Martin's cloak: see CHAPEL〗 **1** a clergyman attached to a chapel, as of a royal court **2** a minister, priest, or rabbi serving in a religious capacity with the armed forces, or in a prison, hospital, etc. **3** a clergyman, or sometimes a layman, appointed to perform religious functions in a public institution, club, etc. —**chap´·laincy** *n.*, *pl.* **-·cies** —**chap´·lain·ship´** *n.*

condemned
(paragraph 5)

con·demn (kən dem´) *vt.* 〖ME *condempnen* < OFr *condemner* < L *condemnare* < *com-*, intens. + *damnare*, to harm, condemn: see DAMN〗 **1** to pass an adverse judgment on; disapprove of strongly; censure **2** *a*) to declare to be guilty of wrongdoing; convict *b*) to pass judicial sentence on; inflict a penalty upon *c*) to doom ☆**3** to take (private property) for public use by the power of eminent domain; expropriate **4** to declare unfit for use or service /to con-*demn* a slum tenement/ —*SYN.* CRITICIZE —**con·dem´·nable** (-dem´nə bəl, -ə bəl) *adj.* —**con·demn´er** *n.*

documentary
(paragraph 2)

docu·men·tary (däk´yōō ment´ə rē, -yə-) *adj.* **1** consisting of, supported by, contained in, or serving as a document or documents **2** designating or of a film, TV program, etc. that dramatically shows or analyzes news events, social conditions, etc., with little or no fictionalization —*n.*, *pl.* **-·ries** a documentary film, TV show, etc.

execution
(paragraph 1)

ex·ecu·tion (ek´si kyōō´shən) *n.* 〖ME *execucion* < Anglo-Fr < OFr *execution* < L *executio*, *exsecutio*: see EXECUTOR〗 **1** the act of executing; specif., *a*) a carrying out, doing, producing, etc. *b*) a putting to death as in accordance with a legally imposed sentence **2** the manner of doing or producing something, as of performing a piece of music or a role in a play **3** [Archaic] effective action, esp. of a destructive nature **4** *Law a*) a writ or order, issued by a court, giving authority to put a judgment into effect *b*) the legal method afforded for the enforcement of a judgment of a court *c*) the act of carrying out the provisions of such a writ or order *d*) the making valid of a legal instrument, as by signing, sealing, and delivering

gurneys
(paragraph 4)

gur·ney (gur´nē) *n.*, *pl.* **-·neys** 〖< ?〗 a stretcher or cot on wheels, used in hospitals to move patients

homicide
(paragraph 5)

homi·cide (häm´ə sīd´, hō´mə-) *n.* **1** 〖ME < OFr < LL *homicidium*, manslaughter, murder < L *homicida*, murderer < *homo*, a man (see HOMO¹) + *caedere*, to cut, kill: see -CIDE〗 any killing of one human being by another: cf. MURDER, MANSLAUGHTER **2** 〖ME < OFr < L *homicida*〗 a person who kills another

horrendous
(paragraph 2)

hor·ren·dous (hô ren´dəs, hə-) *adj.* 〖L *horrendus* < prp. of *horrere*: see HORRID〗 horrible; frightful —**hor·ren´·dously** *adv.*

relentless
(paragraph 5)

re·lent·less (-lis) *adj.* **1** not relenting; harsh; pitiless **2** persistent; unremitting —**re·lent´·lessly** *adv.* —**re·lent´·less·ness** *n.*

sanctioned
(paragraph 5)

sanc·tion (saŋk´shən) *n.* 〖< Fr or L: Fr < L *sanctio* < *sanctus*: see SAINT〗 **1** the act of a recognized authority confirming or ratifying an action; authorized approval or permission **2** support; encouragement; approval **3** something that gives binding force to a law, or secures obedience to it, as the penalty for breaking it, or a reward for carrying it out **4** something, as a moral principle or influence, that makes a rule of conduct, a law, etc. binding **5** *a*) a coercive measure, as a blockade of shipping, usually taken by several nations together, for forcing a nation considered to have violated international law to end the violation *b*) a coercive measure, as a boycott, taken by a group to enforce demands: *often used in pl.* **6** [Obs.] a formal decree; law —*vt.* to give sanction to; specif., *a*) to ratify or confirm *b*) to authorize or permit; countenance —*SYN.* APPROVE —**sanc´·tion·able** *adj.*

19A VOCABULARY

Using the vocabulary words listed on page 267, fill in this crossword puzzle.

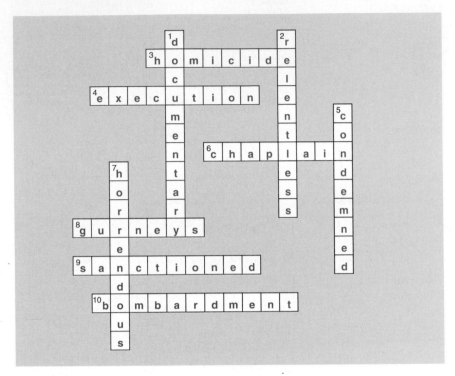

Across

3. murder
4. put to death
6. minister
8. stretchers
9. approved
10. attack

Down

1. program
2. persistent
5. declared guilty
7. horrible

Name

Date

19B   CENTRAL THEME AND MAIN IDEAS

Choose the best answer.

__d__ 1. What is the central theme of "Death Penalty Victims"?
      a. Huntsville is the "prison city" of Texas.
      b. Prison chaplains play a vital role in death row executions.
      c. Media reporters are permitted to witness death row executions.
      d. Death row executions affect both participants and observers.

__b__ 2. What is the main idea of paragraph 5?
      a. Death row inmates have been convicted of murder.
      b. Executing death row inmates is not easy.
      c. Death row inmates are physically healthy human beings.
      d. Executing a death row inmate takes only a few minutes.

19C   MAJOR DETAILS

Decide whether each detail is true (T), false (F), or not discussed (ND).

__F__ 1. Ms. Gideon is a television reporter.

__T__ 2. All of Texas's executions take place in Huntsville, Texas.

__ND__ 3. Death row inmates are permitted to order any food they want for their final meal.

__ND__ 4. Executions of death row inmates occur at 12 midnight.

__T__ 5. The warden signals when the lethal injection is to start.

__T__ 6. Family members of death row inmates are permitted to view the execution.

__T__ 7. More men than women are on Texas's death row.

__ND__ 8. Texas began using the lethal injection for executions in 1982.

19D   INFERENCES

Decide whether each statement below can be inferred (YES) or cannot be inferred (NO) from the reading selection.

__YES__ 1. The death row inmate is strapped to the gurney so he will not jump up or move during the execution procedure.

__NO__ 2. Fred Allen misses his job as a guard at the Huntsville prison.

__NO__ 3. A lethal injection is more humane than execution by electrocution, gas, hanging, or firing squad.

Name   Date

__YES__ 4. Part of the responsibility of a chaplain is to be in the death chamber at the time of execution.

__NO__ 5. Major Kenneth Dean is the head of the tie-down team at the Huntsville prison.

__NO__ 6. Witnessing executions affects the guards more than it does the warden.

19E CRITICAL READING: FACT OR OPINION

Decide whether each statement, even if it quotes someone, contains a FACT or an OPINION.

__FACT__ 1. *From paragraph 1:* "Nowhere in the Western world is the death penalty applied as frequently as in Texas."

__OPINION__ 2. *From paragraph 2:* "You will never hear another sound," Ms. Gideon says, "like a mother wailing whenever she is watching her son be executed."

__OPINION__ 3. *From paragraph 5:* "No one wants to free them [death row inmates]."

__FACT__ 4. *From paragraph 6:* "The Rev. Carroll Picket [. . .] told me in a telephone conversation that symptoms of some kind of distress were common among those who participated in the executions."

__OPINION__ 5. *From paragraph 6:* "There's nothing wrong with an individual spending the rest of his life in prison."

19F CRITICAL READING: THE WRITER'S CRAFT

Choose the best answer.

__c__ 1. In order to develop the essay, the author uses comments from all of the following *except*
a. a chaplain.
b. a guard.
c. a family member.
d. a reporter.

__c__ 2. The sentence "I've walked out of the death chamber numb and my legs feeling like rubber sometimes [. . .]" (paragraph 2) conveys an image of someone who is
a. angry.
b. worried.
c. stunned.
d. scared.

Name   Date

__b__ 3. In the title, "Death Penalty Victims," the author uses the word
   Victims in order to
   a. increase the reader's vocabulary.
   b. affect the reader's viewpoint.
   c. get the reader's attention.
   d. offer an impartial viewpoint.

19G READER RESPONSE: TO DISCUSS OR TO WRITE ABOUT

1. In 1976 the Supreme Court reinstated capital punishment. Today, more than 3,500 inmates sit on Death Row. At least one state, Illinois, has passed a moratorium, a legal delay, on carrying out the death penalty. Are you in favor of such a moratorium for the state where you live? Is your viewpoint based on a moral, ethical, or religious viewpoint? If so, explain in detail. If you are not in favor of a moratorium, why?

2. On the day of execution in Texas, a death row inmate is allowed five witnesses plus a spiritual advisor. The victims are allowed five witnesses. Under what conditions would you attend an execution as a witness for either the inmate or the victim? How do you think viewing an execution would affect you physically, mentally, and emotionally?

3. Just before an execution, the warden asks if the condemned person has any last words. In Texas, a boom microphone comes down from the ceiling so that the inmate's words can be heard by the witnesses. Imagine that you are the condemned person but are being executed for a crime that you did not commit. What would you say in those final seconds?

How Did You Do? 19 Death Penalty Victims

SKILL *(number of items)*	Number Correct		Points for Each		Score
Vocabulary (10)	_____	×	2	=	_____
Central Theme and Main Ideas (2)	_____	×	7	=	_____
Major Details (8)	_____	×	3	=	_____
Inferences (6)	_____	×	3	=	_____
Critical Reading: Fact or Opinion (5)	_____	×	3	=	_____
Critical Reading: The Writer's Craft (3)	_____	×	3	=	_____

(Possible Total: 100) *Total* _____

SPEED

Reading Time: _____ Reading Rate (page 398): _____ Words Per Minute

Name   Date

Should a Wife Keep Her Name?

Norman Lobsenz

(1) Encouraged by feminism to maintain their separate identities, many brides have chosen to keep their maiden name* or to combine it somehow with their husband's name. Yet the emotional and technical problems that arise from this decision have made some women think twice.

(2) "I felt an obligation to carry on the family name and heritage," says Catherine Bergstrom-Katz, an actress. "But I also believed that combining our names was the fair thing to do; if I was going to take my husband's name, the least he could do was take mine." Her husband's legal name now is also Bergstrom-Katz. Though he does not use it at work, it is on all the couple's legal documents—mortgage, house deed, insurance and credit cards. Mail comes addressed to both spouses under their own names, their hyphenated name and, says Catherine, "sometimes to 'Allan Bergstrom.'" The couple's first child was named Sasha Bergstrom-Katz.

(3) Not all wives are so adamant. Some use their maiden name in business and their husband's name socially. And a growing number of women who once insisted on hyphenating maiden and married names have dropped the hyphen and are using the maiden name as a middle name.

(4) Despite the popular use of linked, merged or shared names, "there is still a surprising amount of opposition to the idea," says Terri Tepper, who for many years ran an information center in Barrington, Illinois, advising women who wished to retain their maiden names. Family counselors point out that it triggers highly emotional reactions, not only between the couple but also among parents and in laws. "What about your silver and linens?" one woman asked her daughter. "How can I have them monogrammed if you and Bill have different names?"

(5) While such concerns may seem relatively trivial, there are others that raise significant issues.

- *Control and commitment.* "Names have always been symbols of power," says Constance Ahrons, a therapist at the University of Southern California. "To a modern woman, keeping her name is a symbol of her independence. But a man may feel that implies a lack of commitment to him and to the marriage." Thus when a San Diego

---

*Alternate terms for "maiden name" are often preferred because they are considered less demeaning to women; such terms include "given name," "family name," and "pre-marriage name," although these alternatives are only beginning to come into widespread use.

woman told her fiancé she had decided to keep her name, he was hurt. "Aren't you proud to be my wife?" he asked. Most men are more understanding. When Maureen Poon, a publicist, married Russell Fear, her English-Irish husband sympathized with his wife's desire to preserve her Chinese-Japanese heritage, especially since she was an only child. "We began married life as Poon-Fear," says Maureen. "I've since dropped the hyphen—it just confuses too many people—but Russell continues to use it when we're out together. He feels that we are 'Poon-Fear,' that we are one."

- *Cultural differences.* "Men raised in a macho society find it hard to accept a wife who goes by her own name," says Dr. Judith Davenport, a clinical social worker. For example, New York–born Jennifer Selvy, now a riding instructor in Denver, says her Western-rancher fiancé was horrified that she wanted to keep her name. "What will my friends say?" he protested. "Nobody will believe we're married!" His distress was so real that Selvy reluctantly yielded.

- *What to name the children.* When couples began hyphenating surnames, it was amusing to consider the tongue-twisters that might plague the next generation. But psychologists point out that youngsters with complex names are often teased by classmates or embarrassed if their parents have different names. And how does one explain to grandparents that their grandchild, apple of their eye, will not be carrying on the family name?

- *Technical troubles.* While there are no legal barriers in any state to a woman's keeping her maiden name—or resuming it in mid-marriage—technology can cause complications. Hyphenated names are often too long for computers to handle; others are likely to be filed incorrectly. One reason Maureen Poon-Fear dropped the hyphen in her name was "it created a problem in consistency." She explains: "The Department of Motor Vehicles lists me as POONFEAR. Some of my charge accounts are listed under 'P' and others under 'F,' and I was concerned about the effect on my credit rating if my payments were not properly credited."

(6) Given the difficulties of keeping one's maiden name in a society that has not yet fully adjusted to the idea, should a woman make the effort to do so?

(7) "Clearly, yes, if the name has value to her in terms of personal, family or professional identity," says Alan Loy McGinnis, co-director of the Valley Counseling Center in Glendale, California. "But if keeping one's maiden name makes either spouse feel less secure about the relationship, perhaps the couple needs to find another way to symbolize mutual commitment. After all, marriage today needs all the reinforcement it can get."

(792 words)

Here are some of the more difficult words in "Should a Wife Keep Her Name?"

adamant
(paragraph 3)

ada·mant (ad′ə mənt, -mant′) *n.* [[ME & OFr < L *adamas* (gen. *adamantis*), the hardest metal < Gr *adamas* (gen. *adamantos*) < *a*-, not + *daman*, to subdue: see TAME]] **1** in ancient times, a hard stone or substance that was supposedly unbreakable **2** [Old Poet.] unbreakable hardness —*adj.* **1** too hard to be broken **2** not giving in or relenting; unyielding —*SYN.* INFLEXIBLE —**ad′a·mantly** *adv.*

commitment
(paragraph 5)

com·mit (kə mit′) *vt.* **··mit′·ted**, **··mit′·ting** [[ME *committen* < L *committere*, to bring together, commit < *com*-, together + *mittere*, to send: see MISSION]] **1** to give in charge or trust; deliver for safe-keeping; entrust; consign [we *commit* his fame to posterity] **2** to put officially in custody or confinement [*committed* to prison] **3** to hand over or set apart to be disposed of or put to some purpose [to *commit* something to the trash heap] **4** to do or perpetrate (an offense or crime) **5** to bind as by a promise; pledge; engage [*committed* to the struggle] **6** to make known the opinions or views of [to *commit* oneself on an issue] **7** to refer (a bill, etc.) to a commit-tee to be considered —*vi.* [Informal] to make a pledge or promise: often with *to* —**commit to memory** to learn by heart; memorize —**commit to paper** (or **writing**) to write down; record —**com·mit′·table** *adj.*

SYN.—**commit**, the basic term here, implies the delivery of a person or thing into the charge or keeping of another; **entrust** implies committal based on trust and confidence; **confide** stresses the private nature of information entrusted to another and usually connotes intimacy of relationship; **consign** suggests formal action in transferring something to another's possession or control; **relegate** implies a consigning to a specific class, sphere, place, etc., esp. one of inferiority, and usually suggests the literal or figurative removal of something undesirable

com·mit·ment (-mənt) *n.* **1** a committing or being committed **2** official consignment by court order of a person as to prison or a mental hospital **3** a pledge or promise to do something **4** dedica-tion to a long-term course of action; engagement; involvement **5** a financial liability undertaken, as an agreement to buy or sell secu-rities **6** the act of sending proposed legislation to a committee

feminism
(paragraph 1)

femi·nism (fem′ə niz′əm) *n.* [[< L *femina*, woman + -ISM]] **1** [Rare] feminine qualities **2** *a)* the principle that woman should have political, economic, and social rights equal to those of men *b)* the movement to win such rights for women —**fem′i·nist** *n.*, *adj.* —**fem′i·nis′·tic** *adj.*

heritage
(paragraph 5)

her·it·age (her′ə tij) *n.* [[ME < OFr < *heriter* < LL(Ec) *hereditare*, to inherit < L *hereditas*: see HEREDITY]] **1** property that is or can be inherited **2** *a)* something handed down from one's ancestors or the past, as a characteristic, a culture, tradition, etc. *b)* the rights, burdens, or status resulting from being born in a certain time or place; birthright

SYN.—**heritage**, the most general of these words, applies either to property passed on to an heir, or to a tradition, culture, etc. passed on to a later generation [our *heritage* of freedom]; **inherit-ance** applies to property, a characteristic, etc. passed on to an heir; **patrimony** strictly refers to an estate inherited from one's father, but it is also used of anything passed on from an ances-tor; **birthright**, in its stricter sense, applies to the property rights of a first-born son

Vocabulary List

macho
(paragraph 5)

ma·cho (mä′chō) *n., pl.* **-chos** (-chōz, -chōs) ⟦Sp < Port, ult. < L *masculus,* MASCULINE⟧ **1** an overly assertive, virile, and domineering man **2** MACHISMO —*adj.* exhibiting or characterized by machismo; overly aggressive, virile, domineering, etc.

mutual
(paragraph 7)

mu·tual (myōō′chōō əl) *adj.* ⟦LME *mutuall* < MFr *mutuel* < L *mutuus,* mutual, reciprocal < *mutare,* to change, exchange: see MISS¹⟧ **1** *a)* done, felt, etc. by each of two or more for or toward the other or others; reciprocal *[mutual* admiration*] b)* of, or having the same relationship toward, each other or one another *[mutual* enemies*]* **2** shared in common; joint *[our mutual* friend*]* **3** designating or of a type of insurance in which the policyholders elect the directors, share in the profits, and agree to indemnify one another against loss —**mu′·tu·al′·ity** (-al′ə tē) *n., pl.* **-ties** —**mu′·tu·ally** *adv.*

SYN.—**mutual** may be used for an interchange of feeling between two persons *[John and Joe are mutual* enemies*]* or may imply a sharing jointly with others *[the mutual* efforts of a group*]*; **reciprocal** implies a return in kind or degree by each of two sides of what is given or demonstrated by the other *[a reciprocal* trade agreement*]*, or it may refer to any inversely corresponding relationship *[the reciprocal* functions of two machine parts*]*; **common** simply implies a being shared by others or by all the members of a group *[our common* interests*]*

plague
(paragraph 5)

plague (plāg) *n.* ⟦ME *plage* < MFr < L *plaga,* a blow, misfortune, in LL(Ec), plague < Gr *plēgē, plaga* < IE *plaga,* a blow < base *plag-,* to strike > FLAW²⟧ **1** anything that afflicts or troubles; calamity; scourge **2** any contagious epidemic disease that is deadly; esp., bubonic plague **3** [Informal] a nuisance; annoyance **4** *Bible* any of various calamities sent down as divine punishment: Ex. 9:14, Num. 16:46 —*vt.* **plagued, plagu′·ing 1** to afflict with a plague **2** to vex; harass; trouble; torment —*SYN.* ANNOY —**plagu′er** *n.*

resuming
(paragraph 5)

re·sume (ri zōōm′, -zyōōm′) *vt.* **-sumed′, -sum′·ing** ⟦ME *resumen,* to assume < MFr *resumer* < L *resumere* < *re-,* again + *sumere,* to take: see CONSUME⟧ **1** *a)* to take, get, or occupy again *[to resume* one's seat*] b)* to take back or take on again *[to resume* a former name*]* **2** to begin again or go on with again after interruption *[to resume* a conversation*]* **3** to summarize or make a résumé of —*vi.* to begin again or go on again after interruption —**re·sum′·able** *adj.*

surnames
(paragraph 5)

sur·name (sur′nām′) *n.* ⟦ME < *sur-* (see SUR-¹) + *name,* infl. by earlier *surnoun* < OFr *surnom* < *sur-* + *nom* < L *nomen,* NAME⟧ **1** the family name, or last name, as distinguished from a given name **2** a name or epithet added to a person's given name (Ex.: Ivan *the Terrible*) —*vt.* **-named′, -nam′·ing** to give a surname to

symbolize
(paragraph 7)

sym·bol (sim′bəl) *n.* ⟦< Fr & L: Fr *symbole* < L *symbolus, symbolum* < Gr *symbolon,* token, pledge, sign by which one infers a thing < *symballein,* to throw together, compare < *syn-,* together + *ballein,* to throw: see BALL²⟧ **1** something that stands for, represents, or suggests another thing; esp., an object used to represent something abstract *[the dove is a symbol* of peace*]* **2** a written or printed mark, letter, abbreviation, etc. standing for an object, quality, process, quantity, etc., as in music, mathematics, or chemistry **3** *Psychoanalysis* an act or object representing an unconscious desire that has been repressed —*vt.* **-boled** or **-bolled, -bol·ing** or **-bol·ling** SYMBOLIZE

sym·bol·ize (-līz′) *vt.* **-ized′, -iz′·ing** ⟦Fr *symboliser* < ML *symbolizare*⟧ **1** to be a symbol of; typify; stand for **2** to represent by a symbol or symbols —*vi.* to use symbols —**sym′·boli·za′·tion** *n.* —**sym′·bol·iz′er** *n.*

20A VOCABULARY
Using the vocabulary words listed on pages 275–276, fill in the blanks.

1. Adopting a child demands a tremendous emotional
   __commitment__ .

2. To succeed in getting into better physical shape, amateur athletes
   must be ___adamant___ about exercising regularly, no matter
   how tempted they may be to skip a workout.

3. In successful marriages, the partners realize that they share
   ___mutual___ rights as well as responsibilities.

4. The new owners of the house did not know that mosquitoes would
   ___plague___ them each summer.

5. After working as a clown in a circus for six months, my neighbor recently returned home and is now ___resuming___ his career as a
   stockbroker.

6. Many forms, including employment applications, require people to
   give their ___surnames___ before their first names.

7. Instead of the groom giving the bride a ring, many couples now prefer double-ring ceremonies because they want the exchange of rings
   to ___symbolize___ their equality of partnership.

8. In recent years many people are choosing to study a foreign language, and many select the language of their grandparents as a way
   of preserving their ___heritage___ .

9. Little boys raised in a ___macho___ culture may grow up to
   feel they are superior to women, but such an attitude is resented by
   many women today.

10. Over the last quarter century, the principles of ___feminism___
    have encouraged many women to pursue careers that their mothers
    often did not have the chance to consider.

Name	Date

20B   CENTRAL THEME AND MAIN IDEAS
Choose the best answer.

___c___ 1. What is the central theme of "Should a Wife Keep Her Name?"
   a. The use of hyphenated surnames causes confusion because the wife may seem not to be committed to the marriage, the children face ridicule, and computer errors are likely to occur.
   b. Some men are horrified by their fiancées' wish to keep their maiden names, in part because these men feel their friends will not believe a couple is married unless the woman adopts the man's name.
   c. Technical and emotional problems that sometimes arise when a woman does not take her husband's name are causing some women to think through the issues before they make a decision about their married surnames.
   d. Feminism is seen as the force behind the modern phenomenon of women keeping their maiden names after they get married.

___d___ 2. What is the main idea of paragraph 5?
   a. Many concerns about women's married surnames often seem relatively trivial.
   b. The important issues about women's surnames after marriage are control and commitment, cultural differences, and what to name the children.
   c. Most men are understanding about their wives' desire to keep their maiden names or to hyphenate their maiden and married names.
   d. Some concerns about women's married surnames have raised a number of significant issues.

3. In your own words, give the main idea of paragraph 4.

   There is still a surprising amount of opposition to the

   idea of linked, merged, or shared names.

_____

Name   Date

20C   MAJOR DETAILS

Decide whether each detail is MAJOR or MINOR based on the context of the reading selection.

MAJOR   1. Many brides have chosen to keep their maiden names.

MINOR   2. Catherine Bergstrom-Katz is an actress.

MAJOR   3. Even though her husband does not use their hyphenated name at work, Bergstrom-Katz appears on all the family's legal documents.

MAJOR   4. Some women have decided to use their maiden names as middle names.

MAJOR   5. The issue of linked names can trigger highly emotional reactions.

MINOR   6. One woman is worried about what monograms to put on silver and linens that she wants to give her daughter who is keeping her maiden name.

MINOR   7. Maureen Poon-Fear's husband is of English-Irish descent.

MAJOR   8. Russell Poon-Fear feels he and his wife are one, so he continues to use their hyphenated surnames.

MINOR   9. Jennifer Selvy is now a riding instructor in Denver.

MAJOR 10. Psychologists point out that youngsters with complex names are often teased by classmates.

MAJOR 11. Jennifer Selvy's fiancé worried about what his friends would think if his wife kept her name.

MAJOR 12. Hyphenated surnames sometimes create problems in keeping official government and financial records consistent.

20D INFERENCES

Choose the best answer.

__a__ 1. *Read paragraph 5 again.* Why have names always been symbols of power?
   a. Traditionally, when a woman married and took her husband's name, he gained complete legal and financial control of her life.
   b. Many primitive tribes used to name people after animals, hoping the animals' powers would transfer to their namesakes.
   c. Traditionally, when a husband's surname is associated with great political and financial power, the man feels he is sharing that power with his wife by giving her his name.
   d. Knowing someone's name can enable anyone to look up that person's records and thereby pry into his or her life.

__b__ 2. *Read paragraph 5 again.* What does Russell Poon-Fear think of his marriage?
   a. Because of his own background, he is glad that he has married someone of mixed heritage.
   b. He considers that through marriage his wife has become his partner in all aspects of life.
   c. He feels protective of his wife because she has no other family.
   d. He feels that without his wife he had no identity.

__c__ 3. *Read paragraph 7 again.* Alan Loy McGinnis says "marriage today needs all the reinforcement it can get." He is implying that
   a. people often marry for the wrong reasons, so many marriages are very fragile.
   b. divorce has become too easy, so a couple has to avoid all causes for disagreements if they want their marriage to last.
   c. modern marriages face many pressures from within and from outside sources.
   d. married couples have to resist the influence of people who want to encourage the couple to get divorced.

Name   Date

20E CRITICAL READING: THE WRITER'S CRAFT

Choose the best answer.

___c___ 1. In order to illustrate his point, the author does all of the following *except*
a. give examples.
b. quote women who have used shared names.
c. give statistics.
d. quote authorities on family counseling.

___d___ 2. *Read paragraph 5 again.* The author presents the information in
the form of a list for all these reasons *except* to
a. emphasize main points.
b. achieve conciseness.
c. make reading easier.
d. write sentence fragments.

___d___ 3. The author uses all of the following verbs to connect speakers'
names to their quotations *except*
a. protested.
b. says.
c. explains.
d. stated.

20F READER RESPONSE: TO DISCUSS OR TO WRITE ABOUT

1. Do you think that husbands of women who hyphenate their names
should also hyphenate their names, as Maureen Poon-Fear's husband
did? Why or why not?

2. What influence do you think feminism has had on women? On men?
On children? Using specific examples, explain your point of view.

3. What is the difference between being called equal and being treated as
equal? Using a specific example, describe the difference.

How Did You Do?   20   Should a Wife Keep Her Name?

SKILL *(number of items)*	*Number Correct*		*Points for Each*		*Score*
Vocabulary (10)	_____	×	4	=	_____
Central Theme and Main Ideas (3)	_____	×	8	=	_____
Major Details (12)	_____	×	2	=	_____
Inferences (3)	_____	×	2	=	_____
Critical Reading: The Writer's Craft (3)	_____	×	2	=	_____

(Possible Total: 100) *Total*   _____

SPEED

Reading Time: _____ Reading Rate (page 398): _____ Words Per Minute

Name   Date

Selection 21

Restored to the Sea

Robin Micheli

(1) In the soft orange-and-pink light of dawn, the scene at Seal Rocks on Australia's eastern coast looked like an all-night beach party. People in wet suits warmed themselves before bonfires, as families with small children carried buckets of water from shore to sand, where they worked diligently on what might have been huge sand castles.

(2) But it was rescue, not revelry, on the minds of the hardy souls who had braved the night's 43°F temperatures. An eerie black row of stranded false killer whales (so named because the creatures, though gentle, resemble real killer whales) lay helpless on the sand while beyond them, in the frigid surf, 16 others were held and rocked by shivering divers. The morning before, 49 of the whales had run ashore in New South Wales, and three had died by dusk. The survival of the pod now depended on the ministrations of the residents of the tiny hamlet of Seal Rocks, aided by hundreds of volunteers who had traveled as far as 500 miles.

(3) Why the whales ran aground is a mystery. Experts can only speculate why the creatures, which can grow up to 20' long, sometimes find themselves stranded. "Along shallow beaches, it may be that their sonar doesn't work properly," says Kerrie Haynes-Lovell, a marine-mammal trainer at Sea World in Queensland, who drove 10 hours to assist in the rescue. With no echoes bouncing back from sloping shores to guide it away, a whale may mistakenly head toward land and become disoriented. Disaster may follow. "If one whale gives out distress signals," Haynes-Lovell says, "they may all come in to help."

(4) Humans were quick to answer signals for help after the whales were discovered early on Tuesday morning, July 14, by a visitor walking on the beach. Wayne Kelly, keeper of the Sugarloaf Point Lighthouse, which sits above the rocks and sand where they foundered, says the sight of the bloodied, wailing animals was "pretty distressing. They were writhing around, obviously very uncomfortable." The 200 or so volunteers kept the whales' delicate skin moist in the sun by dousing them continuously with seawater and draping them with soaked towels. Some rescuers, like Susan Clarke, a former registered nurse from nearby Bulahdelah, "adopted" individual whales and became their protectors. "You're a really good boy," Clarke cooed, gently stroking the whale she named Hope as it took a gasping breath from its blowhole. "Hang in there. You'll be in the water soon."

(5) Rescue leaders eventually decided to transport the whales from the rough, open beach to a sheltered cove on the other side of Sugarloaf Point. Teams of 10 to 20 volunteers began hoisting the whales, which weighed as much as 750 lbs., by hand into a trailer. During Tuesday night,

Volunteers try to save a beached whale until they can return it to the sea.

150 volunteers took turns calming the whales in the cove and making sure their blowholes stayed above water. Four people were treated for hypothermia and many others for exhaustion. Kelly Gray, 17, broke her wrist on Tuesday when a whale rolled over on it. But as soon as it was wrapped, she was back at the beach, in the water. "I couldn't leave him," she said. "How could you, when they're so reliant on you and need you so much?"

(6) Volunteers watched helplessly as two of the whales died on Tuesday night. The spent and emotionally drained crowd of volunteers finally had cause for rejoicing late Wednesday afternoon, when 15 of the stranded whales were led out to sea. Three of the largest, dominant bulls were towed in a wire cage a quarter mile from shore, and surfers shepherded the rest after them. Within 24 hours, they had joined another pod of whales and were spotted heading north. In the end, a total of 37 whales were saved.

(7) Their ordeal over, the whales headed east and by midday were swimming freely 12 miles from shore. Homemaker Jenny Mervyn-Jones, who was awake for 36 hours caring for one whale, watched wistfully as they prepared her whale to head out. "You almost don't want to see it go, but you'll do anything you can to save it," she said. "I really can't wait to wave goodbye to the last one and wish it the best of luck."

(697 words)

Craig Bailey/Florida Today

Here are some of the more difficult words in "Restored to the Sea."

blowhole
(paragraph 4)

blow·hole (-hōl′) *n.* **1** a nostril in the top of the head of whales and certain other cetaceans, through which they breathe **2** a hole through which gas or air can escape, esp. in lava **3** a hole in the ice to which seals, whales, etc. come to get air **4** a vertical opening or chimney in the roof of a sea cave through which air and water are forced by the action of the waves and the rising tides **5** a flaw in cast metal caused by an air or gas bubble

disoriented
(paragraph 3)

dis·ori·ent (dis ôr′ē ent′) *vt.* ⟦Fr *désorienter*: see DIS- & ORIENT, *vt.*⟧ **1** to turn away from the east: see ORIENT (*vt.* 1 & 2) **2** to cause to lose one's bearings **3** to confuse mentally, esp. with respect to time, place, and the identity of persons and objects Also **dis·o′ri·en·tate′** (-ən tāt′), **··tat′·ed**, **··tat′·ing** —**dis·o′ri·en·ta′·tion** *n.*

dousing
(paragraph 4)

douse² (dous) *vt.* **doused, dous′·ing** ⟦< ? prec.⟧ **1** to plunge or thrust suddenly into liquid **2** to drench; pour liquid over —*vi.* to get immersed or drenched —*n.* a drenching

eerie
(paragraph 2)

ee·rie or **eery** (ir′ē, ē′rē) *adj.* **··rier**, **··ri·est** ⟦N Eng dial & Scot < ME *eri*, filled with dread, prob. var. of *erg*, cowardly, timid < OE *earg*, akin to Ger *arg*, bad, wicked: for IE base see ORCHESTRA⟧ **1** [Now Rare] timid or frightened; uneasy because of superstitious fear **2** mysterious, uncanny, or weird, esp. in such a way as to frighten or disturb —*SYN.* WEIRD —**ee′·rily** *adv.* —**ee′·ri·ness** *n.*

foundered
(paragraph 4)

foun·der¹ (foun′dər) *vi.* ⟦ME *foundren* < OFr *fondrer*, to fall in, sink < *fond*, bottom < L *fundus*, bottom: see FOUND²⟧ **1** to stumble, fall, or go lame **2** to become stuck as in soft ground; bog down **3** to fill with water, as during a storm, and sink: said of a ship or boat **4** to become sick from overeating: used esp. of livestock **5** to break down; collapse; fail —*vt.* to cause to founder —*n.* ⟦< the *vi.*, 1⟧ LAMINITIS

hypothermia
(paragraph 5)

hypo·ther·mia (-thʉr′mē ə) *n.* ⟦ModL < HYPO- + Gr *thermē*, heat: see WARM⟧ a subnormal body temperature

mammal
(paragraph 3)

mam·mal (mam′əl) *n.* ⟦< ModL *Mammalia* < LL *mammalis*, of the breasts < L *mamma*: see prec.⟧ any of a large class (Mammalia) of warmblooded, usually hairy vertebrates whose offspring are fed with milk secreted by the female mammary glands —**mam·ma·lian** (mə mā′lē ən, ma-) *adj.*, *n.*

ministrations
(paragraph 2)

min·is·tra·tion (min′is trā′shən) *n.* ⟦ME *ministracion* < L *ministratio* < pp. of *ministrare*, to MINISTER⟧ **1** MINISTRY (sense 2*a*) **2** administration, as of a sacrament **3** the act or an instance of giving help or care; service —**min′·is·tra′·tive** *adj.*

pod
(paragraph 2)

☆**pod²** (päd) *n.* ⟦? special use of prec.⟧ a small group of animals, esp. of seals or whales —*vt.* **pod′·ded, pod′·ding** to herd (animals) together

Vocabulary List

revelry
(paragraph 2)

rev·elry (rev′əl rē) *n., pl.* --ries ⟦ME *revelrie*⟧ reveling; noisy merry-making; boisterous festivity

sonar
(paragraph 3)

so·nar (sō′när′) *n.* ⟦*so*(und) *n*(avigation) *a*(nd) *r*(anging)⟧ an apparatus that transmits high-frequency sound waves through water and registers the vibrations reflected from an object, used in finding submarines, depths, etc.

speculate
(paragraph 3)

specu·late (spek′yə lāt′) *vi.* --lat′ed, --lat′·ing ⟦< L *speculatus,* pp. of *speculari,* to view < *specula,* watchtower < *specere,* to see: see SPY⟧ 1 to think about the various aspects of a given subject; meditate; ponder; esp., to conjecture 2 to buy or sell stocks, commodities, land, etc., usually in the face of higher than ordinary risk, hoping to take advantage of an expected rise or fall in price; also, to take part in any risky venture on the chance of making huge profits — *SYN.* THINK[1] —**spec′u·la′·tor** *n.*

writhing
(paragraph 4)

writhe (rīth) *vt.* writhed, writh′·ing ⟦ME *writhen* < OE *writhan,* to twist, wind about, akin to ON *rītha* < IE base *wer-,* to bend, twist > WREATH, WRY⟧ to cause to twist or turn; contort —*vi.* 1 to make twisting or turning movements; contort the body, as in agony; squirm 2 to suffer great emotional distress, as from embarrassment or revulsion —*n.* a writhing movement; contortion —**writh′er** *n.*

21A   VOCABULARY

Choose the best answer.

___c___ 1. **Dousing** as used in "Restored to the Sea" means to
    a. drown out.
    b. keep moist.
    c. pour water over.
    d. splash playfully.

___d___ 2. An **eerie** feeling would best be described as
    a. extremely funny.
    b. heart warming.
    c. suspicious.
    d. frightening or disturbing.

___b___ 3. If the whale **foundered,** it
    a. sank in deep waters.
    b. became stuck or grounded.
    c. traveled in small groups.
    d. rolled all the way over.

Name   Date

_c_   4. A person suffering from **hypothermia** has
      a. a serious lung disease.
      b. a high fever.
      c. extremely low body temperature.
      d. a cold or allergy.

_c_   5. The whale's **blowhole** can best be described as
      a. its dorsal fin.
      b. an opening for taking in water.
      c. a nostril through which it breathes.
      d. an organ used for swimming and balancing.

_b_   6. A **disoriented** person is likely to be
      a. unaccustomed to confusion.
      b. mentally confused.
      c. helplessly nervous.
      d. unfamiliar with directions.

_d_   7. If the editorial writer **speculated** on the senator's problem, she
      a. engaged in a risky business venture with him.
      b. turned all of her information over to the press.
      c. disregarded the likely outcome.
      d. reflected on its various aspects.

_c_   8. **Revelry** at a funeral could best be described as
      a. a violation of the law.
      b. showing respect.
      c. inappropriate.
      d. suspicious behavior.

_d_   9. A **pod** of whales is usually considered to
      a. have identical features.
      b. swim only with their mates.
      c. be dangerous to outsiders.
      d. be a small group.

_a_   10. A **mammal** is a(n)
      a. warmblooded vertebrate.
      b. animal with fins.
      c. ocean-faring fish.
      d. member of the whale family.

_c_   11. A person who is **writhing** in pain
      a. should go to a hospital.
      b. has tremendous will power.
      c. is suffering great distress.
      d. needs to lie down.

___c___ 12. **Ministrations,** as used in "Restored to the Sea," means to
   a. conduct religious services.
   b. give directions or verbal assistance.
   c. administer help or give care.
   d. cure one's illness.

___d___ 13. **Sonar** would most probably be used to
   a. count the number of whales in a pod.
   b. track submarines through the ocean.
   c. calculate ocean depths.
   d. all of the above.

21B   CENTRAL THEME AND MAIN IDEAS

Follow the directions for each item below.

___b___ 1. The story is mainly about
   a. volunteers who have traveled from all over Australia to help.
   b. the rescue of stranded whales by concerned citizens.
   c. the hardships many volunteers endured.
   d. a malfunction in the whales' sonar.

___c___ 2. The underlying central theme of "Restored to the Sea" is that
   a. rescuing stranded false killer whales is dangerous work.
   b. volunteers became attached to the whales and even named them.
   c. caring for creatures in distress can be a rewarding experience.
   d. most of the whales were eventually saved by the volunteers.

3. In your own words, give the main idea of paragraph 3.

   The whales' sonar may have malfunctioned, causing the

   whales to become disoriented.

___c___ 4. What is the main idea of paragraph 5?
   a. The whales were moved from the open beach to a sheltered cove.
   b. Whales weigh as much as 750 lbs. each and were difficult for the volunteers to move.
   c. The volunteers battled exhaustion and cold but were devoted.
   d. Faithful volunteers who were injured returned to the rescue again.

21C MAJOR DETAILS

Decide whether each detail is true (T), false (F), or not discussed (ND).

__F__ 1. Stranded false killer whales are known to attack humans.

__F__ 2. Volunteers from Seal Rocks rescued 37 of the whales.

_ND_ 3. One whale was the cause of the stranding of 49 others.

__T__ 4. Some volunteers traveled great distances to help.

__T__ 5. The whales' malfunctioning sonar may have led them astray.

_ND_ 6. Humans are quick to answer calls to help any animal in distress.

_ND_ 7. The volunteers' previous training prepared them for the rescue attempt.

_ND_ 8. Whales are by nature nervous creatures.

21D INFERENCES

Decide whether each statement below can be inferred (YES) or cannot be inferred (NO) from the reading selection.

__NO__ 1. In paragraph 1 the volunteers were celebrating with a beach party because the work had not yet begun.

__NO__ 2. Scientific studies proved why the whales became stranded.

YES 3. Like humans, whales can become excited and distressed.

__NO__ 4. If a whale's blowhole remains underwater indefinitely, the animal will drown.

YES 5. Watching helpless whales die was an event the volunteers were prepared for when they began the mission.

__NO__ 6. It is common for whales to become stranded.

YES 7. The size of the whales hampered the volunteers' attempts to rescue them.

__NO__ 8. False killer whales become stranded more often than gray whales.

YES 9. The volunteers felt a sense of accomplishment after saving 37 of the whales.

YES 10. Kerrie Haynes-Lovell had worked with whales before.

21E CRITICAL READING: THE WRITER'S CRAFT
Choose the best answer.

__d__ 1. *Read paragraph 4 again.* What would be missing if the description "bloodied, wailing animals" were replaced by the phrase "beached whales"?
a. the drama of the event
b. the visual and auditory impact
c. a sense of desperation
d. all of the above

__d__ 2. *Read paragraph 4 again.* The tone of the "conversation" between Susan Clarke and her whale Hope is
a. pessimistic and sorrowful.
b. impatient yet hopeful.
c. sad but promising.
d. reassuring and optimistic.

__a__ 3. To get the reader's attention, the author starts by
a. contrasting the party atmosphere in paragraph 1 with the somber reality in paragraph 2.
b. explaining the behavior of the people on the beach before introducing the whales to the scene.
c. encouraging the reader to visualize the row of stranded false killer whales.
d. comparing the beach before and after the whales became stranded.

21F READER RESPONSE: TO DISCUSS OR TO WRITE ABOUT

1. Often you read in the newspaper about people who participate in efforts to rescue an animal, such as a cat in a tree or a duckling in a sewer drain. Why do you think people willingly give of their time and effort to rescue stranded animals?

2. Have you ever worked as a volunteer after a natural disaster, such as a flood or tornado? Why did you do this? What were the benefits? Would you do it again? Give specific reasons.

3. In 1985 a humpback whale, later affectionately called Humphrey, made an unprecedented visit to San Francisco Bay, and from there to the Sacramento River Delta region, where he remained for twenty-four days. It took $50,000 and the combined efforts of many individuals to persuade him to return from the water of the Delta to the safety of his natural ocean habitat. Do you think the money and man-hours spent in rescuing this whale were justified? Defend your position with specific reasons.

Name   Date

How Did You Do?　　　　　　　　**21**　Restored to the Sea

SKILL *(number of items)*	Number Correct		Points for Each		Score
Vocabulary (13)	_____	×	2	=	_____
Central Theme and Main Ideas (4)	_____	×	6	=	_____
Major Details (8)	_____	×	3	=	_____
Inferences (10)	_____	×	2	=	_____
Critical Reading: The Writer's Craft (3)	_____	×	2	=	_____

(Possible Total: 100) *Total* _____

SPEED

Reading Time: _____ Reading Rate (page 398): _____ Words Per Minute

Selection 22

I Became Her Target

Roger Wilkins

(1) My favorite teacher's name was "Deadeye" Bean. Her real name was Dorothy. She taught American history to eighth graders in the junior high section of Creston, the high school that served the north end of Grand Rapids, Michigan. It was the fall of 1944. Franklin D. Roosevelt was president; American troops were battling their way across France; Joe DiMaggio was still in the service; the Montgomery bus boycott was more than a decade away, and I was a 12-year-old black newcomer in a school that was otherwise all white.

(2) My mother, who had been a widow in New York, had married my stepfather, a Grand Rapids physician, the year before, and he had bought the best house he could afford for his new family. The problem for our new neighbors was that their neighborhood had previously been pristine (in their terms) and they were ignorant about black people. The prevailing wisdom in the neighborhood was that we were spoiling it and that we ought to go back where we belonged (or alternatively, ought not intrude where we were not wanted). There was a lot of angry talk among the adults, but nothing much came of it.

(3) But some of the kids, those first few weeks, were quite nasty. They threw stones at me, chased me home when I was on foot and spat on my bike seat when I was in class. For a time, I was a pretty lonely, friendless and sometimes frightened kid. I was just transplanted from Harlem, and here in Grand Rapids, the dominant culture was speaking to me insistently. I can see now that those youngsters were bullying and culturally disadvantaged. I knew then that they were bigoted, but the culture spoke to me more powerfully than my mind and I felt ashamed for being different—a nonstandard person.

(4) I now know that Dorothy Bean understood most of that and deplored it. So things began to change when I walked into her classroom. She was a pleasant-looking single woman, who looked old and wrinkled to me at the time, but who was probably about 40. Whereas my other teachers approached the problem of easing in their new black pupil by ignoring him for the first few weeks, Miss Bean went right at me. On the morning after having read our first assignment, she asked me the first question. I later came to know that in Grand Rapids, she was viewed as a very liberal person who believed, among other things, that Negroes were equal.

(5) I gulped and answered her question and the follow-up. They weren't brilliant answers, but they did establish the facts that I had read the assignment and that I could speak English. Later in the hour, when one

Roger Wilkins, distinguished lawyer, award-winning journalist, educator, and civil rights activist, is currently the Clarence J. Robinson Professor of History and American Culture at George Mason University and a commentator for National Public Radio.

© 1998 Arizona State University

of my classmates had bungled an answer, Miss Bean came back to me with a question that required me to clean up the girl's mess and established me as a smart person.

(6) Thus, the teacher began to give me human dimensions, though not perfect ones for an eighth grader. It was somewhat better to be an incipient teacher's pet than merely a dark presence in the back of the room onto whose silent form my classmates could fit all the stereotypes they carried in their heads.

(7) A few days later, Miss Bean became the first teacher ever to require me to think. She asked my opinion about something Jefferson had done. In those days, all my opinions were derivative. I was for Roosevelt because my parents were and I was for the Yankees because my older buddy from Harlem was a Yankee fan. Besides, we didn't have opinions about historical figures like Jefferson. Like our high school building or old Mayor Welch, he just was.

(8) After I had stared at her for a few seconds, she said: "Well, should he have bought Louisiana or not?"

(9) "I guess so," I replied tentatively.

(10) "Why?" she shot back.

(11) Why! What kind of question was that, I groused silently. But I ventured an answer. Day after day, she kept doing that to me, and my answers became stronger and more confident. She was the first teacher to give me the sense that thinking was part of education and that I could form opinions that had some value.

(12) Her final service to me came on a day when my mind was wandering and I was idly digging my pencil into the writing surface on the arm of my chair. Miss Bean impulsively threw a hunk of gum eraser at me. By amazing chance, it hit my hand and sent the pencil flying. She gasped, and I crept mortified after my pencil as the class roared. That was the ice breaker. Afterward, kids came up to me to laugh about "Old Deadeye Bean." The incident became a legend, and I, a part of that story, became a person to talk to. So that's how I became just another kid in school and Dorothy Bean became "Old Deadeye."

(800 words)

Here are some of the more difficult words in "I Became Her Target."

Vocabulary List

bigoted
(paragraph 3)

bigot (big′ət) *n.* [Fr < OFr, a term of insult used of Normans, apparently a Norman oath < ? ME *bi god,* by God] **1** a person who holds blindly and intolerantly to a particular creed, opinion, etc. **2** a narrow-minded, prejudiced person —**SYN.** ZEALOT —**big′·oted** *adj.* —**big′·ot·edly** *adv.*

boycott
(paragraph 1)

boy·cott (boi′kät′) *vt.* [after Capt. C. C. *Boycott,* land agent ostracized by his neighbors during the Land League agitation in Ireland in 1880] **1** to join together in refusing to deal with, so as to punish, coerce, etc. **2** to refuse to buy, sell, or use [to *boycott* a newspaper] —✧*n.* an act or instance of boycotting

Deadeye
(paragraph 1)

dead·eye (-ī′) *n.* **1** a round, flat block of wood with three holes in it for a lanyard, used in pairs on a sailing ship to hold the shrouds and stays taut **2** [Slang] an accurate marksman

derivative
(paragraph 7)

de·riva·tive (də riv′ə tiv) *adj.* [ME *derivatif* < LL *derivativus* < L *derivatus,* pp. of *derivare:* see fol.] **1** derived **2** using or taken from other sources; not original —*n.* **1** something derived **2** *Chem.* a substance derived from, or of such composition and properties that it may be considered as derived from, another substance by chemical change, esp. by the substitution of one or more elements or radicals **3** *Finance* a contract, as an option or futures contract, whose value depends on the value of the securities, commodities, etc. that form the basis of the contract **4** *Linguis.* a word formed from another or others by derivation **5** *Math.* the limiting value of a rate of change of a function with respect to a variable; the instantaneous rate of change, or slope, of a function (Ex.: the derivative of y with respect to x, often written dy/dx, is 3 when $y = 3x$) —**de·riv′a·tively** *adv.*

de·rive (di rīv′) *vt.* **·rived′, ·riv′·ing** [ME *deriven* < OFr *deriver* < L *derivare,* to divert, orig., to turn a stream from its channel < *de-,* from + *rivus,* a stream: see RIVAL] **1** to get or receive (something) *from* a source **2** to get by reasoning; deduce or infer **3** to trace from or to a source; show the derivation of **4** *Chem.* to obtain or produce (a compound) from another compound by replacing one element with one or more other elements —*vi.* to come (*from*); be derived; originate —**SYN.** RISE —**de·riv′·able** *adj.* —**de·riv′er** *n.*

295

Vocabulary List

dominant
(paragraph 3)

domi·nant (däm′ə nənt) *adj.* [[L *dominans*, prp. of *dominari*: see fol.]] **1** exercising authority or influence; dominating; ruling; prevailing **2** *Genetics* designating or relating to that one of any pair of allelic hereditary factors which, when both are present in the germ plasm, dominates over the other and appears in the organism: opposed to RECESSIVE: see MENDEL'S LAWS **3** *Music* of or based upon the fifth tone of a diatonic scale —*n.* **1** *Ecol.* that species of plant or animal most numerous in a community or exercising control over the other organisms by its influence upon the environment **2** *Genetics* a dominant character or factor **3** *Music* the fifth note of a diatonic scale —**dom′i·nantly** *adv.*

SYN.—**dominant** refers to that which dominates or controls, or has the greatest effect [*dominant* characteristics in genetics]; **predominant** refers to that which is at the moment uppermost in importance or influence [the *predominant* reason for his refusal]; **paramount** is applied to that which ranks first in importance, authority, etc. [of *paramount* interest to me]; **preeminent** implies prominence because of surpassing excellence [the *preeminent* writer of his time]; **preponderant** implies superiority in amount, weight, power, importance, etc. [the *preponderant* religion of a country]

groused
(paragraph 11)

grouse[2] (grous) [Informal] *vi.* **groused**, **grous′·ing** [[orig. Brit army slang < ?]] to complain; grumble —*n.* a complaint —**grous′er** *n.*

incipient
(paragraph 6)

in·cipi·ent (in sip′ē ənt) *adj.* [[L *incipiens*, prp. of *incipere*, to begin, lit., take up < *in-*, in, on + *capere*, to take: see HAVE]] in the first stage of existence; just beginning to exist or to come to notice [an *incipient* illness] —**in·cip′i·ence** *n.* or **in·cip′i·ency** —**in·cip′i·ently** *adv.*

insistently
(paragraph 3)

in·sist (in sist′) *vi.* [[MFr *insister* < L *insistere*, to stand on, pursue diligently, persist < *in-*, in, on + *sistere*, to stand, redupl. of *stare*, STAND]] to take and maintain a stand or make a firm demand: often with *on* or *upon* —*vt.* **1** to demand strongly **2** to declare firmly or persistently —**in·sist′er** *n.* —**in·sist′·ingly** *adv.*

in·sist·ent (-tənt) *adj.* [[L *insistens*]] **1** insisting or demanding; persistent in demands or assertions **2** compelling the attention [an *insistent* rhythm] —**in·sist′·ently** *adv.*

mortified
(paragraph 12)

mor·tify (môrt′ə fī′) *vt.* **··fied′**, **··fy′·ing** [[ME *mortifien* < OFr *mortifier* < LL(Ec) *mortificare*, to kill, destroy < L *mors*, death (see MORTAL) + *facere*, to make, DO[1]]] **1** to punish (one's body) or control (one's physical desires and passions) by self-denial, fasting, etc., as a means of religious or ascetic discipline **2** to cause to feel shame, humiliation, chagrin, etc.; injure the pride or self-respect of **3** [Now Rare] to cause (body tissue) to decay or become gangrenous **4** to destroy the vitality or vigor of —*vi.* **1** to practice MORTIFICATION (sense 1*a*) **2** [Now Rare] to decay or become gangrenous —*SYN.* ASHAMED —**mor′·ti·fi′er** *n.*

pristine
(paragraph 2)

pris·tine (pris′tēn′, -tin; pris tēn′; *chiefly Brit* pris′tīn′) *adj.* [[L *pristinus*, former < OL *pri*, before: see PRIME]] **1** characteristic of the earliest, or an earlier, period or condition; original ☆**2** still pure; uncorrupted; unspoiled [*pristine* beauty] —**pris′·tine′ly** *adv.*

ventured
(paragraph 11)

ven·ture (ven′chər) *n.* [[ME, aphetic for *aventure*: see ADVENTURE]] **1** a risky or dangerous undertaking; esp., a business enterprise in which there is danger of loss as well as chance for profit **2** something on which a risk is taken, as the merchandise in a commercial enterprise or a stake in gambling **3** chance; fortune: now only in **at a venture**, by mere chance; at random —*vt.* **··tured**, **··tur·ing** **1** to expose to danger or risk [to *venture* one's life] **2** to expose (money, merchandise, etc.) to chance of loss **3** to undertake the risk of; brave [to *venture* a storm] **4** to express at the risk of criticism, objection, denial, etc. [to *venture* an opinion] —*vi.* to do or go at some risk —**ven′·turer** *n.*

22A   VOCABULARY

From the context of "I Became Her Target," explain the meaning of each of the vo-cabulary words shown in boldface below.

1. *From paragraph 1:* My favorite teacher's name was **"Deadeye"** Bean.

   someone who shoots well

2. *From paragraph 1:* The Montgomery bus **boycott** was more than a decade away, and I was a 12-year-old black newcomer in a school that was oth-erwise all white.

   refusal to use

3. *From paragraph 2:* The problem for our new neighbors was that their neighborhood had previously been **pristine.**

   unspoiled

4. *From paragraph 3:* I was just transplanted from Harlem, and here in Grand Rapids, the **dominant** culture was speaking to me **insistently.**

   prevailing . . . demandingly

5. *From paragraph 3:* I knew then that they were **bigoted.**

   narrow-minded

6. *From paragraph 6:* It was somewhat better to be an **incipient** teacher's pet than merely a dark presence in the back of the room.

   just coming into existence

7. *From paragraph 7:* In those days, all my opinions were **derivative.**

   not original

8. *From paragraph 11:* What kind of question was that, I **groused** silently. But I **ventured** an answer.

   complained . . . risked

   _____

   _____

   _____

9. *From paragraph 12:* I crept **mortified** after my pencil as the class roared.

   ashamed

   _____

22B   CENTRAL THEME AND MAIN IDEAS

Choose the best answer.

___c___ 1. What is the central theme of "I Became Her Target"?
   a. Roger Wilkins' teacher did not like him and asked him trick questions because he was black and she was a racist.
   b. Roger Wilkins' classmates had been raised by their parents to be racists, and until they were forced to be nice to Wilkins they had no idea what black people were really like.
   c. Roger Wilkins' teacher helped him realize his worth and get the respect of the other students by challenging him to show his intelligence and answer hard questions.
   d. Roger Wilkins' classmates became his friends once they realized that he and they shared a dislike of their American history teacher.

___d___ 2. What is the main idea of paragraph 7?
   a. Roger Wilkins did not like being called upon to answer hard questions.
   b. Roger Wilkins did not know anything about President Jefferson.
   c. All of Roger Wilkins' opinions were derived from his parents or friends.
   d. Roger Wilkins was not used to being asked to think and form his own opinions.

Name   Date

__a__ 3. What is the main idea of paragraph 12?
  a. Miss Bean helped Roger Wilkins gain his classmates' acceptance by throwing an eraser at him when his attention wandered.
  b. Miss Bean always looked for opportunities to embarrass her students by throwing erasers at them.
  c. Miss Bean had only pretended to be interested in Roger Wilkins' education, but she was a racist underneath.
  d. Roger Wilkins was accepted by his classmates only after he mortified Miss Bean in front of them.

22C MAJOR DETAILS

Decide whether each detail is true (T), or false (F), or not discussed (ND).

__T__ 1. Roger Wilkins' favorite teacher was Dorothy Bean.

__T__ 2. He was in her eighth grade American history class in 1944.

__ND__ 3. Before Wilkins, no black student had ever attended Creston High School in Grand Rapids, Michigan.

__ND__ 4. Wilkins' mother met his stepfather in New York.

__F__ 5. The adults in Wilkins' new neighborhood threw stones at his house because they wanted his family to move away.

__T__ 6. Miss Bean asked Roger Wilkins the very first question on the very first assignment.

__T__ 7. Dorothy Bean was viewed as a very liberal person, who believed, among other things, that blacks were equal to whites.

__F__ 8. Roger Wilkins had never been to Harlem.

__T__ 9. Miss Bean kept asking Roger Wilkins questions day after day until his answers became increasingly confident.

__ND__ 10. It was the tradition at Creston High School to give teachers nicknames.

22D INFERENCES

Choose the best answer.

__b__ 1. *Read paragraphs 1, 2, and 4 again.* Why does the author change from using the word "black" in these paragraphs to using the word "Negroes" in the last sentence of paragraph 4?
   a. By using the word "Negroes," the author shows that he is prejudiced against his own black people.
   b. The preferred, formal term for blacks was "Negroes" in 1944, and the author wants to recreate that time for the reader.
   c. The author assumes that the words "Negroes" and "blacks" are interchangeable, although today the preferred term is "blacks."
   d. The author prefers the word "Negroes," even though in 1987, when he wrote this essay, the preferred word was "blacks."

__d__ 2. *Read paragraph 3 again.* What is the author implying when he calls the white students "culturally disadvantaged," a term that is usually applied to undereducated minority people?
   a. The author is not aware of how the term is usually used.
   b. The author is implying that the students at Creston High School had not gotten a good education and had not developed good study habits.
   c. The author is trying to be polite by using a nice word for "stupid."
   d. The author is being mildly sarcastic, applying a term to these students that they or their parents might have applied to him.

__a__ 3. *Read paragraph 6 again.* Why did Roger Wilkins feel "it was somewhat better to be an incipient teacher's pet than merely a dark presence in the back of the room"?
   a. He preferred being liked by the teacher to being liked by no one at all.
   b. He felt that being teacher's pet might result in his getting special privileges or a higher grade.
   c. He did not like the other students and did not care what they thought of him.
   d. He did not like sitting in the back of the room, and he hoped that Miss Bean would change his seat.

Name   Date

22E CRITICAL READING: THE WRITER'S CRAFT
Choose the best answer.

___a___ 1. The author gives Dorothy Bean's nickname in paragraph 1 in order to
a. immediately arouse the reader's curiosity.
b. add to the list of historic facts.
c. give an anecdote.
d. make a comparison.

___b___ 2. *Read paragraphs 8 to 10 again.* The author includes this dialogue for all of the following reasons *except* it
a. was typical of his early questioning by Miss Bean.
b. shows how she tried to embarrass him in front of the other students.
c. demonstrates Miss Bean's personality as a teacher.
d. shows how Miss Bean forced him to think.

___c___ 3. *Read paragraph 10 again.* If the phrase "shot back" were replaced by the word "asked," Miss Bean's response would seem *less*
a. cruel.
b. humble.
c. dramatic.
d. professional.

___d___ 4. *Read paragraph 12 again.* This anecdote accomplishes all of the following *except* to
a. explain how Dorothy Bean earned her nickname.
b. show that Miss Bean was a tough disciplinarian.
c. tell how the other students came to accept the author by identifying with his embarrassment.
d. demonstrate that the author felt comfortable with Miss Bean.

22F READER RESPONSE: TO DISCUSS OR TO WRITE ABOUT

1. Suppose the "best house" you could "afford" (paragraph 2) were in a neighborhood where people of your race, religion, or ethnic background are not wanted. Would you move into that neighborhood? Explain your point of view fully.

2. Discuss a teacher or other adult who had a big impact on you when you were growing up. Using specific details and examples, describe the way in which he or she affected you.

3. Does calling someone by a nickname usually indicate a feeling of affection or ridicule? Think of someone you have known who had a nickname. Did the nickname reveal something about that person's physical features or personality? If not, what was the basis for the nickname? Be specific with your explanation.

How Did You Do?   **22** I Became Her Target

SKILL *(number of items)*	Number Correct		Points for Each		Score
Vocabulary (11)	_____	×	3	=	_____
Central Theme and Main Ideas (3)	_____	×	4	=	_____
Major Details (10)	_____	×	4	=	_____
Inferences (3)	_____	×	1	=	_____
Critical Reading: The Writer's Craft (4)	_____	×	3	=	_____

(Possible Total: 100) *Total* _____

SPEED

Reading Time: _____ Reading Rate (page 399): _____ Words Per Minute

Name   Date

She Made Her Dream Come True

Michael Ryan

(1) To appreciate where Maria Vega is today, you have to understand where she was 22 years ago. "My family and I traveled up the East Coast throughout the growing season," this daughter of migrant workers recalled. "I went to five or six schools a year, from Florida to Pennsylvania."

(2) Maria Vega's view of life was formed in transient shacks with communal baths. In most schools she attended, Maria was placed in remedial classes, falling further behind in her studies. Homework, if any was assigned, was difficult to finish. "There was a lot of noise at night from the men who got drunk after work to forget about their troubles," she said. But every few months visitors from a different kind of world arrived. "Toward the end of the season in each state, the doctors and nurses would come," she said. These public health workers brought young Maria comfort—and relief from the frequent infections that have left a welter of scar tissue in her ear canals. They also brought her an idea: "I started to have this dream that I would become a doctor," she recalled. "But I never thought it was possible."

(3) Although Maria's two brothers, two sisters and parents formed a close-knit, supportive family, they had nothing in the way of financial resources. "During the holidays, my mom would sit us down and give us the same speech every year: 'There are no gifts under the tree—there is no tree,'" Maria said. What her family did give her was its support for her dream. "They told me to do what I wanted," she said, "and if it didn't work out, I could always come home to them."

(4) When Maria was in the 10th grade, her mother decided to stay in one place for a season, finding farm work around Homestead, Fla., so that Maria and her older sister could spend the year in one school. "Until that year, I had never taken a final exam," Maria told me. She worked so hard in high school that she earned a scholarship to Miami-Dade Community College. But even the basic, introductory chemistry course at Miami-Dade was difficult for her. "I had to take it twice," she said. "But I learned how to ask for help." As she recounted her story, Maria frequently talked about the people who helped her. "I know I didn't get here on my own," she said. Her junior college teachers provided extra assistance. They helped her get into the University of Miami, where she entered the pre-med program, supporting herself by working as a waitress and an aerobics instructor. School administrators, impressed by her effort, helped arrange scholarships and loans. Some professors even lent Maria textbooks. She graduated from Miami on time, with a Bachelor of Science in psychology.

(5) But her bachelor's degree was not an automatic ticket to medical school. Her scores on the Medical College Admissions Test, the standard

medical school admissions test, were mediocre. "I guess I panicked when I took it the first time," she said. "Or maybe I didn't know enough." Maria applied to 20 medical schools, but she was rejected everywhere. "I didn't give up," Maria said. "I thought I'd try again next year." She took a job as a receptionist, then applied to a program at Boston University that helps prepare bright but disadvantaged students for medical school. "Her enthusiasm, and her determination to achieve her goal, showed that she is a remarkable young woman," said Dr. Kenneth Edelin, the dean who administers the program.

(6) Finally, Maria was admitted to Boston University's medical school. She is now a second-year student. "It's hard," Maria said, "but I'll do what it takes to get through." Maria isn't sure yet about her eventual medical specialty, but she already knows what her approach to doctoring is going to be. "I think I can relate to patients who don't live in middle-class conditions," she said. "If somebody comes in and says they don't have the money to get medicine, I've been there. Victims of violence or alcohol or drug abuse—I grew up surrounded by that."

(7) Every September, Maria Vega's parents come to the end of their circuit—picking tomatoes in Pennsylvania before going back to Florida to begin the process again. Someday, Maria hopes to be able to help them to a better life. But for now, when her parents come north, she takes a bus to see them. "When I get there, my mom says, 'Here grab a bucket,' so I do," Maria said. For a few days, Maria Vega, medical student, is once again Maria Vega, migrant worker, holding on to her history and her values. As Maria's anatomy professor, Linda Wright, told me: "She's going to be a fantastic doctor."

(803 words)

Vocabulary List

Here are some of the more difficult words in "She Made Her Dream Come True."

anatomy
(paragraph 7)

anato·my (ə nat′ə mē) *n., pl.* **··mies** ⟦ME & OFr *anatomie* < LL *anatomia* < Gr *anatomia, anatomē,* a cutting up < *anatemnein* < *ana-,* up + *temnein,* to cut: see -TOMY⟧ **1** the dissecting of an animal or plant in order to determine the position, structure, etc. of its parts **2** the science of the morphology or structure of animals or plants **3** the structure of an organism or body **4** a detailed analysis **5** [Archaic] a skeleton

circuit
(paragraph 7)

cir·cuit (sur′kit) *n.* ⟦ME < OFr < L *circui̇us,* a going around, circuit < *circumire* < *circum* (see CIRCUM-) + *ire,* to go: see YEAR⟧ **1** the line or the length of the line forming the boundaries of an area **2** the area bounded **3** the act of going around something; course or journey around /the moon's *circuit* of the earth/ **4** *a)* the regular journey of a person performing certain duties, as of an itinerant preacher or a judge holding court at designated places *b)* the district periodically traveled through in the performance of such duties *c)* the route traveled ☆**5** the judicial district of a U.S. Court of Appeals **6** *a)* a number of associated theaters at which plays, movies, etc. are shown in turn *b)* a group of nightclubs, resorts, etc. at which entertainers appear in turn ☆*c)* a sequence of contests or matches held at various places, in which a particular group of athletes compete; also, an association or league of athletic teams /the professional bowlers' *circuit*/ **7** *Elec. a)* a complete or partial path over which current may flow *b)* any hookup, wiring, etc. that is connected into this path, as for radio, television, or sound reproduction —*vi.* to go in a circuit —*vt.* to make a circuit about —SYN. CIRCUMFERENCE —**cir′·cuital** *adj.*

communal
(paragraph 2)

com·mu·nal (kə myōōn'əl, käm'yə nəl) *adj.* [ME & OFr < LL *communalis*] **1** of a commune or communes **2** of or belonging to the community; shared, or participated in, by all; public **3** designating or of social or economic organization in which there is common ownership of property —**com·mu·nal·i·ty** (käm'yōō nal'ə tē) *n.* —**com'·mu·nally** *adv.*

mediocre
(paragraph 5)

me·dio·cre (mē'dē ō'kər, mē'dē ō'kər) *adj.* [Fr *médiocre* < L *mediocris* < *medius*, middle (see MID[1]) + *ocris*, a peak < IE base **ak-*, sharp > L *acer*] **1** neither very good nor very bad; ordinary; average **2** not good enough; inferior

migrant
(paragraph 1)

mi·grant (mī'grənt) *adj.* [L *migrans,* prp. of *migrare*] migrating; migratory —*n.* **1** a person, bird, or animal that migrates ☆**2** a farm laborer who moves from place to place to harvest seasonal crops

specialty
(paragraph 6)

spe·cialty (spesh'əl tē) *n., pl.* ·**·ties** [ME *specialte* < OFr *especialté*] **1** a special quality, feature, point, characteristic, etc. **2** a thing specialized in; special interest, field of study or professional work, etc. **3** the state of being special **4** an article or class of article characterized by special features, superior quality, novelty, etc. [a bakery whose *specialty* is pie] **5** *Law* a special contract, obligation, agreement, etc. under seal, or a contract by deed —*adj.* **1** designating or of a store or stores that specialize in selling certain types of goods or to certain types of customers **2** of such goods or customers

transient
(paragraph 2)

tran·sient (tran'shənt, -sē ənt; -zhənt, -zē ənt) *adj.* [L *transiens,* prp. of *transire*: see TRANSIT] **1** *a)* passing away with time; not permanent; temporary; transitory *b)* passing quickly or soon; fleeting; ephemeral ☆**2** staying only for a short time [the *transient* population at resorts] —*n.* ☆**1** a transient person or thing [transients at a hotel] **2** *Elec.* a temporary component of a current, resulting from a voltage surge, a change from one steady-state condition to another, etc. —**tran'·sience** *n.* or **tran'·sien·cy** —**tran'·sient·ly** *adv.*

welter
(paragraph 2)

wel·ter (wel'tər) *vi.* [ME *weltren* < MDu *welteren*, freq. formation akin to OE *wealtan*, to roll, boil up: for IE base see WELL[1]] **1** *a)* to roll about or wallow, as a pig does in mud *b)* to be deeply or completely involved [to *welter* in work] **2** to be soaked, stained, or bathed [to *welter* in blood] **3** to tumble and toss about: said as of the sea —*n.* **1** a tossing and tumbling, as of waves **2** a confusion; turmoil

23A VOCABULARY

From the context of "She Made Her Dream Come True," explain the meaning of each vocabulary word shown in boldface below.

1. *From paragraph 1:* "My family and I traveled up the East Coast throughout the growing season," this daughter of **migrant** workers recalled.

   farm laborer who moves

2. *From paragraph 2:* Maria Vega's view of life was formed in **transient** shacks with **communal** baths.

   temporary . . . public

3. *From paragraph 2:* . . . frequent infections that left a **welter** of scar tissue in her ear canals.

   a roll

4. *From paragraph 5:* Her scores on the MCAT . . . were **mediocre.**

   average

5. *From paragraph 6:* Maria isn't sure yet about her eventual medical **specialty. . . .**

   field of study

6. *From paragraph 7:* Every September, Maria Vega's parents come to the end of their **circuit. . . .**

   regular journey

7. *From paragraph 7:* As Maria's **anatomy** professor, Linda Wright, told me: "She's going to be a fantastic doctor."

   an animal's structure

Name   Date

23B CENTRAL THEME AND MAIN IDEAS

Choose the best answer.

__c__ 1. What is the central theme of "She Made Her Dream Come True"?
   a. Given financial support and encouragement, migrant workers can succeed in medical school.
   b. Maria Vega's overcoming problems related to finance, health, and education will help her be a sympathetic doctor.
   c. Through determination Maria Vega overcame poverty and educational disadvantages to qualify for medical school.
   d. Maria Vega plans to provide her family a better lifestyle when she becomes a doctor.

   2. In your own words, give the main idea of paragraph 4.

   Teachers and college administrators were impressed with Maria

   Vega's hard work so they provided her moral support and finances

   to realize her goal of graduating from college as a pre-medical major.

__d__ 3. What is the main idea of paragraph 5?
   a. Maria Vega's Bachelor of Science degree did not assure her admission to a medical school.
   b. Twenty medical schools rejected Maria Vega's application to enroll.
   c. Maria Vega's enrolling in a Boston University program for disadvantaged students helped prepare her for medical school.
   d. Maria Vega's determination and enthusiasm helped her to achieve her goal to enroll in medical school.

23C MAJOR DETAILS

Decide whether each detail is MAJOR or MINOR based on the context of the reading selection.

MAJOR 1. Public health workers influenced Maria Vega's dream to become a doctor.

MINOR 2. Maria Vega's family consisted of her parents, two brothers, and two sisters.

MAJOR 3. Maria Vega learned to ask for help when she had difficulties with her studies.

MINOR 4. Maria Vega's college major was psychology.

MINOR 5. After graduating from the University of Miami, Maria Vega worked as a receptionist

MINOR 6. Maria Vega borrowed textbooks from college professors.

MAJOR 7. Maria Vega's parents are migrant workers.

MAJOR 8. Maria Vega took her college chemistry course twice before she passed it.

MINOR 9. Maria takes a bus when she goes to visit her parents.

MAJOR 10. Maria Vega was placed in remedial classes at most schools she attended.

23D INFERENCES

Decide whether each statement below can be inferred (YES) or cannot be inferred (NO) from the reading selection.

NO 1. Maria Vega was twenty-two years old when this was written.

NO 2. Maria Vega thought her ear infections would prevent her from becoming a doctor.

YES 3. Frequent moves to different states negatively affected Maria Vega's academic performance in school.

NO 4. Maria Vega resented her parents' not giving her presents at Christmas.

NO 5. Because of Maria Vega's health problems, her mother decided to stay in one location when Maria was a sophomore.

NO 6. Maria Vega's staying in one school for an entire year allowed her to make lifelong friends.

NO 7. Maria Vega's employment as a waitress and aerobics instructor was good preparation for her becoming a doctor.

YES 8. Maria Vega's willingness to help her family harvest crops when she visits them indicates she upholds her family's history and values.

YES 9. Maria Vega will most likely not become wealthy when she becomes a doctor.

Name   Date

23E CRITICAL READING: FACT OR OPINION

Decide whether each statement, even if it quotes someone, contains a FACT or an OPINION.

<u>FACT</u> 1. *From paragraph 2:* During their visits, the health workers brought relief and comfort to Maria Vega.

<u>FACT</u> 2. *From paragraph 5:* "Her enthusiasm, and her determination to achieve her goal, showed that she is a remarkable woman [. . .]."

<u>OPINION</u> 3. *From paragraph 7:* Maria Vega's family harvested crops from Florida to Pennsylvania.

<u>OPINION</u> 4. *From paragraph 7:* "She's going to be a fantastic doctor."

23F CRITICAL READING: THE WRITER'S CRAFT

Choose the best answer.

  <u>c</u> 1. *Read paragraph 1 again.* The author gets the reader's attention in this paragraph through the use of
  a. comparison and contrast.
  b. a question.
  c. quotations.
  d. details related to the five senses.

  2. Repeating a key word in an essay helps the flow of thought. What key word is repeated in the topic sentence of every paragraph *except* paragraph 5?

  Maria

23G READER RESPONSE: TO DISCUSS OR TO WRITE ABOUT

1. Some children have to change schools one or more times between kindergarten and the twelfth grade. If this happened to you, what effect did such moving have on you? If this did not happen to you, what do you imagine the effect on you would have been?

2. If you knew that a doctor had once failed the medical school entrance exam before passing it the second time and the doctor found the course-work difficult, would you want to be this doctor's patient? Citing specific reasons, explain why you would or would not consider being a patient of this doctor.

3. Many college students are required or strongly urged to take one or more "remedial" courses (such as Developmental Reading, Basic Writing, Basic Math). If this has happened to you, what do you think are the advantages and disadvantages, both academic and social, of taking such courses? If this did not happen to you, what do you imagine would have been the academic and social advantages and disadvantages for you?

How Did You Do? 23 She Made Her Dream Come True

SKILL (number of items)	Number Correct		Points for Each		Score
Vocabulary (8)	_____	×	2	=	_____
Central Theme and Main Ideas (3)	_____	×	7	=	_____
Major Details (10)	_____	×	3	=	_____
Inferences (9)	_____	×	3	=	_____
Critical Reading: Fact or Opinion (4)	_____	×	1	=	_____
Critical Reading: The Writer's Craft (2)	_____	×	1	=	_____

(Possible Total: 100) *Total* _____

SPEED

Reading Time: _____ Reading Rate (page 399): _____ Words Per Minute

Name   Date

Selection 24

From In Search of Bernabé

Graciela Limón

(1) Luz and Arturo arrived at the Tijuana bus terminal forty hours later, exhausted and bloated from sitting in their cramped seats. As soon as they stepped out of the bus, they were approached by a woman who asked them if they wanted to cross the border that night. Without waiting for an answer, she told them she could be their guide. The price was five hundred American dollars apiece.

(2) Luz stared at the woman for a few moments, caught off guard by the suddenness of what was happening. More than her words, it was the woman's appearance that held Luz's attention. She was about thirty-five. Old enough, Luz figured, to have experience in her business. The woman was tall and slender, yet her body conveyed muscular strength that gave Luz the impression that she would be able to lead them across the border. The *coyota* returned Luz's gaze, evidently allowing time for the older woman to make up her mind. She took a step closer to Luz, who squinted as she concentrated on the woman's face. Luz regarded her dark skin and high forehead, and the deeply set eyes that steadily returned her questioning stare. With a glance, she took in the *coyota's* faded Levi's and plaid shirt under a shabby sweatshirt, and her eyes widened when she saw the woman's scratched, muddy cowboy boots. She had seen only men wear such shoes.

(3) Luz again looked into the woman's eyes. She was tough, and Luz knew that she had to drive a hard bargain. She began to cry. *"¡Señora, por favor!"* Have a heart! How can you charge so much? We're poor people who have come a long way. Where do you think we can find so many *dólares?* All we have is one hundred dollars to cover the two of us. Please! For the love of your mamacita!" The woman crossed her arms over her chest and laughed out loud as she looked into Luz's eyes. She spoke firmly. "Señora, I'm not in the habit of eating fairy tales for dinner. You've been in Mexico City for a long time. I have eyes, don't I? I can tell that you're not starving. Both of you have eaten a lot of enchiladas and tacos. Just look at those *nalgas!"* She gave Luz a quick, hard smack on her behind. Then, ignoring the older woman's look of outrage, the *coyota* continued to speak rapidly. "Look, Señora. Just to show you that I have feelings, I'll consider guiding the both of you at the reduced rate of seven hundred dollars. Half now; the rest when I get you to Los Angeles. Take it or leave it!" Luz knew that she was facing her match. She answered with one word, *"Bueno."*

(4) The *coyota* led them to a man who was standing nearby. He was wearing a long overcoat, inappropriate for the sultry weather in Tijuana. The coat had a purpose, though, for it concealed deep inner pockets which

were filled with money. The *coyota* pulled Luz nearer to the man, then whispered into her ear. "This man will change your pesos into American dollars. A good rate, I guarantee." When Arturo began to move closer, the *coyota* turned on him. "You stay over there!" Arturo obeyed.

(5) Even though she felt distrust, Luz decided that she and Arturo had no alternative. However, she needed to speak with him, so she pulled him to the side. "Hijo, we're taking a big chance. We can be robbed, even killed. Remember the stories we've been hearing since we left home. But what can we do? We need someone to help us get across, so what does it matter if it's this one, or someone else? What do you say?" Arturo agreed with her. "Let's try to make it to the other side. The sooner the better. I think you made a good bargain. We have the money, don't we?" "With a little left over when we get to Los Angeles."

(6) Before they returned to where the others were waiting, she turned to a wall. She didn't want anyone to see what she was doing. Luz withdrew the amount of pesos she estimated she could exchange for a little more than seven hundred American dollars. She walked over to the money vendor, and no sooner had the man placed the green bills on her palm than she heard the *coyota*'s sharp voice. "Three hundred and fifty dollars, *por favor!*" She signaled Luz and Arturo to follow her to a waiting car. They went as far as Mesa Otay, the last stretch of land between Mexico and California. There, the *coyota* instructed them to wait until it got dark. Finally, when Luz could barely see her hand in front of her, the woman gave the signal. "*¡Vámonos!*"

(7) They walked together under the cover of darkness. As Luz and Arturo trekked behind the woman, they sensed that they were not alone, that other people were also following. Suddenly someone issued a warning, "*¡La Migra! ¡Cuidado!*" The *coyota* turned with unexpected speed, and murmured one word, "*¡Abajo!*" All three fell to the ground, clinging to it, melting into it, hoping that it would split open so that they could crawl into its safety. Unexpectedly a light flashed on. Like a giant eye, it seemed to be coming from somewhere in the sky, slowly scanning the terrain. No one moved. All that could be heard were the crickets and the dry grass rasping in the mild breeze. The light had not detected the bodies crouched behind bushes and rocks. It flashed out as suddenly as it had gone on.

(8) "*¡Vámonos!*" The *coyota* was again on her feet and moving. They continued in the dark for hours over rough, rocky terrain. The *coyota* was sure-footed but Luz and Arturo bumped into rocks and tripped over gopher holes. Luz had not rested or eaten since she had gotten off the bus. She was fatigued but she pushed herself fearing she would be left behind if she stopped. Arturo was exhausted too, but he knew that he still had reserves of energy, enough for himself and for Luz.

(9) Dawn was breaking as they ascended a hill. Upon reaching the summit, they were struck with awe at the sight that spread beneath their feet. Their heavy breathing stopped abruptly as their eyes glowed in disbelief. Below, even though diffused by dawn's advancing light, was an il-

A sign near the United States/Mexico border warns illegal immigrants of the dangers in crossing the Yuha desert. The sign reads, "Careful! Don't risk your life to the elements. It's not worth the hardship!" Symbols represent, clockwise from left, sunstroke, mountains, rattlesnakes, canals, lack of water, and desert habitat.

© David McNew/Newsmakers/Getty Images

luminated sea of streets and buildings. A blur of neon formed a mass of light and color, edged by a highway that was a ribbon of liquid silver. Luz and Arturo wondered if fatigue had caused their eyes to trick them because as far as they could see there was brilliance, limited only in the distance by a vast ocean. To their left, they saw the lights of San Diego unfolding beneath them, and their heart stopped when they realized that farther north, where their eyes could not see, was their destination. Without thinking, Luz and Arturo threw their arms around one another and wept.

(10) The lights of San Diego receded behind them. The *coyota* had guided Luz and Arturo over an inland trail, taking them past the U.S. Immigration station at San Onofre, and then down to connect with the highway. A man in a car was waiting for them a few yards beyond Las Pulgas Road on California Interstate 5. The driver got out of the car as they approached, extending a rough hand first to Luz, and then to Arturo. "*Me llamo Ordaz.*" Ordaz turned to the *coyota* and spoke in English. His words were casual, as if he had seen her only hours before. "You're late. I was beginning to worry."

(11) "The old bag slowed me down." The *coyota* spoke to the man in English, knowing that her clients were unable to understand her. Then, she switched to Spanish to introduce herself to Luz and Arturo. "*Me llamo Petra Traslaviña*. I was born back in San Ysidro on a dairy farm. I speak English and Spanish." There was little talk among them beyond this first encounter. The four piled into a battered Pontiac station wagon, and with Ordaz at the wheel, they headed north. The woman pulled out a pack of Mexican cigarettes, smoking one after the other, until Ordaz started to cough. He opened the window complaining, "*Por favor*, Petra, you wanna choke us to death?" "Shut up!" she retorted rapidly, slurring the English *sh*. The phrase engraved itself in Luz's memory. She liked the sound of it. She liked its effect even more, since she noticed that Ordaz was silenced by the magical phrase. Inwardly, Luz practiced her first English words, repeating them over and again under her breath.

(12) Luz and Arturo were quiet during the trip mainly because they were frightened by the speed at which Ordaz was driving. As she looked out over the *coyota*'s shoulder, Luz knew that she didn't like what she was feeling and hearing. She even disliked the smell of the air, and she felt especially threatened by the early morning fog. When the headlights of oncoming cars broke the grayness, her eyes squinted with pain. The hours seemed endless, and they were relieved when Ordaz finally steered the Pontiac off the freeway and onto the streets of Los Angeles. Like children, Luz and Arturo looked around craning their necks, curiously peering through the windows and seeing that people waited for their turn to step onto the street. Luz thought it was silly the way those people moved in groups. No one ran out onto the street, leaping, jumping, dodging cars as happened in Mexico City and back home. Right away, she missed the vendors peddling wares, and the stands with food and drink.

(13) Suddenly, Luz was struck by the thought that she didn't know where the *coyota* was taking them. As if reading Luz's mind, the woman asked, "Do you have a place you want me to take you to?" Rattled by the question, Luz responded timidly. "No. We didn't have time to think." "I thought so. It's the same with all of you."

(14) The *coyota* was quiet for a while before she whispered to Ordaz, who shook his head in response. They engaged in a heated exchange of words in English, the driver obviously disagreeing with what the *coyota* was proposing. Finally, seeming to have nothing more to say, Ordaz shrugged his shoulders, apparently accepting defeat. The *coyota* turned to her passengers. "*Vieja*, I know of a place where you two can find a roof and a meal until you find work. But . . ." She was hesitating. "¡*Mierda!* . . . just don't tell them I brought you. They don't like me because I charge you people money."

(15) What she said next was muttered and garbled. Luz and Arturo did not understand her so they kept quiet, feeling slightly uneasy and confused. By this time Ordaz was on Cahuenga Boulevard in Hollywood. He turned up a short street, and pulled into the parking lot of Saint Turibius

Church, where the battered wagon spurted, then came to a stand-still. "*Hasta aquí.* You've arrived."

(16) The *coyota* was looking directly at Luz, who thought she detected a warning sign in the woman's eyes. "It was easy this time, Señora. Remember, don't get caught by *la Migra*, because it might not be so good next time around. But if that happens, you know that you can find me at the station in Tijuana." Again, the *coyota* seemed to be fumbling for words. Then she said, "Just don't get any funny ideas hanging around these people. I mean, they love to call themselves *voluntarios*, and they'll do anything for nothing. *Yo no soy así.* I'll charge you money all over again, believe me!" The *coyota* seemed embarrassed. Stiffly, she shifted in her seat, pointing at a two-story, Spanish-style house next to the church. "See that house?" Luz nodded. "*Bueno.* Just walk up to the front door, knock, and tell them who you are, and where you're from. They'll be good to you. But, as I already told you, don't mention me."

(17) She turned to Arturo. "Take care of yourself, *muchacho*. I've known a few like you who have gotten themselves killed out there." With her chin, she pointed toward the street. When Arturo opened his mouth to speak, the *coyota* cut him off curtly. "My three hundred and fifty dollars, *por favor*." She stretched out her hand in Luz's direction without realizing that her words about other young men who resembled Arturo had had an impact on Luz. "Petra, have you by any chance met my son? His name is Bernabé and he looks like this young man."

(18) The *coyota* looked into Luz's eyes. When she spoke her voice was almost soft. "They all look like Arturo, Madre. They all have the same fever in their eyes. How could I possibly know your son from all the rest?" Luz's heart shuddered when the *coyota* called her madre. Something told her that the woman did know Bernabé. This thought filled her with new hope, and she gladly reached into her purse. She put the money into the *coyota*'s hand, saying, "*Hasta pronto.* I hope, Petra, that our paths will cross again sooner or later."

(19) Luz and Arturo were handed the small bundles they had brought with them from Mexico City. As they stepped out of the car, the engine cranked on, backfiring loudly. When it disappeared into the flow of traffic, both realized that even though only three days had passed since they had left Mexico, they had crossed over into a world unknown to them. They were aware that they were facing days and months, perhaps even years, filled with dangers neither of them could imagine.

(20) Feeling apprehensive, they were silent as they approached the large house that their guide had pointed out. They didn't know that the building had been a convent and that it was now a refuge run by priests and other volunteers. Neither realized that they were entering a sanctuary for the displaced and for those without documents or jobs. When they were shown in, Luz and Arturo were surprised at how warmly they were received. No one asked any questions. Afterwards, they were given food to eat and a place to sleep.

(2,382 words)

Here are some of the more difficult words in "In Search of Bernabé."

apprehensive
(paragraph 20)

ap·pre·hen·sive (-hen′siv) *adj.* 〖ME < ML *apprehensivus* < pp. of L *apprehendere*, APPREHEND〗 **1** able or quick to apprehend or understand **2** having to do with perceiving or understanding **3** anxious or fearful about the future; uneasy —**ap′·pre·hen′·sively** *adv.* —**ap′·pre·hen′·sive·ness** *n.*

clients
(paragraph 11)

cli·ent (klī′ənt) *n.* 〖OFr < L *cliens*, follower, retainer < IE base **klei-*, to lean, as in L *clinare* (see INCLINE); basic sense, "one leaning on another (for protection)"〗 **1** [Archaic] a person dependent on another, as for protection or patronage **2** a person or company for whom a lawyer, accountant, advertising agency, etc. is acting **3** a customer **4** a person served by a social agency **5** a nation, state, etc. dependent on another politically, economically, etc.: also **client state** **6** *Comput.* a terminal or personal computer that is connected to a SERVER (sense 3) —**cli·en·tal** (klī′ən təl, klī en′təl) *adj.*

convent
(paragraph 20)

con·vent (kän′vənt, -vent′) *n.* 〖OFr < L *conventus*, assembly (in ML(Ec), religious house, convent), orig. pp. of *convenire*, CONVENE〗 **1** a community of nuns or, sometimes, monks, living under strict religious vows **2** the building or buildings occupied by such a community —*SYN.* CLOISTER

diffused
(paragraph 9)

dif·fuse (di fyo͞os′; *for v.*, -fyo͞oz′) *adj.* 〖ME < L *diffusus*, pp. of *diffundere*, to pour in different directions < *dis-*, apart + *fundere*, to pour: see FOUND²〗 **1** spread out or dispersed; not concentrated **2** using more words than are needed; long-winded; wordy —*vt., vi.* **-·fused′, -·fus′·ing 1** to pour, spread out, or disperse in every direction; spread or scatter widely **2** *Physics* to mix by diffusion, as gases, liquids, etc. —*SYN.* WORDY —**dif·fuse′·ly** *adv.* —**dif·fuse′·ness** *n.*

pesos
(paragraph 4)

peso (pā′sō; *Sp* pe′sô) *n., pl.* **-·sos′** (-sōz′; *Sp*, -sôs) 〖Sp, lit., a weight < L *pensum*, something weighed < neut. pp. of *pendere*: see PENSION〗 the basic monetary unit of: *a)* Argentina *b)* Chile *c)* Colombia *d)* Cuba *e)* the Dominican Republic *f)* Mexico *g)* the Philippines *h)* Uruguay: see the table of monetary units in the Reference Supplement

sultry
(paragraph 4)

sul·try (sul′trē) *adj.* **-·trier, -·tri·est** 〖var. of SWELTRY〗 **1** oppressively hot and moist; close; sweltering **2** extremely hot; fiery **3** *a)* hot or inflamed, as with passion or lust *b)* suggesting or expressing smoldering passion —**sul′·trily** *adv.* —**sul′·tri·ness** *n.*

terrain
(paragraph 7)

ter·rain (tə rān′) *n.* 〖Fr < L *terrenum* < *terrenus*, of earth, earthen < *terra*, TERRA〗 **1** ground or a tract of ground, esp. with regard to its natural or topographical features or fitness for some use **2** *Geol.* TERRANE (sense 1)

trekked
(paragraph 7)

trek (trek) *vi.* **trekked, trek′·king** 〖Afrik < Du *trekken*, to draw; akin to MHG *trecken*〗 **1** [South Afr.] to travel by ox wagon **2** to travel slowly or laboriously **3** [Informal] to go, esp. on foot —*vt.* [South Afr.] to draw (a wagon): said of an ox —*n.* **1** [South Afr.] a journey made by ox wagon, or one leg of such a journey **2** any journey or leg of a journey **3** a migration **4** [Informal] a short trip, esp. on foot —**trek′·ker** *n.*

vendor
(paragraph 6)

ven·dor (ven′dər, ven dôr′) *n.* 〖Anglo-Fr < Fr *vendre*〗 **1** one who vends, or sells; seller **2** VENDING MACHINE

wares
(paragraph 12)

ware¹ (wer) *n.* 〖ME < OE *waru*, merchandise, specialized use of *waru*, watchful care, in the sense "what is kept safe": for IE base see GUARD〗 **1** any piece or kind of goods that a store, merchant, peddler, etc. has to sell; also, any skill or service that one seeks to sell: *usually used in pl.* **2** things, usually of the same general kind, that are for sale; a (specified) kind of merchandise, collectively: generally in compounds *[hardware, earthenware, glassware]* **3** dishes made of baked and glazed clay; pottery, or a specified kind or make of pottery

316

24A VOCABULARY

Using the vocabulary words listed on page 316, fill in this crossword puzzle.

Across

2. extremely hot
6. fearful
7. home for religious persons
8. tract of ground
10. unit of money in Latin America

Down

1. customers
3. anything for sale
4. traveled slowly
5. seller
9. spread out

24B CENTRAL THEME AND MAIN IDEAS
Choose the best answer.

__d__ 1. What is the central theme of "In Search of Bernabé"?
  a. Luz bargains with a *coyota* to take her and Arturo across the Mexican border to the United States.
  b. Petra Traslaviña is a *coyota* who makes her living by serving as a border guide.
  c. Luz and Arturo have over a forty-hour bus ride from their home to the Tijuana terminal.
  d. Luz and Arturo cross the United States-Mexican border illegally with the help of a *coyota* to find a missing relative.

__b__ 2. What is the main idea of paragraph 2?
  a. Luz is afraid of the woman who approaches her at the Tijuana bus terminal.
  b. Luz carefully inspected the woman's appearance to determine her skill as a guide.
  c. The *coyota* was a tall, slim, and muscular woman who wore Levi's and a plaid shirt under a sweatshirt.
  d. Luz is surprised to see a woman wearing scratched, muddy cowboy boots generally worn by a male.

__a__ 3. What is the main idea of paragraph 7?
  a. Luz, Arturo, and the *coyota* walked cautiously across the Mexican-United States border at night to avoid detection by the border patrol.
  b. Besides Luz and Arturo, there were others who crossed the border on foot.
  c. The immigration authorities used bright lights to search for illegal immigrants.
  d. The immigrants clung to the ground when someone issued a warning about the presence of the immigration authorities.

24C MAJOR DETAILS
Decide whether each detail is true (T), false (F), or not discussed (ND).

__F__ 1. Luz and Arturo's home was in Mexico City.

__F__ 2. Luz brought the equivalent of only seven hundred American dollars to pay for a border guide.

__F__ 3. The *coyota*, Luz, and Arturo trekked on foot across the border from Tijuana to Los Angeles.

__T__ 4. Luz and Arturo spoke only Spanish.

Name   Date

___T___   5. The first English words Luz practiced were *shut up.*

___T___   6. Ordaz and Petra argued about the location where he was to take Luz and Arturo.

___F___   7. Luz and Artuo brought a lot of clothes with them.

__ND__   8. The *coyota* gave Ordaz half of the seven hundred dollar guide fee.

24D   INFERENCES

Decide whether each statement below can be inferred (YES) or cannot be inferred (NO) from the reading selection.

__YES__   1. *Coyota* is a word used to refer to a smuggler of illegal aliens.

__YES__   2. A *coyota* generally expects to bargain with the illegal aliens for the guide fee.

__NO__   3. Because the *coyota* was a United States citizen, she wanted to be paid in American dollars.

__YES__   4. Luz and Arturo would not have been able to cross the border successfully without the *coyota*'s help.

__NO__   5. As a border guide, the *coyota* had never been caught by immigration authorities.

__NO__   6. The *coyota* used a fictitious name when she identified herself to Luz and Arturo.

__YES__   7. Ordaz was a nonsmoker.

__NO__   8. Luz and Arturo had never seen pedestrians observe traffic signals in Mexico.

__YES__   9. Bernabé was Arturo's brother.

__NO__ 10. The *coyota* had been Bernabé's guide when he crossed the Mexican-United States border.

__NO__ 11. The *coyota* always took her clients to the convent in Los Angeles if they had no destination.

__NO__ 12. The people at the refuge center assisted illegal aliens in getting United States visas.

24E   CRITICAL READING: FACT OR OPINION

Decide whether each statement, even if it quotes someone, contains a FACT or an OPINION.

FACT   1. *From paragraph 3:* From looking into the eyes of the *coyota,* Luz knew she had to drive a hard bargain.

FACT   2. *From paragraph 4:* "The coat had a purpose, though, for it concealed deep inner pockets which were filled with money."

FACT   3. *From paragraph 8:* "The *coyota* was sure-footed but Luz and Arturo bumped into rocks and tripped over gopher holes."

FACT   4. *From paragraph 9:* "Upon reaching the summit, they were struck with awe at the sight that spread beneath their feet."

OPINION   5. *From paragraph 11:* "The old bag slowed me down."

OPINION   6. *From paragraph 14:* "They don't like me because I charge you people money."

OPINION   7. *From paragraph 16:* "I mean, they love to call themselves *voluntarios,* and they'll do anything for nothing."

FACT   8. *From paragraph 17:* "I've known a few like you who have gotten themselves killed out there."

24F   CRITICAL READING: THE WRITER'S CRAFT

Choose the best answer.

___c___   1. Throughout the essay, the author italicizes the word *coyota* because it is
   a. a grammar rule.
   b. alternate spelling for "coyote."
   c. a Spanish word.
   d. a slang term.

___d___   2. *Read paragraph 9 again.* The author provides a vivid description of San Diego to
   a. appeal to the reader's sensory image of sound.
   b. compare the brightness of the neon signs with the dawning of a new day.
   c. prove that San Diego is a city of bright lights and modern buildings.
   d. to describe what Luz and Arturo felt upon first seeing the city's morning glow.

Name   Date

__a__ 3. To develop the central theme, the author
   a. tells a story.
   b. contrasts good and evil.
   c. uses Mexico as the setting.
   d. makes use of Spanish words.

24G READER RESPONSE: TO DISCUSS OR TO WRITE ABOUT

1. Approximately 3.5 million to 4 million Mexicans live and work illegally in the United States. In California, these migrants often work at low-paying jobs: restaurants, car washes, and construction and landscape companies. Many managers say that Americans will not take these jobs. Have you ever turned down a job because of the low wage? What was the job? The duties? The pay? If you have not turned down a low-paying job, then what is your opinion of someone who needs work but declines such a job offer?

2. Mexican migrants who try to enter the United States through treacherous deserts or across dangerous rivers may now encounter their own government agents: Group Beta, a migrant protection group whose purpose is to keep migrants from crossing the border. In the past, however, the Mexican government had the long-standing tradition of allowing its citizens to cross unhindered into the United States. Why do you support or not support that tradition? Be specific with your reasons. Would your view be the same if you were a native Mexican? Explain.

3. In recent years the Border Patrol has used personnel, equipment, technology, and tactics across the United States' most vulnerable cross points to reduce the number of illegal migrants. This has forced them to seek routes that are dangerous—across deserts and rivers. As a result, many migrants hire *coyotes* or *polleros*, names given the smugglers who sometimes charge as much as $1,200 for their services. In some cases, the *coyotes* have abandoned their clients in the desert without food or water when they could not keep up the pace. If you were a Mexican without the proper papers and identification to enter the United States, would you consider hiring a *coyote*? Why? Luz looked directly into the eyes of the *coyote* to determine Petra's skill as a guide. How would you go about choosing a guide? How would you prepare yourself for the trip, which can take several days across the desert? What would you take with you? Be specific.

How Did You Do?   **24**   In Search of Bernabé

SKILL *(number of items)*	Number Correct		Points for Each		Score
Vocabulary (10)	_____	×	2	=	_____
Central Theme and Main Ideas (3)	_____	×	5	=	_____
Major Details (8)	_____	×	2	=	_____
Inferences (12)	_____	×	2	=	_____
Critical Reading: Fact or Opinion (8)	_____	×	2	=	_____
Critical Reading: The Writer's Craft (3)	_____	×	3	=	_____

(Possible Total: 100) *Total*   _____

SPEED

Reading Time: _____ Reading Rate (page 399): _____ Words Per Minute

Name   Date

▪ Part 6 ▪

Thinking: Getting Started

In Part 6 you will encounter a wider variety of types of reading than before in this book. Try to use these selections to the fullest: They are challenging so that you can stretch. You may find that your comprehension, your exercise scores, your reading rate, or other areas slip back somewhat at first. Do not be discouraged. Some kinds of reading are supposed to be slower than other kinds. Also, mistaken answers give you a chance to learn and to catch on to the more subtle aspects of reading. If you have worked through most of Parts 2–5 in this book, you are ready to dig into material that will help you grow stronger as a reader.

Selection 25 will particularly engage you—and your sense of humor—on, between, and beyond the lines. Selection 26 will demand close reading, probably at a somewhat slower pace, and particular attention to vocabulary and to understanding the author's attitude. Selections 28 and 29 taken from textbooks used in college courses, offer you opportunities to practice and reinforce your knowledge of the SQ3R technique, as discussed in the opening chapter of this book. Selection 30 has many unspoken subtexts only hinted at by the story, so it allows you, the reader, one of the special joys of reading: the chance to compose a world in the privacy of your mind

Buy recycled. It would mean the world to them.

Recycling keeps working to protect their future when you buy products made from recycled materials. So celebrate America Recycles Day on November 15th. For a free brochure, call 1-800-CALL-EDF or visit our web site at www.edf.org

© 1997 EDF

The Ad Council

If your area has a recycling program, explain why you do or do not participate. (See "Houses to Save the Earth.")

By permission of Johnny Hart and Creators Syndicate, Inc.

Now that medicines are available today to treat physical and emotional problems, do you think we need medicines to make people fall permanently into love with one person? (See "The Chaser.")

A blood clot the size of this dot can cause a Heart Attack.

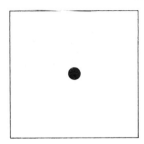

Or a stroke.

Every year, thousands die because of a blood clot. Thousands more become disabled, some permanently.

What's being done to stop it.

Plenty.

We're the American Heart Association. We're giving scientists the chance to find out more about blood clots.

How to detect them. How to treat them. How to keep them from happening.

We're fighting hard. With new drugs. New kinds of treatment. Better ways to help heart attack and stroke victims return to a normal life.

And it's only a part of the total war we're waging against the number one cause of death in this country: heart disease and stroke.

But we can't fight without your money. When the Heart Association volunteer asks for your dollars, be generous.

The blood clot is small, the problem is enormous.

Please give generously to the American Heart Association ♥

WE'RE FIGHTING FOR YOUR LIFE

How much are you willing to give up to help you live a longer life?
(See "How to Stay Alive.")

More on next page . . .

In what ways do you work to strengthen and improve your ability to remember what you learn in school and what you need to do in daily life? (See "Long-Term Memory.") What techniques do you know about for reducing stress in your life? Which of them do you use regularly? (See "A Personal Stress Survival Guide.")

© Kip Aoki

Why do drivers need to use self-control when they are angered by aggressive drivers? (See "Collegians Predisposed to Road Rage.")

How to Stay Alive

Art Hoppe

Once upon a time there was a man named Snadley Klabberhorn who was the healthiest man in the whole wide world.

Snadley wasn't always the healthiest man in the whole wide world. When he was young, Snadley smoked what he wanted, drank what he wanted, ate what he wanted, and exercised only with young ladies   5
in bed.

He thought he was happy. "Life is absolutely peachy," he was fond of saying. "Nothing beats being alive."

Then along came the Surgeon General's Report linking smoking to lung cancer, heart disease, emphysema, and tertiary coreopsis.   10

Snadley read about The Great Tobacco Scare with a frown. "Life is so peachy," he said, "that there's no sense taking any risks." So he gave up smoking.

Like most people who went through the hell of giving up smoking, Snadley became more interested in his own health. In fact, he became fas-   15
cinated. And when he read a WCTU tract which pointed out that alcohol caused liver damage, brain damage, and acute *weltanschauung*, he gave up alcohol and drank dietary colas instead.

At least he did until The Great Cyclamate Scare.

"There's no sense in taking any risks," he said. And he switched to   20
sugar-sweetened colas, which made him fat and caused dental caries. On realizing this he renounced colas in favor of milk and took up jogging, which was an awful bore.

That was about the time of The Great Cholesterol Scare.

Snadley gave up milk. To avoid cholesterol, which caused atheroscle-   25
rosis, coronary infarcts, and chronic chryselephantinism, he also gave up meat, fats, and dairy products, subsisting on a diet of raw fish.

Then came the Great DDT Scare.

"The presence of large amounts of DDT in fish . . ." Snadley read with anguish. But fortunately that's when he met Ernestine. They were made   30
for each other. Ernestine introduced him to home-ground wheat germ, macrobiotic yogurt, and organic succotash.

They were very happy eating this dish twice daily, watching six hours of color television together, and spending the rest of their time in bed.

They were, that is, until The Great Color Television Scare.   35

"If color tee-vee does give off radiations," said Snadley, "there's no sense taking risks. After all, we still have each other."

And that's about all they had. Until The Great Pill Scare.

On hearing that The Pill might cause carcinoma, thromboses, and lin-
40 gering stichometry, Ernestine promptly gave up The Pill—and Snadley.
"There's no sense taking any risks," she said.

Snadley was left with jogging. He was, that is, until he read somewhere that 1.3 percent of joggers are eventually run over by a truck or bitten by rabid dogs.

45 He then retired to a bomb shelter in his back yard (to avoid being hit
by a meteor), installed an air purifier (after The Great Smog Scare) and
spent the next 63 years doing Royal Canadian Air Force exercises and por-
ing over back issues of The Reader's Digest.

"Nothing's more important than being alive," he said proudly on
50 reaching 102. But he never did say anymore that life was absolutely
peachy.

* * *

CAUTION: Being alive may be hazardous to your health.

(520 words)

Vocabulary List

Here are some of the more difficult words in "How to Stay Alive."

carcinoma
(line 38)

car·ci·noma (kär′sə nō′mə) *n., pl.* **-mas** or **-mata** (-mə tə) [[L < Gr *karkinōma*, cancer < *karkinoun*, affect with a cancer < *karkinos*, crab: see CANCER]] any of several kinds of cancerous growths deriving from epithelial cells: see SARCOMA —**car′·ci·nom′a·tous** (-näm′ə təs, -nō′mə-) *adj.*

chronic
(line 25)

chronic (krän′ik) *adj.* [[Fr *cronique* < L *chronicus* < Gr *chronikos*, of time < *chronos*, time]] **1** lasting a long time or recurring often: said of a disease, and distinguished from ACUTE **2** having had an ailment for a long time [a *chronic* patient] **3** continuing indefinitely; perpetual; constant [a *chronic* worry] **4** by habit, custom, etc.; habitual; inveterate [a *chronic* complainer] —*n.* a chronic patient —**chron′i·cally** *adv.* —**chro·nic·ity** (krə nis′ə tē) *n.*

SYN.—**chronic** suggests long duration or frequent recurrence and is used especially of diseases or habits that resist all efforts to eradicate them [*chronic* sinusitis]; **inveterate** implies firm establishment as a result of continued indulgence over a long period of time [an *inveterate* liar]; **confirmed** suggests fixedness in some condition or practice, often from a deep-seated aversion to change [a *confirmed* bachelor]; **hardened** implies fixed tendencies and a callous indifference to emotional or moral considerations [a *hardened* criminal]

coronary
(line 25)

coro·nary (kôr′ə ner′ē, kär′-) *adj.* [[L *coronarius:* see CROWN]] **1** of, or in the form of, a crown **2** *Anat. a)* like a crown; encircling *b)* designating or relating to either of two arteries, or their branches, coming from the aorta and supplying blood directly to the heart muscle —☆*n., pl.* **-nar′·ies** CORONARY THROMBOSIS

DDT
(line 28)

DDT (dē′dē′tē′) *n.* [[*d(ichloro)d(iphenyl)t(richloroethane)*]] a powerful insecticide (ClC_6H_4)$_2$CHCCl$_3$, effective upon contact: its use is restricted by law due to damaging environmental effects

emphysema
(line 9)

em·phy·sema (em′fə sē′mə; -zē′-) *n.* ⟦ModL < Gr *emphysēma*, inflation < *emphysaein*, to inflate, blow in < *en-*, in + *physaein*, to blow < IE *phus- < base *pu-*, *phu-*, echoic of blowing with puffed cheeks⟧ **1** an abnormal swelling of body tissues caused by the accumulation of air; esp., such a swelling of the lung tissue, due to the permanent loss of elasticity, or the destruction, of the alveoli, which seriously impairs respiration **2** HEAVES —em′·phy·se′ma·tous (-sē′mə təs, -sem′-) *adj.* —em′·phy·se′mic *adj., n.*

macrobiotic
(line 31)

macro·bi·ot·ics (mak′rō bī ät′iks) *pl.n.* ⟦see prec. & -BIOTIC⟧ [*with sing. v.*] the study of prolonging life, as by special diets, etc. — mac′ro·bi·ot′ic *adj.*

weltanschauung
(line 16)

Welt·an·schau·ung (velt′än shou′oon) *n.* ⟦Ger, world view⟧ a comprehensive, esp. personal, philosophy or conception of the universe and of human life

"How to Stay Alive" has many unusual words in it. To help you read the essay easily, here are some quick definitions.

tertiary	(line 10)	third
coreopsis	(line 10)	tickseed plant
WCTU	(line 16)	Women's Christian Temperance Union
cholesterol	(line 24)	fatty substances in the blood
atherosclerosis	(line 25-26)	hardening of the arteries
infarcts	(line 26)	obstruction of blood vessels
chryselephantinism	(line 26)	being overlaid with gold and ivory
yogurt	(line 32)	a fermented milk food
succotash	(line 32)	lima beans and corn cooked together
thromboses	(line 39)	blood clots
stichometry	(line 40)	practice of writing prose

25A VOCABULARY

Choose the best answer.

__b__ 1. If you had **emphysema** you would
   a. be breaking the law.
   b. have trouble breathing.
   c. get frequent headaches.
   d. be unable to digest food.

__d__ 2. The word **weltanschauung** is closest in meaning to
   a. peptic ulcers.
   b. a passion for German opera.
   c. cruelty to children.
   d. a personal philosophy of life.

_a_ 3. The word **coronary** refers to
   a. the arteries leading to the heart.
   b. a medical examiner.
   c. kidney disease.
   d. the arteries leading to the brain.

_c_ 4. A **chronic** illness is best described as
   a. painful.
   b. extremely expensive to treat.
   c. continuing indefinitely.
   d. likely to result in death.

_b_ 5. **DDT** is best known as
   a. the FBI's list of "most wanted" criminals.
   b. a deadly insecticide.
   c. the cause of high blood pressure.
   d. a foreign sports car.

_a_ 6. Anything that is **macrobiotic** is
   a. believed to prolong life.
   b. hazardous to your health.
   c. very delicious.
   d. pornographic.

_b_ 7. **Carcinoma** is a medical term for
   a. tuberculosis.
   b. cancer.
   c. heart disease.
   d. measles.

25B CENTRAL THEME
Choose the best answer.

_b_ 1. What is the central theme of "How to Stay Alive"?
   a. The secret of living to a ripe old age is avoiding indulgences that are hazardous to your health.
   b. Snadley Klabberhorn enjoyed life until he changed his habits in reaction to every health scare.
   c. Snadley Klabberhorn's main goal was to live to 102 without giving up smoking, drinking, sweets, and color television.
   d. Everyone should disregard health scares and live life to its fullest.

Name   Date

25C   MAJOR DETAILS

Decide whether each detail is true (T), false (F), or not discussed (ND).

_T_   1. Snadley liked to say, "Nothing beats being alive."

_T_   2. With each new health scare, Snadley altered his life to avoid the danger.

_ND_   3. The Great Noise Scare led Snadley to wear ear plugs all the time.

_F_   4. Snadley's wife, Ernestine, refused to give up The Pill even after hearing about its health hazards.

_F_   5. Snadley liked to say, "Nothing beats being healthy."

_T_   6. Snadley finally retired to his bomb shelter to avoid all hazards.

_T_   7. By the time Snadley reached the age of 102, he no longer said that life was absolutely peachy.

25D   INFERENCES

Choose the best answer.

_c_   1. "How to Stay Alive" implies that people
   a. should avoid anything that might cause disease.
   b. should live recklessly.
   c. cannot expect to avoid all health hazards.
   d. cannot live long in today's world.

_d_   2. *Read lines 9, 25, and 39 again.* The author uses the words "tertiary coreopsis," "chronic chryselephantinism," and "stichometry," which are not medical terms. Why does he use them?
   a. He thinks big words will impress the reader.
   b. He likes to teach his readers difficult words.
   c. He thinks that they are connected with good health and staying alive.
   d. He is poking fun at the use of big technical words to name well-known diseases.

25E   CRITICAL READING: THE WRITER'S CRAFT

Choose the best answer.

_b_   1. The author starts with the words "once upon a time" because he is writing
   a. a story for young children.
   b. in the style of a fable.
   c. a story for adults.
   d. in the style of a short story.

  b   2. The author ends with a "caution" that is
         a. a call for government regulations.
         b. a humorous summary.
         c. a key question.
         d. a forecast of the future.

25F   READER RESPONSE: TO DISCUSS OR TO WRITE ABOUT

1. Have you ever changed your habits because of health warnings? Using a specific example of a health warning, explain why you did or did not change your habits.

2. Why do you think food additives are so common today? What steps, if any, can you take to avoid consuming the additives?

3. If the statement is true that you are what you eat, what are the best foods for you? Why?

How Did You Do?   **25** How to Stay Alive

SKILL (number of items)	Number Correct		Points for Each		Score
Vocabulary (7)	_____	×	5	=	_____
Central Theme (1)	_____	×	7	=	_____
Major Details (7)	_____	×	6	=	_____
Inferences (2)	_____	×	4	=	_____
Critical Reading: The Writer's Craft (2)	_____	×	4	=	_____

(Possible Total: 100) *Total* _____

SPEED

Reading Time: _____ Reading Rate (page 399): _____ Words Per Minute

---

Name   Date

Houses to Save the Earth

Seth Shulman

(1) "You are walking on the casings of used fluorescent bulbs," says Steven Loken pointing to the ceramic floor tiles in his master bathroom. The rich blue tiles around the tub were made from recycled car windshield glass. It's the kind of detail Loken loves to volunteer about the dream house he built on the outskirts of Missoula, Montana. In the kitchen, the sink looks like it is made of stone, but Loken explains that it was molded from epoxy and granite dust—a byproduct left when granite is quarried. The carpets upstairs were once plastic milk jugs. From the foundation to the roof tiles, the split-level house is made almost entirely of recycled materials.

(2) Despite the sound of it, the house doesn't look newfangled or avant-garde. In fact, without Loken's animated descriptions, a visitor would never guess the origins of the materials—a feature he says was important when he set out in 1990 to build his "recycled" house. "I wanted to show that you could use recycled building materials without making any compromises on the type of house most Americans want," says Loken, 45. "This meant that the place had to look like any other house if the ideas behind it were going to catch on." Since his house was completed in 1992, Loken's efforts have caught on in ways he never imagined, helping to spawn one of the country's hottest trends in house construction. In fact, over the past few years, Loken has become something of a guru to an alternative-materials movement among builders. He travels the country regularly giving lectures about his building techniques. So far, 12,000 people, including architects and builders from around the world, have made the pilgrimage to his Missoula home.

(3) Why make houses from recycled materials? To Loken it is a question of using our resources efficiently. The average wood-framed house, after all, uses an astonishing 11,000 board feet of lumber—enough, stacked end to end, to top the Empire State Building and both World Trade Center towers combined—but the stock of large-diameter trees has steadily declined. In addition to the environmental consequences, the diminishing supply has led to a significant rise in the average price of lumber. But, as Loken puts it, builders are a "conservative bunch who tend to favor old reliables" when choosing materials. He realized that, if he was going to change attitude, he would have to do something about it himself. "I realized I was part of the problem every time I blindly followed building practices that were inherently wasteful," he says.

(4) The result was Loken's own path-breaking house, in which he incorporated recycled materials into virtually every facet of construction. The house's insulation, for instance, is made from blown bits of cellulose derived from shredded newspaper. Instead of using cement to mix the

foundation's concrete, fly ash was added. (Fly ash is a waste product from incinerators and coal burning power stations. Generally hazardous, it is harmless when fused into concrete.) Loken used one-sixth of the wood required to frame a conventional house of the same size. The wood he did use was either salvaged or "composite" lumber made from the chips of slender trees, which normally are discarded.

(5) For Loken, an important part of the project has been to live in the house with his family (wife, Christine; daughter, Kira, 7; and son, Rye, 5), testing the products over time. Loken says he has learned some lessons the hard way: The recycled sawdust and cement tiles he used on his roof look identical to slate and came with a 50-year guarantee. But they are beginning to flake after five years of Montana's brutal, freeze-thaw climate. "It is sad," Loken says, "but this is how you learn." So far, however, most of the products Loken used have worked flawlessly. And though it has a furnace, the house is so energy-efficient that it can stay comfortable in winter with just ambient heat (from cooking, body heat, and other existing sources) and solar heat (enhanced by the home's southern exposure).

(6) As an outgrowth of his building efforts, Loken founded a Missoula-based organization called the Center for Resourceful Building Technology in 1990. The center serves as a clearinghouse for new ideas about building materials, replete with samples of everything from "strawboard" (a plywood substitute made from straw) to a paintable, woodlike material made from soybeans. Tracy Mumma, the research coordinator at the center, keeps close track of changes in the use of materials by the construction industry. "Recycled carpets are really catching on," she says, "as are some of the lumber products made from recycled plastics."

(7) Meanwhile, in the past several years, a half-dozen demonstration homes like Loken's have followed his initial effort—including houses in Arizona, Oregon, Massachusetts, and Minnesota. All have offered builders a look at the new materials and have proved that competitively priced homes—which look and feel as solid, safe, and appealing as any on the market—can be built today from recycled materials. "Efforts like these help contractors to see the new materials and talk with other builders who have learned to work with them," says Kate Warner, an architect who employed Loken's help to build a "resource-efficient" house on Martha's Vineyard, Massachusetts. "We ask people to recycle, but then we don't know what to do with the stuff," she says. Warner's sentiments are echoed by builders across the country. For instance, Brian Paul Sweeney, a Washington-based architect, recently finished a model conservation house in downtown Seattle. He believes designers and contractors eventually will adapt to what he terms "issues of sustainability," just as they have to stringent energy codes and to the Americans With Disabilities Act, which requires public buildings and bathrooms to be accessible by wheelchair. "My hope," Sweeney says, "is that these materials and building techniques will become so commonplace that contractors won't see them as extra demands."

Steve Loken made his home almost entirely from recycled materials.

Michael G. Garland

(8) But the demonstration homes of Loken, Warner, and Sweeney alone don't nearly convey the growing popularity of the new building materials and techniques that Loken has helped pioneer. The real action is happening at thousands of other new homes that are starting to incorporate some of the new materials and techniques into their designs. And many more recycled products have become available in the last few years, as wood prices have risen steeply. Just five years ago, Loken explains, many recycled building materials were relatively overpriced and hard to come by. Amid all the attention to his ideas, Loken keeps a frenetic building pace. His construction firm currently is rehabilitating Missoula's oldest commercial building downtown. And he is focusing more on affordability in his latest project—building a new, low-cost, resource-efficient house. Like his own home, this one uses considerable less wood than the average home and incorporates many recycled products. This time, Loken says, the goal is also to meet or beat the cost of a comparable home using conventional materials.

(9) Today, Loken notes proudly, he has prospective clients from as far away as Atlanta and New York. He says he is happy to see many recycled building materials being used but views some of them as only interim solutions. "I'm interested in cutting down on waste altogether and making more intelligent use of our resources," he says. The key is turning one industry's waste into another's raw materials. "If we could master this," he says, "our environment and our society would be a lot better off."

(1,239 words)

Here are some of the more difficult words in "Houses to Save the Earth."

Vocabulary List

avant-garde
(paragraph 2)

avant-garde (ə vänt′gärd′, ä′-, a′-; *Fr* à vän gård′) *n.* [Fr, lit., advance guard] the leaders in new or unconventional movements, esp. in the arts; vanguard —*adj.* of such movements, ideas, etc. — **avant′-gard′ism′** *n.* —**avant′-gard′ist** *n.*

by-product
(paragraph 1)

by·product or **by-product** (-präd′əkt) *n.* anything produced in the course of making another thing; secondary or incidental product or result

composite
(paragraph 4)

com·pos·ite (kəm päz′it) *adj.* [L *compositus*, pp. of *componere*, to put together < *com-*, together + *ponere*, to place: see POSITION] **1** formed of distinct parts; compound **2** [C-] designating or of a classical Roman order of architecture, in which the scroll-like ornaments of the Ionic capital are combined with the acanthus design of the Corinthian: see ORDER, illus. **3** *Bot.* designating the largest family (Asteraceae, order Asterales) of dicotyledonous plants, including the daisy, thistle, artichoke, and chrysanthemum, characterized by flower heads composed of dense clusters of small flowers surrounded by a ring of small leaves or bracts —*n.* **1** a thing of distinct parts; compound; esp., any of a class of high-strength, lightweight engineering materials consisting of various combinations of alloys, plastics, and ceramics **2** *Bot.* a composite plant — **com·pos′·itely** *adv.*

compromise
(paragraph 2)

com·pro·mise (käm′prə mīz′) *n.* [ME & OFr *compromis* < LL *compromissum*, a compromise, mutual promise < L *compromissus*, pp. of *compromittere*, to make a mutual promise to abide by an arbiter's decision < *com-*, together + *promittere*, to PROMISE] **1** a settlement in which each side gives up some demands or makes concessions **2** *a)* an adjustment of opposing principles, systems, etc. by modifying some aspects of each *b)* the result of such an adjustment **3** something midway between two other things in quality, effect, etc. **4** *a)* exposure, as of one's reputation, to danger, suspicion, or disrepute *b)* a weakening, as of one's principles —*vt.* **-mised′, -mis′ing 1** to settle or adjust by concessions on both sides **2** to lay open to danger, suspicion, or disrepute **3** to weaken or give up (one's principles, ideals, etc.) as for reasons of expediency **4** *Med.* to weaken or otherwise impair [drugs that *compromised* his immune system] —*vi.* to make a compromise or compromises —**com′·pro·mis′er** *n.*

conventional
(paragraph 4)

con·ven·tional (kən ven′shə nəl) *adj.* [LL *conventionalis*] **1** having to do with a convention or assembly **2** of, sanctioned by, or growing out of custom or usage; customary **3** *a)* depending on or conforming to formal or accepted standards or rules rather than nature; not natural, original, or spontaneous [*conventional* behavior] *b)* not unusual or extreme; ordinary **4** stylized; conventionalized **5** nonnuclear [*conventional* weapons] **6** *Law* based on an agreement between parties; contractual —**con·ven′·tion·al·ism′** *n.* —**con·ven′·tion·al·ist** *n.* —**con·ven′·tion·ally** *adv.*

fluorescent
(paragraph 1)

fluo·res·cent (-ənt) *adj.* **1** producing light when acted upon by radiant energy **2** glowing and vivid [*fluorescent* colors]

frenetic
(paragraph 8)

fre·netic (frə net′ik) *adj.* [see PHRENETIC] frantic; frenzied: also **fre·net′i·cal** —**fre·net′i·cally** *adv.*

guru
(paragraph 2)

guru (g $\overline{oo}$'r $\overline{oo}$', goor' $\overline{oo}$'; *also* g oo r $\overline{oo}$', gə-) *n.* ⟦Hindi *guru* < Sans *guruh*, venerable, orig. heavy < IE **gweru-* < base **gwer-* > GRAVE[1]⟧ **1** in Hinduism, one's personal spiritual advisor or teacher **2** any leader highly regarded by a group of followers: sometimes used derisively

inherently
(paragraph 3)

in·her·ency (-ən sē) *n.* **1** INHERENCE **2** *pl.* **-cies** something inherent
in·her·ent (-ənt) *adj.* ⟦L *inhaerens*, prp. of *inhaerere*: see INHERE⟧ existing in someone or something as a natural and inseparable quality, characteristic, or right; innate; basic; inborn —**in·her'·ently** *adv.*

interim
(paragraph 9)

in·ter·im (in'tər im) *n.* ⟦L, meanwhile < *inter*: see INTER-⟧ the period of time between; meantime —*adj.* for or during an interim; temporary; provisional /an *interim* council/

pilgrimage
(paragraph 2)

pil·grim·age (pil'grə mij) *n.* ⟦ME *pilgrymage* < OFr *pelegrinage* < *pelegrin*, prec.⟧ **1** a journey made by a pilgrim, esp. to a shrine or holy place **2** any long journey, as to a place of historical interest

recycled
(paragraph 1)

re·cy·cle (rē sī'kəl) *vt.* **-cled, -cling 1** to pass through a cycle or part of a cycle again, as for checking, treating, etc. **2** to use again and again, as a single supply of water in cooling, washing, diluting, etc. **3** *a*) to treat or process in order to use again /*recycle* aluminum cans/ *b*) to gather up and turn in (empty bottles and cans, old newspapers, etc.) to be so treated or processed **4** to alter or adapt to a new use or function /*recycle* an old tenement into condominiums/ **5** to use again; bring back; reuse /*recycle* a speech from a previous campaign/ —*vi.* **1** to pass through a cycle, system, etc. and return to the starting point again or repeatedly /the electronic flash *recycles* in 5 seconds; the water *recycles* through the cooling system/ **2** to engage in recycling empty bottles, old newspapers, etc. —**re·cy'·cla·ble** (-klə bəl) *adj.* —**re·cy'·cler** (-klər, -kəl ər) *n.*

stringent
(paragraph 7)

strin·gent (strin'jənt) *adj.* ⟦L *stringens*, prp. of *stringere*, to draw tight: see STRICT⟧ **1** rigidly controlled, enforced, etc.; strict; severe ☆**2** tight in loan or investment money /a *stringent* money market/ **3** compelling; convincing /*stringent* reason/ —**strin'·gently** *adv.* —**strin'·gent·ness** *n.*

26A VOCABULARY

Choose the best answer.

___d___ 1. A **stringent** law is
  a. unjust.
  b. impractical.
  c. praiseworthy.
  d. strict.

___c___ 2. In manufacturing, a **by-product** refers to
  a. an item sold at discount during special sales.
  b. a thing made by machinery on an assembly line.
  c. something made as an offshoot of something else.
  d. inventory stored in a warehouse.

___b___ 3. A **guru** is a person who is considered
  a. an outcast.
  b. a leader.
  c. a fighter.
  d. an artist.

___b___ 4. Plywood is a **composite** because it
  a. results from a mixture of decayed bark and leaves.
  b. combines several layers of wood glued together.
  c. is used as a building material.
  d. is a strong but lightweight material.

___b___ 5. **Recycled** paper indicates the product has undergone
  a. proper disposal.
  b. treatment for reuse.
  c. curbside collection.
  d. return to the original manufacturer.

___c___ 6. **Avant-garde** clothing is best described as
  a. unattractive.
  b. unoriginal.
  c. unconventional.
  d. unimportant.

___d___ 7. **Frenetic** as used in this story means
  a. freely.
  b. punctual.
  c. angry.
  d. excited.

Name   Date

a 8. An argument settled by **compromise** indicates
   a. giving up part of the demands.
   b. hiring an attorney to represent the parties.
   c. having witnesses to present their opinions.
   d. receiving money for the damages sustained.

a 9. A **pilgrimage** is a journey made
   a. to a sacred or holy place.
   b. by bus to take criminals to prison.
   c. by pilgrims to a new land.
   d. to a foreign land.

b 10. "Good morning" is a **conventional** greeting in that it is
   a. polite.
   b. customary.
   c. convenient.
   d. thoughtful.

c 11. An **interim** college president is one who is
   a. retired.
   b. likeable.
   c. temporary.
   d. capable.

d 12. A characteristic of a living thing held **inherently** is
   a. inactive.
   b. inhuman.
   c. inadequate.
   d. inborn.

d 13. **Fluorescent** bulbs are recognized by their
   a. color.
   b. dimness.
   c. odor.
   d. brightness.

26B CENTRAL THEME AND MAIN IDEAS
Choose the best answer.

d 1. Another title for this story could be
   a. The Earth and Its Resources
   b. A Dangerous Montana Home
   c. Trends in Building Construction
   d. New Homes from Old Materials

Name   Date

_a_ 2. What is the main idea of paragraph 1?
   a. Recycled materials were used almost exclusively to build Steve Loken's home.
   b. Builder Steve Loken built his dream home in Montana.
   c. Glass and plastic are recyclable materials.
   d. Recycled fluorescent bulbs were used to make the ceramic tile in the master bathroom.

_c_ 3. What is the main idea of paragraph 7?
   a. Homes built of recycled materials cost about the same as conventional homes.
   b. Appearance and safety will determine the popularity of the "resource-efficient" homes.
   c. Steve Loken's use of recycled materials and his building techniques are becoming more acceptable to builders.
   d. Steve Loken was the first builder to construct a home of recycled materials.

26C MAJOR DETAILS

Decide whether each detail is MAJOR or MINOR based on the context of the reading selection.

MAJOR 1. The upstairs carpets were once plastic milk jugs.

MAJOR 2. Visitors to Steve Loken's home cannot distinguish between natural and recycled materials.

MAJOR 3. Architects and builders from around the world have traveled to see Steve Loken's home.

MAJOR 4. The lumber supply to build wood-framed homes is dwindling.

MAJOR 5. Steve Loken and his family live in his resource-efficient home.

MINOR 6. Steve Loken's home has a furnace.

MINOR 7. Missoula, Montana, is the city in which the Center for Resourceful Building Technology is located.

MINOR 8. Architect Brian Paul Sweeney built a model conservation home in Seattle, Washington.

MAJOR 9. Steve Loken's construction firm is rehabilitating Missoula's oldest commercial building downtown.

MAJOR 10. Recently, Steve Loken's firm has begun to build a more affordable yet resource-efficient home.

Name   Date

26D INFERENCES

Decide whether each statement can be inferred (YES) or cannot be inferred (NO) from the reading selection.

__NO__ 1. Steve Loken used recycled materials in building homes because he wanted to make a big profit.

__YES__ 2. Steve Loken's Montana home was the first home to be constructed almost completely from recycled materials.

__NO__ 3. In the future Steve Loken plans to use traditional slate roof materials because his roof of recycled materials began to flake.

__YES__ 4. The money saved by the energy efficiency of Steve Loken's home is an appealing feature to prospective homeowners.

__YES__ 5. People like getting attention for living in a home made of recycled materials.

26E CRITICAL READING: FACT OR OPINION

Decide whether each statement, even if it quotes someone, contains a FACT or an OPINION.

FACT 1. *From paragraph 2:* "He travels the country regularly giving lectures about his building techniques."

OPINION 2. *From paragraph 3:* "[. . .] builders are a conservative bunch who tend to favor old reliables when choosing materials."

OPINION 3. *From paragraph 5:* "And though it has a furnace, the house is so energy-efficient that it can stay comfortable in winter with just ambient heat [. . .] solar heat [. . .]."

OPINION 4. *From paragraph 7:* "[. . .] designers and contractors eventually will adapt to what he terms 'issues of sustainability' [. . .]."

OPINION 5. *From paragraph 9:* "The key is turning one's industrial waste into another's raw materials."

26F CRITICAL READING: THE WRITER'S CRAFT

Choose the best answer.

__c__ 1. To get the reader's attention, the author begins the story with
   a. historical information.
   b. a definition.
   c. specific examples.
   d. a question.

Name   Date   341

   _a_   2. To make his point, the author uses all of these techniques *except*
          a. dramatic incidents.
          b. statistics.
          c. definitions of key terms.
          d. professional opinions.

   _b_   3. *Reread paragraph 9.* The author concludes his story by
          a. summarizing his main points.
          b. making a recommendation.
          c. asking a question.
          d. drawing on personal experiences.

26G READER RESPONSE: TO DISCUSS OR TO WRITE ABOUT

1. Many communities now have recycling centers for collecting recyclable glass, plastic, aluminum and tin cans, and newspapers. If your community has such a program, what are some specific reasons either for or against participating in this effort?

2. If you had the choice of purchasing a home built of either standard building materials or recycled materials, which house would you buy? To what extent would your choice be influenced by appearance, cost, safety, and durability? Why?

3. Since the late 1960s there has been a growing concern over the dwindling supply of our natural resources of timber, water, land, and minerals. To help conserve timber, some families, for example, use cloth napkins instead of paper. What are some specific practices you can recommend to help save our natural resources?

          Name   Date

How Did You Do?   **26** Houses to Save the Earth

SKILL (number of items)	Number Correct		Points for Each		Score
Vocabulary (13)	_____	×	2	=	_____
Central Theme and Main Ideas (3)	_____	×	6	=	_____
Major Details (10)	_____	×	3	=	_____
Inferences (5)	_____	×	3	=	_____
Critical Reading: Fact or Opinion (5)	_____	×	1	=	_____
Critical Reading: The Writer's Craft (3)	_____	×	2	=	_____

(Possible Total: 100) *Total*   _____

SPEED

Reading Time: _____ Reading Rate (page 399): _____ Words Per Minute

Collegians Predisposed to Road Rage

Andrew J. Pulskamp

(1) It's quite easy to push the pedal to the metal, flip off that tailgater and scream a string of obscenities at no one in particular while you're driving. It's also easy for that tailgater to get out of his or her car at the next light and start threatening you. Road rage is becoming increasingly common on America's streets and highways and though college students may be the victims of it, often times they are the aggressors.

(2) Leon James, a social psychologist at the University of Hawaii, who is also a traffic psychologist, known as Dr. Driving, says, "even though incidences of road rage are rare in the newspapers—there might be a thousand a year—millions of aggressive exchanges take place on the roads every day." In extreme cases of road rage, people can end up dead—or their passengers can. In September 1999, two brothers were charged with stabbing a man to death in front of his wife and five daughters in a horrific road rage incident in Seattle. In October 1999 a Las Vegas woman was indicted after she allegedly cut off a tractor-trailer that was driving too slowly, then slammed on her brakes. A motorcyclist following that truck crashed into it and died of massive head injuries. Last February a still unidentified man got out of his car after a fender bender in San Jose, California. He approached the other driver, reached inside her car, grabbed her dog and threw the bichon frisé into oncoming traffic. The canine was killed after being run over. Although the perpetrators in none of these instances were college-age, James says college students are among a segment of the population that comprises the most aggressive drivers. Basically in the world of road rage, the younger the driver the more aggressive. James explains: "In college, students still have a tendency to act like teenagers in that they take a lot of risks. The question is when do we learn as drivers not to take risks? That's after the college years."

(3) John Richardson, a student at Birmingham Southern College, considers himself to be a good and courteous driver. Even though he's proud of his own habits behind the wheel and relates that his friends are pretty good drivers, too, he says, "There are some good reasons to the notion that [students] are younger and therefore more carefree and less aware of consequences. So they might drive faster and show less caution." Age isn't the only factor in aggressive driving. James' research also shows that being a road hog has a lot to do with gender and what kind of car a person drives. James says, in general, men are more aggressive drivers than women. And as far as cars go, if the highways were oceans then sports cars, trucks, and sports utility vehicles would be the sharks, whereas economy cars, family cars, and vans would be the angel fish. There are no hard-line explanations

A California trooper looks over the remains of a vehicle in which two women died when their car was struck after they had entered Interstate 5, going in the wrong direction. The highway patrol is looking into the possibility that the women were being chased by another vehicle and are investigating the accident as a case of road rage.

as to why different cars are driven more or less aggressively, but James thinks most likely there are multiple factors at play. It might have to do with the idea that more aggressive people are drawn to certain cars, and it could also mean that certain vehicles make drivers feel more aggressive. After all, it's easier to feel like the king of the road when one is cruising around in a Ford Explorer rather than a Dodge Neon.

(4) Driving for most folks is a very personal thing, which means emotions run high. "Driving is a particularly dramatic and challenging experience for most people," James says. "Things happen fast and whatever happens could cost you money and physical injury." When people feel threatened on the roads, their first instinct is to lash out. James offers, "We want to retaliate and punish these persons and let them know they've done something wrong and make sure they're not going to get away with it. We may want to prove that we're not a wimp. There are a thousand reasons and all of them are cultural." Those cultural reasons were at play when Richardson got into a little accident shortly after he got his license. He says, "I was on my way to school, and there was a solid green light ahead of me. . . . Someone was coming from the other road and wanted to go left in front of me. I had the right of way, but I could have avoided the other person if I just had slowed down. But I felt I was right and I went through; they turned and we had a little fender bender." Richardson's experience certainly doesn't qualify as road rage, but the feelings that contributed to his accident, that he was right and therefore had a right to keep going, are the same emotions that road rage feeds on.

(5) "When something happens that threatens you, you are challenged emotionally to respond. But you have to respond intelligently rather than provocatively," says James. One way to behave intelligently is to drive defensively. Be on the lookout for others who might be on the edge. James created a list of behaviors that correlate to aggressive driving syndrome, which can be a precursor to road rage. Signs of aggressive driving are drivers who speed, drivers who yell at other drivers, drivers who make a lot of insulting gestures or honk a lot, and drivers who tailgate and cut people off.

(6) James says it's best not to retaliate when you're behind the wheel. Patience is the key to avoiding road rage, but such a virtue can be hard to come by when one is behind the wheel, especially considering that most drivers have their own traffic pet peeves. Those little things can light a fire beneath bedraggled commuters. "I've gotten irritated with drivers, especially when I'm running late and want to get somewhere in a hurry," says Allison Richards, a student at the University of Arkansas. Among Richards' pet peeves, "People below the speed limit and people who turn on their turn signal and never turn it off." Commuters' top pet peeves, according to James, are putting on the turn signal long before they need to, cutting off someone then slowing down, tailgating, aggressive braking or acceleration, and late merging. All these behaviors do nothing but agitate drivers. But do not retaliate. One has to take a step back when these behaviors emerge on the highway. James says the first step to changing a driver's warlike ways on the road is to take a look in the mirror. It's not always the other guy's fault.

(7) "Just like alcoholics have to acknowledge that they have a problem, traffic emotions need to be acknowledged," says James. He also says a lot of people don't even realize how they're behaving on the roads. One way to find out is to record yourself on the next commute. "I discovered a whole new world while talking on my tape recorder. I was swearing a lot, and I don't swear. I'm against it for religious reasons. I got angry and really hostile. I was yelling at people and behaving very negatively," James says.

(8) Along with taking personal responsibility, James also proposes a policy of lifetime driver education to combat the enormous negative education that drivers have received from the first moment they were placed in a car. He says learning how to behave on the roads starts with examples set by mom and dad and from watching those edge-of-your-seat car chases in the movies and on television.

(9) Ultimately the way to combat the highway mania that has taken hold of many drivers is just to be nice and courteous. And though the likes of Madonna and others have encouraged students to express themselves, James doesn't always think this is the best idea when on the road. He says, "Most students believe it's better to express anger than to hold it in. That's a big mistake. When you express your anger you basically multiply it. Expressing it is like putting your anger in an amplifier. It's not that holding it in is what matters, but it's better to transform it and turn it into something positive."

(1,360 words)   347

Here are some of the more difficult words in "Collegians Predisposed to Road Rage."

bedraggled
(paragraph 6)

be·drag·gle (bē drag′əl, bi-) *vt.* --gled, --gling to make wet, limp, and dirty, as by dragging through mire —be·drag′·gled *adj.*

correlate
(paragraph 5)

cor·re·late (kôr′ə lāt′, kär′-) *n.* ⟦back-form. < fol.⟧ either of two interrelated things, esp. if one implies the other —*adj.* closely and naturally related —*vi.* --lat′ed, --lat′·ing to be mutually related (*to* or *with*) —*vt.* to bring (a thing) into mutual relation (*with* another thing); calculate or show the reciprocal relation between; specif., to bring (one of two related or interdependent quantities, sets of statistics, etc.) into contrast (*with* the other)

incidences
(paragraph 2)

in·ci·dence (in′sə dəns) *n.* ⟦ME (North) < OFr < LL *incidentia*⟧ 1 the act, fact, or manner of falling upon or influencing 2 the degree or range of occurrence or effect; extent of influence 3 [Informal] an individual or particular occurrence or happening; instance or occasion [several *incidences* of the disease in our village] 4 *Geom.* partial coincidence between two figures, as of a line and a point contained in it 5 *Physics a)* the falling of a line, or a ray of light, projectile, etc. moving in a line, on a surface *b)* the direction of such falling See also ANGLE OF INCIDENCE

obscenities
(paragraph 1)

ob·scen·ity (äb sen′ə tē, əb-; *also, chiefly Brit*, -sēn′-) *n.* ⟦Fr *obscénité* < L *obscenitas*⟧ 1 the state or quality of being obscene 2 *pl.* -ties an obscene remark, act, event, etc.

perpetrators
(paragraph 2)

per·pe·trate (pur′pə trāt′) *vt.* --trat′ed, --trat′·ing ⟦< L *perpetratus*, pp. of *perpetrare*, to commit, perpetrate, orig., to bring about, achieve < *per*, thoroughly + *patrare*, to effect, prob. orig. a ritual term < *pater*, FATHER, priest⟧ 1 to do or perform (something evil, criminal, or offensive); be guilty of 2 to commit (a blunder), impose (a hoax), etc. —per′·pe·tra′·tion *n.* —per′·pe·tra′·tor *n.*

precursor
(paragraph 5)

pre·cur·sor (prē kur′sər, pri-; prē′kur′-) *n.* ⟦L *praecursor* < *praecurrere*, to run ahead: see PRE- & CURRENT⟧ 1 a person or thing that goes before; forerunner; harbinger 2 a predecessor, as in office 3 a substance that precedes and is the source of another substance

predisposed
(title)

pre·dis·pose (prē′dis pōz′) *vt.* --posed′, --pos′·ing to dispose, or make receptive, beforehand; make susceptible [fatigue *predisposes* one to illness]

provocatively
(paragraph 5)

pro·voca·tive (prə väk′ə tiv, prō-) *adj.* ⟦ME *prouocatyue*, aphrodisiac < LL *provocativus* < L *provocare*: see fol.⟧ provoking or tending to provoke, as to action, thought, feeling, etc.; stimulating, erotic, irritating, etc. —*n.* something that provokes —pro·voc′a·tive·ly *adv.* —pro·voc′a·tive·ness *n.*

retaliate
(paragraph 4)

re·tali·ate (ri tal′ē āt′) *vi.* --at′ed, --at′·ing ⟦< LL *retaliatus*, pp. of *retaliare*, to require, retaliate < L *re-*, back + *talio*, punishment in kind, akin to Welsh *tāl*, compensation⟧ to return like for like; esp., to return evil for evil; pay back injury for injury —*vt.* to return an injury, wrong, etc. for (an injury, wrong, etc. given); requite in kind —re·tal′ia′·tion *n.* —re·tal′ia·tive *adj.* or re·tal′ia·to′ry (-tal′yə tôr′ē, -tal′ē ə-)

segment
(paragraph 2)

seg·ment (seg′mənt; *for v.*, -ment) *n.* ⟦L *segmentum* < *secare*, to cut: see SAW¹⟧ 1 any of the parts into which a body is separated or separable; division; section 2 *Geom. a)* a part of a figure, esp. of a circle or sphere, marked off or made separate by a line or plane, as a part of a circular area bounded by an arc and its chord (see CIRCLE, illus.) *b)* any of the finite sections of a line 3 *Linguis.* a phone, or single sound, in the stream of speech 4 *Zool. a)* METAMERE *b)* the part of an arthropod appendage between joints —*vt.*, *vi.* to divide into segments —SYN. PART¹ —seg′·men·tar′y *adj.*

syndrome
(paragraph 5)

syn·drome (sin′drōm′) *n.* ⟦ModL < Gr *syndromē* < *syn-*, with + *dramein*, to run: see DROMEDARY⟧ **1** a number of symptoms occurring together and characterizing a specific disease or condition **2** any set of characteristics regarded as identifying a certain type, condition, etc. —**syn·drom′ic** (-drō′mik, -dräm′ik) *adj.*

tailgater
(paragraph 1)

☆**tail·gate** (-gāt′) *n.* a board or gate at the back of a wagon, truck, station wagon, etc., designed to be removed or swung open on hinges for loading or unloading —*vt.* ·**·gat′ed**, ·**·gat′·ing** to drive too closely behind (another vehicle) —*vi.* **1** to drive too closely behind another vehicle **2** ⟦so called because the meal was orig. served on the tailgate⟧ to picnic at or near one's automobile or in a parking lot, as before a sporting event —**tail′·gat′er** *n.*

Vocabulary List

27A VOCABULARY

Using the words listed on pages 348–349, fill in the blanks.

1. A person who is a ___tailgater___ is someone who drives too closely to another car.

2. Rashunda tried to ___correlate___ her knowledge of mathematics with her knowledge of music.

3. In a tornado, the ___incidences___ of widespread destruction are very likely.

4. Eating-between-meals ___syndrome___ can result in a weight gain.

5. After Alicia came in from the pie throwing contest, she tried to comb her ___bedraggled___ hair.

6. A sore throat can be a ___precursor___ to a sinus infection.

7. Reade's malnutrition ___predisposed___ her to many childhood illnesses.

8. Responding intelligently, not ___provocatively,___ is best in incidences of road rage.

9. A ___segment___ of a local newspaper is the weather.

10. Yelling ___obscenities___ at another driver could evoke road rage.

| Name | Date |

11. The perpetrators of the kidnapping were featured on *America's Most Wanted*.

12. If insulted, aggressive drivers will possibly   retaliate .

27B CENTRAL THEME AND MAIN IDEAS
Choose the best answer.

  d   1. What is the central theme of "Collegians Predisposed to Road Rage"?
    a. The roots of aggressive driving begin in childhood.
    b. Male drivers are more aggressive in all driving behaviors than female drivers.
    c. Aggressive driving can be attributed to drivers' lack of patience.
    d. Aggressive driving is common throughout the United States, especially among younger drivers.

  c   2. What is the main idea of paragraph 3?
    a. John Richardson is proud of his driving habits behind the wheel of his car.
    b. Younger drivers drive faster and show less caution than older drivers.
    c. Age, gender, and type of car are factors in aggressive driving.
    d. A driver of a Ford Explorer is more aggressive than a driver of a Dodge Neon.

27C MAJOR DETAILS
Decide whether each detail is true (T), false (F), or not discussed (ND).

  F   1. Dr. Leon James is a psychiatrist at the University of Hawaii.

  ND 2. A truck ran over the dog that was pulled from the owner's lap during a California road rage incident.

  T   3. In the world of road rage, the younger the driver, the more aggressive the driver.

  ND 4. John Richardson, a college student, was involved in a traffic accident in Birmingham, Alabama.

  T   5. Certain behaviors, such as drivers who yell at other drivers, correlate to aggressive driving syndrome.

Name   Date

_ND_ 6. Men who drive family cars see themselves as less aggressive than women who drive family cars.

_T_ 7. One way to determine your behavior behind the wheel is to carry a tape recorder and tape your thoughts out loud as you drive.

_F_ 8. Like Madonna, Dr. Leon James agrees that students need to express their anger rather than hold it in.

27D INFERENCES

Decide whether each statement below can be inferred (YES) or cannot be inferred (NO) from the reading selection.

_NO_ 1. Incidences of road rage occur more frequently in western states, such as California and Nevada.

_NO_ 2. The best way to prevent aggressive drivers from pushing you around is to block their way or give them a scare.

YES 3. Leon James earned the title of "Dr. Driving" because of his expertise on drivers' road habits.

_NO_ 4. People who drive below the speed limit create a driving hazard.

_NO_ 5. An alcoholic is most likely an aggressive driver.

YES 6. Many children are exposed to years of aggressive driving attitudes as they ride in their parents' cars.

27E CRITICAL READING: FACT OR OPINION

Decide whether each statement, even if it quotes someone, contains a FACT or an OPINION.

OPINION 1. *From paragraph 1:* "It's quite easy to push the pedal to the metal, flip off that tailgater, and scream a string of obscenities [. . .]."

FACT 2. *From paragraph 2:* "In extreme cases of road rage, people can end up dead—or their passengers can."

FACT 3. *From paragraph 3:* "Age isn't the only factor in aggressive driving."

FACT 4. *From paragraph 5:* "One way to behave intelligently is to drive defensively."

OPINION 5. *From paragraph 6:* "James says the first step to changing a driver's warlike ways on the road is to take a look in the mirror."

27F   CRITICAL READING: THE WRITER'S CRAFT

Choose the best answer.

__d__ 1. Who is the intended audience of this essay?
  a. aggressive drivers
  b. elderly drivers
  c. road rage victims
  d. all drivers

__b__ 2. *Read paragraph 2 again.* The author uses which of the following to develop the topic of road rage?
  a. statistics
  b. examples
  c. definitions
  d. story

__c__ 3. The author concludes the essay with which of the following?
  a. a prediction
  b. a summary
  c. a recommendation
  d. a question

27G   READER RESPONSE: TO DISCUSS OR TO WRITE ABOUT

1. Rage is not limited just to the road. Other types of rage include parking, air, bicycle, boat, fishing, jogger, truckers, cell phone, supermarket, shopping mall, shopper, etc. Have you ever been involved in a rage of some kind? Were you the victim or the perpetrator? What happened? How was the incident resolved?

2. Car society is in its second century. In the first century, we licensed drivers through minimal training and examination. This approach worked until manufacturers began making faster moving vehicles in the 1950s. Today there are over 40,000 traffic fatalities each year. What can be done to reverse this trend? What part do parents play? Higher insurance rates? Excessive fines? On-going driver education programs? Patience and self-control?

Name   Date

3. During an argument over a fender bender, a man grabbed a white bichon frisé from the owner's lap and tossed it into traffic, where the dog was struck and killed. Within weeks, the road rage death of Leo generated donations of more than $100,000 to a reward fund. The San Jose, California, police said the amount topped previous sums offered in child molestation and rape cases. Why do you think people were so generous? Do you think the donors placed more importance on finding the person responsible for the pet's death than that of persons responsible for sex crimes? Discuss whether you would or would not have contributed to a reward fund for this dog.

How Did You Do?   **27** Collegians Predisposed to Road Rage

SKILL (number of items)	Number Correct		Points for Each		Score
Vocabulary (12)	_____	×	2	=	_____
Central Theme and Main Ideas (2)	_____	×	5	=	_____
Major Details (8)	_____	×	3	=	_____
Inferences (6)	_____	×	3	=	_____
Critical Reading: Fact or Opinion (5)	_____	×	3	=	_____
Critical Reading: The Writer's Craft (3)	_____	×	3	=	_____

(Possible Total: 100) *Total* _____

SPEED

Reading Time: _____ Reading Rate (page 399): _____ Words Per Minute

Name   Date

Long-Term Memory

in Fundamentals of Psychology

Joseph Calkin and Richard S. Perrotto

(1) Everything you know—every word, name, fact, date, experience, definition, and skill—is contained in your long-term memory (LTM), where information is stored unconsciously for an extended period of time. How long do your memories last in LTM? No precise answer can be given. LTM duration can be as brief as a few minutes and as long as a lifetime. Many people believe that LTM is permanent, but the evidence is not conclusive. The duration of LTM depends on several factors, including the strength of the memory, its meanings, and how much it is used.

(2) How much do you know? If you started to remember everything in your LTM right now, you would probably spend the rest of your life and not finish. If short-term memory (STM) is a memory workbench where information is stored for a short period of time and in limited space, your LTM is a vast warehouse of information with no apparent limit. Surely there are millions of items stored in your LTM, but researchers have no way of estimating the maximum capacity of LTM. Although its upper limit is unknown, your everyday experience tells you that LTM holds an astounding amount of information.

THE ORGANIZATION OF LONG-TERM MEMORY

(3) The enormous LTM warehouse contains many types of knowledge, and its contents are highly organized in terms of several qualities of those memories. Four aspects of LTM have been identified and named: **semantic, episodic, procedural,** and **implicit** memory. These aspects of LTM organization are summarized in Table 1.

(4) Language is an essential part of your memory. Factual knowledge based on words, phrases, sentences, and other verbal information is contained in your **semantic memory.** Like a dictionary, semantic memory is based on **semantic codes,** representations of information in terms of the meaning of words. To appreciate the scope of semantic memory, just consider the many definitions, names, formulas, and other facts that you have learned since elementary school. Your semantic memory does not exist as thousands of independent bits of knowledge, but is organized by complex **association networks,** or groups of memories linked together on the basis of meaning.

Semantic Memory
Memory for factual knowledge based on verbal information

Table 1 Organization of Long-Term Memory

Semantic memory	Impersonal facts based on semantic, or verbal, codes
Episodic memory	Personal, autobiographical facts; flashbulb memories
Procedural memory	Skills, habits, stimulus-response associations
Implicit memory	Memories learned and retrieved without conscious effort

(5) As a demonstration, start with a familiar word, *dog* and call to mind every word association you can, for example, *pet, companion, mammal,* and so on. Then, do the same for each of those associations, and for all the associations linked to them, and so on. Before long, you will realize that the web of your word associations is almost endless. These complex semantic associations control your ability to understand and remember language-based facts. Your semantic memory is impersonal, lacking any obvious connection with specific life experiences. For instance, when you remember 2 + 2 = 4 you probably do not connect it with the situation in which you first learned it.

(6) By contrast, your **episodic memory** contains very personal, auto-biographical facts—facts that are tied to episodes in your life and often ones that contain significant emotional meaning. Think of the birth of your young siblings, a great party you attended, a family tragedy, and other events from your personal past—these recollections reveal your episodic memory.

Episodic (epp-ee-sod-ik) Memory
Memory for personal, autobiographical facts

(7) A special type of episodic memory is a **flashbulb memory,** a vivid recollection of an emotionally powerful event. Your flashbulb memories seem like moments frozen in time, and their emotional associations are thought to be responsible for their vividness. For example, some people report flashbulb memories for January 28, 1986, the day the space shuttle *Challenger* exploded, killing the crew, while broadcast nationwide on television. Many flashbulb memories are more personal, such as the death of a close friend or the day you won the lottery. Although they seem very clear, flashbulb memories are not necessarily accurate, and people often recall with confidence false details of those events.

(8) Your memory for learned responses and action patterns is **procedural memory.** Learned skills and behaviors, as well as stimulus-response associations, are contained in your procedural memory. Countless everyday activities depend on procedural memory, as when you drive a car, play the piano, use a tool, or carry on a conversation.

Procedural Memory
Memory for learned responses and action patterns

Such behavior may be acquired through conditioning and cognitive learning. In addition, procedural memory controls your automatic conditioned responses to stimuli. The next time you experience fear upon entering your dentist's office, you can thank your procedural memory for the reminder.

(9) Semantic and episodic memories taken together are sometimes called **declarative memory,** which requires conscious effort to learn and retrieve. For example, you must exert conscious effort to memorize a new formula in math (semantic memory).

(10) Many memories, however, are acquired and remembered automatically with little or no conscious involvement. These make up your **implicit memory.** In fact, a lot of procedural memory is implicit, such as conditioned fears and other emotional responses. You do not consciously control their acquisition or activation by stimuli.

Implicit (im-**pliss**-it) **Memory**
Memories learned and retrieved without conscious effort

(11) Research on the **priming effect** illustrates that implicit memory controls your unconscious retrieval of stored information. In a typical study, subjects are "primed" by exposure to some stimuli, and later their memory is tested without asking them to consciously remember the stimuli. Priming improves their memory despite the subjects' lack of awareness of learning or remembering the stimuli. Imagine that you are in such a study: You are shown some words (the priming list), which you must identify as nouns or verbs (Refer to Table 2). Later, another series of words (the test list) is presented very rapidly, and you are asked simply to indicate which words you perceive. You are most likely to perceive the test list words that were on the priming list even though you did not try to memorize or retrieve them.

(12) Although implicit and declarative (semantic and episodic) memory have distinctive features, they are not completely independent. Rather, these aspects of LTM interact to provide you with richly integrated memories. Do you remember how to ride a bicycle? If you can describe this skill in words (semantic memory), recall yourself doing it in a specific situation (episodic memory), and show it in action (procedural memory), you are illustrating the integrated facets of your LTM. Recent studies suggest that declarative and implicit memory work together to create complex abilities and knowledge, such as learning the rules of language usage and classifying your experiences into organized concepts.

Table 2 Priming Effect Study of Implicit Memory

Priming List	Test List	Primed Implicit Memory
rabbit	bird	rabbit
swim	rabbit	write
car	write	
write	house	

LONG-TERM MEMORY PROCESSES

(13) As you have learned, LTM contains many types of stored information. The complex organization of knowledge in LTM depends on a number of factors. The **depth-of-processing** model explains the strength and durability of LTM as the result of encoding processes. In this view, a "deep" memory is acquired by semantic codes that represent facts through language. Without semantic codes, memory is "shallow" and quite easily forgotten. A deep memory is more lasting and meaningful than a shallow one, and it is easier to recollect. This model suggests that memories based on several codes are deeper than those based on a single code.

Depth-of-Processing Model
View that memory strength depends on encoding processes

(14) Research on combined semantic codes and imagery supports this notion. This effect may be illustrated by a **paired-associates recall task,** in which you are given word pairs to remember (for example, house-pencil, fish-tree), and later you must recall one of the words when the other is presented. For instance, when shown *tree* you must say *fish*. If you use visual images along with the words to encode the paired associates, your recall is improved, especially for concrete words like those in Figure 1.

Figure 1 Imagery in a Paired-Associates Recall Task

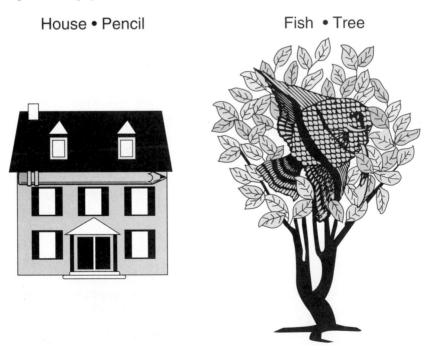

House • Pencil
Fish • Tree

The depth-of-processing model suggests that a combination of semantic and image codes will produce a deeper memory than will a single code. When subjects use visual images and word pairs to encode the information, their memory for the word association improves.

(15) In 1932, British psychologist Frederick Bartlett proposed that memories are reconstructions of events based partly on fact and partly on schemas, or personal beliefs about reality. In his classic study, he read a Native American folktale to his English subjects and later asked them to remember it. Their memories of the story showed changes that reflected their culture-based schemas. For instance, instead of recalling that the Indians hunted for seals in canoes, some subjects remember that they were fishing in boats.

(16) In the tradition of Bartlett, many psychologists today consider **reconstructive memory** to be an act of remembering in which facts, personal beliefs, and inferences are all woven together. In reconstructing a past event, you often fill in the gaps with "facts" that you believe, on the basis of your personal schemas, might have occurred. In addition, you rely on familiar patterns of events stored as **memory scripts** that give you a framework for remembering.

> **Reconstructive Memory**
> Remembering affected by schemas, personal beliefs, and inferences

Try to remember what you did at 4:00 P.M. exactly six months ago. If it was a Wednesday during the school year, you might find yourself using your "typical-Wednesday-afternoon-at-school" script to reconstruct what you probably did. Have you ever noticed that each time you tell a story it is a little different than the last time because you add new elements or drop old details with each telling? Facts learned after a memory is formed can change it, and even the act of remembering sometimes alters the memory being recalled. Reconstructive memory is also open to the power of suggestion, as shown in a study by psychologists Elizabeth Loftus and John Palmer in which subjects saw a filmed car accident and were later asked how fast the cars were going. The questions were phrased either in terms of when the cars "hit" or when they "crashed." Subjects who were asked the "crashed" version recalled much higher speeds because the wording suggests that the cars were moving faster.

(17) Your ability to retrieve a memory often depends on having the proper cues at the time you try to remember. When your retrieval is influenced by stimulus cues, you show evidence of **cue-dependent memory.** Two forms of cue-dependent memory are **context-dependent memory** and **state-dependent memory.**

> **Cue-Dependent Memory**
> Memory influenced by cues in the situation or emotional state

If you try to recall some information in a situation that is similar to the one in which you learned that information, you tend to perform better than when you try in a situation that differs from the learning one. This phenomenon, called **context-dependent memory,** is the result of associations formed between situation cues and the information at the time it is learned. An example of context-dependent memory is a study of scuba divers who learned some words under water and later recalled them better when under water than on land. You can examine **context-dependent memory** in yourself by studying some material while listening to music and later testing yourself on half of the material with the same music playing and on the

359

other half without any music. You should find that your memory is better when the music is playing.

(18) The power of situational cues may explain a curious phenomenon called déjà vu (French for "already seen") in which you feel that you recognize someone or some place with no basis for the memory in your experience. For example, on entering a house for the first time, it may seem familiar, as if you had been there before. Déjà vu is a false recognition due to subtle cues in the situation. Perhaps something about the house, such as an odor or room design, triggers partial memory of another place in which similar cues were present, thus giving you the feeling of familiarity.

(19) Have you ever noticed that when you are happy you remember many experiences with a similar happy feeling, or that when depressed you recall other depressing events? Such observations point to **state-dependent memory;** your state of mind influences you to retrieve memories that were formed in a similar state. Studies of state-dependent memory show that emotional states prime your retrieval of experiences with similar emotional features.

(1,949 words)

Vocabulary List

Here are some of the more difficult words in "Long-Term Memory."

cognitive
(paragraph 8)

cog·ni·tion (käg nish′ən) *n.* 〚ME *cognicioun* < L *cognitio,* knowledge < *cognitus,* pp. of *cognoscere,* to know < *co-,* together + *gnoscere,* KNOW〛 **1** the process of knowing in the broadest sense, including perception, memory, and judgment **2** the result of such a process; perception, conception, etc. —**cog·ni′·tional** *adj.* —**cog′·ni·tive** (-nə tiv) *adj.*

conclusive
(paragraph 1)

con·clu·sive (-siv) *adj.* 〚LL *conclusivus* < pp. of L *concludere,* CONCLUDE〛 that settles a question; final; decisive —**con·clu′·sively** *adv.* —**con·clu′·sive·ness** *n.*

duration
(paragraph 1)

du·ra·tion (doo rā′shən, dyoo-) *n.* 〚ME *duracioun* < ML *duratio* < pp. of L *durare:* see DURABLE〛 **1** continuance in time **2** the time that a thing continues or lasts

encoding
(paragraph 13)

en·code (en kōd′, in-) *vt.* ·-**cod′ed,** ·-**cod′·ing 1** to convert (a message, information, etc.) into code **2** to convert (data) by applying an electronic code —**en·cod′er** *n.*

imagery
(paragraph 14)

im·agery (im′ij rē, -ər ē) *n., pl.* **--ries** ⟦ME *imagerie* < OFr⟧ **1** [Now Rare] images generally; esp., statues **2** mental images, as produced by memory or imagination **3** descriptions and figures of speech

perceive
(paragraph 11)

per·ceive (pər sēv′) *vt., vi.* **--ceived′, --ceiv′·ing** ⟦ME *perceyven* < OFr *perceivre* < L *percipere,* to take hold of, feel, comprehend < *per,* through + *capere,* to take: see HAVE⟧ **1** to grasp mentally; take note (of); observe **2** to become aware (of) through one of the senses, esp. through sight —*SYN.* DISCERN —**per·ceiv′·able** *adj.* —**per·ceiv′·ably** *adv.* —**per·ceiv′er** *n.*

retrieve
(paragraph 9)

re·trieve (ri trēv′) *vt.* **--trieved′, --triev′·ing** ⟦ME *retreven* < inflected stem of OFr *retrouver* < *re-,* again + *trouver,* to find: see TROVER⟧ **1** to get back; recover **2** to restore; revive /to *retrieve* one's spirits/ **3** to rescue or save **4** to set right or repair (a loss, error, etc.); make good **5** to recall to mind ☆**6** *Comput.* to gain access to (data) that is on a floppy disk, hard drive, etc. **7** *Hunting* to find and bring back (killed or wounded small game): said of dogs **8** *Racket Sports* to return (a ball that is hard to reach) —*vi. Hunting* to retrieve game —*n.* **1** any retrieval ☆**2** a retrieving of the ball in tennis, etc. —*SYN.* RECOVER —**re·triev′·able** *adj.*

schemas
(paragraph 15)

schema (skē′mə) *n., pl.* **--mata** (-mə tə) ⟦Gr *schēma:* see SCHEME⟧ **1** an outline, diagram, plan, or preliminary draft **2** *Psychol.* a mental image produced in response to a stimulus, that becomes a framework or basis for analyzing or responding to other related stimuli

siblings
(paragraph 6)

sib·ling (sib′liŋ) *n.* ⟦20th-c. revival of OE, a relative: see SIB & -LING¹⟧ one of two or more persons born of the same parents or, sometimes, having one parent in common; brother or sister

stimulus-response
(paragraph 8)

stimu·lus (-ləs) *n., pl.* **-u·li′** (-lī′) ⟦L, a goad, sting, torment, pang, spur, incentive: see STYLE⟧ **1** something that rouses or incites to action or increased action; incentive **2** *Physiol., Psychol.* any action or agent that causes or changes an activity in an organism, organ, or part, as something that excites an end organ, starts a nerve impulse, activates a muscle, etc.

subtle
(paragraph 18)

sub·tle (sut′'l) *adj.* **sub′·tler** (-lər, -'l ər), **sub′·tlest** ⟦ME *sotil* < OFr *soutil* < L *subtilis,* fine, thin, precise, orig., closely woven < *sub-* (see SUB-) + *tela,* web < *texla < texere,* to weave: see TECHNIC⟧ **1** thin, rare; tenuous; not dense or heavy /a *subtle* gas/ **2** *a)* capable of making or noticing fine distinctions in meaning, etc. /a *subtle* thinker/ *b)* marked by or requiring mental keenness /subtle reasoning/ **3** delicately skillful or clever; deft or ingenious /a *subtle* filigree/ **4** not open or direct; crafty; sly **5** delicately suggestive; not grossly obvious /a *subtle* hint/ **6** working insidiously; not easily detected /a *subtle* poison/ —**sub′·tle·ness** *n.* —**sub′·tly** *adv.*

Vocabulary List

28A1 VOCABULARY

From the context of "Long-Term Memory," explain the meaning of each of the vocabulary words shown in boldface below.

1. *From paragraph 1:* **LTM duration** can be as brief as a few minutes and as long as a lifetime.

   continuance in time

2. *From paragraph 1:* Many people believe that LTM is permanent, but the evidence is not **conclusive.**

   final

3. *From paragraph 6:* Think of the birth of your young **siblings,** a great party you attended, a family tragedy . . .

   brothers or sisters

4. *From paragraph 8:* Learned skills and behaviors, as well as **stimulus-response** associations, are contained in your procedural memory.

   something that causes an action

5. *From paragraph 8:* Such behavior may be acquired through conditioning and **cognitive** learning.

   knowing process

6. *From paragraph 9:* Semantic and episodic memories taken together are called declarative memory, which requires conscious effort to learn and **retrieve.**

   recover

7. *From paragraph 11:* You are most likely to **perceive** the test list words that were on the priming list even though you did not try to memorize or retrieve them.

   grasp mentally

Name   Date

8. *From paragraph 13:* The depth-of-processing model explains the strength and durability of LTM as the result of **encoding** processes.

   converting information
   _____

   _____

9. *From paragraph 14:* Research on combined semantic codes and **imagery** supports this notion.

   mental images
   _____

   _____

10. *From paragraph 15:* Their memories of the story showed changes that reflected their culture-based **schemas.**

    plans
    _____

    _____

11. *From paragraph 18:* **Déjà vu** is a false recognition due to subtle cues in the situation.

    thin
    _____

    _____

28A2 SPECIAL TEXTBOOK VOCABULARY

Key terms in this textbook selection are explained as they are discussed. Referring to "Long-Term Memory," fill in the blanks.

1. _____Semantic_____ memory contains factual knowledge based on words, phrases, sentences, and other verbal information.

2. The memory for very personal, autobiographical facts is

   _____episodic_____ .

3. A _____flashbulb_____ memory is a vivid recollection of a more personal, emotionally powerful event.

4. Your memory for learned responses and action patterns is

   _____procedural_____ memory.

5. _____Declarative_____ memory requires a conscious effort to learn and retrieve.

6. _____Implicit_____ memory is learned and retrieved without conscious effort.

7. The view that memory strength depends on encoding processes is the depth-in-processing model.

8. Remembering affected by schemas, personal beliefs, and inferences is __reconstructive__ memory.

9. _Cue-dependent__ memory is influenced by cues in the situation or emotional state.

10. Context-dependent memory results from associations formed between cues and the information learned at the time.

11. Your mind's ability to retrieve memories that were formed in a similar state is __state-dependent__ memory.

28B CENTRAL THEME AND MAIN IDEAS
Choose the best answer.

__c__ 1. The textbook selection "Long-Term Memory" covers a topic that could be part of a course in
   a. physics.
   b. mathematics.
   c. study skills.
   d. writing.

__b__ 2. The main purpose of paragraphs 3 through 11 is to
   a. show the differences between long-term memory and short-term memory.
   b. name and explain how the four types of long-term memory are organized in humans.
   c. discuss the importance of language in stimulating the memory process in humans.
   d. list methods to help people retain information in long-term memory.

Name   Date

__a__ 3. The main idea of paragraph 13 is the view that
   a. memories based on several semantic codes are deeper than those based on a single code.
   b. long-term memory contains many types of information stored in the human brain.
   c. short-term memory is "shallow" and is easy to remember.
   d. the organization of knowledge in long-term memory is complex so it is usually forgotten.

28C   MAJOR DETAILS

Decide whether each detail is true (T), false (F), or not discussed (ND).

__ND__ 1. Information stored in short-term memory is stored for twenty-four hours and then forgotten.

__F__ 2. Semantic memory exists as thousands of independent bits of knowledge.

__T__ 3. Flashbulb memories are not necessarily accurate.

__ND__ 4. Eyewitness memories are just as prone to error as other memories are.

__T__ 5. According to Figure 1, a deeper memory is possible through combining semantic and visual codes.

__ND__ 6. Memories grow weaker over time.

__F__ 7. Flashbulb memories do not involve emotions.

__ND__ 8. Memories are stored in both the left side and the right side of the brain.

28D   CRITICAL READING: FACT OR OPINION

Decide whether each statement contains a FACT or an OPINION.

OPINION 1. *From paragraph 1:* "Many people believe that long-term memory is permanent [. . .]."

FACT 2. *From paragraph 5:* "Your semantic memory is impersonal [. . .]."

FACT 3. *From paragraph 8:* Everyday activities, such as driving a car or playing the piano, depend on your procedural memory.

FACT 4. *From paragraph 11:* "Research on the priming effect illustrates that implicit memory controls your unconscious retrieval of stored information."

OPINION 5. *From paragraph 17:* "You should find that your memory is better when the music is playing."

28E CRITICAL READING: THE WRITER'S CRAFT

Choose the best answer.

___e___ 1. Expressions that communicate connections may contain one word or several words. You can find an abundance of such connections in paragraphs 13 through 18 of this selection. Which of the following is *not* used to show connections?
a. "In this view" (paragraph 13)
b. "later" (14)
c. "For instance" (15)
d. "In addition" (16)
e. "This" (17)
f. "For example" (18)
g. "thus" (18)

___a___ 2. To explain the organization of long-term memory and its processes, the authors use all these techniques *except*
a. quotations.
b. tables.
c. definitions of key terms.
d. research study by experts.

___d___ 3. The authors' goal in this selection is to
a. convince readers of the importance of semantic codes as the major factor in building LTM.
b. provide readers with techniques for strengthening abilities to retrieve information in LTM.
c. show readers that information is more easily retrieved when it is learned in both words and pictures.
d. inform readers about the storage and retrieval of information in long-term memory.

28F READER RESPONSE: TO DISCUSS OR TO WRITE ABOUT

1. Memory experts believe people can increase their ability to remember with memory aids, such as a mnemonic device. Mnemonic devices include rhymes, clues, mental pictures, and other methods. For example, many people remember the number of days in a month by using a verse that begins, "Thirty days hath September . . ." What are some mnemonic devices you use or know of to recall information?

2. Using paragraph 14 as a model, create a list of ten sets of words for a paired-association recall task. Then administer it to four people, and tell only two to use images to associate the words. Then test their recall and see whether the two who used images do better, worse, or the same as the other two.

Name   Date

3. If there were a drug available that claimed to improve memory, would you take it? If not, why? Should it be available to everyone? Would you support its use for victims of assault, sexual abuse, natural disaster, or terrible accidents? Why or why not?

How Did You Do?   **28** Long-Term Memory

SKILL (number of items)	Number Correct		Points for Each		Score
Vocabulary (11)	_____	×	2	=	_____
Special Textbook Vocabulary (11)	_____	×	2	=	_____
Central Theme and Main Ideas (3)	_____	×	7	=	_____
Major Details (8)	_____	×	2	=	_____
Critical Reading: Fact or Opinion (5)	_____	×	2	=	_____
Critical Reading: The Writer's Craft (3)	_____	×	3	=	_____

(Possible Total: 100) *Total* _____

SPEED

Reading Time: _____ Reading Rate (page 399): _____ Words Per Minute

A Personal Stress Survival Guide

in *An Invitation to Health*

Dianne Hales

(1) Although stress is a very real threat to emotional and physical well-being, its impact depends not just on what happens to you, but on how you handle it. If you tried to predict who would become ill based simply on life-change units or other stressors, you'd be correct only about 15% of the time. The inability to feel in control of stress, rather than stress itself, is often the most harmful.

(2) In studying individuals who manage stress so well that they seem "stress-resistant," researchers have observed that these individuals share many of the following traits:

- They respond actively to challenges. If a problem comes up, they look for resources, do some reading or research, and try to find a solution rather than giving up and feeling helpless. Because they've faced numerous challenges, they have confidence in their abilities to cope.

- They have personal goals, such as getting a college degree or becoming a better parent.

- They rely on a combination of planning, goal setting, problem solving, and risk taking to control stress.

- They use a minimum of substances such as nicotine, caffeine, alcohol, or drugs.

- They regularly engage in some form of relaxation, from meditation to exercise to knitting, at least fifteen minutes a day.

- They tend to seek out other people and become involved with them.

(3) In order to achieve greater control over the stress in your life, start with some self-analysis: If you're feeling overwhelmed, ask yourself: Are you taking an extra course that's draining your last ounce of energy? Are you staying up late studying every night and missing morning classes? Are you living on black coffee and jelly doughnuts? While you may think that you don't have time to reduce the stress in your life, some simple changes can often ease the pressure you're under and help you achieve your long-term goals. One of the simplest, yet most effective, ways to work through stress is by putting your feelings into words that only you will read. The more honest and open you are as you write, the better. In studies at Southern Methodist University, psychologist James Pennebaker, Ph.D., found that college

Chart 1: How to Cope with Stress

A. Recognize your stress signals. Is your back bothering you more? Do you find yourself speeding or misplacing things? Force yourself to stop whenever you see these early warnings and say, "I'm under stress; I need to do something about it."

B. Keep a stress journal. Focus on intense emotional experiences and "autopsy" them away to try to understand why they affected you the way they did. Rereading and thinking about your notes may help you discern the underlying reasons for your response and garner insights that can help you cope better in the future.

C. Try "stress-inoculation." Rehearse everyday situations that you find stressful, such as speaking in class. Think of how you might handle the situation, perhaps by breathing deeply before you talk, or visualizing yourself speaking with confidence.

D. Put things in proper perspective. When you're feeling hassled, stop and breathe deeply and slowly five times. Ask yourself: Will I remember what's made me so upset a month from now? If you had to rank this problem on a scale of 1 to 10, with worldwide catastrophe as 10, where would it rate? If this were the worst thing to happen to you this year, would you feel lucky?

E. Think of one simple thing that could make your life easier. What if you put up a hook to hold your keys so that you didn't spend five minutes searching for them every morning? Doing something, however small, will boost your sense of control.

students who wrote in their journals about traumatic events felt much better afterward than those who wrote about superficial topics. Recording your experiences and feelings on paper or audiotape may help decrease stress and enhance well-being. Since the small ups and downs of daily life have an enormous impact on psychological and physical well-being, getting a handle on daily hassles will reduce your stress load.

POSITIVE COPING MECHANISMS

(4) After a perfectly miserable, aggravating day, a teacher comes home and yells at her children for making too much noise. Another individual, after an equally stressful day, jokes about what went wrong during the all-time most miserable moment of the month. Both of these people are using **defense mechanisms**—actions or behaviors that help protect their sense of self-worth. The first is displacing anger onto someone else; the second uses humor to vent frustration.

(5) Under great stress, we all may turn to negative defense mechanisms to alleviate anxiety and eliminate conflict. These can lead to maladaptive behavior, such as rationalizing overeating by explaining to yourself that you need the extra calories to cope with the extra stress in your life. **Coping mechanisms** are healthier, more mature and adaptive ways of dealing with stressful situations. While they also ward off unpleasant emotions, they usually are helpful rather than harmful. The most common are:

(6) ■ **Sublimation,** the redirection of any drives considered unacceptable into socially acceptable channels. For example, someone who is furious with a friend or relative may go for a long run to sublimate anger.

(7) ■ **Religiosity,** in which one comes to terms with a painful experience, such as a child's death, by experiencing it as being in accord with God's will.

(8) ■ **Humor,** which counters stress by focusing on comic aspects. Medical students, for instance, often make jokes in anatomy lab as a way of dealing with their anxieties about working with cadavers.

(9) ■ **Altruism,** which takes a negative experience and turns it into a positive one. For example, an HIV-positive individual may talk to teenagers about AIDS (Acquired Immune Deficiency Syndrome) prevention.

MANAGING TIME

(10) Every day you make dozens of decisions, and the choices you make about how to use your time directly affect your stress level. If you have a big test on Monday and a term paper due Tuesday, you may plan to study all weekend. Then, when you're invited to a party Saturday night, you go. Although you set the alarm for 7:00 A.M. on Sunday, you don't pull yourself out of bed until noon. By the time you start studying, it's 4:00 P.M., and anxiety is building inside you. How can you tell if you've lost control of your time? The following are telltale symptoms of poor time management:

■ Rushing.

■ Chronic inability to make choices or decisions.

■ Fatigue or listlessness.

■ Constantly missed deadlines.

■ Not enough time for rest or personal relationships.

■ A sense of being overwhelmed by demands and details and having to do what you don't want to do most of the time.

One of the hard lessons of being on your own is that your choices and your actions have consequences. Stress is just one of them. But by thinking ahead, being realistic about your workload, and sticking to your plans, you can gain better control over your time and your stress levels.

OVERCOMING PROCRASTINATION

(11) Putting off until tomorrow what should be done today is a habit that creates a great deal of stress for many students. The three most common types of procrastination are: putting off unpleasant things, putting off difficult tasks, and putting off tough decisions. Procrastinators are most likely to delay by wishing they didn't have to do what they must or by telling themselves they "just can't get started," which means they never do.

(12) People procrastinate, not because they're lazy, but to protect their self-esteem and make a favorable impression. "Procrastinators often perceive their worth as based solely on task ability, and their ability is determined only by how well they perform on completed tasks," notes psychologist Joseph Ferrari, Ph.D. "By never completing the tasks, they are never judged on their ability, thus allowing them to maintain an illusion of competence."

Chart 2: Breaking Out of the
Procrastination Trap

A. Keep track of the tasks you're most likely to put off, and try to figure why you don't want to tackle them. Think of alternative ways to get tasks done. If you put off library readings, figure out if the problem is getting to the library or the reading itself. If it's the trip to the library, arrange to walk over with a friend whose company you enjoy.

B. Keep a daily "To Do" list. Rank items according to priorities: A, B, C. Evaluate the items. Should any B's be A's? Schedule your days so the A's get accomplished.

C. Try not to fixate on half-completed projects. Divide large tasks, such as a term paper, into smaller ones, and reward yourself when you complete a part.

D. Do what you like least first. Once you have it out of the way, you can concentrate on the tasks you do enjoy.

E. Build time into your schedule for interruptions, unforeseen problems, unexpected events, and so on, so you aren't constantly racing around.

F. Beware of overcommitment. Establish ground rules for meeting your own needs (including getting enough sleep and making time for friends) before saying yes to any activity.

G. Learn to live according to a three-word motto: Just do it!

GOING WITH THE FLOW

(13) Americans enjoy less free time than people in many other societies—and we often don't know how to make the most of the free time we do have. According to the Americans' Use of Time Project, when we don't have to do anything else, most Americans mainly watch television: an average of 15.1 hours every week—compared with 4.9 hours visiting friends, 4.3 talking, 3.1 traveling, 2.8 reading, and 2.2 for either sports or hobbies. Yet when asked what they like to do, men and women rank playing with children, active sports, socializing and talking with family members much higher than watching TV. Three quarters of Americans believe the amount of stress in their lives is within their control. How do they prefer to handle stress? Exercise, 42%; Slowing down, 17%; Taking time off, 11%; Watching television, 7%; and Meditating, 3%.

(14) So why do we end up in front of the tube? Often it's simply because, while we carefully schedule our weekdays, we let our weekends and other free time drift. "Everybody who works looks forward to time off to do something they really enjoy, but very few do," observes psychologist Mihaly Czikszentmihalyi, Ph.D., author of *Flow: The Psychology of Optimal Experience*. "When you get home, you feel listless, so you fall into the passive leisure trap of watching television—even though it isn't a really satisfying form of relaxation."

(15) There is an alternative, but it requires two things: prior planning and organization. "It's difficult to enjoy leisure time unless you prepare for it," says Czikszentmihalyi. "Left to themselves, things turn into a muddle; they deteriorate. To get any real psychological benefit from your free time, you have to invest some energy into it. Quality relaxation takes what I call spontaneous coordination." The first step is making leisure a priority. Too often, in our work-obsessed culture, we feel bad about simply feeling good. "We greatly undervalue relaxation," observes David Sobel, M.D., a specialist in behavioral medicine and coauthor of *Healthy Pleasures*. "It requires a certain amount of self-esteem to believe that you deserve to do something just because you enjoy it."

(16) But don't assume that the best leisure activities are expensive or elaborate. Often they're not. What they offer is flow, which Czikszentmihalyi defines as a state of altered consciousness that occurs when we are so focused, so immersed in what we're doing that we lose sense of time or anything else. The moment becomes everything. People find this sort of transcendental experience in different ways: playing chess, dancing, listening to music. Very often flow involves being outdoors—gardening, hiking, biking, sitting under a shady tree, looking for falling stars on a summer night, crunching through newly fallen snow. "Nature has a measurable restorative effect with respect to stress," says environmental psychologist Robert Ulrich, Ph.D., of Texas A&M University. Follow your own inclinations, whether or not they lead outdoors, to find your personal sources of flow.

RELAXATION TECHNIQUES

(17) Relaxation is the physical and mental state opposite that of stress. Rather than gearing up for fight or flight, our bodies and minds grow calmer and work more smoothly. We're less likely to become frazzled and more capable of staying in control. The most effective relaxation techniques include progressive relaxation, visualization, meditation, mindfulness, and biofeedback.

(18) **Progressive relaxation** works by intentionally increasing and then decreasing tension in the muscles. While sitting or lying down in a quiet, comfortable setting, you tense and release various muscles, beginning with those of the hand, for instance, and then proceeding to the arms, shoulders, neck, face, scalp, chest, stomach, buttocks, genitals, and so on, down each leg to the toes. Relaxing the muscles can quiet the mind and restore internal balance.

(19) **Visualization** or guided memory involves creating mental pictures that calm you down and focus your mind. Some people use this technique to promote healing when they are ill. The Glaser study showed that elderly residents of retirement homes in Ohio who learned progressive relaxation and guided imagery enhanced their immune function and reported better health than did the other residents. Visualization skills require practice and, in some cases, instruction by qualified health professionals.

(20) **Meditation** has been practiced in many forms over the ages, from the yogic techniques of the Far East to the Quaker silence of more modern times. Meditation helps a person reach a state of relaxation, but with the goal of achieving inner peace and harmony. There is no one right way to meditate, and many people have discovered how to meditate on their own, without even knowing what it is they are doing. Among college students, meditation has proven especially effective in increasing relaxation. Most forms of meditation have common elements: sitting quietly for fifteen to twenty minutes once or twice a day, concentrating on a word or image, and breathing slowly and rhythmically. If you wish to try meditation, it often helps to have someone guide you through your first sessions. Or try tape recording your own voice (with or without favorite music in the background) and playing it back to yourself, freeing yourself to concentrate on the goal of turning the attention within.

(21) **Mindfulness** is a modern-day form of an ancient Asian technique that involves maintaining awareness in the present moment. You tune in to each part of your body, scanning from head to toe, noting the slightest sensation. You allow whatever you experience—an itch, an ache, a feeling of warmth—to enter your awareness. Then you open yourself to focus on all the thoughts, sensations, sounds, and feelings that enter your awareness. Mindfulness keeps you in the here-and-now, thinking about what is rather than about "what if" or "if only."

(22) **Biofeedback** is a method of obtaining feedback, or information, about some physiological activity occurring in the body. An electronic

monitoring device attached to a person's body detects a change in an internal function and communicates it back to the person through a tone, light, or meter. By paying attention to this feedback, most people can gain some control over functions previously thought to be beyond conscious control, such as body temperature, heart rate, muscle tension, and brain waves. Biofeedback training consists of three stages:

A. Developing increased awareness of a body state or function.

B. Gaining control over it.

C. Transferring this control to everyday living without use of the electronic instrument.

The goal of biofeedback for stress reduction is a state of tranquility, usually associated with the brain's production of alpha waves (which are slower and more regular than normal waking waves). After several training sessions, most people can produce alpha waves more or less at will.

(2,646 words)

Here are some of the more difficult words in "A Personal Stress Survival Guide."

alleviate
(paragraph 5)

al·le·vi·ate (ə lē'vē āt') *vt.* ·-at'ed, ·-at'·ing [ME *alleviaten* < LL *alleviatus*, pp. of *alleviare*, for L *allevare* < *ad-*, to + *levis*, LIGHT²] **1** to make less hard to bear; lighten or relieve (pain, suffering, etc.) **2** to reduce or decrease [to *alleviate* poverty] —*SYN.* RELIEVE —al·le'·via'·tor *n.* —al·le'·via·to·ry (-ə tôr'ē)

discern
(Chart 1, Item B)

dis·cern (di surn', -zurn') *vt.* [ME *discernen* < OFr *discerner* < L *discernere* < *dis-*, apart + *cernere*, to separate: see HARVEST] **1** to separate (a thing) mentally from another or others; recognize as separate or different **2** to perceive or recognize; make out clearly —*vi.* to perceive or recognize the difference —dis·cern'·ible *adj.* —dis·cern'·ibly *adv.*

garner
(Chart 1, Item B)

gar·ner (gär'nər) *n.* [ME *gerner* < OFr *grenier* < L *granarium*, granary < *granum*, GRAIN] a place for storing grain; granary —*vt.* **1** to gather up and store in or as in a granary **2** to get or earn **3** to collect or gather

immersed
(paragraph 16)

im·merse (i murs') *vt.* ·-mersed', ·-mers'·ing [< L *immersus*, pp. of *immergere*, to dip, plunge into: see IN-¹ & MERGE] **1** to plunge, drop, or dip into or as if into a liquid, esp. so as to cover completely **2** to baptize by submerging in water **3** to absorb deeply; engross [*immersed* in study]

maladaptive
(paragraph 5)

mal·ad·ap·ta·tion (mal'ad əp tā'shən) *n.* inadequate or faulty adaptation —mal'·adap'·tive (-ə dap'tiv) *adj.*

ad·ap·ta·tion (ad'əp tā'shən) *n.* [Fr < ML *adaptatio*: see ADAPT] **1** an adapting or being adapted **2** a thing resulting from adapting [this play is an *adaptation* of a novel] **3** a change in structure, function, or form that improves the chance of survival for an animal or plant within a given environment **4** the natural reactions of a sense organ to variations in the degree of stimulation **5** *Sociology* a gradual change in behavior to conform to the prevailing cultural patterns —ad'·ap·ta'·tional *adj.*

Vocabulary List

Vocabulary List

physiological
(paragraph 22)

physi·ol·ogy (fiz'ē äl'ə jē) *n.* ⟦Fr *physiologie* < L *physiologia* < Gr: see PHYSIO- & -LOGY⟧ **1** the branch of biology dealing with the functions and vital processes of living organisms or their parts and organs **2** the functions and vital processes, collectively (of an organism, or of an organ or system of organs) —**phys'i·ol'o·gist** *n.*

procrastination
(paragraph 11)

pro·cras·ti·nate (prō kras'tə nāt', prə-) *vi.*, *vt.* **-·nat'ed**, **-·nat'ing** ⟦< L *procrastinatus*, pp. of *procastinare* < *pro-*, forward (see PRO-²) + *crastinus*, belonging to the morrow < *cras*, tomorrow⟧ to put off doing (something unpleasant or burdensome) until a future time; esp., to postpone (such actions) habitually —**pro·cras'·ti·na'·tion** *n.* —**pro·cras'·ti·na'·tor** *n.*

psychological
(paragraph 3)

psycho·logi·cal (sī'kə läj'i kəl) *adj.* **1** of psychology **2** of the mind; mental **3** affecting or intended to affect the mind Also **psy'cho·log'ic** —**psy'cho·log'i·cally** *adv.*

superficial
(paragraph 3)

su·per·fi·cial (sōō'pər fish'əl) *adj.* ⟦ME *superficyall* < L *superficialis* < *superficies*: see fol.⟧ **1** *a*) of or being on the surface [a *superficial* burn] *b*) of or limited to surface area; plane [*superficial* measurements] **2** concerned with and understanding only the easily apparent and obvious; not profound; shallow **3** quick and cursory [a *superficial* reading] **4** seeming such only at first glance; merely apparent [a *superficial* resemblance] —**su'·per·fi'·ci·al'·ity** (-ē al'ə tē) *n.*, *pl.* **-ties** —**su'·per·fi'·cially** *adv.* —**su'·per·fi'·cial·ness** *n.*
SYN.—**superficial** implies concern with the obvious or surface aspects of a thing [*superficial* characteristics] and, in a derogatory sense, lack of thoroughness, profoundness, significance, etc. [*superficial* judgments]; **shallow**, in this connection always derogatory, implies a lack of depth of character, intellect, meaning, etc. [*shallow* writing]; **cursory**, which may or may not be derogatory, suggests a hasty consideration of something without pausing to note details [a *cursory* inspection] —*ANT.* **deep, profound**

tranquility
(paragraph 22)

tran·quil·lity or **tran·quil·ity** (traŋ kwil'ə tē, tran-) *n.* the quality or state of being tranquil; calmness; serenity

transcendental
(paragraph 16)

tran·scen·den·tal (tran'sen dent''l) *adj.* ⟦ML *transcendentalis*⟧ **1** *a*) TRANSCENDENT (sense 1) *b*) SUPERNATURAL **2** abstract; metaphysical **3** of or having to do with transcendentalism **4** in Kantian philosophy, based on those elements of experience which derive not from sense data but from the inherent organizing function of the mind, and which are the necessary conditions of human knowledge; transcending sense experience but not knowledge **5** *Math. a*) not capable of being a root of any algebraic equation with rational coefficients *b*) of, pertaining to, or being a function, as a logarithm, trigonometric function, exponential, etc., that is not expressible algebraically in terms of the variables and constants (opposed to ALGEBRAIC, sense 2)) —**tran'·scen·den'·tally** *adv.*

vent
(paragraph 4)
[*vt. form*]

vent¹ (vent) *n.* ⟦ME *venten* < OFr *venter*, to blow (or aphetic < OFr *esventer*, to expose to the air, let out < *es-*, out + *venter*) < VL **ventare* < L *ventus*, WIND²⟧ **1** [Rare] the action of escaping or passing out, or the means or opportunity to do this; issue; outlet **2** expression; release [giving *vent* to emotion] **3** *a*) a small hole or opening to permit passage or escape, as of a gas ☆*b*) a small triangular window or, now esp., an opening on or beneath the dashboard, for letting air into the passenger compartment of a motor vehicle **4** in early guns, the small hole at the breech through which a spark passes to set off the charge **5** the opening in a volcano from which gas and molten rock erupt **6** *Zool.* the excretory opening in animals; esp., the external opening of the cloaca in birds, reptiles, amphibians, and fishes —*vt.* **1** to make a vent in or provide a vent for **2** to allow (steam, gas, etc.) to escape through an opening **3** to give release or expression to **4** to relieve or unburden by giving vent to feelings [to *vent* oneself in curses]

29A1 VOCABULARY

From the context of "A Personal Stress Survival Guide," explain each of the vocabulary words shown in boldface below.

1. *From paragraph 3:* . . . college students who wrote in their journals about traumatic events felt much better afterward than those who wrote about **superficial** topics.

   shallow

2. *From paragraph 3:* Since the small ups and downs of daily life have an enormous impact on **psychological** and physical well-being, getting a handle on daily hassles will reduce your stress load.

   mental

3. *From Chart 1, Item B:* Rereading and thinking about your notes may help you **discern** the underlying reasons for your response and **garner** insights that can help you cope better in the future.

   recognize . . . get insights

4. *From paragraph 4:* The second [person] uses humor to **vent** frustration.

   release

5. *From paragraph 5:* Under great stress, we all may turn to negative defense mechanisms to **alleviate** anxiety and eliminate conflict.

   relieve

6. *From paragraph 5:* These can lead to **maladaptive** behavior, such as overeating. . . .

   unsuitable

7. *From paragraph 11:* The three most common types of **procrastination** are putting off unpleasant things, putting off difficult tasks, and putting off tough decisions.

   postponing actions

Name   Date

8. *From paragraph 16:* What they offer is flow, which Czikszentmihalyi defines as a state of altered consciousness that occurs when we are so focused, so **immersed** in what we're doing that we lose sense of time or anything else.

   absorbed

9. *From paragraph 16:* People find this sort of **transcendental** experience in different ways.

   supernatural

10. *From paragraph 22:* Biofeedback is a method of obtaining feedback, or information, about some **physiological** activity occurring in the body.

    organic

11. *From paragraph 22:* The goal of biofeedback for stress reduction is a state of **tranquility.**

    calmness

29A2   SPECIAL TEXTBOOK VOCABULARY

Key terms in this textbook selection are explained as they are discussed. Referring to "A Personal Stress Survival Guide," fill in the blanks.

1. Defense mechanisms are actions or behaviors that people use to protect their sense of self-worth.

2. Redirecting an unacceptable drive into a socially acceptable channel is

   sublimation .

3. Religiosity is the practice of one's trying to accept a painful experience as being in agreement with God's will.

4. Medical students use jokes, or humor , to counteract stress they encounter during anatomy lab.

5. Turning a negative experience into a positive one is

   altruism .

Name   Date

6. <u>Progressive relaxation</u> occurs when a person intentionally increases and then decreases tension in various muscles according to a set sequence.

7. One's creating and using mental pictures to calm oneself and focus the mind is <u>   visualization   </u> .

8. <u>   Meditation   </u> can involve sitting quietly, concentrating, or breathing slowly and rhythmically to achieve a state of relaxation.

29B   CENTRAL THEME AND MAIN IDEAS

Choose the best answer.

__b__   1. The central theme of "A Personal Stress Survival Guide" is
a. how unbalanced stress distribution on metal parts can cause failure of machinery resulting in serious accidents.
b. how important is the maintenance of good mental health through all stages of life, from childhood through old age.
c. how people can learn to handle stress: first, by learning the types of stress and, second, by using ways to minimize their effects.
d. how to handle the trauma that can follow having almost died in a major disaster, such as a tornado, flood, or hurricane.

__b__   2. The main purpose of paragraph 2 is to
a. describe and discuss the possible signals of stress overload.
b. identify the common traits found in those who control stress.
c. describe and discuss the behaviors that lead to stress.
d. recommend involvement with other people to avoid stress.

__d__   3. The main idea of paragraph 4 is that
a. teachers may take out their stress from work by yelling at their own children.
b. joking about a stressful day at work can relieve stress.
c. protecting one's sense of self-worth is necessary during stressful times.
d. people use defense mechanisms to protect against stress.

29C MAJOR DETAILS
Fill in the word or words that correctly complete each statement.

1. The impact of stress depends not just on what ___happened___ to you, but on how you ___handle___ it.

2. An effective way to deal with stress is writing about your ___feelings___ into ___words___ that only you will read.

3. Some strategies to help you cope with stress include __ ___recognizing___ your stress signals, ___keeping___ a stress journal, ___trying___ "stress-inoculation," ___putting___ things in proper perspective, and ___thinking___ of one thing to simplify your life.

4. Symptoms of ___poor time management___ include rushing, the inability to make choices, fatigue, missed deadlines, and not enough time for rest.

5. The Americans' Use of Time Project showed that Americans spend the greater amount of their free time ___watching television___ .

6. To make effective use of free time requires ___prior planning___ and ___organization___ .

7. In our work-obsessed culture, David Sobel observes "we greatly undervalue ___relaxation___ ."

29D INFERENCES
Decide whether each statement can be inferred (YES) or cannot be inferred (NO) from the reading selection.

__YES__ 1. Stress management includes striving for a personal goal because it provides reasons for choices made.

__YES__ 2. Stress management includes using a minimum of substances, such as nicotine and caffeine, because these stimulants can affect a person's thought processes.

__NO__ 3. Procrastinators have high self-esteem.

__NO__ 4. Stress counseling is available through many resources.

Name   Date

29E   CRITICAL READING: FACT OR OPINION
Decide whether each statement contains a FACT or an OPINION.

OPINION 1. *From paragraph 1:* "The inability to feel in control of stress, rather than stress itself, is often the most harmful."

FACT 2. *From paragraph 11:* "Putting off until tomorrow what should be done today is a habit that creates a great deal of stress for many students."

OPINION 3. *From paragraph 12:* "People procrastinate, not because they're lazy, but to protect their self-esteem and make a favorable impression."

FACT 4. *From paragraph 13:* "Three-quarters of Americans believe the amount of stress in their lives is within their control."

FACT 5. *From paragraph 14:* "Everybody who works looks forward to time off to do something they really enjoy [. . .]."

FACT 6. *From paragraph 19:* "The Glaser study of elderly residents of retirement homes in Ohio showed that residents who practiced progressive relaxation and guided imagery enhanced their immune function and reported better health than the other residents."

OPINION 7. *From paragraph 20:* "Among college students meditation has proven especially effective in increasing relaxation."

29F   CRITICAL READING: THE WRITER'S CRAFT
Choose the best answer.

c 1. Expressions that show connections between ideas may contain one word or several words. Which of the following is *not* used to show connections?
   a. "One of the simplest"   (paragraph 3)
   b. "Another individual"   (4)
   c. "Under great stress"   (5)
   d. "Then"   (10)
   e. "The three most common types" (11)
   f. "but"   (15)

a 2. Why are bullets used in the essay?
   a. to make reading each list easier and more efficient
   b. to indicate what should be memorized
   c. to show what is the most important information in the chapter
   d. to alert readers that they can skip the information if they wish

29G READER RESPONSE: TO DISCUSS OR TO WRITE ABOUT

1. Stress can either help or hurt a person. Good stress provides a challenge. Bad stress is harmful physically and/or psychologically. Discuss several situations that illustrate either good or bad stress in your life or in a friend's life.

2. Give an example of a stressful situation involving you and a family member, coworker, friend, or classmate. Were you able to change the situation? If so, explain what you did. If not, explain the coping techniques you used to handle the situation.

3. Every student knows that examinations can be a source of stress. What are some ways a student can manage stress before, during, and after the exam? Give specific suggestions.

How Did You Do?   29 A Personal Stress Survival Guide

SKILL (number of items)	Number Correct		Points for Each		Score
Vocabulary* (12)	_____	×	2	=	_____
Special Textbook Vocabulary (8)	_____	×	2	=	_____
Central Theme and Main Ideas (3)	_____	×	5	=	_____
Major Details** (14)	_____	×	2	=	_____
Inferences (4)	_____	×	1	=	_____
Critical Reading: Fact or Opinion (7)	_____	×	1	=	_____
Critical Reading: The Writer's Craft (2)	_____	×	3	=	_____
			(Possible Total: 100) *Total*		_____

SPEED

Reading Time: _____ Reading Rate (page 400): _____ Words Per Minute

*Question 3 in this exercise calls for two separate answers. In computing your score, count each separate answer toward your number correct.

**Questions 1, 2, and 6 in this exercise call for two separate answers. Question 3 calls for five separate answers. In computing your score, count each separate answer toward your number correct.

Name   Date

Selection 30

The Chaser

John Collier

(1) Alan Austen, as nervous as a kitten, went up certain dark and creaky stairs in the neighborhood of Pell Street, and peered about for a long time on the dim landing before he found the name he wanted written obscurely on one of the doors.

(2) He pushed open this door, as he had been told to do, and found himself in a tiny room, which contained no furniture but a plain kitchen table, a rocking-chair, and an ordinary chair. On one of the dirty buff-colored walls were a couple of shelves, containing in all perhaps a dozen bottles and jars.

(3) An old man sat in the rocking-chair, reading a newspaper. Alan, without a word, handed him the card he had been given. "Sit down, Mr. Austen," said the man very politely. "I am glad to make your acquaintance."

(4) "Is it true," asked Alan, "that you have a certain mixture that has—er—quite extraordinary effects?"

(5) "My dear sir," replied the old man, "my stock in trade is not very large—I don't deal in laxatives and teething mixtures—but such as it is, it is varied. I think nothing I sell has effects which could be precisely described as ordinary."

(6) "Well, the fact is—" began Alan.

(7) "Here, for example," interrupted the old man, reaching for a bottle from the shelf. "Here is a liquid as colorless as water, almost tasteless, quite imperceptible in coffee, milk, wine, or any other beverage. It is also quite imperceptible to any known method of autopsy."

(8) "Do you mean it is a poison?" cried Alan, very much horrified.

(9) "Call it a glove-cleaner if you like," said the old man indifferently. "Maybe it will clean gloves. I have never tried. One might call it a life-cleaner. Lives need cleaning sometimes."

(10) "I want nothing of that sort," said Alan.

(11) "Probably it is just as well," said the old man. "Do you know the price of this? For one teaspoonful, which is sufficient, I ask five thousand dollars. Never less. Not a penny less."

(12) "I hope all your mixtures are not as expensive," said Alan apprehensively.

(13) "Oh dear, no," said the old man. "It would be no good charging that sort of price for a love potion, for example. Young people who need a love potion very seldom have five thousand dollars. Otherwise they would not need a love potion."

(14) "I am glad to hear that," said Alan.

(15) "I look at it like this," said the old man. "Please a customer with one article, and he will come back when he needs another. Even if it is more costly. He will save up for it, if necessary."

(16) "So," said Alan, "you really do sell love potions?"

(17) "If I did not sell love potions," said the old man, reaching for another bottle, "I should not have mentioned the other matter to you. It is only when one is in a position to oblige that one can afford to be so confidential."

(18) "And these potions," said Alan. "They are not just—just—er—"

(19) "Oh, no," said the old man. "Their effects are permanent, and extend far beyond casual impulse. But they include it. Bountifully, insistently. Everlastingly."

(20) "Dear me!" said Alan, attempting a look of scientific detachment. "How very interesting!"

(21) "But consider the spiritual side," said the old man.

(22) "I do, indeed," said Alan.

(23) "For indifference," said the old man, "they substitute devotion. For scorn, adoration. Give one tiny measure of this to the young lady—its flavor is imperceptible in orange juice, soup, or cocktails—and however gay and giddy she is, she will change altogether. She will want nothing but solitude, and you."

(24) "I can hardly believe it," said Alan. "She is so fond of parties."

(25) "She will not like them any more," said the old man. "She will be afraid of the pretty girls you may meet."

(26) "She will actually be jealous?" cried Alan in rapture. "Of me?"

(27) "Yes, she will want to be everything to you."

(28) "She is, already. Only she doesn't care about it."

(29) "She will, when she has taken this. She will care intensely. You will be her sole interest in life."

(30) "Wonderful!" cried Alan.

(31) "She will want to know all you do," said the old man. "All that has happened to you during the day. Every word of it. She will want to know what you are thinking about, why you smile suddenly, why you are looking sad."

(32) "That is love!" cried Alan.

(33) "Yes," said the old man. "How carefully she will look after you! She will never allow you to be tired, to sit in a draught, to neglect your food. If you are an hour late, she will be terrified. She will think you are killed, or that some siren has caught you."

(34) "I can hardly imagine Diana like that!" cried Alan, overwhelmed with joy.

(35) "You will not have to use your imagination," said the old man. "And, by the way, since there are always sirens, if by any chance you should, later on, slip a little, you need not worry. She will forgive you, in the end. She will be terribly hurt, of course, but she will forgive you—in the end."

(36) "That will not happen," said Alan fervently.

(37) "Of course not," said the old man. "But, if it did, you need not worry. She would never divorce you. Oh, no! And, of course, she herself will never give you the least, the very least, grounds for—uneasiness."

(38) "And how much," said Alan, "is this wonderful mixture?"

(39) "It is not as dear," said the old man, "as the glove-cleaner, or life-cleaner, as I sometimes call it. No. That is five thousand dollars, never a penny less. One has to be older than you are, to indulge in that sort of thing. One has to save up for it."

(40) "But the love potion?" said Alan.

(41) "Oh, that," said the old man, opening the drawer in the kitchen table, and taking out a tiny, rather dirty-looking phial. "That is just a dollar."

(42) "I can't tell you how grateful I am," said Alan, watching him fill it.

(43) "I like to oblige," said the old man. "Then customers come back, later in life, when they are rather better off, and want more expensive things. Here you are. You will find it very effective."

(44) "Thank you again," said Alan. "Good-by."

(45) "Au revoir," said the old man.

(1,075 words)

Here are some of the more difficult words in "The Chaser."

au revoir
(paragraph 45)

au re·voir (ō′rə vwär′) ⟦Fr < *au*, to the + *revoir*, seeing again < L. *revidere*, see again < *re-*, again + *videre*, see: see VISION⟧ until we meet again; goodbye: implies temporary parting

autopsy
(paragraph 7)

au·top·sy (ô′täp′sē, ôt′əp sē) *n.*, *pl.* **-sies** ⟦ML & Gr *autopsia*, a seeing with one's own eyes < Gr *autos*, self + *opsis*, a sight < *ōps*, EYE⟧ **1** an examination and dissection of a dead body to discover the cause of death, damage done by disease, etc.; postmortem **2** a detailed critical analysis of a book, play, etc., or of some event —*vt.* **-sied**, **-sy·ing** to examine (a body) in this manner

bountifully
(paragraph 19)

boun·ti·ful (-tə fəl) *adj.* **1** giving freely and graciously; generous **2** provided in abundance; plentiful —**boun′·ti·fully** *adv.* —**boun′·ti·ful·ness** *n.*

chaser
(title)

chaser[1] (chā′sər) *n.* ⟦CHASE[1] + -ER⟧ **1** a person or thing that chases or hunts; pursuer **2** a gun formerly placed on the stern (**stern chaser**) or bow (**bow chaser**) of a ship, used during pursuit by or of another ship ☆**3** a mild drink, as water, ginger ale, or beer, taken after or with whiskey, rum, etc.

confidential
(paragraph 17)

con·fi·den·tial (kän′fə den′shəl) *adj.* **1** told in confidence; imparted in secret **2** of or showing trust in another; confiding **3** entrusted with private or secret matters *[a confidential agent]* — SYN. FAMILIAR —**con′·fi·den′·ti·al′·ity** (-shē al′ə tē) *n.* or **con′·fi·den′·tial·ness** —**con′·fi·den′·tially** *adv.*

Vocabulary List

Vocabulary List

draught
(paragraph 33)

draught (draft, dräft) *n., vt., adj.* now chiefly Brit. sp. of DRAFT

draft (draft, dräft) *n.* [ME *draught*, a drawing, pulling, stroke < base of OE *dragan*, DRAW] **1** *a*) a drawing or pulling, as of a vehicle or load *b*) the thing, quantity, or load pulled **2** *a*) a drawing in of a fish net *b*) the amount of fish caught in one draw **3** *a*) a taking of liquid into the mouth; drinking *b*) the amount taken at one drink **4** *a*) a portion of liquid for drinking; specif., a dose of medicine *b*) [Informal] a portion of beer, ale, etc. drawn from a cask **5** *a*) a drawing into the lungs, as of air or tobacco smoke *b*) the amount of air, smoke, etc., drawn in **6** a rough or preliminary sketch of a piece of writing **7** a plan or drawing of a work to be done **8** a current of air, as in a room, heating system, etc. **9** a device for regulating the current of air in a heating system **10** a written order issued by one person, bank, firm, etc., directing the payment of money to another; check **11** a demand or drain made on something

imperceptible
(paragraph 7)

im·per·cep·tible (im′pər sep′tə bəl) *adj.* [Fr < ML *imperceptibilis*: see IN-² & PERCEPTIBLE] not plain or distinct to the senses or the mind; esp., so slight, gradual, subtle, etc. as not to be easily perceived —**im′·per·cep′·tibil′·ity** *n.* —**im′·per·cep′·tibly** *adv.*

obscurely
(paragraph 1)

ob·scure (əb skyoor′, äb-) *adj.* [OFr *obscur* < L *obscurus*, lit., covered over < *ob-* (see OB-) + IE **skuro-* < base **(s)keu-*, to cover, conceal > HIDE¹, SKY] **1** lacking light; dim; dark; murky [the *obscure* night] **2** not easily perceived; specif., *a*) not clear or distinct; faint or undefined [an *obscure* figure or sound] *b*) not easily understood; vague; cryptic; ambiguous [an *obscure* explanation] *c*) in an inconspicuous position; hidden [an *obscure* village] **3** not well-known; not famous [an *obscure* scientist] **4** *Phonet.* pronounced as (ə) or (i) because it is not stressed; reduced; neutral: said of a vowel —*vt.* **-·scured′, -·scur′·ing** [L *obscurare* < the adj.] **1** to make obscure; specif., *a*) to darken; make dim *b*) to conceal from view; hide *c*) to make less conspicuous; overshadow [a success that *obscured* earlier failures] *d*) to make less intelligible; confuse [testimony that *obscures* the issue] **2** *Phonet.* to make (a vowel) obscure —*n.* [Rare] OBSCURITY —**ob·scure′·ly** *adv.* —**ob·scure′·ness** *n.*

SYN.—**obscure** applies to that which is perceived with difficulty either because it is concealed or veiled or because of obtuseness in the perceiver [their reasons remain *obscure*]; **vague** implies such a lack of precision or exactness as to be indistinct or unclear [a *vague* idea]; **enigmatic** and **cryptic** are used of that which baffles or perplexes, the latter word implying deliberate intention to puzzle [*enigmatic* behavior, a *cryptic* warning]; **ambiguous** applies to that which puzzles because it allows of more than one interpretation [an *ambiguous* title]; **equivocal** is used of something ambiguous that is deliberately used to mislead or confuse [an *equivocal* answer] —*ANT.* **clear, distinct, obvious**

phial
(paragraph 41)

phial (fī′əl) *n.* [ME *fiole* < OFr < Prov *fiola* < ML < L *phiala* < Gr *phialē*, broad, shallow drinking vessel] a small glass bottle; vial

rapture
(paragraph 26)

rap·ture (rap′chər) *n.* [ML *raptura:* see RAPT & -URE] **1** the state of being carried away with joy, love, etc.; ecstasy **2** an expression of great joy, pleasure, etc. **3** a carrying away or being carried away in body or spirit: now rare except in theological usage —*vt.* **-·tured, -·tur·ing** [Now Rare] to enrapture; fill with ecstasy —*SYN.* ECSTASY —**the rapture** [often the R-] in some Christian theologies, the bodily ascent into heaven just before Armageddon of those who are saved (see SAVE¹, *vt.* 8) —**rap′·tur·ous** *adj.* —**rap′·tur·ously** *adv.*

siren
(paragraph 33)

si·ren (sī′rən) *n.* [ME *syrene* < OFr < LL *Sirena*, for L *Siren* < Gr *Seirēn* < ? *seira*, cord, rope (hence, orig. ? one who snares, entangles) < IE base **twer-*, to grasp] **1** *Gr. & Rom. Myth.* any of several sea nymphs, represented as part bird and part woman, who lure sailors to their death on rocky coasts by seductive singing **2** a woman who uses her sexual attractiveness to entice or allure men; a woman who is considered seductive **3** *a*) an acoustical device in which steam or air is driven against a rotating, perforated disk so as to produce sound; specif., such a device producing a loud, often wailing sound, used esp. as a warning signal *b*) an electronic device that produces a similar sound **4** any of a family (Sirenidae) of slender, eel-shaped salamanders without hind legs; esp., the mud eel

30A VOCABULARY

Using the vocabulary words listed on pages 385–386, fill in this crossword puzzle.

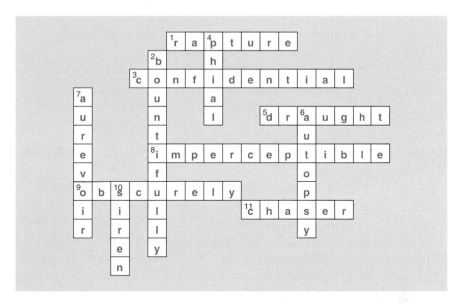

Across

1. an expression of great happiness and delight
3. told or divulged in secret
5. air current
8. insignificant or not easily perceived
9. not distinctly or clearly
11. The _____ following his beer was simply a glass of water.

Down

2. given freely or graciously; abundantly
4. a small glass container
6. An _____ determined the cause of death.
7. the French expression for "farewell"
10. an enchantress or seductive woman

Name   Date

30B CENTRAL THEME AND MAIN IDEAS
Choose the best answer.

___c___ 1. The central theme of "The Chaser" is that
      a. an old man sells only two types of potions.
      b. love potions may cause distinct personality changes.
      c. "true love" may also have a dark side.
      d. there are inherent dangers involved in using potions.

___b___ 2. What is the underlying assumption of "The Chaser"?
      a. The effects of love potions are permanent and irreversible.
      b. People will resort to even more drastic measures to get out of a love relationship than to get into one.
      c. Young people have less money than older people to buy what they want.
      d. A love potion may cause unfounded jealousy and unsolicited adoration.

___a___ 3. The unexpected main idea of paragraph 9 is
      a. the old man's cavalier attitude toward poisoning people.
      b. the unusual names the old man chooses to disguise his poison.
      c. the philosophy that lives sometimes need to be "cleaned out."
      d. that of the two potions the old man sells, one is poison.

___c___ 4. The main idea of paragraph 43 is that
      a. the old man is pleased that his customers are happy with his potions.
      b. the old man is aware that he has a tremendous service to offer his customers.
      c. the old man is willing to give his customers what they think they want now, knowing that they'll be back later for a more expensive deadly potion.
      d. the old man is anxious for his customers to return so that he can sell them more of the same potion at a higher price.

30C MAJOR DETAILS
Decide whether each detail is MAJOR or MINOR based on the context of the reading selection.

MINOR 1. The potion seller's tiny room was at the top of the dark and creaky stairs.

MAJOR 2. There was a tremendous difference in price between the two potions.

MAJOR 3. The old man refers to his poison as a "life-cleaner."

Name   Date

MAJOR 4. The effects of the love potion are permanent.

MAJOR 5. Diana will forgive Alan's indiscretions, "in the end."

MINOR 6. The potion seller is an old man.

MAJOR 7. The old man sells only two potions.

MINOR 8. The potion seller's room contained only the barest of furniture and shelves hung on dirty buff-colored walls.

MAJOR 9. The poison is imperceptible in any autopsy.

MAJOR 10. Of his two potions, the old man tells Alan about his "life-cleaner" first.

MINOR 11. Diana is very fond of parties.

MAJOR 12. The old man hints that all customers who purchase the first potion return later in life for the second.

30D INFERENCES

Choose the best answer.

__b__ 1. The word "chaser" in the title refers to
   a. the orange juice, soup, or cocktail mixed with the love potion.
   b. the poisonous potion taken to counter the effects of the love potion.
   c. a mild drink taken following a stronger alcoholic drink.
   d. the love potion purchased from the old man by young customers.

__c__ 2. *Read paragraph 13 again.* The author implies that
   a. young people seldom have a need for love potions.
   b. young people in love are generally poor but are mostly indifferent to their poverty.
   c. anyone with $5000 will have no need for a love potion because his money will make him desirable.
   d. expensive love potions would be wasted on young people, who rarely have much money anyway.

__c__ 3. *Read paragraph 17 again.* The old man is implying that
   a. his potions can be very expensive and are a well-kept secret.
   b. if he did not sell love potions, Alan would not have come to see him in the first place.
   c. if he did not sell love potions, he would have no need to sell another potion to "cure" the effects of love potions.
   d. admitting to the need for a love potion is a very confidential matter.

__a__ 4. *Read paragraphs 31–33 again.* Alan's exclamation of "That is love!" is answered with a flat "Yes." The old man's lack of enthusiasm is likely the result of
   a. his awareness that this love will eventually become clinging, possessive, and destructive.
   b. his belief that true love does not truly exist.
   c. his own experience with a past tragic love.
   d. his lack of interest in Alan's reaction to the potion's effects.

__c__ 5. *Read paragraph 35 again.* The author uses the expression "in the end" twice, each time following the statement "She will forgive you." He does this because
   a. Alan must be persistent in asking Diana for forgiveness.
   b. Alan should be careful of these sirens and try to avoid them.
   c. Diana is likely to play the martyr first and inflict some guilt before granting forgiveness.
   d. Diana will be slow to forgive because of her confusion over Alan's unfaithfulness.

__a__ 6. *Read paragraph 39 again.* The author implies that
   a. the poison is more expensive because people want it more badly than the love potion.
   b. young people have not lived long enough to have the problems associated with needing a "life-cleaner."
   c. older people can expect to need "life-cleaners" and are more willing to use poisons.
   d. the poison is a precious commodity because of its inherently expensive ingredients.

__d__ 7. *Read paragraphs 44–45 again.* While Alan bids the old man "goodby," the old man responds with "au revoir," implying that
   a. he is more sophisticated than Alan.
   b. he has not been in the United States long enough yet to converse easily in English.
   c. Alan is also fluent in French and understands the exchange.
   d. the parting is not permanent and Alan will be coming back.

Name   Date

30E CRITICAL READING: THE WRITER'S CRAFT
Choose the best answer.

_a_ 1. Irony in fiction is the use of scenes, actions, or dialogue that convey to the reader the opposite of their literal meaning, often for comic effect. Which of the following statements by the two characters in "The Chaser" is best described as *ironic* in its effect?
   a. (paragraph 3) "Is it true," asked Alan, "that you have a certain mixture that has—er—quite extraordinary effects?"
   b. (paragraph 11) "For one teaspoonful, which is sufficient, I ask five thousand dollars. Never less. Not a penny less."
   c. (paragraph 32) "That is love!" cried Alan.
   d. (paragraph 39) "One has to be older than you are, to indulge in that sort of thing."

_a_ 2. Fiction writers often create dramatic effects by giving the reader crucial pieces of knowledge that are not available to characters in the story. By the end of "The Chaser," who is meant to understand the full significance of the second potion?
   a. the old man and the reader
   b. Alan and the reader
   c. the old man, Alan, and the reader
   d. the reader and the author

30F READER RESPONSE: TO DISCUSS OR TO WRITE ABOUT

1. In your opinion, is it reasonable for the "glove-cleaner" to be so much more expensive than the love potion? Why or why not?

2. Assume a friend came to you for advice about marriage. Would you encourage the person to marry for love, money, or some other factor? Explain fully.

3. Do you believe in the manufacture and distribution of a medication, such as a love potion, to affect a person's feelings for someone else? This medication might be prescribed in a situation of unrequited love. What are the advantages of such a medication? Are there any dangers? To whom would this be prescribed? Give specific support to convince your audience to consider your point of view.

Name   Date   391

How Did You Do?   **30** The Chaser

SKILL (number of items)	Number Correct		Points for Each		Score
Vocabulary (11)	_____	×	2	=	_____
Central Theme and Main Ideas (4)	_____	×	5	=	_____
Major Details (12)	_____	×	2	=	_____
Inferences (7)	_____	×	4	=	_____
Critical Reading: The Writer's Craft (2)	_____	×	3	=	_____

(Possible Total: 100) *Total*   _____

SPEED

Reading Time: _____ Reading Rate (page 400): _____ Words Per Minute

Name   Date

Appendix

Progress Charts

TOTAL SCORE ON SKILL-BUILDING EXERCISES GRAPH*

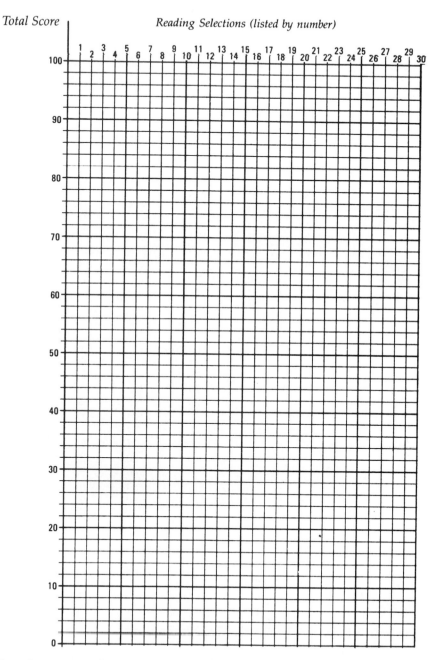

Total Score

Reading Selections (listed by number)

*Put a dot at your total score from the "How Did You Do?" box at the end of each reading selection. Connect the dots with a line to see your progress.

READING RATE TABLE

Here's how to figure your reading rate. Time your reading to the nearest half-minute. Next, locate your time in the left column of this table. Then, stay on the line that lists your time and move to the right to locate the column for

Time in half-minute intervals	Reading Selections (listed by number)						
	PART 2						PART 3
	1	2	3	4	5	6	7
1	498	527	563	775	1121	1259	215
1.5	332	351	375	517	747	839	143
2	249	264	282	388	561	630	108
2.5	199	211	225	310	448	504	86
3	166	176	188	258	374	420	72
3.5	142	151	161	221	320	360	61
4	125	132	141	194	280	315	54
4.5	111	117	125	172	249	280	48
5	97	105	113	155	224	252	
5.5	91	96	102	141	204	230	
6	83	88	94	129	187	210	
6.5	77	81	87	111	172	194	
7	71	75	80	103	160	180	
7.5	66	70	75	97	149	168	
8		66	70	91	140	157	
8.5			66	86	132	148	
9				82	125	140	
9.5				78	118	133	
10				74	112	126	
10.5				70	107	120	
11				67	102	114	
11.5				65	97	109	
12					93	105	
12.5					90	101	
13					86	97	
13.5					83	93	
14					80	90	
14.5					77	87	
15					75	84	
15.5					72	81	
16					70	79	
16.5					68	76	
17						74	
17.5						72	
18						70	
18.5							
19							
19.5							
20							

396

the particular reading selection you have just completed. The number you meet is the number of words per minute you read in that reading selection. **This number of words per minute is your reading rate.** (If you would like to chart your reading rate, you can use the graph on page 401.)

Time in half-minute intervals			*Reading Selections (listed by number)*				
						PART 4	
	8	*9*	*10*	*11*	*12*	*13*	*14*
1	850	894	1004	1396	1775	694	773
1.5	567	596	669	931	1183	463	515
2	425	447	502	698	888	342	387
2.5	340	358	402	558	710	278	309
3	283	298	335	465	592	231	258
3.5	243	255	287	399	507	198	221
4	213	224	251	349	444	174	193
4.5	189	199	223	310	394	154	172
5	170	179	201	279	355	139	155
5.5	155	163	183	254	323	126	141
6	141	149	167	233	296	116	129
6.5	131	138	155	215	273	107	119
7	121	128	143	199	253	99	110
7.5	113	119	134	186	237	93	103
8	106	112	126	175	222	87	97
8.5	100	105	118	164	209	82	91
9	94	99	112	155	197	77	86
9.5	89	94	106	147	187	73	81
10	85	89	100	140	176	69	77
10.5	81	85	96	133	169	66	74
11	77	81	91	127	161	63	70
11.5	74	78	87	121	154		67
12	71	75	84	116	148		64
12.5	68	72	80	112	142		62
13	65	69	77	107	137		
13.5			74	103	131		
14			72	98	127		
14.5			69	96	122		
15			67	93	118		
15.5			65	90	115		
16				87	111		
16.5				85	108		
17				82	104		
17.5				80	101		
18				78	99		
18.5				75	96		
19				73	93		
19.5				72	91		
20				69	89		

Time in half-minute intervals	Reading Selections (listed by number)				PART 5		
	15	16	17	18	19	20	21
1	950	1197	1235	2008	763	792	697
1.5	633	798	823	1339	509	528	465
2	475	599	618	1004	381	396	349
2.5	388	479	494	803	305	317	279
3	317	399	412	669	254	264	232
3.5	271	342	353	574	218	226	199
4	238	299	309	502	191	198	174
4.5	211	266	274	446	170	176	155
5	190	239	247	402	153	158	139
5.5	173	218	224	365	139	144	127
6	158	200	206	335	127	132	116
6.5	146	184	190	309	117	122	107
7	136	171	176	287	109	113	100
7.5	127	168	165	267	102	106	93
8	119	150	154	251	95	99	87
8.5	112	141	145	236	90	93	82
9	106	133	137	223	85	88	77
9.5	100	126	130	211	80	83	73
10	95	120	124	200	76	79	70
10.5	90	114	118	191	73	75	66
11	86	109	112	183	69	72	63
11.5	83	104	107	175	66	69	61
12	79	100	103	167	64		
12.5	76	96	99	161			
13	73	92	95	154			
13.5	70	89	91	149			
14	68	86	88	143			
14.5	66	83	85	138			
15	63	80	82	134			
15.5	61	77	80	130			
16		75	77	125			
16.5		73	75	122			
17		70	73	118			
17.5		68	71	115			
18		67	69	112			
18.5			68	109			
19			65	106			
19.5			63	103			
20			62	100			

Time in half-minute intervals	Reading Selections (listed by number)						
				PART 6			
	22	*23*	*24*	*25*	*26*	*27*	*28*
1	800	803	2382	520	1239	1360	1949
1.5	533	535	1588	346	826	907	1299
2	400	402	1191	260	620	680	975
2.5	320	321	953	208	496	544	780
3	267	268	794	173	413	453	650
3.5	229	229	681	149	354	389	557
4	200	201	596	130	310	340	487
4.5	178	178	529	116	275	302	433
5	160	161	476	104	248	272	390
5.5	145	146	433	95	225	247	354
6	133	134	397	87	207	227	325
6.5	123	124	366	80	191	209	300
7	114	115	340	74	177	194	278
7.5	107	107	318	69	165	181	260
8	100	100	298	65	155	170	244
8.5	94	94	280	61	145	160	229
9	89	89	265		138	151	217
9.5	84	85	251		130	143	205
10	80	80	238		124	136	195
10.5	76	76	227		118	130	186
11	73	73	217		113	124	177
11.5	70	70	207		108	118	169
12	67	67	199		103	113	162
12.5		64	191		99	109	156
13			183		95	105	150
13.5			176		92	101	144
14			170		89	97	139
14.5			164		85	94	134
15			159		83	91	130
15.5			154		80	88	126
16			149		77	85	122
16.5			144		75	82	118
17			140		73	80	115
17.5			136		71	78	111
18			132		69	76	108
18.5			128		67	74	105
19			125		65	72	103
19.5			122			70	100
20			119			68	97
20.5			116				95
21			113				93
21.5			111				91
22			108				89
22.5			106				87
23			104				85
23.5			101				83
24			99				81
24.5			97				80
25			95				78

Time in half-minute intervals	Reading Selections (listed by number)				
	29	30	continued	29	30
1	2646	1075	16	165	67
1.5	1764	717	16.5	160	65
2	1323	538	17	156	63
2.5	1058	430	17.5	151	61
3	882	358	18	147	60
3.5	756	307	18.5	143	
4	662	269	19	139	
4.5	588	239	19.5	136	
5	529	215	20	132	
5.5	481	196	20.5	129	
6	441	179	21	126	
6.5	407	165	21.5	123	
7	378	154	22	120	
7.5	353	143	22.5	118	
8	331	134	23	115	
8.5	311	127	23.5	113	
9	294	119	24	110	
9.5	279	113	24.5	108	
10	265	108	25	106	
10.5	252	102	25.5	103	
11	241	98	26	102	
11.5	230	94	26.5	100	
12	221	90	27	98	
12.5	212	86	27.5	96	
13	204	83	28	95	
13.5	196	80			
14	189	77	28.5	93	
14.5	182	74	29	91	
15	176	72	29.5	90	
15.5	171	69	30	88	

(continued at upper right)

READING RATE GRAPH*

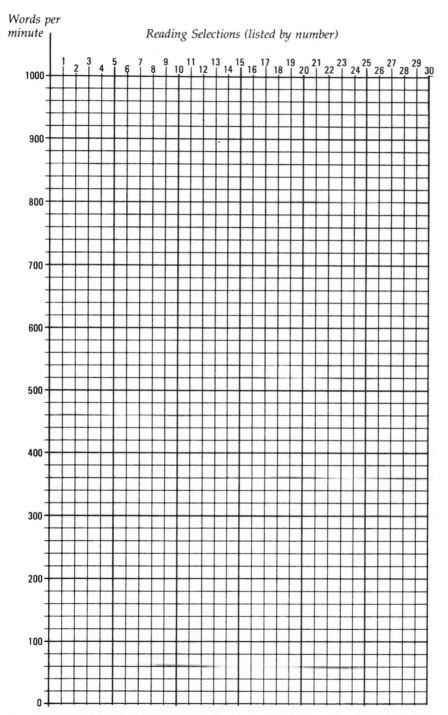

Words per minute

Reading Selections (listed by number)

*Put a dot at the number of words you read per minute (reading rate) for each reading selection. 401
Use pages 396–400 to compute your rate. Connect the dots with a line to see your progress.

Guide to Dictionary Use*

With a good dictionary you can do much more than check the meanings or spellings of words. The Fourth Edition of *Webster's New World College Dictionary,* the dictionary featured in *Structured Reading,* is an example of a very good dictionary. The entries are clearly written, and they offer many resources of particular interest to students. This Guide to Dictionary Use can help you understand the basic features of the entries so that you can use them fully. For more details, consult the explanatory material in the front and back sections of the dictionary itself.

Main Entry Word

The technical term for each word included in the dictionary is **main entry word.** When you look up a word, the list of main entry words is what you consult. Listed alphabetically, they stand out because they are set in dark print (called *boldface*). If more than one spelling is given for a main entry word, the first spelling shown is the one more widely used. **Dictionary entry** is the technical term for the paragraph of information given for a main entry word. This textbook contains 315 entries from the Fourth Edition of *Webster's New World College Dictionary.*

Definitions

If a word has more than one meaning, its various **definitions** are listed in numerical order. The original meaning of the word (which is sometimes—but not always—outdated) comes first. The most recent meaning of the word appears last. Sometimes added information is given at the end of the entry, after the most recent meaning. You can tell this is happening because labels precede such information. The labels are explained here in the sections "Parts of Speech Labels," "Usage Labels," and "Field of Study Labels." For example, in the entry for *asset* (used with Selection 2 in this textbook), definition 2 gives the most recent general meaning. The third definition gives a special meaning, as the label *Accounting* indicates; and the fourth definition gives a special meaning for the *Law.* Then verb definitions and a noun form are given.

as·set (as′et) *n.* ⟦earlier *assets* < Anglo-Fr *assetz* (in legal phrase *aver assetz*, to have enough) < OFr *assez*, enough < VL **ad satis,* sufficient < L *ad,* to + *satis,* enough: see SAD⟧ **1** anything owned that has exchange value **2** a valuable or desirable thing to have [charm is your chief *asset*] **3** [pl.] *Accounting* all the entries on a balance sheet showing the entire resources of a person or business, tangible and intangible, including accounts and notes receivable, cash, inventory, equipment, real estate, goodwill, etc. **4** [pl.] *Law* a) property, as of a business, a bankrupt, etc. b) the property of a deceased person available to his or her estate for the payment of debts and legacies

*Based on "Guide to the Use of the Dictionary," *Webster's New World College Dictionary,* Fourth Edition.

To decide which meaning of a word fits your situation, review the context in which the word is being used. The context can tell you whether an older or recent meaning of a word applies. Ways to figure out a word's meaning from its context are discussed in this textbook on pages 19–28.

Americanisms

An open star (☆) in front of a word tells you that the word is an **Americanism.** This means that the word has its origins in the United States. The entry for *chute* (used with Selection 2 in this textbook) shows that the word itself, but not necessarily all the definitions, are Americanisms.

> ☆**chute**[1] (sho͞ot) *n.* [[Fr, a fall < OFr *cheute* < *cheoite*, pp. of *cheoir*, to fall < L *cadere*: see CASE[1]] **1** *a*) a waterfall *b*) rapids in a river **2** an inclined or vertical trough or passage down which something may be slid or dropped [laundry *chute*] **3** a steep slide, as for tobogganing

Syllabification

For pronunciation and writing purposes, words can be divided into syllables, unless a word has a single vowel sound, such as *kiss.* Each syllable represents a single vowel sound and usually its adjacent consonants. **Syllabification,** also called **word division,** becomes important for writers when space runs out at the end of a line and a word has to be carried over onto the next line. Words can be divided only at breaks for syllables.

In *Webster's New World College Dictionary,* the parts of boldface entry words are separated by a heavy centered period [•]. The heavy centered period indicates one or more places where a word can be acceptably divided at the end of a line. The entry for *deteriorate* (used with Selection 2 in this book) illustrates the heavy centered period for word division.

> **de·te·rio·rate** (dē tir′ē ə rāt′, di-) *vt., vi.* **··rat′ed, ··rat′·ing** [[< LL *deterioratus,* pp. of *deteriorare,* to make worse < L *deterior,* worse, inferior < *deter,* below < de-, from + *-ter,* compar. suffix]] to make or become worse; lower in quality or value; depreciate —**de·te′rio·ra′·tion** *n.*

Pronunciation

The symbols in parentheses immediately following the main entry word show **pronunciation.** You can figure out the sound indicated by each symbol by consulting a dictionary's key to pronunciation. A "Key to Pronunciation" from *Webster's New World College Dictionary* is shown here. A more complete "Guide to Pronunciation" appears on pp. xxii–xxiv of this

403

dictionary. To get used to the key, practice first with entries for words familiar to you. Then once you are comfortable with the key, practice with entries for words that are new to you. You can practice with the sample entries in this guide and with the entries with each selection in this textbook.

PRONUNCIATION KEY

Symbol	Key Words	Symbol	Key Words
a	asp, fat, parrot	b	bed, fable, dub, ebb
ā	ape, date, play, break, fail	d	dip, beadle, had, dodder
ä	ah, car, father, cot	f	fall, after, off, phone
		g	get, haggle, dog
e	elf, ten, berry	h	he, ahead, hotel
ē	even, meet, money, flea, grieve	j	joy, agile, badge
		k	kill, tackle, bake, coat, quick
i	is, hit, mirror	l	let, yellow, ball
ī	ice, bite, high, sky	m	met, camel, trim, summer
		n	not, flannel, ton
ō	open, tone, go, boat	p	put, apple, tap
ô	all, horn, law, oar	r	red, port, dear, purr
oo	look, pull, moor, wolf	s	sell, castle, pass, nice
o͞o	ooze, tool, crew, rule	t	top, cattle, hat
yo͞o	use, cute, few	v	vat, hovel, have
yoo	cure, globule	w	will, always, swear, quick
oi	oil, point, toy	y	yet, onion, yard
ou	out, crowd, plow	z	zebra, dazzle, haze, rise
u	up, cut, color, flood	ch	chin, catcher, arch, nature
ur	urn, fur, deter, irk	sh	she, cushion, dash, machine
		th	thin, nothing, truth
ə	a in ago	th	then, father, lathe
	e in agent	zh	azure, leisure, beige
	i in sanity	ŋ	ring, anger, drink
	o in comply	'	[indicates that a following l
	u in focus		or n is a syllabic consonant,
ər	perhaps, murder		as in cattle (kat''l), Latin
			(lat''n); see full explanation
			on p. xiii]

Parts of Speech Labels

The first **part of speech** of a word is given after the pronunciation information in an entry. Parts of speech are abbreviated in the dictionary. They are shown in dark italic print. Here are major abbreviations and their meanings.

n.	noun
n. pl.	plural noun
vt.	transitive verb
vi.	intransitive verb
v. aux.	auxiliary verb
adj.	adjective

adv.   adverb
prep.   preposition
conj.   conjunction
pron.   pronoun
interj.   interjection

Some words are used as more than one part of speech. If you are unsure which part of speech applies to the word in the context you are dealing with, look at all the definitions in an entry to see what works for your context. To help you work with context, use the information about using context to figure out a word's meaning, discussed in this textbook on pages 19–25.

The entry for *harvest* (used with Selection 2 in this textbook) illustrates that one word can have multiple meanings. The meanings differ according to the part of speech (noun, verb) and within a part of speech.

> **har·vest** (här′vist) *n.* ⟦ME *hervest* < OE *hærfest*, akin to Ger *herbst* (OHG *herbist*) < IE *(s)kerp-* < base *(s)ker-*, to cut > SHEAR, SHORT, L *caro*, flesh, *cernere* & Gr *krinein*, to separate, *karpos*, fruit: basic sense "time of cutting"⟧ **1** the time of the year when matured grain, fruit, vegetables, etc. are reaped and gathered in **2** a season's yield of grain, fruit, etc. when gathered in or ready to be gathered in; crop **3** the gathering in of a crop **4** the outcome or consequence of any effort or series of events /the tyrant's *harvest* of hate/ —*vt.*, *vi.* **1** to gather in (a crop, etc.) **2** to gather the crop from (a field) **3** to catch, shoot, trap, etc. (fish or game), usually in an intensive, systematic way, as for commercial purposes **4** to get (something) as the result of an action or effort **5** to remove (body parts) for transplantation —**har′·vest·able** *adj.*

Inflected Forms

The form of a word when it becomes plural or a participle or when it changes its tense is called its **inflected form.** Information about inflected forms comes after the part of speech label. Inflected forms are shown in small dark print. Information for *heresy* (used with Selection 16 in this textbook) illustrates the plural noun form of the word; information for *dispel* (used with Selection 11 in this textbook) illustrates letter doubling when *-ed* is added and when *-ing* is added.

> **her·esy** (her′ə sē) *n.*, *pl.* **-sies** ⟦ME *heresie* < OFr < L *haeresis*, school of thought, sect, in LL(Ec), heresy < Gr *hairesis*, a taking, selection, school, sect, in LGr(Ec), heresy < *hairein*, to take⟧ **1** *a)* a religious belief opposed to the orthodox doctrines of a church; esp., such a belief specifically denounced by the church *b)* the rejection of a belief that is a part of church dogma **2** any opinion (in philosophy, politics, etc.) opposed to official or established views or doctrines **3** the holding of any such belief or opinion

> **dis·pel** (di spel′) *vt.* **··pelled′**, **··pel′·ling** ⟦ME *dispellen* < L *dispellere* < *dis-*, apart + *pellere*, to drive: see FELT⟧ to scatter and drive away; cause to vanish; disperse —*SYN.* SCATTER

Word History

For most main entry words, the **word history,** known as **etymology,** is given in brackets after the main entry word, its pronunciation, and any inflected forms. Abbreviations and symbols present information and origins, and words from languages other than English appear in italics. Etymology often suggests a word's flavor. The sample dictionary entries in this Guide use these frequently used symbols and abbreviations.

<	derived from
+	plus
Fr	French (MFr = Middle French; OFr = Old French)
Gr	classical Greek
IE	Indo-European
ME	Middle English
L	Latin (LL = Late Latin; VL = Vulgar Latin)
OE	Old English

Usage Labels

The customary way words are used—their **usage**—depends on many factors. The two major influences are the formality of occasion on which the word is used and the location where the word is used. Whenever a word or sense may not be appropriate for formal writing, the dictionary entry gives usage information. Usage labels are shown in brackets following a main entry word or one of its numbered definitions. Here are the most frequently seen usage labels and their meanings.

[Brit.]	*British:* commonly accepted meaning in British English
[Informal]	*informal:* used in conversation and informal writing
[Dial.]	*dialect:* used in certain geographical areas of the United States
[Obs.]	*obsolete:* no longer in use
[Old Poet.]	*poetic:* used chiefly in earlier poetry or for poetic meaning
[Slang]	*slang:* highly informal and generally considered not standard; acceptable when used for effect or mood to convey a highly informal context

The entry for *rumpus* (used with Selection 18 in this textbook) indicates that it has an informal sense. The entry for *deadeye* (used with Selection 22 in this textbook) says that one of its meanings (definition 2) is slang.

rum·pus (rum′pəs) *n.* ⟦< ?⟧ [Informal] an uproar or commotion

dead·eye (-ī′) *n.* **1** a round, flat block of wood with three holes in it for a lanyard, used in pairs on a sailing ship to hold the shrouds and stays taut **2** [Slang] an accurate marksman

Field of Study Labels

Many words have special meanings when used in the context of various **fields of study.** For example, the entry for *derivative* (used in Selection 22 of this textbook) starts with its usual meanings as an adjective and then as a noun. Then come abbreviated labels that indicate special meanings from various fields of study: chemistry, linguistics, and math.

> **de·riva·tive** (də riv′ə tiv) *adj.* ⟦ME *derivatif* < LL *derivativus* < L *derivatus*, pp. of *derivare*: see fol.⟧ **1** derived **2** using or taken from other sources; not original **3** of derivation —*n.* **1** something derived **2** *Chem.* a substance derived from, or of such composition and properties that it may be considered as derived from, another substance by chemical change, esp. by the substitution of one or more elements or radicals **3** *Finance* a contract, as an option or futures contract, whose value depends on the value of the securities, commodities, etc. that form the basis of the contract **4** *Linguis.* a word formed from another or others by derivation **5** *Math.* the limiting value of a rate of change of a function with respect to a variable; the instantaneous rate of change, or slope, of a function (Ex.: the derivative of *y* with respect to *x*, often written dy/dx, is 3 when y = 3x) —**de·riv′a·tively** *adv.*

Synonyms

When a word has **synonyms** whose meanings may or may not be interchanged with it, the dictionary entry ends with the symbol **SYN.** followed by a word in small capital letters. When you look up that word, you will find at the end of its entry a **synonymy**—a list of synonyms with definitions that explain slight differences in meaning, among the words listed. The synonymy is signaled by the symbol *SYN.-.* To decide which synonym fits your situation, review the context in which the word appears and match it to the definitions in the synonymy. The entry for *latent* (used with Selection 14 in this textbook) offers a synonymy of four words.

> **la·tent** (lāt′′nt) *adj.* ⟦L *latens*, prp. of *latere*, to lie hidden, lurk < IE *lāidh-* < base *lā-*, to be hidden > ON *lōmr*, deception, Gr *lēthē*, forgetfulness, *lanthanein*, to be hidden⟧ **1** present but invisible or inactive; lying hidden and undeveloped within a person or thing, as a quality or power **2** *Biol.* dormant but capable of normal development under the best conditions: said of buds, spores, cocoons, etc. **3** *Psychol.* unconsciously but not actively so [a *latent* homosexual] —*n.* a fingerprint found on an object as at the scene of a crime — **la′·tency** *n.* —**la′·tently** *adv.*
>
> *SYN.*—**latent** applies to that which exists but is as yet concealed or unrevealed [his *latent* ability]; **potential** applies to that which exists in an undeveloped state but which can be brought to development in the normal course of events [a *potential* concert pianist]; **dormant** suggests a lack of visible activity, as of something asleep [a *dormant* volcano]; **quiescent** implies a stopping of activity, usually only temporarily [the raging sea had become *quiescent*] —*ANT.* active, actual, operative

The following three pages show a sample dictionary page, with labels for your reference.

Cerritos / cevitamic acid   230

Cer·ri·tos (se rē'tōs) [Sp, little hills] city in SW Calif.: suburb of
Los Angeles: pop. 53,000   ——— American place name with etymology

Cerro de Pasco (ser'ō dä päs'kō) mining town in the mountains of
WC Peru: alt. *c.* 14,000 ft. (4,250 m): pop. 72,000

cert 1 certificate 2 certified

cer·tain (surt'n) *adj.* [ME & OFr < VL *certanus* < L *certus*,
determined, fixed, orig. pp. of *cernere*, to distinguish, decide, orig.,
to sift, separate: see HARVEST] 1 fixed, settled, or determined 2
sure (to happen, etc.); inevitable 3 not to be doubted; unquestiona-
ble *[certain* evidence] 4 not failing; reliable; dependable *[a certain*
cure] 5 controlled; unerring *[his certain* aim] 6 without any
doubt; assured; sure; positive *[certain* of his innocence] 7 not
named or described, though definite and perhaps known *[a certain*
person] 8 some, but not very much; appreciable *[to a certain*
extent] —*pron.* [with pl. u] a certain indefinite number; certain
ones (of) —**SYN.** SURE **for certain** as a certainty; without doubt   ——— Idiomatic phrase

cer·tain·ly (-lē) *adv.* beyond a doubt; surely

cer·tain·ty (-tē) *n.* [ME *certeinte* < OFr *certaineté*] 1 the quality,
state, or fact of being certain 2 *pl.* **-ties** anything certain; definite
act —**of a certainty** [Archaic] without a doubt; certainly

SYN.—**certainty** suggests a firm, settled belief or positiveness in the truth
of something; **certitude** is sometimes distinguished from the preceding as
implying an absence of objective proof, hence suggesting unassailable blind
faith; **assurance** suggests confidence, but not necessarily positiveness, usually in something that is yet to happen *[I* have *assurance* of his continuing
support]; **conviction** suggests a being convinced because of satisfactory
reasons or proof and sometimes implies earlier doubt —**ANT.** doubt, skep-
ticism   ——— Synonymy

cer·tes (sur'tēz') *adv.* [ME & OFr < VL *certas*, for L *certo*, surely
< *certus*: see CERTAIN] [Archaic] certainly; verily

cer·ti·fi·able (surt'ə fī'ə bəl) *adj.* that can be certified —**cer·ti·fi·ably**
(-blē) *adv.*

cer·tif·i·cate (sər tif'i kit; *for v.,* -kāt') *n.* [ME & OFr *certificat* < ML
certificatum < LL *certificatus,* pp. of *certificare,* CERTIFY] a written
or printed statement by which a fact is formally or officially certi-   ——— Part-of-speech labels
fied or attested; specif., *a)* a document certifying that one has met
specified requirements, as for teaching *b)* a document certifying
ownership, a promise to pay, etc. —*vt.* **-cat·ed, -cat·ing** to attest or
authorize by a certificate; issue a certificate to —**cer·tif'i·ca·tor** *n.*   ——— Derived entries
—**cer·tif'i·ca·to·ry** (-kə tôr'ē) *adj.*

certificate of deposit a certificate issued by a bank or a savings
and loan association acknowledging the receipt of a specified sum of
money in a special kind of time deposit drawing interest and requiring written notice for withdrawal

certificate of incorporation a legal document stating the name
and purpose of a proposed corporation, the names of its incorpora-
tors, its stock structure, etc.

certificate of origin a certificate submitted by an exporter to those
countries requiring it, listing goods to be imported and stating their
place of origin

cer·ti·fi·ca·tion (surt'ə fi kā'shən) *n.* [Fr] 1 a certifying or being
certified 2 a certified statement

cer·ti·fied (surt'ə fīd') *adj.* 1 vouched for; guaranteed 2 having, or
attested to by, a certificate

☆certified check a check for which a bank has guaranteed pay-   ——— Americanism
ment, certifying there is enough money on deposit to cover the
check

☆certified mail 1 a postal service for recording the mailing and
delivery of a piece of first-class mail 2 mail recorded by this service: it is not insurable

☆certified public accountant a public accountant certified by a
State examining board as having met the requirements of State law

Inflected forms ——— **cer·ti·fy** (surt'ə fī') vt. **-fied', -fy'ing** [ME *certifien* < OFr *certifier* < LL *certificare* < L *certus*, CERTAIN + -FY] **1** to declare (a thing) true, accurate, certain, etc. by formal statement, often in writing; verify; attest **2** to declare officially insane and committable to a mental institution ☆**3** to guarantee the quality or worth of (a check, document, etc.); vouch for **4** to issue a certificate or license to **5** [Archaic] to assure; make certain —*vi.* to testify (*to*) —**SYN.**

Usage label ———— APPROVE —**cer·ti·fi'er** *n.*

cer·ti·o·ra·ri (surʹshē ə rerʹē) *n.* [ME < LL, lit., to be made more certain: a word in the writ] *Law* a discretionary writ from a higher

Field label ———— court to a lower one, or to a board or official with some judicial power, requesting the record of a case for review

cer·ti·tude (surtʹə tōōd', -tyōōd') *n.* [OFr < LL(Ec) *certitudo* < L *certus*, CERTAIN] **1** a feeling of absolute sureness or conviction **2** sureness; inevitability —**SYN.** CERTAINTY

ce·ru·le·an (sə rōōʹlē ən) *adj.* [L *caeruleus*; prob. < *caelulum*, dim. of *caelum*, heaven: for IE base see CESIUM] sky-blue; azure

ce·ru·men (sə rōōʹmən) *n.* [< L *cera*, wax; sp. infl. by ALBUMEN] EARWAX —**ce·ru'mi·nous** (-mə nəs) *adj.*

ce·ruse (sirʹōōs', sə rōōs') *n.* [OFr < L *cerussa* < ? Gr *kēroessa*, waxlike < *kēros*, wax] **1** WHITE LEAD **2** a former cosmetic containing white lead

ce·rus·site (sirʹə sīt', sə rusʹīt') *n.* [< L *cerussa* (see prec.) + -ITE¹] native lead carbonate, PbCO₃, widely distributed in crystalline or massive form

Biographical ——— **Cer·van·tes** (Sa·a·ve·dra) (ther vänʹtes säʹä vedʹrä; *E* sər vanʹtēz'),
entry **Mi·guel de** (mē gelʹ the) 1547-1616; Sp. novelist, poet, & playwright; author of *Don Quixote*

cer·ve·lat (ser və läʹ, -lätʹ) *n.* [Fr] a dry, smoked sausage of beef and pork Also sp. **cer·ve·las'** (-läʹ)

cer·vi·cal (surʹvi kəl) *adj.* [< L *cervix* (gen. *cervicis*), the neck + -AL] *Anat.* of the neck or cervix

cer·vi·ces (sər vīʹsēz', surʹvə-) *n.* alt. pl. of CERVIX

cer·vi·ci·tis (surʹvə sītʹis) *n.* [see -ITIS] inflammation of the cervix of the uterus

cervico- (surʹvi kō', -kə) [< L *cervix*, neck] *combining form* cervical [*cervicitis*] Also, before a vowel, **cer'vic-**

cer·vid (surʹvid') *adj.* [< ModL *Cervidae*, name of the family (< L *cervus*, stag, deer < IE *kerewos*, horned, a horned animal < base *ker-*, HORN) + -ID] of the deer family

Cer·vin (môn ser vanʹ), **Mont** *Fr.* name of the MATTERHORN

Main entry word ——— **cer·vine** (surʹvīn', -vin) *adj.* [L *cervinus* < *cervus*: see CERVID] of or like a deer

cer·vix (surʹviks') *n., pl.* **cer·vi·ces** (sər vīʹsēz', surʹvə-) or **-vix·es** [L, the neck] **1** the neck, esp. the back of the neck **2** a necklike part, as of the uterus or urinary bladder

Ce·sar·e·an or **Ce·sar·i·an** (sə zerʹē ən) *adj., n.* CAESAREAN

ce·si·um (sēʹzē əm) *n.* [ModL, orig. neut. of L *caesius*, bluish-gray
Etymology ——— (< IE base *(s)kāi-*, bright > -HOOD): so named (1860) by Robert Wilhelm BUNSEN because of the blue line seen in the spectroscope] a soft, silver-white, ductile, metallic chemical element, the most electropositive of all the elements: it ignites in air, reacts vigorously with water, and is used in photoelectric cells: symbol, Cs; at. wt., 132.905; at. no., 55; sp. gr., 1.892; melt. pt., 28.64°C; boil. pt., 670°C: a radioactive isotope (**cesium-137**) with a half-life of 30.17 years is a fission product and is used in cancer research, radiation therapy, etc.

Ces·ké Bu·dě·jo·vi·ce (chesʹke bōōʹde yōʹvit sə) city in SW Czechoslovakia, on the Vltava River: pop. 93,000

Ces·ko·slo·ven·sko (chesʹkô slô venʹskô) Czech name of CZECHOSLOVAKIA

ces·pi·tose (sesʹpə tōs') *adj.* [ModL < L *caespes*, turf, grassy field + -OSE²] growing in dense, matlike clumps without creeping stems, as moss, grass, etc.

cess (ses) *n.* [prob. < ASSESS] in Ireland, an assessment; tax: now used only in **bad cess to bad luck to** —————— Pronunciation

ces·sa·tion (se sā'shən) *n.* [L *cessatio* < pp. of *cessare*, CEASE] a ceasing, or stopping, either forever or for some time

ces·sion (sesh'ən) *n.* [OFr < L *cessio* < *cessus*, pp. of *cedere*, to yield: see CEDE] a ceding or giving up (of rights, property, territory, etc.) to another

ces·sion·ary (sesh'ə ner'ē) *n.*, *pl.* **-aries** *Law* ASSIGNEE

cess·pit (ses'pit') *n.* [< fol. + PIT²] a pit for garbage, excrement, etc.

cess·pool (-pōōl') *n.* [< ? It *cesso*, privy < L *secessus*, place of retirement (in LL, privy, drain): see SECEDE] **1** a deep hole or pit in the ground, usually covered, to receive drainage or sewage from the sinks, toilets, etc. of a house **2** a center of moral filth and corruption —————— Definitions

ces·ta (ses'tə) *n.* [Sp, basket < L *cista*: see CHEST] in jai alai, the narrow, curved, basketlike racket strapped to the forearm, in which the ball is caught and hurled against a wall

c'est la vie (se lä vē') [Fr] that's life; such is life

ces·tode (ses'tōd') *n.* [CEST(US)¹ + -ODE²] any of a class (Cestoda) of parasitic flatworms, with a ribbonlike body and no intestinal canal; tapeworm —*adj.* of such a worm —————— Scientific name

ces·toid (-toid') *adj.* ribbonlike, as a tapeworm

ces·tus¹ (-təs) *n.* [L < Gr *kestos*, a girdle; akin to *kentein*, to stitch: see CENTER] in ancient times, a woman's belt or girdle

ces·tus² (-təs) *n.* [L *caestus* < *caedere*, to strike, cut down: see -CIDE] a contrivance of leather straps, often weighted with metal, worn on the hand by boxers in ancient Rome

ce·su·ra (si zyoor'ə, -zhoor'ə) *n.*, *pl.* **-ras** or **-rae** (-ē) CAESURA

CETA Comprehensive Employment and Training Act

ce·ta·cean (sə tā'shən) *n.* [< ModL < L *cetus*, large sea animal, whale < Gr *kētos* + -ACE(A) + -AN] in some systems of classification, any of an order (Cetacea) of nearly hairless, fishlike water

CESTUS —————— Illustration with caption

mammals, lacking external hind limbs, but having paddlelike forelimbs, including whales, porpoises, and dolphins —*adj.* of the cetaceans Also **ce·ta'ceous** (-shəs)

ce·tane (sē'tān') *n.* [< L *cetus* (see prec.) + -ANE] a colorless, liquid alkane, $C_{16}H_{34}$, found in petroleum and, sometimes, in vegetable matter, and used to test fuel oils

cetane number a number that increases with higher quality, representing the ignition properties of diesel engine fuel oils: it is determined by the percentage of cetane that must be mixed with a standard liquid to match the fuel oil's performance in a standard test engine: see OCTANE NUMBER —————— Foreign phrase

ce·ter·is pa·ri·bus (set'ər is par'ə bəs) [L, other things being equal] all else remaining the same

ce·tol·o·gy (sə täl'ə jē) *n.* [< L *cetus*, whale (see CETACEAN) + -OLOGY] the branch of zoology that deals with whales —**ce·to·log·i·cal** (sēt'ə läj'i kəl) *adj.* —**ce·tol'o·gist** *n.*

Ce·tus (sēt'əs) [L, whale] an equatorial constellation near Pisces

Ceu·ta (syoot'ə; *Sp* thā'ōō tä') Spanish seaport in NW Africa, opposite Gibraltar: an enclave in Morocco: pop. 71,000

Cé·vennes (sā ven') mountain range in S France, west of the Rhone: highest peak, 5,755 ft. (1,754 m)

ce·vi·che (sə vē'chä', -chē') *n.* [Sp SEVICHE] —————— Cross-reference

ce·vi·tam·ic acid (sē'vi tam'ik, -vi-) [< C + VITAM(IN) + -IC] ASCORBIC ACID

410

Credits

Dictionary entries and "Guide to Dictionary Use" based on "Guide to the Use of the Dictionary" from *Webster's New College World Dictionary, Third Edition.* Copyright © 1997, 1996, 1994, 1991, 1988 by Simon & Schuster, Inc. Reprinted with the permission of Hungry Minds, Inc.

Brandeis Review, excerpt from "Bees" from *Brandeis Review,* Vol. 20, No. 2. Reprinted with the permission of Cliff Haptman, *Brandeis Review,* Brandeis University.

Kitty Crider, excerpt from "Fish for All Seasons" from *Austin American-Statesman* (August 15, 2001). Copyright © 2001. Reprinted by permission.

Bill and Sonia Freedman, excerpts from "People Are the Attraction" from *The Denver Post* (1976). Reprinted with the permission of the authors.

Jack London, excerpt from a letter to his daughter Joan, from *The Letters of Jack London,* edited by Earle Labor, Robert C. Leitz, and I. Milo Shepard. Copyright © 1988 by The Board of Trustees of the Leland Stanford Jr. University. Reprinted with the permission of Stanford University Press, www.sup.org.

Daniel Okrent and Steve Wulff, excerpt from the Preface to *Baseball Anecdotes.* Copyright © 1989 by Daniel Okrent and Steve Wulff. Reprinted with the permission of HarperCollins Publishers, Inc.

Andrew X. Pham, excerpt from *Catfish and Mandala.* Copyright © 1999 by Andrew X. Pham. Reprinted with the permission of Farrar, Straus & Giroux, LLC.

Sylvia Resnick, "Noise It Can Kill You." Reprinted with the permission of the author.

Richard Selzer, M.D., excerpt from *Mortal Lessons: Notes on the Art of Surgery* (New York: Simon & Schuster, 1976). Copyright © 1976 by Richard Selzer. Reprinted with the permission of Georges Borchart, Inc. for the author.

Paul Taylor, excerpts from "Coretta Scott King: A Woman of Courage." Reprinted with the permission of Creative Education, Inc.

Selection 1 A Real Loss

Fern Kupfer, "A Real Loss" from *Newsday* (September 27, 1987) Copyright © 1987 by Fern Kupfer. Reprinted with the permission of the author.

Selection 2 The Death of a Farm

Amy Joe Keifer, "The Death of a Farm" from *The New York Times* (June 30, 1991). Copyright © 1991 by The New York Times Company. Reprinted by permission.

Selection 3 Tyranny of Weakness

Eda LeShan, "Tyranny of Weakness" from *New York Newsday* (January 19, 1991). Copyright © 1991 by Eda LeShan. Reprinted with the permission of Rosenstone/Wender, New York.

Selection 4 Darkness at Noon

Harold Krents, "Darkness at Noon" from *The New York Times* (May 26, 1976), Op-Ed. Copyright © 1976 by The New York Times Company. Reprinted by permission.

Selection 5 My World Now

Anna Mae Halgrim Seaver, "My World Now" from *Newsweek* (June 27, 1994). Copyright © 1994 by Anna Mae Halgrim Seaver. Reprinted with the permission of Richard Seaver.

Selection 6 My Mother's Blue Bowl

Alice Walker, "My Mother's Blue Bowl" from *Anything We Love Can Be Saved: A Writer's Activism*. Copyright © 1997 by Alice Walker. Reprinted with the permission of Random House, Inc.

Selection 7 Summer

Jonathan Schwartz, "Summer" from *The New York Times* (June 22, 1975). Copyright © 1975 by The New York Times Company. Reprinted by permission.

Selection 8 The Girl with the Large Eyes

Julius Lester, "The Girl with the Large Eyes" from *Black Folktales* (New York: Grove Press, 1992). Copyright © 1969 and 1991 by Julius Lester. Reprinted with the permission of the author.

Selection 9 You Are How You Eat

Enid Nemy, "You Are How You Eat" from *The New York Times* (September 20, 1987). Copyright © 1987 by The New York Times Company. Reprinted by permission.

Selection 10 Flour Children

Lexine Alpert, "Flour Children" from *In Health* (January/February 1990). Copyright © 1990. Reprinted with the permission of the author.

Selection 11 The Magic Words Are "Will You Help Me?"

Michael Ryan, "The Magic Words Are 'Will You Help Me?'" from *Parade* (May 5, 1996). Copyright © 1996 by Michael Ryan. Reprinted with the permission of Scovil Chichak Galen Literary Agency on behalf of the author.

Selection 12 Mute in an English-Only World

Chang-rae Lee, "Mute in an English-Only World" from *The New York Times* (April 18, 1996). Copyright © 1996 by The New York Times Company. Reprinted by permission.

Selection 13 Genes and Behavior: A Twin Legacy

Selection 14 Every Kid Needs Some Manual Arts

Selection 15 Richard Cory, All Over Again

Selection 16 Escaping the Daily Grind for Life as a House Father

Selection 17 Forty Acres and a Holiday

Selection 18 Out of Their Element

Selection 19 Death Penalty Victims

Selection 20 Should a Wife Keep Her Name?

Selection 21 Restored to the Sea

Selection 22 I Became Her Target

Roger Wilkins, "I Became Her Target" from *Newsday* (September 6, 1987). Copyright © 1987 by Roger Wilkins. Reprinted with the permission of the author.

Selection 23 She Made Her Dream Come True

Michael Ryan, "She Made Her Dreams Come True" from *Parade* (May 7, 1995). Copyright © 1995 by Michael Ryan. Reprinted with the permission of Scovil Chichak Galen Literary Agency on behalf of the author.

Selection 24 From *In Search of Bernabé*

Graciela Limón, excerpt from *In Search of Bernabé*. Copyright © 1993 by Graciela Limón. Reprinted with the permission of Arte Publico Press.

Selection 25 How to Stay Alive

Arthur Hoppe, "How to Stay Alive" from *San Francisco Chronicle* (1970). Copyright © 1970 by Chronicle Publishing Company. Reprinted with the permission of the author.

Selection 26 Houses to Save the Earth

Seth Shulman, "Houses to Save the Earth" from *Parade* (March 3, 1996): 4–5. Copyright © 1996 by Seth Shulman. Reprinted with the permission of the author.

Selection 27 Collegians Predisposed to Road Rage

Andrew J. Pulskamp, "Collegians Predisposed to Road Rage," from *U. Magazine*. Reprinted with permission.

Selection 28 Long-Term Memory

Joseph Calkin and Richard S. Perrotto, "Long-Term Memory" from *Fundamentals of Psychology: Applications for Life and Work*. Copyright © 1996 by South-Western Educational Publishing, a division of International Thomson Publishing, Inc. Reprinted with the permission of South-Western Educational Publishing, a division of Thomson Learning, Fax 800 730-2215.

Selection 29 A Personal Stress Survival Guide

Dianne Hales, "A Personal Stress Survival Guide" from *An Invitation to Health, Seventh Edition*. Copyright © 1997, 1994, 1992, 1989, 1986, 1983, and 1980 by The Benjamin/Cummings Publishing Company, Inc. Reprinted with the permission of Wadsworth, an imprint of the Wadsworth Group, a division of Thomson Learning. Fax 800 730-2215.

Selection 30 The Chaser

John Collier, "The Chaser" from *The John Collier Reader* (New York: Alfred A. Knopf, 1972). Originally published in *The New Yorker* (December 28, 1940). Copyright 1940 and renewed © 1968 by John Collier. Reprinted with the permission of Harold Matson Company, Inc.

Vocabulary Index

General Index

Instructor's Guide

The major features of this Instructor's Guide include the following:

- "Readability" offers a discussion of what a readability index is and the limitations that operate with all readability indexes. Also, the cloze procedure is described as an alternative way for teachers to assess the suitability of reading material. Finally, a complete list of readability statistics and related profile data is presented for each of the thirty reading selections in the text.

- "Reading Selections Listed by Types and Themes" helps instructors match readings to student interest and also serves as an aid to help students experience different readings of the same type: narration, exposition, argumentation, and textbook extracts.

- "How to Use *Structured Reading* in a Variety of Instructional Settings" suggests the effective use of the text in the classroom, in labs, and for self-instruction.

- "Teaching Strategies for *Structured Reading*" discusses specific instructional techniques for using the text. These expand the ideas presented to the student in the text's opening chapter, Part One, Skills for Reading. Included are teaching approaches for reading speed, vocabulary study, predicting, the comprehension skills of reading on, between, and beyond the lines, and exploring the writer's craft and helping students make informed opinions about what they read.

We have continued to find that research in the teaching of reading to adults demonstrates that the reading skills treated in depth in *Structured Reading* are precisely those which are most effective in helping students improve their reading skills. Studies indicate among other findings that:

- grade point averages rise when students are in reading courses that emphasize finding main ideas, recognizing and interpreting inferences, and differentiating fact from opinion.

- students improve in reading when they assess their own difficulties and chart their progress.

- students improve when reading skills are applied to material in content areas.

Structured Reading and the material in this Instructor's Guide incorporate the findings of these studies in its teaching strategies and reading content.

Capable and confident readers are one of our nation's best resources. *Structured Reading* is intended to help prepare students to become effective, literate participants in our nation's future. This Instructor's Guide strives to help teachers use the text as effectively and easily as possible. We hope the added resources for this Sixth Edition prove useful and stimulating.

READABILITY

To help instructors predict students' ability to read the selections in this text, we provide readability indexes on the next page. The indexes are based on the fact that certain features of any reading selection can be counted. These features include the average number of words per sentence, syllables per word, and sentences per a given block of words. These counts can be combined in a variety of ways to yield a readability index. Many readability indexes are available, and although there is some correlation among the indexes, their findings vary.

In addition to variations among indexes, all readability indexes have important limitations. Many aspects of a reading selection cannot be quantified. Content load, complexity of thought, humor and irony cannot be reduced to numbers. Thus, for example, while the selection "Richard Cory, All Over Again," with its frequent one and two syllable words, has a Fry readability index equivalent to a 5.0, its sentence structure and detail make the material much too difficult for a student finishing fifth grade.

A further limitation of readability indexes derives from their necessary overemphasis on product rather than process. Reading is the result of a powerful interaction between the written page, the eye, and the brain. Thus, reading ability is affected by the prior knowledge that a reader brings to a given reading selection, as well as other factors. The classic source for teachers wanting to learn more about this psycholinguistic analysis of the reading process is Frank Smith's *Understanding Reading* (third edition, 1982: Holt, Rinehart and Winston), available in many libraries.

The Cloze Procedure

An alternative way for teachers to assess the suitability of reading material—this time for individual students—is the cloze procedure. The cloze procedure is based on the theory that human beings dislike fragmentation and tend to bring unity and wholeness to anything that seems fragmented. In the reading process, this same idea operates. When words are omitted from a sentence, readers try to supply them in order to make sense out of the passage. This ability to logically complete the author's idea is an indication of a student's reading ability.

To prepare cloze materials, the teacher types a section of a reading as follows: (1) type the first and last sentence; (2) beginning with the second sentence, delete every fifth word and indicate the deletion with a blank line, which should be a standard length no matter how long the word that is being deleted; (3) do not stop until you have at least fifty blanks—which means a passage of about 250 words. Then the student reads the passage aloud and supplies the missing words or writes them in the blanks. For testing purposes, cloze procedures demand that the exact word be supplied. For teaching purposes, however, a suitable synonym is acceptable. If a student can supply words for 65% of the blanks, that student can work independently with the material. If the student can give words for 41% to 64% of the blanks, the material is at a suitable instructional level. If the student can provide words for only 40% or less of the blanks, that student will find the material frustrating.

The Statistics

With this perspective about readability indexes and with the knowledge that there are alternative individualized methods of determining suitability of materials, instructors can use the data that follow as *one* measure of the difficulty level of the reading selections in *Structured Reading*. The readabilities for the Dale Index were calculated using a computer program, *Readability Calculations,* by Michael Schuyler. The readability for the Flesch Reading Ease Index was calculated by using Microsoft Word. From the computer generated sentence/syllable information, the Fry Index was determined using the *Fry Readability Scale* (Extended).

Definitions of the Fry, Dale, and Flesch Indexes

Each test is a sampling of running words which are analyzed according to frequency, complexity, and sentence length. The Fry Index is more efficient to use at the primary level whereas the Dale and Flesch indexes rank higher readability level because of their complexity. Independently, these reading indexes measure readability through distinct methods and formulas. In total, these three reading indexes depend on the 100 word count procedure for readability, yet their formulas are quite distinct. In essence, each relies on two factors: word difficulty and sentence length and complexity.

HOW TO USE THE FRY INDEX

Select three 100-word passages from the beginning, middle, and end of a book. Skip proper nouns. Now count the total number of sentences in each word passage (estimating to the nearest tenth of a sentence). Average these three numbers by adding them and dividing by three. Next, count the total number of syllables in each 100 word sample. There is a syllable for each vowel sound and word endings such as T, ED, EL, or LE. For convenience, count every syllable over one in each word and add 100. Average the total number of syllables for the three samples. Plot on the Fry Readability Estimate the average number of sentences and the average number of syllables per 100 words. Perpendicular lines mark off approximate grade-level areas.

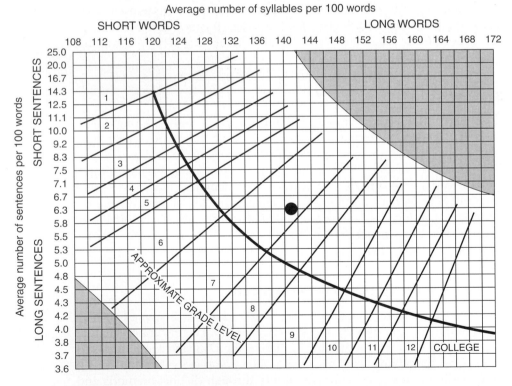

Fry Readability Estimate
by Edward Fry, Rutgers University Reading Center, New Brunswick, NJ 08904

HOW TO USE THE DALE-CHALL FORMULA (FOR GRADES 4–16)

Dale-Chall involves mathematical computations partly validated by teachers' and librarians' judgments of material difficulty, which is arbitrary. This index calls for 100 word counts, sentence complexity, and vocabulary. The vocabulary portion relies on a set list of 3000 words and words not on the list that are declared unfamiliar; it is this percentage of "unfamiliar" words that determines the difficulty level of the passage. Dale-Chall uses sentence length as the simplest measure of grammatical complexity. Grammatical studies of difficulty level (counting prepositional phrases, adverbial clauses, and other various grammatical matters) rank higher because of their complexity.

HOW TO USE FLESCH

There are two formulas for calculating Flesch: Formula A and Formula B. For our purposes, we will discuss only Formula A. Formula A assesses R.E.: "reading ease." Take 3–5 samples from a book; these may be taken from every third paragraph or every other page. Count 100 words. Count contractions and hyphenated words as one and count as words numbers or letters separated by a space. Compute the number of syllables per 100 words and then figure the average sentence length within this sample. Now divide the number of words in the sentences by the number of sentences.

The "reading ease" score puts your sample on a scale between 0 (which means practically unreadable) to 100 (which is supposedly easy for any literate person).

Readability Statistics

	Average Sentence Length	Average Syllables per Word	Flesch Reading Ease Index	Dale Index	Fry Index (Hand Calculated)
PART 2					
1. A Real Loss	22.2	1.2	81.3	7.22	7
2. The Death of a Farm	N/A	1.3	81.1	N/A	6
3. Tyranny of Weakness	N/A	1.3	64.4	N/A	7
4. Darkness at Noon	N/A	1.4	74.8	7.76	8
5. My World Now	N/A	N/A	83.5	N/A	5
6. My Mother's Blue Bowl	N/A	N/A	70.8	N/A	6
AVERAGES					**6.5**
PART 3					
7. Summer	16.6	1.5	74.6	8.07	7
8. The Girl with the Large Eyes	20.8	1.2	81.4	7.05	7

Readability Statistics (continued)

	Average Sentence Length	*Average Syllables per Word*	*Flesch Reading Ease Index*	*Dale Index*	*Fry Index (Hand Calculated)*
9. You Are How You Eat	17.4	1.3	63.4	7.55	7
10. Flour Children	N/A	1.5	85.1	N/A	7
11. The Magic Words Are "Will You Help Me?"	N/A	N/A	81.1	N/A	7
12. Mute in an English-Only World	N/A	N/A	62.99	6.4	8.3
AVERAGES					**7.2**
PART 4					
13. Genes and Behavior: A Twin Legacy	17.5	1.5	48.4	8.13	9
14. Every Kid Needs Some Manual Arts	N/A	N/A	68.7	N/A	9
15. Richard Cory, All Over Again	8.3	1.4	69.3	7.34	5
16. Escaping the Daily Grind for Life as a House Father	N/A	1.3	68.0	N/A	8
17. Forty Acres and a Holiday	N/A	N/A	62.6	8	9
18. Out of Their Element	N/A	N/A	57.5	N/A	8
AVERAGES					**8**
PART 5					
19. Death Penalty Victims	N/A	N/A	60.91	7.4	10
20. Should a Wife Keep Her Name?	15.0	1.5	69.6	8.22	8
21. Restored to the Sea	N/A	1.4	57.1	N/A	8
22. I Became Her Target	15.1	1.4	73.4	7.78	9
23. She Made Her Dream Come True	N/A	N/A	71.6	N/A	9
24. From *In Search of Bernabé*	N/A	N/A	68.77	6.1	6.6
AVERAGES					**8.4**
PART 6					
25. How to Stay Alive	12.0	1.5	64	7.73	7
26. Houses to Save the Earth	N/A	N/A	54.9	N/A	11
27. Collegians Predisposed to Road Rage	N/A	N/A	58.39	6.6	10.6
28. Long-Term Memory	N/A	N/A	32.2	N/A	13
29. A Personal Stress Survival Guide	N/A	N/A	47.8	N/A	9
30. The Chaser	N/A	1.3	73.9	N/A	5
AVERAGES					**9.2**

READING LEVELS: ACTIVITY PASSAGES, CHS. 10–14, PART ONE

Chapter 10: Central Theme and Main Ideas

- *Activity M:* "Dealing with Unhappy and Difficult Customers" from *Investing for Dummies:* 9.0

- *Activity N:* From *Direct from Dell,* by Michael Dell with Catherine Fredman: 9.8

- *Activity O:* From *Catfish and Mandala,* by Andrew X. Pham: 4

- *Activity P:* From *Fish For All Seasons,* by Kitty Crider: 7.9

Chapter 11: Major Details

- *Activity Q:* From *Learn Horseback Riding in a Weekend* by Mark Gordon Watson: 6.9

- *Activity R:* From *Manchester Mammoth Book of Fascinating Information,* by Richard B. Manchester: 8.7

- *Activity S:* From *The Cake Mix Doctor,* by Anne Byrn: 9.6

- *Activity T:* From *Careers and Occupations,* by Catherine Dubiec Holm: 10.4

Chapter 12: Inferences

- *Activity U:* From *Travels with Lizbeth,* by Lars Eighner: 7.4

- *Activity V:* From *Let's Get Well,* by Adelle Davis: 8.6

- *Activity W:* From the *New Yorker,* "Saint Valentine's Day." 1949; reprinted in Josephine Ohayan, ed. *All For Love:* 8.8

- *Activity X:* From *Computers,* 7th edition, by Larry Long and Nancy Long: 8.9

Chapter 13: Critical Reading

FACT OR OPINION

- *Activity Y:* From *Warriors Don't Cry,* by Melba Pattillo Beals: 8.2

- *Activity Z:* From *Words Still Count with Me,* by Herbert Mitgang: 8.2

- *Activity AA:* From *Hispanics,* "Top Ten Cities for Hispanics," by Diana A. Terry-Azios: 11.3

- *Activity BB:* From *Total Television, 4th edition,* by Alex McNeil: 11.3

THE WRITER'S CRAFT

- *Activity CC:* From *Yellow Woman and A Beauty of Spirit*, by Leslie Marmon Silko: 4.8

- *Activity DD:* From *A Lady's Life in the Rocky Mountains*, by Isabella L. Bird: 6.8

- *Activity EE:* Letter by Jack London (to his daughter Joan). From *The Letters of Jack London*, ed. Earle Labor, Robert C. Leitz, and I. Milo Shepard: 7.7

- *Activity FF:* From *Baseball Anecdotes*, by Daniel Okrent and Steve Wulff: 9.0

READING SELECTIONS LISTED BY TYPES AND THEMES

In *Structural Reading, Sixth Edition,* the reading selections are grouped into five parts, each of increasing difficulty according to their readability statistics and teacher judgments. Within each section, the selections are presented according to their length, from shortest to longest. This is done so that students can systematically develop their reading skills.

At times, however, teachers want to capture and expand upon their students' interests by assigning reading selections according to their types or their related themes. This list will help such an approach. Because most of the reading selections fit into many different categories, most of the selections are listed here more than once.

Types

Narration

2   The Death of a Farm, p. 95

5   My World Now, p. 117

6   My Mother's Blue Bowl, p. 127

7   Summer, p. 141

8   The Girl with the Large Eyes, p. 147

16   Escaping the Daily Grind for Life as a House Father, p. 227

18   Out of Their Element, p. 249

22   I Became Her Target, p. 293

25   How to Stay Alive (satire), p. 327

30   The Chaser, p. 383

Themes

Unusual People

Family

City Life

Rural Life

Nature

School

HOW TO USE *STRUCTURED READING* IN A VARIETY OF INSTRUCTIONAL SETTINGS

Structured Reading offers a systematized program for the development of reading skills. The book is designed to engage students through hands-on practice of skills using the strategies presented in Part One and by working with the exercises that follow each reading selection. The logical sequence of exercises that consistently follows each selection is constructed to lead students to discover insights into the reading process and into the critical thinking processes involved in reading.

Because *Structured Reading* is basically an anthology-style book, it could be misused as a workbook in which students simply read selections and complete exercises. This is not the intention of the book. *Structured Reading* is designed to engage students' thinking processes as they improve their comprehension skills by cumulative exposure to questions that delve beneath the surface.

Structured Reading can be used effectively in various types of reading programs, including those based in the classroom or lab. The following suggestions are intended to provide you with ideas for using the text in those settings.

The Classroom

Reading selections at various levels of readability and of different types and themes help make *Structured Reading* a useful resource for both large- and small-group classroom instruction. Here are some ideas for using the text in a classroom setting:

1. **Introduction of instructional strategies.** Introduce systematically each of the strategies discussed in Part One, beginning on page 3 in the text: reading speed, vocabulary, predicting, and the comprehension skills of reading on, between, and beyond the lines. Incorporate a vocabulary card system as a strand throughout the entire text. Use the "Thinking: Getting Started" ideas at the beginning of each section in the text as organizers for the skills you can present to the entire class in discussion. Encourage thorough discussion of the questions following each reading selection. Help develop evaluative skills and divergent thinking by insisting that students explain why wrong options are not correct.

2. **Teaching strategies.** Use the teaching ideas in the next section of this Guide as you work with *Structured Reading*.

3. **Writing.** Incorporate writing into your reading class. Writing helps students learn by putting material into their own language. *Structured Reading* makes connections between reading and writing in two concrete ways. First, an exercise on "Critical Reading: The Writer's Craft" is included in the set of exercises that follow each of the text's reading selections. Here the focus is on how the writer achieves his or her effect on the reader. Students are asked to analyze the choice of words, development techniques, devices of emphasis, and other writing techniques.

Second, the "Reader Response" exercise that follows each of the reading selections suggests topics for writing or discussion based on the subjects in the reading selection.

Reading teachers who integrate writing into their courses find that students' overall language abilities are strengthened. Students discover the relationships between the composing process and the reading process, so their skills improve more quickly. A rich compendium of practical ideas for incorporating writing into the curriculum can be found in *How to Handle the Paper Load*, published by the National Council of Teachers of English in 1979. Some basic suggestions include:

a. Writing is best taught as a process. The stages of prewriting, drafting, and revising are similar to these reading steps: prereading, reading for the general content, and reviewing for clarification.

b. Reading teachers can use the process model of writing. Teachers can ask students for a prewriting think sheet instead of a finished assignment. This shows students how important prewriting is. Also, such a think sheet assignment requires the teacher only to read it, jot any added ideas to help, and return it. Correcting is not the point here.

Teachers can ask students to hand in a draft of an assignment. Because a draft is only the first written version, teachers can read the assignments and make suggestions about how the writer might further develop his or her content. Correcting is not the point here either. Correcting is one of the points for teachers when revised, final versions are asked for. This must be done from time to time, but not for every assignment.

c. Classroom peers can help in the revision process. Groups of three to five students can be formed for the purpose of reviewing each other's work based on a teacher-prepared guide sheet for listening and responding.

d. Grading can be focused. Focused grading means that only certain features are selected for attention. The focus can be on quality of ideas (basic premise and support given for it), or on variety of language (strong verbs, nongeneral adjectives, good

437

metaphors), or on grammar, and so on. Instructors who feel hesitant to return a paper unless every error has been corrected can rest assured that error correction does not guarantee that students will not repeat the same mistakes. If each returned assignment contains a photocopied sheet explaining that the grading focused on a particular aspect of the writing, students will be clear about the requirements.

Ten-Step Procedure for Classroom Instruction

1. **Preview vocabulary.** Begin the assignment with instructor-led pronunciation of vocabulary.

   Being able to pronounce words correctly is a first step in building self-confidence in the reading process. It decreases oral reading reluctance among students when called on to read. After pronunciations, students may work with definitions individually or in small groups to complete vocabulary cards and to practice word usage.

2. **Complete a five-to-ten minute prereading activity.** Make predictions and/or conduct a brainstorming activity (freewriting, asking questions, or making a list) related to the selection title or to an instructor query related to the subject contents.

   Such an activity activates the mind for further discovery and reading. It serves as an advanced organizer, and, more importantly, it allows students to make connections and to construct relationships. Thus, students become actively involved in the reading process by (1) establishing a purpose for reading and (2) bringing background knowledge to the forefront for better comprehension. For Selection 8, "The Girl with the Large Eyes," students are asked to brainstorm everything they can think of related to African culture.

3. **Make the assignment to read the selection and to answer the comprehension questions.** Because student reading rates vary, this works more effectively as an out-of-class assignment. Such an approach allows for reading rate flexibility among students and more quality time in the classroom.

4. **Begin class with instructor-led pronunciation of vocabulary.** Have students repeat word pronunciations several times.

   Students who experience difficulty with reading often become too preoccupied with pronunciations to the extent of losing out on the more important aspect—comprehension. By taking care of this problem on the front end, the student is freed to focus on the issue at hand.

5. **Survey the selection.** Call on volunteer(s) to conduct the survey: read (1) the title, (2) the entire first and last paragraphs, and (3) the

first sentences of paragraphs in between—all as they appear in the selection.

This is of special importance if the selection is read as a home-work assignment. Surveying whets the appetite and refreshes the memory.

6. **Conduct a vocabulary review.** Answer vocabulary questions and spend time with usage.

7. **Discuss answers to follow-up questions.** Call on volunteers or "round robin" to answer follow-up questions from the selection and to give support for answers. (See suggestions in the Strategies section of this Guide.)

Student should read questions and possible answers and discuss reasons for choosing and/or not choosing an answer.

8. **Complete "Comprehension Boosters."** Depending on the selection, students should complete these short information processing exercises in the *Instructor's Resource Manual* either *before* or *after* responses are given to the follow-up questions to each selection. Boosters vary in function as follows:
   a. to assist students in comprehension of some of the more difficult follow-up questions (see "The Girl with the Large Eyes" and "Genes: A Twin Legacy").
   b. to highlight a reading concept not focused on in the text (see "A Real Loss," "My Mother's Blue Bowl," "Every Kid Needs Some Manual Arts," "Out of Their Element").
   c. to assess overall understanding and effectiveness of instruction (see "Flour Children," "A Personal Stress Survival Guide," and "The Magic Words Are 'Will You Help Me?'").
   d. to develop proficiency in identifying language concepts (see "A Real Loss," "Escaping the Daily Grind for Life as a House Father," "Richard Cory, All Over Again," "Tyranny of Weakness," and "My Mother's Blue Bowl").
   e. to serve as a culminating activity testing mental alertness (see "Genes: A Twin Legacy," "How to Stay Alive," and "Long-Term Memory").
   f. to fill a void (see "You Are How You Eat," "Restored to the Sea," and "The Chaser").
   g. to vary the classroom routine (see "The Chaser," "Restored to the Sea," and "A Personal Stress Survival Guide").

9. **Complete supplementary vocabulary and/or writing activities.** Additional vocabulary exercises in the *Instructor's Resource Manual* may be completed and checked on an on-going basis or held over as a review prior to tests. The writing activities are quite useful in that they assist in the debriefing process that aids in storage of knowledge for future use.

10. **Chart progress.** Encourage students to keep a record of their performance on the graphs in the back section of the text.

For variety, try one or all of the following:

I. **Student-led class discussions—**

After completing at least Part 2 of the *Structured Reading* text, students may either choose or be assigned a reading selection of interest. The student assumes responsibility for this selection when it is scheduled for review in class. The student completes the assignment early and confers with the instructor on pronunciations, definitions, comprehension and instructional strategies to be employed prior to the date of presentation. This individualized instructional conference gives the instructor a valid assessment of the student's current status and overall concept development in the course.

On the day of the presentation, the student takes charge: sits up front with the instructor (who will assist as needed with the selection), leads vocabulary, summarizes the selection, distributes extra activities, calls on respondents to answer questions, and awards bonus points for special activities or difficult questions. The student receives bonus points for participation.

II. **Detonator (most difficult question = bonus points)**

Students may work individually or in groups to answer the most difficult question (as identified by the instructor) in some selections. One by one or group-by-group, students take answer(s) to the instructor for a "quick check." For a correct response, students may earn bonus points to be added to their reading comprehension test score and either dismissed or paired with a student who finds the activity academically challenging. If incorrect, students must remain in class for more in-depth study and/or assistance. This type of activity not only rewards the more advanced student but also provides extra attention to the academically challenged student in areas of need. Moreover, this personal contact with the instructor or a mentor can prove invaluable to the student's progress.

III. **Collaboration**

Collaborative learning is based on the idea that learning is a natural, social act. Thus, by talking and discussing among themselves, students can share ideas that may assist them in solving problems, answering comprehension questions, and, in some instances, even creating new knowledge. Involving peer critiquing, this exchange of ideas during group discussions is motivational to students and quite appropriate to the reading selections in the *Structured Reading* text. For this reason, a procedure for ease of implementation follows:

Objective: Students of varying abilities will work together in small groups to discuss comprehension questions and to generate consensus answers.

A. *Preparation*

1. **Materials**—In addition to the *Structured Reading* text, a routing chart is essential to determine where each student is at all times. (See Tables 1 and 2 and explanation below.)

2. **Initial Grouping Activity**—Group students so that each group of four or five represents a microcosm of the class (age, race, gender, ability). Plan for groups to participate in an initial group activity **to get acquainted, to identify roles** (recorder, leader, timer, etc.) and **to practice consensus building.** The members of this group make up the primary group below.

B. *Implementation*

1. **Assignment**—Each student is responsible for reading the selection and answering follow-up questions.

2. **Primary Group**—This is the principal group to which each student belongs. Given about twenty minutes per selection, students discuss questions, verify answers, reach consensus, and record consensus answers to be turned in to the instructor.

3. **Expert Group (Optional)**—At least one member from each primary group makes up the expert group membership. This group meets for about ten minutes to verify primary group consensus answers related to only one skill category: (1) Main Idea and Central Theme, (2) Details, (3) Inferences, or (4) Critical Reading. Each representative records expert group consensus answers and returns to the primary group to present findings.

4. **Primary Group Revisited**—Back in the primary group, members listen to reasons given for different responses. They either accept or reject the representative's findings before submitting final consensus responses to the instructor.

5. **Wrap-up**—The instructor checks and returns responses to each group, awards bonus points, and leads class discussion as needed. Problem areas are clarified and any questions are answered, either by instructor or selected group members.

C. *Evaluation*

1. **Formative**—Some type of monitoring is the key to effective collaborative groups, checking for total team involvement and appropriate social interactions. Therefore, following each collaborative activity, students should evaluate individual and group effectiveness and determine avenues for improvement.

2. **Summative**—Individual students should complete the reading comprehension test and turn it in. Before receiving a test grade, group members work together to produce consensus

441

answers for that same test. Students' final grade is an average of the two scores.

Table 1: Principle Routing Chart (4-Member Groups)

Expert Groups	Primary Groups				
	1	2	3	4	5
A	1	2	3	4	5
B	6	7	8	9	10
C	11	12	13	14	15
D	16	17	18	19	20

Explanation of Table 1

Table 1 shows a class of 20 students—each given a number and divided into five, four-member primary groups, shown vertically. For example, Primary Group 1 consists of students numbered 1, 6, 11, and 16; Group 2, 2, 7, 12, and 17; Group 3, 3, 8, 13, and 18; Group 4, 4, 9, 14, and 19; and Group 5, 5, 10, 15, and 20. These same students in the four, five-member horizontal groups (A–D) represent the expert groups, showing at least one representative from each primary group.

Table 2: Expert Group Weekly Rotations

Concept Skills	Week Number			
	1	2	3	4
Central Theme & Main Idea	A	B	C	D
Details	B	C	D	A
Inferences	C	D	A	B
Critical Reading	D	A	B	C

Explanation of Table 2

Table 2 shows that same class of 20 students from the Primary Groups being rotated in Expert Groups over a four-week period so that all students are given an opportunity to be exposed to focused group work on a particular concept skill (Central Theme and Main Ideas, Details, Inferences, and Critical Reading) during the four-week cycle. For example, during Week 1, students in Expert Group A (numbers 1–5) from Table 1 will focus on central theme and main ideas during their ten-minute stay in the expert group. During this same time, Expert Group B (students 6–10) will focus on details, and so on. However, during Week 2, the concept skill for each expert group changes. Expert Group B students will work on central theme and main ideas, and Expert Group C will focus on details.

The Lab and Self-Instruction

Structured Reading can be used in reading labs or for self-instruction in individualized programs when students have controlled access to the Answer Key in the *Instructor's Edition.* Here are some suggestions for effectively using the text in this setting:

1. **Access to the Answer Key.** Instruct students to finish the reading and exercises before they check the answers. Some of the readings and exercises might be reserved for assessment purposes; thus part of the key should be under the Supervisor's control.

2. **Written answers.** Ask students occasionally to write out why they chose a particular answer. Instruct students to support their answer with specific references to the reading selection and to share their reasoning for eliminating the alternative answers in multiple choice items. This works well because much of the emphasis in the text is on reasoning and evaluation.

3. **Group discussion.** Integrate small group discussion with lab-based and individualized programs. Base the discussions on reading selections in the text. Encourage students to share their answers, discuss their disagreements, and offer informed opinions about what they read. A teacher-prepared guide sheet can help students organize the discussion session.

4. **Poll sheets.** If student groups are not feasible, post "poll sheets" in the lab asking students to enter their opinions about issues raised in the reading selections. This helps motivate students who have not read particular selections to investigate them, and it also provides readers with a forum to express their opinions.

TEACHING STRATEGIES FOR *STRUCTURED READING*

Part One of *Structured Reading* introduces several instructional strategies to the student (pages 3–77). That section is a central component of the text. The purpose is to explain to students the process of reading and then to provide students with practical techniques to apply to the readings and to the practice exercises in the text.

This section of the *Instructor's Guide* offers teachers objectives for the student related to each of the strategies. This section also provides additional teaching ideas to implement classroom instruction of the strategies.

Reading Speed

Objective for the student: To understand the key factors that affect reading rate and to learn practical techniques to achieve increases in speed and improvement in comprehension.

443

Structured Reading emphasizes that reading is a meaning-making process. Researchers in reading speed have demonstrated that the mind does about 90 to 95 percent of the work in reading while the eyes contribute only about 5 to 10 percent. Rather than focusing on training eye movement, instruction in reading speed is therefore most effective when it helps students discover how best to extract meaning from print. The text's section on reading speed, pages 8–18, gives the student information about the many factors that affect reading speed: vocabulary level, background knowledge of the subject being read about, purposes for reading a particular selection, the difficulty of the material, and ways people actually read. Here are some ways instructors can help students come to understand some of these concepts and, in the process, establish new habits to increase reading rate:

1. **Inventory of interests.** Take an informal inventory of interests in the class. Consult the "Themes" list in the "Reading Selections Listed by Types and Themes" in this Guide. Find out which students, for example, have an interest or background in human behavior, health, or multi-cultural topics. First, assign readings in the student's area of interest. Next, have the students read in an area they know little about. Compare the influence of background knowledge (and interest) on reading rates and comprehension scores. Discuss problems with concentration and comprehension on unfamiliar material. Suggest ways to solve the problems (for example, finding easier-to-read material on a subject to increase prior knowledge before reading the less accessible material).

2. **Types.** Assign readings of the same type as listed in "Reading Selections Listed by Types and Themes" in this Guide. Using the statistics in the "Readability" section choose selections at differing levels of readability. For example, assign the two narratives "The Death of a Farm" (readability: 6) and "I Became Her Target" (readability: 9). Discuss how length of the article, vocabulary level, sentence length, and other factors affect the difficulty of the material and therefore influence speed and comprehension. The goal here is not to imply that students stay with only easy material; the goal is to urge students to take risks and not get discouraged. When students know why they are running into difficulty, they can mobilize to overcome it.

3. **Cloze exercises.** Develop cloze exercises as explained in "Readability" in this Guide. Develop cloze paragraphs from readings with differing readability levels. Show students that the ability to complete an author's idea logically indicates whether or not the material is too hard or too easy for each reader.

4. **Vocabulary exercises.** Identify readings of the same type at differing levels as described in item 2 above. Administer the vocabulary exercises that follow each reading selection and group of dictionary

entries. The "Additional Vocabulary Exercises" in the *Instructor's Resource Manual* are an alternate source. Use the vocabulary exercise as a pretest prior to the reading of the selection. Discuss how the results of this pretest can help a student predict his or her ability to comprehend the article. Explain that one useful technique to help reading comprehension is to preview the vocabulary before reading the selection, and if many words are difficult, to scan their definitions before reading. Additionally, show students that a preview provides a way to help them understand ideas prior to the reading of a selection.

5. **Purpose.** Assign three readings of various types (consult "Reading Selections Listed by Types and Themes" in this Guide). One might be a narrative like "My Mother's Blue Bowl," another an argumentative essay like "Every Kid Needs Some Manual Arts," and another a textbook extract like "Long-Term Memory." Referring to the chart in the text on page 9, have students decide their purposes for reading. Discuss the concept of **reading flexibility,** that is, efficient readers learn to develop various reading rates depending on their **purpose** for reading particular material. Skillful readers also learn to slow down or speed up within a particular reading as they meet unfamiliar or familiar material.

6. **Rate-building techniques.** Integrate the teaching of rate-building techniques with each new reading in the text. These techniques, discussed in the text on pages 14–16, are eliminating "white space," reading by clustering ideas, and pacing through print. To demonstrate these techniques, write the first two paragraphs of "I Became Her Target," p. 293, on the chalkboard. Then, incorporate the following procedure into your introduction of each of the new reading selections: Have the students "prepare the print" prior to the reading of each selection (if you prefer, this procedure can come after a vocabulary preview). Now instruct the student to:

   • draw margin lines about five letter spaces in from each margin throughout the entire reading;
   • cluster ideas using slash marks throughout the first few paragraphs of each selection;
   • pace through the print as a preread by taking one or two minutes using a hand to move through the entire reading to develop the mechanics of the technique.

   The key to helping students eliminate poor habits is to teach them how to establish new good ones. The above procedure will help students establish a productive reading routine.

   As the students apply the procedure, discuss the importance of developing a "soft focus" when working with margin lines as slash marks. Rather than "stare" at the boundary lines as they read, students need to be aware that they are searching for ideas that connect. The artificial marks and the hand will seem less of a distraction if instructors focus students' attention back on the fact that they are trying to get meaning from the print.

7. **Seeing more than one word.** Respond to those students who may insist that it is necessary to focus on every word when they read, and that their peripheral vision simply cannot see more than one word at a time. Develop an easy cloze paragraph at the independent reading level of students in the class (see "Readability" in this Guide for instructions on developing a cloze exercise). Use the results of this exercise to demonstrate that the mind can "fill in the blanks" even when some of the words are missing. Also, ask the students to infer the point of the material before they fill in the words.

Use another method to demonstrate the mind's ability to take in more than one word at a time by putting the following on the board:

educational	(takes up 11 letter spaces)
in the past	(takes up 11 letter spaces including breaks between words)

Explain to students that if they focus in the middle of the word "educational" they can "see" it all at once. Most students will acknowledge they read it as one word, not syllable by syllable (ed/u/ca/tion/al). Next, point out that the idea cluster "in the past" also takes up eleven letter spaces. Have students "soft focus" on the phrase so that they will "see" it. Then, most importantly, show that they read it in one cluster as well: educational; in the past.

8. **Rate goals.** Help students set reasonable goals for improving their reading rates: 25 to 50 words per minute faster each session for reading material of the same type and level of difficulty. Clarify that speed without comprehension is meaningless, and explain that increases in reading speed usually go hand in hand with better comprehension. Researchers find that with slow reading, the mind has time to wander and take "mental vacations." It is important, then, that students strive to keep their minds working to full potential.

Discuss the fact that students who balk at taking risks by speeding up generally have concentration difficulties, and often they regress and subvocalize to aid their comprehension. These are major crutches which work against efficient reading. Subvocalization is appropriate about 50 percent of the time—when a reader encounters a new word, unfamiliar idea, or key concept. Regression is appropriate only when it is conscious—when the reader chooses to reread a particularly difficult passage, for example. Help students break the habits of subvocalizing every word and rereading sentences by encouraging them to do the following:

- Use a blank 3 × 5 card as a pacer. The chard should move **down** the print, not follow under the lines of print. The card should move at a consistent pace, not moving back to allow rereading of a missed sentence. This helps focus the reader's attention on the task. It also helps readers become aware of "mental vacations" while reading. For students who seem frustrated with the technique, have them use the card only on the first few paragraphs of a reading to set the pace.
- Have students avoid focusing on the problem of subvocalization. Instead encourage them to push themselves to read slightly faster than the rate at which they "hear" all the words. The rate should be slightly uncomfortable, but comprehension adequate. Subvocalization lessens when rates go above about 250 wpm, or the fastest rate at which a person can comprehend individual words being said.

Vocabulary

Objective for the student: To learn how to use context clues, word parts, the dictionary, and a personal vocabulary card system to effect an increase in word knowledge.

In *Structural Reading,* new vocabulary words are presented in context and a complete dictionary entry is provided for each new word. The concept is that because words are handles for ideas, an understanding of key vocabulary is crucial for good comprehension and reading rate. For each reading selection the vocabulary list might often be presented prior to reading. The words should be discussed as part of the preview. The "Additional Vocabulary Exercises" in the *Instructor's Resource Manual* provide practice and reinforcement for the vocabulary list for each reading.

But only adding new words to students' vocabulary is not enough. Students need to learn strategies that they can use when they encounter words they do not know whether in the reading selections in this text or in any other material. Here are some strategies students can use:

CONTEXT CLUES

The text's section on vocabulary, pages 19–28, provides students with four types of context clues: a restatement clue, a contrast clue, an example clue, and a definition context clue.

Students will need **practice** with context, however, to master the concept fully. Weak readers rarely realize that awareness of context plays a pivotal role in the reading process. For example, when a reader sees the words "once upon a," that reader always knows from the context that there is a 99% chance that the next word will be "time." This ability to predict what words will come next becomes easier as a reader becomes more experienced. This ability to use context to predict is indispensable for efficient comprehension and good reading speeds.

Some students need help discovering the concept of context, and most need practice in using clues to help predict the meaning of words. Here are some ideas for implementing the teaching of context clues:

1. **Concept of context.** Demonstrate the concept of context by designing short cloze passages (see "Readability" in this Guide). Instruct students to fill in the blanks according to the meaning of the surrounding words. You can simplify this task for the student by using the maze technique. Delete every fifth word, but instead of leaving only a blank for the deletion, provide three alternative responses.

2. **Importance of context.** Try to convince students of the importance of learning a word in context. Demonstrate the importance of knowing the context by asking students to define some simple words: for example, **fox, good, island.** Then give students sentences, each using the word in a different context. Ask students how the definitions change depending on the context:

   Define **fox:**
   Define **fox** in "Senator White is certainly a political **fox.**"
   Define **fox** in "I saw a dead **fox** on the side of the road this morning."
   Define **good:**
   Define **good** in "**Good** children never stay out past 2:00 A.M."
   Define **good** in "Now is the time for all **good** men to come to the aid of their country."
   Define **good** in "All I need to be happy is **good** food, **good** drink, and **good** company."
   Define **island:**
   Define **island** in "No man is an **island** unto himself."
   Define **island** in "I saw a blind woman stranded on the pedetrian **island.**"

3. **Sophisticated language and context.** Help students become aware that sophisticated language demands a careful look at the context. Subtle differences in definitions may not always reveal whether a word is used incorrectly or not. For example, the dictionary lists the definition of **sift** as **examine** for the sentence, "The Senate investigators had to **sift** through many Presidential papers to find the evidence they needed." Yet it would be incorrect to use the word **sift** as a synonym for **examine** in this sentence: "I took my dog to the vet so he could **sift** his eye."

Many words in *Structured Reading* can have various meanings depending on the context. Encourage students to develop sentences using the words listed below in various contexts to examine the differences in meaning:

> antennae, p. 86; carriage, p. 253; circuit, p. 304; consensus, p. 167; craned, p. 86; draught, p. 386; lobby, p. 221; reared, p. 97; siren, p. 386.

4. **Context clue exercises.** Develop context clue exercises based on the vocabulary words from the reading selections in the text. Give students practice with the four types of clues.

   Emphasize the importance of students determining the correct meaning of the word, rather than only identifying the types of clues.

5. **Context clues and other strategies.** Make students aware that the meaning of all words cannot always be figured out from the context. Weak readers are often discouraged when they discover that examining the context will not always yield meaning. Help such students learn that professional writers try to be as clear and accessible to their readers as possible, but many concepts need sophisticated words that do not have simple substitutes. Explain that students can use other resources to help them out, particularly analysis of the word parts and dictionary entries.

DICTIONARY

Dictionary entries are provided for each of the vocabulary words identified for study from the reading selections in *Structured Reading*. Using the dictionary entries with the students, instructors can read through each entry to help students discover which meaning of the word fits the context of the sentence. Vocabulary entries in *Webster's New World College Dictionary, Fourth Edition,* use dots for syllabification. The dots indicate where a word can be acceptably divided at the end of a line.

The Sixth Edition of *Structured Reading* provides an updated "Guide to the Dictionary" written in language understandable to the developmental reader. It appears in the Appendix to the text. To help instructors give students practice in its principles, this Guide offers exercises in using the pronunciation guide, understanding syllabification, finding synonyms, determining the correct forms of infected nouns and verbs, as well as prefix and suffix practice in the "Dictionary Skills Exercises" in the *Instructor's Resource Manual.* Dictionary skills are taught most effectively when they relate to a real task of discovering meaning, but these exercises can provide preliminary practice.

449

"Transparency Masters: Dictionary Entries," in the *Instructor's Resource Manual*, are provided to help instructors lead discussions on the various elements of a dictionary entry.

The entries for **crane** and for **missionaries** (with **mission**) demonstrate that many words have multiple meanings and that students must consider context when they use a dictionary entry. The entry for **contingent** shows that one word can occur as many different parts of speech. The entries for **derivative** (with **derive**) and for **anomaly** illustrate the varying fields of study that call upon a single word in different ways. The entry for **exclude** offers synonyms that list and explain subtle differences among synonyms. The presentation of these entries follows the order of explanation offered in *Structured Reading*'s "Guide to Dictionary Use" that appears in the Appendix to the text. Also, the entries **crane** and **derivative** (with **derive**) are illustrations of information presented in the "Guide to Dictionary Use." The pronunciation key shown on one of the transparency masters in the *Instructor's Resource Manual* also appears in the text's "Guide to Dictionary Use." It is offered to help instructors lead students to the correct pronunciation of the entries from *Webster's New World College Dictionary, Fourth Edition,* reproduced in *Structured Reading*.

As students learn to use context clues, word parts, and the dictionary as useful resources while working with the vocabulary in *Structured Reading,* they will need a personal system of regular vocabulary study to help them learn new words. One method of developing and practicing with vocabulary cards is described for the student on pages 26–27 of the text. A sample vocabulary card also appears on page 26 and is reproduced in the "Transparency Masters: Vocabulary Study" section of the *Instructor's Resource Manual*. Here are ways to incorporate a vocabulary card practice system into classroom instruction:

Introduction of the Technique

Introduce the format of the vocabulary cards and point out all the elements that make up the study of a word. When planning a lecture and discussion involving your students, choose one word to examine with the class, such as the word **aggressive** (which appears on page 104 in the text). Make up numbered envelopes and in each write on a piece of paper one element of the vocabulary cards. Do not identify on the envelope which element is contained inside.

In envelope 1 put the word to be studied, **aggressive.**

In envelope 2 put the pronunciation of the word as listed in the dictionary.

In envelope 3 put the context in which the word appeared.

In envelope 4 put all the definitions of the word.

In envelope 5 put the word broken down into its word parts.

In envelope 6 put the word used in a student-designed sentence.

Hand out the six envelopes randomly to the class without explanation. Draw a large vocabulary card on the board. Use the sample card on page 26 in the text as a model. Then ask for the student with envelope 1 to read what is inside. Enter the word on the card drawn on the board. Then ask the student with envelope 2 to do the same, but since it is the pronunciation, you will have to spell it out. Ask the class if anyone recognizes what it is, and what the symbols mean. You can lead this discussion by referring students to the pronunciation key in the text's Appendix "Guide to Dictionary Use" (also a transparency master in the *Instructor's Resource Manual*). Proceed with all of the other envelopes in the same manner, taking time to discuss each element of vocabulary study as you enter the information on the board. For example, when the students have revealed all of the definitions, have the class examine which one best fits the context. Eliminate all the other definitions so that students learn that the definition of a word in context should not be encumbered with several definitions to learn at one time. When the word parts are revealed, discuss the basics of word part analysis and show how when combined with context, the word parts contribute to help determine the meaning of a word.

At the end of the discussion, you will have a very complete vocabulary card on the board. Turn the students' attention to page 26 in the text which summarizes how to make a vocabulary card (you can add or delete some of the elements as you see fit).

Structured Reading recommends that students choose ten words each week found in their readings. In addition to the method for study explained in the text, a regular practice routine in the classroom can help students as paired teams. Develop a check list by expanding the sample of the one below. Have students orally "practice test" each other. Instruct them to read the word and context clue from their partner's cards, asking the partner for definitions. Have the students keep track of their own results so they can learn which words are particularly difficult to master. Once or twice during the semester, use this list and the cards to test students individually on their personal vocabulary list.

PERSONAL VOCABULARY WORD LIST

		Team Practice Dates			
Date entered	Word to learn	Results of practices			
1.					
2.					
3.					

Key: "✓" = correct, "-" = incorrect; definition correct 3 times in a row indicates mastery.

Predicting

Objective for the student: To learn the preparation step for reading—predicting—for greater concentration and comprehension.

Predicting is presented in *Structured Reading* on pages 29–30 as a pre-reading step crucial to active reading and good comprehension. One approach that emphasizes the use of predictions in reading comprehension, the Directed Thinking and Reading Activity, was developed by Russell D. Stauffer. The approach is explained in his book, *Directing the Reading-Thinking Process* (Harper and Row, 1975). This approach calls for a predict-read-prove cycle. The student consciously predicts what a selection will be about after reading the title or other introductory material. Then the student guesses what will come next based on reading the first few paragraphs. These predictions are hypotheses which are confirmed or rejected as the reading continues.

The DTRA derives from two research-based findings about the reading process. First, that reading requires the active participation of the reader—making predictions, checking them out for accuracy, refining them, and moving along. Second, the approach allows for trial and error and risk-taking. When students share their predictions, they see that several answers are possible. This encourages divergent thinking. It allows a student to think, "Well, I made a decent guess but I guessed wrong; now that I know something about the selection, maybe my next guess will be more on target." The atmosphere of right-or-wrong shifts to an atmosphere of open investigation.

In reading fiction, predicting involves thinking about what will happen next. In reading nonfiction, predicting additionally involves summoning up whatever prior knowledge the students have about the subject at hand and predicting from the title what the main idea of the piece will be. Here are some suggestions for encouraging students to practice predicting:

1. **Introduction of predicting.** Introduce the technique to the class by asking students how they usually begin a textbook assignment. Most will answer that they simply pick it up and start to read it. Then ask the athletes in the class how they start out their activity for the day. The joggers and dancers might say they stretch, the football players might say they run short sprints, and so on. Conduct a discussion of what happens if athletes do not warm up in these ways. Injuries and poor performance are among the possible answers. Make the point that in reading, to start out "cold" without a warmup—previewing the title, predicting the main point, reading the first few paragraphs and making further predictions about the content—will result in lack of concentration and focus. Also, emphasize that one of the advantages of the predicting step is to refocus attention from a previous activity to the one at hand. When making

predictions after reading the title and first few paragraphs, the reader can know that his or her mind is on the reading and not on a prior telephone conversation, math paper, or stack of unpaid bills.

2. **Prediction examples.** Get students thinking about predictions concretely by bringing to class four different types of empty picture frames in different sizes, for example a modern chrome frame, an old-looking etched wood frame, a highly-decorative gilt frame, and a plain white plastic frame. Ask students what they can predict about the picture that might be placed in each frame. Students might mention size, style, age, and color. Compare the predictions they made to the "frame" they will get when they read the title and first few paragraphs of a reading—the "complete picture," the main ideas and details, will fit into that frame when they do the thorough reading.

3. **Visuals.** Use the "Thinking: Getting Started" sections of visuals and questions that precede each of the five parts in the text to help students think about the prior knowledge they have on the subjects they will read about. Each poster, ad, or cartoon refers to one or more of the reading selections that follow in that part. For each selection, there is a question to lead students into making a connection between the visual and the reading selection.

4. **Reading selections.** To demonstrate how reading the title and first few paragraphs can help with accurate predictions of some of the main points, several readings in this text can be used for this purpose. Some of these include:

> "The Death of a Farm," p. 95; "Escaping the Daily Grind for Life as a House Father," p. 227; "Darkness at Noon," p. 109; "Houses to Save the Earth," p. 333; "Genes and Behavior: A Twin Legacy," p. 199; "Restored to the Sea," p. 283; and "Long-Term Memory," p. 355.

Other reading selections do not reveal the main points in such an obvious way, but will engage interest when the students find that what they thought to be true may not be true at all. Some examples are:

> "A Real Loss," p. 85: The beginning of this essay describes a pleasant scene between a man and a girl. What is "the real loss?" Will it be the loss of life of the girl? A loss of innocence? Will the man cause the loss?

> "The Girl with the Large Eyes," p. 147: This symbolic tale does not have its true meaning revealed until the unusual characters and events are analyzed.

> "Summer," p. 141: What seems to begin as a description of a boyhood summer turns into a tragedy that makes an unforgettable impression on the author.

"How to Stay Alive," p. 327: It is often difficult to predict the main point of a satiric piece. The phrase "Once upon a time . . ." may clue the reader that there is more to this essay than is exactly stated.

On, Between, and Beyond the Lines

Objective for the student: To learn how to determine central theme, main ideas and images; identify key details; draw correct inferences; distinguish fact from opinion; understand how the writer's craft influences the reader; and make judgments about what has been read.

Chapter 9, Part One, pages 39–40, in *Structured Reading* discusses the three major comprehensions levels students will encounter: literal, critical, and analytical. Each reading selection contains follow-up questions that deal with those levels. Here are some ways to help students learn to apply them.

1. **Literal.** Encourage students not to skip illustrations, charts, and graphs when they read. Examine with them the illustration in selection 28. "Transparency Masters: Reading Illustrations" in the *Instructor's Resource Manual* are also provided for you to help students analyze information contained in this visual. After a survey of the textbook extract from which it is taken, ask students to interpret the illustration about how it supports the main idea of the chapter. You also might discuss how a visual helps the mind remember since the mind thinks in pictures.

2. **Critical.** Some reading selections in the text are particularly useful in bringing the student beyond only a literal understanding. If the symbolism is not understood, "The Girl with the Large Eyes" could be read as a ludicrous story of a woman marrying a fish. In "How to Stay Alive," the satire must be appreciated to correctly identify the main point. In "You Are How You Eat," the humor has to be recognized or the material might be mistaken as trivial. Have the students read each of these essays, and using the questions on page 59 of the text on "Inferences," take students through the process of analyzing the essays in order to draw valid conclusions.

3. **Analytical.** Engage students in close reading and careful analysis by having them make up their own questions about a reading selection using the questions categories in the book such as Central Theme and Main Ideas, Major Details, Inferences, and so on. Then distribute the questions to the rest of the class for discussion and answering while the "author" of the questions checks the answers. This activity also promotes debate about the questions in the book, and it encourages students to see questions as not merely tests of their understanding, but springboards to further analysis.

4. **Critical and Analytical.** Make students aware of the connotations of words. The readings "Tyranny of Weakness," page 103, or "Out of Their Element," page 249, provide useful practice in eliminating opinionated words. Instruct students to edit the opinionated words, then revise the articles using only factual statements. This helps the student recognize how the author's choice of words may help to persuade the reader.

5. **Critical and Analytical.** Help students become aware that many essays and articles are made up primarily of opinionated statements. Using the guidelines for qualifying a statement as a fact listed on page 67 of the text, have the students look at opening paragraphs from essays that promote a particular point of view. Ask students to make judgments about the statements in those paragraphs. Some useful reading selections for this are: "The Death of a Farm," p. 95; "Tyranny of Weakness," p. 103; "My World Now," p. 117; "Should a Wife Keep Her Name?" p. 273; and "Every Kid Needs Some Manual Arts," p. 209.

Using the same type of analysis, compare the above reading selections to the textbook extracts in Part 6 of the text. This helps students clarify the importance of understanding the author's purpose for writing and the techniques he or she uses to develop the work. Help students recognize that if the author's primary purpose is to inform as in a textbook, he or she will use factual statements; if the purpose is to persuade or influence as in an argumentative essay, the author will use opinions as well as facts and choose words which promote a particular point of view.

Objective for the student: To apply a systematic approach to determine central theme, main ideas and images; identify key details; draw correct inferences; distinguish fact from opinion; and evaluate the writer's craft.

Here are some strategies, along with sample questions and answers, and brief explanations to help students answer follow-up questions from the reading selections.

I. CENTRAL THEME AND MAIN IDEA

The **central theme** tells what the entire selection is about. In answering this type of question, students should:

1. look away from the text after reading a selection.

2. write a one-sentence statement that explains to someone else what the selection is all about. (This statement should resemble a movie description in the *TV Guide*.)

3. compare this sentence with the four options in a multiple choice question. (The correct answer is probably the one which most closely matches one of the options.)

The **main idea** tells what a paragraph or group of paragraphs is about. Encourage students to

1. determine the topic or subject.

2. determine the point the author attempts to make about the subject.

3. use the process of elimination for multiple-choice options that may be too specific, too narrow, or maybe even false.

4. analyze the paragraph. Many of the multiple-choice options for these questions are often sentences, or details, taken from the paragraph in question. By taking the paragraph apart sentence by sentence, students can often see the topic as well as the major point unfold.

EXAMPLE: The following brief explanations relate to central theme and main idea exercises from Selection 1, "A Real Loss."

__d__ 1. What is the central theme of "A Real Loss"?
  a. **These are trying times for men. . . .** is incorrect because the story focuses on one man, and not one media account of child molestation is mentioned.
  b. **The author felt sorry. . . .** is incorrect because there is no evidence to support this sentiment.
  c. **Child molesters can find victims everywhere. . . .** is also incorrect because this issue is not discussed. Only two women are concerned here, and the airplane is the only place mentioned where a possible victim could be found.
  d. **Because of her increased awareness that some . . .** is the correct choice because it more appropriately summarizes the point the author makes. When the man befriended the little girl, the author watched suspiciously to see what his actions would be. Her alarm heightened when the bathroom issue surfaced, and she became even more suspect. Once she saw that his intentions were honorable, she realized that she had missed out on something beautiful, a very special moment.

    When students look away from the text after reading the selection and write as though they are telling someone else what the selection is about, they tend never to mention ideas presented in options a, b, or c.

__c__ 2. What is the main idea of paragraph 6?
  a. **Airplane passengers often listen to other. . . .** This is too narrow a focus to be the point here.
  b. **Becoming suspicious, the author leaned far. . . .** This is another detail, not the paragraph essence, leading to the main idea.
  c. **As she waited to see what the man would do. . . .** This is the correct answer because it best makes the author's point and summarizes the key ideas in options a, b, and d.

    d. **The man opened the bathroom door for the little. . . .** This is another detail which answers "as she waited to see what the man would do."

II. DETAILS

Two of the three types of detail questions will be analyzed in this section: (1) distinguishing between major and minor details and (2) true, false, and not discussed.

A. Major and Minor Details

In distinguishing between major and minor details, students might follow these suggestions:

1. Reread the central theme.

2. Determine the following:
   a. If the detail supports the central theme.
      ASK: Is the detail an example, a clarifying definition, a fact, a statistic, a reason, or a quotation related to some aspect of the central theme?
   b. If a relationship exists between the central theme and the detail.
      ASK: Does the detail answer who, what, when, where, why, or how about any aspect of the central theme?

3. Conclude that if some supporting relationship exists between the central theme and the detail, then the detail is most likely major; if not, then it is minor.

EXAMPLE 1: This sample major details exercise is taken from Selection 1, "A Real Loss."

Central Theme: Because of her increased awareness that some people are child molesters, the author now realizes that she has become suspicious of people who are kind to children they do not know.

1. The author was sitting in back of a little girl who was flying alone.
   Major—This identifies the setting and presents a fact about the author (who) and her seating (where), in a position to observe what was taking place.

2. The little girl's mother placed a Care Bear in the girl's arms.
   Minor—Who cares?—no bearing on the story line—could be omitted.

3. The little girl was going to California.
   Minor—(same as #2)

4. The little girl knew how to adjust her seat belt.
   Minor—(same as #2)

5. The bear's name was Furry.
   Minor—(same as #2)

6. Both the girl and the man's daughter were six years old.
   Major—Because of his experience with six-year-olds, the man knew how to gain the little girl's confidence.

7. The little girl announced that she had to go to the bathroom.
   Major—This tells what aroused the author's suspicion.

8. At that moment, the flight attendants were busy collecting lunch trays, so the man offered to take the girl to the bathroom.
   Major—This tells why the man accepted the challenge.

9. The man showed the girl how the lock worked, and then he waited for her outside the door.
   Major—This is climax, indicating what happened.

10. The other woman sighed in relief.
    Minor—(Same as #2)

11. The author's image of the man and the little girl on the plane left her with a feeling of loss.
    Major—This is the essence of the story, telling how the author felt about her needless suspicions.

12. A new heightened consciousness about child molestation is in itself a good thing.

    Major—The author draws this conclusion from the experience.

EXAMPLE 2: This sample major details exercise is taken from Selection 4, "Darkness at Noon."

Central Theme: People often assume that because blind people cannot see, they cannot hear, learn, or work.

1. The author has been blind from birth.
   Major—This fact provides evidence (credibility) about the author (who) and tells why he can attest to the central theme.

2. People often shout at blind people and pronounce every word with great care.
   Major—This example supports the "cannot hear" aspect.

3. Airline personnel use a code to refer to blind people.
   Minor—The emphasis here is on identification of the blind.

4. The author goes out to dinner with his wife Kit.
   Minor—The emphasis here is on dining and socializing.

5. If a blind person and a sighted person are together, other people will usually communicate with them by talking. . . .
   Major—This example supports the "cannot hear" aspect.

6. The author was given a year's leave of absence from his Washington law firm to study for a diploma-in-law degree. . . .
   Minor—This emphasizes his ability, not his disability.

7. The author had to be hospitalized while studying in England.
   Minor—The emphasis here is on health.

8. In 1975 the Department of Labor issued regulations that require equal employment opportunities for the handicapped.
   Major—This is an effect of the "work" aspect of the central theme (cause) which indicates why.

9. On the whole, the business community's response to offering employment of the handicapped has been enthusiastic.
   Major—This fact supports the "work" aspect of the central theme.

10. The author and his father played basketball in the backyard using a special system they had worked out.
    Minor—This is about recreation.

11. The author's father shot for the basket and missed completely.
    Minor—This is about the father's disability.

12. The neighbor's friend was not sure if the author on his father was blind.
    Major—This statement ironically summarizes the essence of the selection (the author's hope) and connects the assumption made here (was not sure if) with that (assume) in the central theme.

B. True, False, Not Discussed

Close reading requires verifying information. Students may apply the following techniques in answering true, false, and not discussed type questions.

1. If the statement is **True,** verify its validity in the text by locating and reading the supporting sentence(s). (e.g., Paragraph 6, Sentence 2)

2. If the statement is **False,** locate reference sentence(s) in the text. Then, cross out the incorrect part of the sentence(s) and substitute the correct information.

3. If the statement is **Not Discussed,** there should be no reference to the key idea in the text.

4. To verify responses, convert statements into questions and answer them: Yes (same as True), No (same as False), and Not Sure (same as Not Discussed).

EXAMPLE 1: This sample major details exercise is taken from Selection 13, "Genes and Behavior: A Twin Legacy."

1. Thomas J. Bouchard is the director of the Minnesota Center for Twin and Adoption Research.
   Q: Is Thomas J. Bouchard the director of the Minnesota Center for Twin and Adoption Research?
   Yes/True (Paragraph 1, Sentence 3)

2. The behavior of separated twins is being compared with the behavior of a *group of 25 pairs of twins* raised together.
   Q: Is the behavior of separated twins being compared with the behavior of a group of 25 pairs of twins raised together?
   No/False: The behavior of separated twins is being compared with the behavior of a *comparison group* reared together.

3. Even though many of the separated twins have different jobs, they often share the same hobbies and interests.
   Q: Do separated twins who have different jobs share the same hobbies and interests?
   Yes/True (Paragraph 4, Sentence 1)

4. One pair of identical twins who burst into tears easily both cried *when asked to appear* on a talk show.
   Q: Did one pair of identical twins who burst into tears easily both cry when asked to appear on a talk show?
   No/False: . . . both cried *in response to one of the questions.*

5. Twins who are afraid of water are usually also afraid of the dark and of animals.
   Q: Are twins who are afraid of water also afraid of the dark and of other animals?
   *Not sure—can't find answer in selection/***Not Discussed**

6. One set of separated fraternal twins both had antisocial personalities and grew up to be criminals.
   Q: Did one set of separated fraternal twins with antisocial behavior grow up to be criminals?
   Yes/True (Paragraph 6, Sentence 3)

7. *A woman's twin sons* won mathematics competitions. . . .
   Q: Did a woman's twin sons win a mathematics competition in Wyoming and Texas?
   No/False: *Two identical twin women* each had a son who won. . . .

460

8. Social closeness is essential for happiness in humans.

   Q: Is social closeness essential for happiness in humans?

   Not sure—can't locate answer in selection/**Not Discussed**

9. *Environmental influences* are the most important shapers of personality.

   Q: Are environmental influences the most important shapers of personality?

   <u>No</u>/**False:** *Genes* . . . **primary shaping forces of personality.**

10. Genes determine *almost all* personality traits.

    Q: Do genes determine almost all personality traits?

    <u>No</u>/**False: Genes determin***e about 11 p***ersonality traits.**

EXAMPLE 2: This sample major details exercise is taken from Selection 21, "Restored to the Sea."

1. Stranded false killer whales are known to attack humans.

   Q: Do *false* killer whales attack humans?

   <u>No</u>/**False: The word** *false* **suggests they are** *not* **killers. (Paragraph 2, Sentence 2)**

2. Volunteers from Seal Rocks rescued 37 of the whales.

   Q: Did volunteers from Seal Rocks rescue 37 whales?

   <u>No</u>/**False: Rescuers from as far as 500 miles from Seal Rocks participated in the rescue. (Paragraph 2, Sentence 4)**

3. One whale was the cause of the stranding of 49 others.

   Q: Did one whale cause 49 other whales to be stranded?

   Not sure—Why the whales ran aground is a mystery/**Not Discussed**

4. Some volunteers traveled great distances to help.

   Q: Did some volunteers travel great distances to help?

   <u>Yes</u>/**True: Some volunteers traveled over 500 miles.**

5. The whales' malfunctioning sonar may have led them astray.

   Q: Did the whales' malfunctioning sonar lead them astray?

   <u>Yes</u>/**True: Only know that along shallow beaches malfunctioning sonar may lead them astray. (Paragraph 3, Sentence 2)**

6. Humans are quick to answer calls to help any animal in distress.

   Q: Are humans quick to answer calls to help any animal in distress?

   Not sure—Only know that humans responded quickly to this call/**Not Discussed (Paragraph 4, Sentence 1)**

7. The volunteers' previous training prepared them for the rescue attempt.

   Q: Did the volunteers have any previous training to prepare them for this?

Not sure—No mention is made of volunteers' previous training for rescuing preparing them for this rescue/**Not Discussed**

8. Whales are by nature nervous creatures.
   Q: Are whales nervous creatures by nature?
   Not sure—Volunteers sought to calm the creatures but no mention is made that whales are nervous by nature/**Not Discussed**

III. INFERENCES

In making **inferences,** students must be able to identify the part of the selection (words, sentences, thought groups) that supports a particular response. To do this, students must also read between the lines and supply information the author assumes they know already. The following steps are useful for students in answering inference type questions:

1. Make sure you understand what is stated on the lines.

2. Find evidence to support your position.

3. Use reasoning and background knowledge to bring it all together.

4. Remember: Your thoughts alone are not sufficient; base your response on evidence from the selection.

EXAMPLE 1: This sample exercise is taken from Selection 1, "A Real Loss." (There is no evidence to support unlisted distractors.)

1. Why did the little girl's mother tell her to remind Daddy to call?
   b. The mother wanted to know that the girl. . . .
      Evidence: Care Bear—indicates concern for child.

2. Why did the man say Furry was a good name?
   c. He wanted to make her feel comfortable and secure.
      Evidence: "Nodded in approval"

3. Why did the little girl's announcement that she had to go to the bathroom wake up the author?
   d. As a mother, the author was used to listening—even in sleep—for children's calls for help.
      Evidence: "My mother instinct"

4. By saying "Well, you can't be too careful these days" the woman was communicating that she was
   c. slightly embarrassed that she had worried about what the man might do to the little girl.
      Evidence: "sighed in relief"

5. What does the author mean when she says "there is a real loss here for us all when we must always be wary of the kindness of strangers"?
    a. ... from enjoying some of the pleasanter moments. ...
       Evidence: "saddens me"

6. The *loss* used in the title refers to the
    a. author's loss of trust of adults who are kind to children.
       Evidence: This is what the selection is about: the author's inability to appreciate the adult (man and stranger) being kind to a little girl.

EXAMPLE 2: This sample inference exercise is taken from Selection 4, "Darkness at Noon."

1. The title of the essay suggests that it is sighted people, not blind people, who cannot "see."
   YES: Darkness at noon (the brightest time of the day).

2. The author feels that he is greatly admired. ...
   NO: "I have never had the opportunity to see myself and have been completely dependent on the image I create in the eye of the observer. To date it has not been narcissistic."

3. The author feels that he can make his point more effectively with humor than with a stern lecture.
   YES: He gives several humorous examples—in the airport, restaurant, and hospital—related to people's assumptions: can't hear (yell at him, enunciate carefully, and whisper), can't talk and needs an interpreter (communications with wife and orderly), can't work (cum laude graduate with law degree rejected by over 40 law firms and told that he could not practice law).

4. The author often eats in restaurants with his wife Kit.
   NO: Often when he and his wife Kit go out to dinner, the same thing happens.

5. The author was highly entertained by the conversation. ...
   NO: ... "even my saint-like disposition deserted me."

6. The author got good grades at Harvard Law School because he was given special privileges reserved for blind students.
   NO: Evidence to the contrary—cum laude degree from Harvard College, a good ranking at Harvard, received a year's leave of absence to study for a diploma-in-law degree at Oxford University.

7. The April 10, 1976, Department of Labor regulations were. ...
   NO: No Evidence to support this.

8. The author's father was a much better basketball player. . . .
   NO: No Evidence—they both shot and missed; "Dad missed the garage entirely."

IV. FACT OR OPINION

For *opinions*, encourage students to determine if there are differing opinions in the classroom and if any of the following terms/conditions exist:

1. possibility words (apparently, appears, possibly, potentially, probably, seems, suppose, think)

2. conditional words (should, could, may, prefer, might, suppose, if, believe)

3. abstract terms (exhausted, loyalty, democracy, love, expensive, tentative)

4. someone is speaking for another (you, they, everybody)

5. any future reference (will, in the future, tomorrow)

For *facts*, test the statement using the three tests for verification: research, observation, or experimentation.

1. Research requires paying particular attention to references to written record, statistics and concrete terms.

2. Observation may be anything perceived by the senses: smell, taste, touch, see, hear.

3. Experimentation involves manipulation: testing, weighing, counting, etc.

NOTE: Students are to be reminded that their agreement with a statement only makes it a fact for them but not necessarily for anybody else—and this is the concern. The statement remains an opinion if it cannot be verified.

The following three (3) sample fact or opinion exercises come from (a) Selection 1, "A Real Loss," (b) Selection 3, "Tyranny of Weakness," and (c) Selection 4, "Darkness at Noon." The brief explanations attempt to apply the strategies above to show their effectiveness in unraveling this type of exercise. Some of the key words are highlighted in opinion sentences.

EXAMPLE 1: This sample fact or opinion exercise is taken from Selection 1, "A Real Loss."

1. The girl adjusted her seat belt and sniffed back a tear.
   Fact—Observation (see)

2. He asked her how much money the tooth fairy was giving out in New York these days.
   Fact—Observation (hear)

3. She revealed to him the names of her favorite friends.
   Fact—Observation (hear)

4. She *looked tentative.*
   Opinion—Abstraction

5. He became transformed in my eyes.
   Fact—Observation (The author sees and speaks for herself.)

6. The *dark* business suit *looked sinister.*
   Opinion—Abstraction

7. The woman and I sighed in relief.
   Fact—Observation (see)

8. *"You* can't be *too careful these days."*
   Opinion—Someone is speaking for someone else.

9. A new *heightened consciousness* about child molestation is in itself a *good thing.*
   Opinion—Maybe for you but not for the child molester.

10. These are *trying times* for men.
    Opinion—Abstraction (trying times)

   EXAMPLE 2: This sample fact or opinion exercise is taken from Selection 2, "Tyranny of Weakness."

1. The most *aggressive,* the *strongest* people *we* know are the *weak* ones.
   Opinion—Abstractions and speaking for someone else.

2. *I suppose* it begins in childhood when a child realizes that *helplessness* is a way of *controlling* parents.
   Opinion—Possibility phrase and abstract terms.

3. The man wanted a quiet, shy, helpless wife because his mother had been aggressive and overpowering.
   Fact—Ask the man; he can verify if this is what he wants.

4. She said she was too tired.
   Fact—The lady is speaking for herself. We hear her voice.

5. A *competent* mother can turn into a *weak, helpless* widow.
   Opinion—A general abstract statement about someone else.

6. *It seemed* to break a pattern that was *bad* for *both of us.*
   Opinion—Possibility phrase with abstract terms and speaking for someone else.

EXAMPLE 3: This sample fact or opinion exercise is taken from Selection 4, "Darkness at Noon."

1. Blind from birth, I have never had the opportunity to see myself.
   Fact—Verifiable (The author speaks for himself.)

2. *They fear* that *if* the *dread word* is spoken, the ticket agent's retina *will* immediately detach.
   Opinion—Speaking for someone else, abstractions and possibility.

3. I had been given a year's leave of absence from my Washington law firm to study for a diploma-in-law degree at Oxford.
   Fact—(same as #1)

4. I was turned down by over forty law firms because of my blindness.
   Fact—The author can verify this with written evidence (rejection letters).

5. By and large, the business community's response to offering employment to the *disabled* has been *enthusiastic.*
   Opinion—general statement with abstract terms.

6. Dad shot [the basketball] and missed the garage entirely.
   Fact—Observable (see)

V. CRITICAL READING: THE WRITER'S CRAFT

The writer's craft shows how the author captures the reader's attention and gets him/her involved in the story. Encourage students to evaluate the choice of answers carefully, paying particular attention to:

1. ridiculous options,

2. author's choice of words,

3. images conveyed, and

4. overall good writing techniques.

Style and audience are good clues to understanding these types of questions as well.

EXAMPLE 1: The sample "Writer's Craft" exercise examined here is taken from Selection 1, "A Real Loss."

1. To get the reader's attention, the author opens with
   a. a brief anecdote. **YES—She tells a short story.**
   b. a description. **NO**
   c. a startling fact. **NO**
   d. a quotation. **NO**

2. To show how the man gains the little girl's trust, the author describes how he
   a. tells the girl jokes. **NO**
   b. asks the girl questions about herself. **YES—Asked name of her bear, how much money the tooth fairy was giving out . . .**
   c. shows her pictures of his own daughter. **NO**
   d. talks to her stuffed bear. **NO**

3. The author uses dialogue here
   a. to show she has a detailed, reliable memory of the event. **NO (Ridiculous answer)**
   b. to highlight that this was the most important part of the conversation. **YES—This definitely shows this to be important.**
   c. to demonstrate how to write direct dialogue. **NO—This is no demonstration.**
   d. because every story should have at least one passage of direct dialogue. **NO—(Ridiculous)**

4. The author concludes her essay with
   a. a dramatic call to action. **NO**
   b. a forecast of the future. **NO**
   c. an evaluation of the situation. **YES—"These are trying times for men. We women say. . . ."**
   d. a final example of the problem. **NO**

   EXAMPLE 2: The sample "Writer's Craft" exercise examined here is taken from Selection 4, "Darkness at Noon."

1. The author shows the connections between each of his ideas with all of these words except
   a. "to date"—blind from birth
   b. **"obviously"—shows emphasis—no connection**
   c. "also"—I can't see
   d. "conversely"—converse with me at the top of their lungs
   e. "for example"—whisper, "Hi, Jane . . . "
   f. "on the other hand"—I cannot hear
   g. "therefore"—believe I can't talk
   h. "finally"— . . . for approximately five minutes

2. In paragraph 3, rather than telling what happened in his own words, the author uses diagloue. He does this for all of these reasons except
   a. to help the reader experience the situation. **YES**
   b. to illustrate exactly how foolishly the people behaved. **YES— The author paints a picture with dialogue.**
   c. to impress the reader with his ability to recall the exact words in a conversation. **NO—This is not impressive (rather ridiculous)**
   d. to dramatize the frustration he felt. **YES**

EXAMPLE 3: The sample "Writer's Craft" exercise examined here is taken from Selection 8, "The Girl with the Large Eyes."

1. "The Girl with the Large Eyes" is a folk tale. . . . The purpose of this folk tale is to
   a. teach the history of an African tribe.
      NO—No history is being taught here.
   b. warn people not to trust fish.
      NO—There is no such warning presented here.
   c. explain the effects of a drought.
      NO—Though one or two effects are given, this is not the major emphasis of the story.
   d. illustrate the destructive power of prejudice.
      YES—This is the best answer because it shows clearly that prejudice can lead to death (a loved one dies).

2. The word "embrace" in paragraph 7 means to
   a. kiss.
      NO—There is no evidence to support this.
   b. hug.
      YES—This action occurred before the ensuing major action.
   c. make love with.
      NO—This is the major action following the embrace—they consummate the marriage (and she became his wife).
   d. become close friends with.
      NO—This entails more than just friendship.

3. If the word "flung" in paragraph 10 were replaced by the word "placed," what feelings would be missing?
   a. love and concern
      NO—This would show a certain gentleness.
   b. anger and triumph
      NO—They were perhaps triumphant but certainly not angry.
   c. embarrassment and fear
      YES—They took their kill home to the village to show that they did not condone the girl's actions. "Placed" would show that they were not embarrassed by the girl's actions and not fearful of being put out of the village in disgrace.
   d. tenderness and disappointment
      NO—This would indicate a softening of expression.

4. Water appears often . . . in connection with all these except
   a. the fish's voice
      NO—There is no reference to water.
   b. the girl's tears.
      YES—are made *of water*
   c. the drought.
      YES—is a condition *without water*

d. the girl's death
   YES—occurred *in water*

Reader Response

Objective for the student: To learn to shape an informed opinion and to make valid oral or written judgments about a written work.

Structured Reading makes a point of helping students appreciate why recognizing good writing enhances reading. The text also encourages students to make judgments that go beyond, "I agree or disagree with the author" by providing open-ended questions at the end of each selection for oral or written response.

The appreciation of good writing is sometimes lost on students who struggle with some of the mechanics of the reading process. One technique that often ends in elementary school is reading out loud to students, yet it has validity with older readers as well as reported by Charlotte Huck in the Autumn, 1982 issue of *Theory into Practice*. Instructors ask students to follow along as they read out loud. These "read-alongs" help students develop reading fluency, and they provide models that allow readers to hear how fluent readers sound. "Read-alongs" also help readers see writing as live communication, or "talk written down." Students discover the drama in what is being read by hearing the author's voice. Some of the reading selections in *Structured Reading* that particularly lend themselves to "read-alongs" are:

"My Mother's Blue Bowl," p. 127; "The Girl with the Large Eyes," p. 147; "The Chaser," p. 383; "Summer," p. 141; and "My World Now," p. 117.